非洲经济评论

本项目受上海市高原学科世界史建设项目、
国家社科基金重大项目"多卷本《非洲经济史》"
（项目批准号：14ZDB063）、
教育部国别和区域研究基地经费资助。

教育部"国别和区域研究基地"
外交部"中非智库10+10合作伙伴计划"单位
上海师范大学非洲研究中心

非洲经济评论

2020
African
Economic
Review

舒运国 张忠祥 刘伟才 主编

上海三联书店

上海师范大学非洲研究中心简介

上海师范大学非洲研究中心成立于 1998 年，2011 年被教育部评为"国别和区域研究基地"，2014 年入选外交部"中非智库 10+10 合作伙伴计划"。

中心由中国非洲史研究会顾问、国内著名非洲研究专家舒运国教授一手创办。目前，中心有专职研究人员 5 名、特别研究员 3 名、兼职研究员 6 名。

中心长期致力于非洲历史、非洲经济及中非关系等研究，先后完成国家社科基金项目、教育部项目、上海哲社项目、上海市教委项目多项。目前在研国家社科基金重大项目 1 项（舒运国教授主持的"多卷本《非洲经济史》"）、国家社科基金一般项目 1 项（刘伟才副教授主持的"19 世纪英国人非洲行居记录研究"）。

中心成员出版专著十余部，发表论文百余篇。2012 年以来，张忠祥教授、舒运国教授、刘伟才副教授先后出版了《中非合作论坛研究》、《20 世纪非洲经济史》、《泛非主义史》、《非行者言： 19 世纪英国人非洲行居记录的史料价值及其利用》、《大津巴布韦学术史论》等著作，均在国内具有开创性。中心组织译介国外非洲研究成果，搭建"非洲经济史译丛""非洲历史人物传记译丛""非洲国别和区域历史丛书"等平台，已出版《非洲经济史： 内部发展与外部依赖》、《作为历史的口头传说》、《20 世纪前中部与东部非洲的贸易》等多部译著。

中心注重发挥自身专业特色，积极为中非合作献言献策，完成外交部"中非联合研究交流计划"项目多项，为相关政府部门提供决策咨询报告多篇。中心注重配合中非关系发展，通过在报刊媒体刊文以及在公众教育场合授课等形式进行非洲知识传播和中非关系宣传工作。中心注重发挥非洲经济研究特色，自 2012 年起编辑出版《非洲经济评论》，该书已成为国内非洲经济研究的重要阵地之一。

在当前中非交流蓬勃发展的大背景下，顺应当前教育和学术研究国际化趋势，针对非洲研究注重实地调查的特点，中心注重国际交流，每年举办国际学术研讨会或工作坊，邀请国外学者来中心交流、讲学。中心研究人员均多次赴非考察，中心多名研究生也在国家留学基金委、教育部、国家汉办、外交部等多种中非交流平台的资助下赴非访问和学习。

目前，中心已与博茨瓦纳大学、内罗毕大学、赞比亚大学、津巴布韦大学以及南非、尼日利亚、贝宁等非洲国家的多所大学和研究机构建立学术和人员交往机制，并与英、法、美等国家非洲研究学者保持密切联系，努力走在国际学术科研的前沿，为中非关系的长期稳定发展献计献策。

前　言

《非洲经济评论》于 2012 年正式创立,每年出版一本,本书是第九本。

本书所选文章全部来自津巴布韦学者,这些学者或是来自津巴布韦大学经济史系,或是曾在津巴布韦大学经济史系学习或工作。文章主要关注津巴布韦经济史,也兼及一些社会史方面的内容。文章以英文原文发布。

本书源起于近年来上海师范大学非洲研究中心与津巴布韦大学经济史系和津巴布韦大学历史系的交流与合作,同时也是上海师范大学非洲研究中心舒运国教授主持的国家社科基金重大项目"多卷本《非洲经济史》"在中非学术合作层面的一项成果。

本书共含导言一篇、论文十二篇、书评一篇。

在题为《津巴布韦社会经济史的回顾》的导言中,尼亚萨·布舒(Nyasha Bushu)、乌谢维杜·库法库里纳尼(Ushehwedu Kufakurinani)和戈弗雷·霍夫(Godfrey Hove)对津巴布韦的殖民占领、殖民地经济的建立以及"二战"、"单方面独立"(UDI, Unilateral Declaration of Independence)、①民族解放运动框架下津巴布韦社会经济的发展与变迁进行了回顾,对津巴布韦社会经济史研究的发展及其特点进行了论述,最后还对本书的基本情况进行了介绍。

在题为《性别与殖民时期的劳工市场:罗得西亚公共服务部门中的女性职员》的论文中,乌谢维杜·库法库里纳尼对白人妇女进入劳工市场的动因和情况进行了论述。作者指出,白人妇女进入劳工市场受到像"一战"和"二战"这种历

---

① 罗得西亚在实际地位上相当于英国的自治领,有高度自主权,但理论上仍应接受英国管辖。在 20 世纪 50—60 年代的非洲民族主义浪潮中,英国力图推动罗得西亚白人移民统治集团做出让步,与黑人和解,但始终未能达成一致,白人移民统治集团遂在 1965 年 11 月 11 日单方面宣布独立,这被英国视为"叛乱",罗得西亚也因此受到英国等方面的制裁。

史背景的推动,因此一些人认为所谓白人妇女进入劳工市场不过是特殊条件的产物,妇女属于家庭的观念和实际并没有得到根本改变。但是,简单地认为妇女属于家庭的观念和表达并不确切。并且,即便是承认推动条件的特殊性,也仍需要正视妇女进入劳工市场的上升趋势、妇女自身观念的改变、妇女越来越倾向于通过主动行动来争取自己在劳工市场中的地位和影响力等事实。

在题为《水与电:联邦电力局与卡里巴大坝的水电政治(1956—1963)》的论文中,马西林·鲁温戈(Massiline Ruvingo)以中非联邦电力局(Federal Power Board)为切入点,从政治经济学的角度对卡里巴大坝水电项目进行了分析。作者对中非联邦电力局的缘起、运行以及联邦解体后的改造转型进行了介绍和论述。作者指出,尽管中非联邦本身存在诸多问题,但电力局对水电项目的管理仍是比较成功的,并且使它能够在联邦解体后延续。作者认为,对卡里巴大坝水电项目进行研究,既可以深入认识项目本身,也有助于理解中非联邦的政治经济历史。

在题为《殖民时期哈拉雷非洲人市政职工劳工史(1945—1979)》的论文中,布莱辛·迪利瓦约(Blessing Dhliwayo)和埃里克·库辛加·马科姆贝(Eric Kushinga Makombe)对1945—1979年间索尔兹伯里(Salisbury。今哈拉雷)的非洲人市政职工的工作条件进行了考察。作者从请假权、养老金、医疗和福利安排等方面对非洲人市政职工的工作条件进行了介绍和分析,对非洲人市政职工对相关工作条件的反应进行了论述,特别是对具体的反应形式如罢工、参与非正式经济活动、加入工会性组织、从事农业活动进行贴补、借贷、盗窃、改换职业等进行了介绍和分析。

在题为《罗得西亚咖啡种植园的农业资本主义与劳工关系发展》的论文中,塔克苏雷·塔林加纳(Takesure Tarigana)对津巴布韦殖民时期咖啡产业发展中的劳工问题进行了论述。作者对咖啡种植园中劳工生态的形成进行了分析,指出殖民政府通过剥夺非洲人的主要生产资源迫使他们以较低的价格受雇于白人移民是劳工关系形成的一个基本出发点,咖啡种植园中的劳工关系发展实际上呈现的是殖民政府将生产资源从非洲人手中转到白人移民手中的过程。

在题为《津巴布韦殖民时期的技术培训:历史视野下的白人矿工培训机构

(1923—1948)》的论文中,尼亚萨·布舒对南罗得西亚的第一批矿工培训学校的建立和运行情况进行了介绍和分析。作者指出,南罗得西亚的白人移民试图建设一个"白人国家",他们把设立本国矿工学校培养本国白人年轻人当作建设"白人国家"的重要一环,但国际矿业资本更倾向于更多地使用更廉价的非洲人劳工以获取更高利润,虽然在殖民主义体系下,二者的追求仍有可契合之处,但二者之间也存在冲突,而国际矿业资本往往能在冲突中占据优势。作者认为,尽管南罗得西亚白人移民从政治和情感方面追求种族主义,但仍可以从单纯经济的角度去理解整体的殖民统治。

在题为《气象服务与白人移民农业发展:以南罗得西亚气象服务局为例(1897—1945)》的论文中,特里希·马乔里·帕伊达·贡贝(Trish Marjory Paida Gombe)对南罗得西亚殖民时期白人移民农业发展中的气象服务问题进行了分析。作者叙述了南罗得西亚气象服务局产生和发展的过程,介绍了气象服务局提供的信息和服务方面的情况,分析了气象服务局的存在和发展对白人农业发展的影响。作者认为,气象服务局对白人移民农业发展起到了重要的积极推动作用,并且也推动了重视气象服务传统在津巴布韦的形成。

在题为《南罗得西亚与单方面独立时期的税务专员:受制约经济的改革与转型》的论文中,鲁姆比扎伊·奇陶基雷(Rumbidzai Chitaukire)以税务专员(Commissioner of Taxes Department)的活动为切入点,对"单方面独立"时期罗得西亚当局应对外部世界制裁的努力进行了分析。作者论述了中非联邦解体、"单方面独立"后被制裁的情况下罗得西亚经济发展的挑战,对税务专员应对这些挑战的举措进行了分析,强调了机构和机构改革在经济事务特别是应对特定经济问题中的作用,并提出了要进一步重视通过研究殖民时期相关的机构遗产来探讨非洲经济史的问题。

在题为《国家角色与马塔贝莱兰地区的干旱管理:以 1960 年干旱为例》的论文中,曾格塔伊·姆斯卡法纽(Chengetai Musikavanhu)对 1960 年马塔贝莱兰(Matabeleland)的干旱及其对农业、牧业的影响进行了介绍,对当时殖民政府采取的各种措施进行了论述,特别是对干旱对养牛业的影响以及相应的应对进行了介绍和分析。作者认为,殖民政府的干旱管理措施多样,尽管一些措施因为执行不力和资源不足而未能凑效,但殖民政府整体的应对还是比较有效地缓解了干旱的消极影响。作者认为,从历史研究的层面来看,政府在农业面临灾害时能发挥关键的作用,现实和未来的农业生产和粮食安全问题解决应注重这一点。

在题为《利润与实用主义:口蹄疫与南罗得西亚的牛产业(20世纪30年代—40年代)》的论文中,艾莎·马辛高塔(Aisha Mashingauta)和戈弗雷·霍夫对南罗得西亚牛产业中的口蹄疫问题进行了研究。作者指出,口蹄疫在社会经济和政治方面的影响最为突出,它不光塑造了南罗得西亚牛产业本身的发展,还影响了南罗得西亚的政治和社会。通过分析口蹄疫爆发、传播以及牛产业各相关方的反应,作者发现,当口蹄疫爆发时,养牛者往往倾向于隐瞒疫情或者转嫁责任,这直接导致疫情难以控制,进一步还会恶化养牛者与政府之间的关系,有时还会造成与周边国家关系的紧张。作者认为,加强对殖民时期牲畜疫情和防疫问题的研究对当下津巴布韦牲畜产业发展中相关问题的应对仍有借鉴意义。

在题为《诺顿工业区与南罗得西亚的公路基础设施发展(1923—1965)》的论文中,沙洛特·尼亚拉佐·内特(Shalot Nyaradzo Nhete)和贝纳德·库塞纳(Bernard Kusena)以索尔兹伯里城郊的诺顿(Norton)工业区为切入点,对南罗得西亚的公路基础设施规划建设和制造业扩展之间的相互作用进行了研究。作者认为,资金限制和劳工供给不足使诺顿地区的公路建设不如预期,这是限制诺顿地区工业化发展的一个关键因素。

在题为《"二战"后南罗得西亚的工业化:以工业发展委员会为切入点(1945—1949)》的论文中,伊文尼·姆罗姆博(Iviny Murombo)对工业发展委员会(IDC, Industrial Development Commission)在推动工业发展中做的工作进行了分析。作者指出,南罗得西亚的工业发展受到市场、资源和资金等方面的限制,工业发展委员会通过建立或资助工业企业、推进工业企业现代化、协调各领域发展等方式,努力突破这些限制。工业发展委员会的举措取得了一定的成绩,也仍存在一些问题。作者认为,像工业发展委员会这种形式的国家介入仍是工业发展的一个重要推动因素。

在题为《理解"1947年三方劳工协议":中部非洲劳工问题与南罗得西亚劳工需求》的论文中,彼得·乌莱迪(Peter Uledi)对中部非洲三"领地"——南罗得西亚、北罗得西亚、尼亚萨兰的《三方劳工协议》的签订、谈判、修改、实施等进行了介绍和分析,对中部非洲区域经济发展中的劳工问题进行了解读。作者认为,南罗得西亚一直关注并一直追求有利于自身的解决方案,但另两方的诉求和行动也发挥着作用,可以说,劳工问题是中部非洲区域发展中的关键问题。

本书的最后一篇是尼亚萨·布舒对《津巴布韦制造业史(1890—1995)》的书评。书评作者认为,该书对津巴布韦殖民时期以及之后一段时间内的制造业发展进行了比较全面的论述,对理解殖民时代开始以来津巴布韦制造业发展的经济史和政策机制颇有帮助。

目录 | Contents

Introduction: Revisiting the Colonial Social and Economic History of Zimbabwe

Nyasha Bushu, Ushehwedu Kufakurinani and Godfrey Hove

The social and economic history of Zimbabwe and colonial Africa generally has undergone constant reinterpretation and revision in recent years. In Zimbabwe, colonial historiographies have been concerned with discourses around capital accumulation, agriculture, mining, land, labour, gender, migration, racial segregation and inequality, unionism and worker militancy, nationalist movements, regional as well as international relations among many others. [1] These elements are deeply engraved in the country's political and economic history which, among many things, reveals the radical nature of capitalism which guided colonial policy. Assembling essays that bring in novel case studies and themes in the social and economic history of

---

[1] On these aspects see works by: A. Mlambo, "Building a Whiteman's Country: Aspects of White Immigration into Rhodesia up to World War 2", *Zambezia*, vol. 25, no. 2, 1998, pp. 123 – 46; P. Mosley, *The settler economies: studies in the economic history of Kenya and Southern Rhodesia*, Cambridge, Cambridge University Press, 1963; C. Van Onselen, *Chibaro: African Mine Labour in Southern Rhodesia*, London, Pluto Press, 1976; I. R. *An Economic and Social History of Zimbabwe*, 1890 – 1948: *Capital Accumulation and Class Struggle*. London, Longman, 1988; G. Arrighi. "Labour supplies in historical perspective: a study of the proletarianization of the African peasantry in Rhodesia", *The Journal of Development Studies*, vol. 6, no. 3, 1970; R. H. Palmer. "War and land in Rhodesia." *Transafrican Journal of History*, vol. 1, no. 2, 1971; D. J. Murray, Governmental Systems in Southern Rhodesia, Oxford: Clarendon Press, 1970; T. O. Ranger, *Peasant Consciousness and Guerrilla War in Zimbabwe: A Comparative Study*, London, James, Currey, 1985; B. Raftopoulos and A. Mlambo (eds), *Becoming Zimbabwe: A History from the Pre-colonial Period to 2008*, Harare, Weaver Press, 2009.

Zimbabwe, this Special Issue revisits Zimbabwe's social and economic history emphasising discourses that have not received attention in mainstream historical research. For instance, in this collection, authors write about gender discourses, labour relations, hydro-politics and critical government departments which have all, hitherto, received little, if any scholarly attention. In this introduction, we provide a social, economic and political context of the colonial process which birthed the various dynamics that authors in this issue discuss.

Occupation of Zimbabwe

The story of Zimbabwe's colonial occupation has been widely covered by historians, but here we make an overview of this tale so that readers appreciate the broader context of this process. The colony was occupied by the British South Africa Company (BSAC) in 1890 through a charter granted to Cecil John Rhodes by the British government. Various parts of the continent were similarly occupied by different European powers. [1] Rhodes and his BSAC ear marked the territory lying between the Zambezi and Limpopo Rivers in Southern Africa to develop on the basis of gold mining, similar to developments in South Africa after the Mineral Revolution from the mid-19th century. [2] Armed with the charter, Rhodes assembled a group of white settlers who came to be known as the Pioneer Column to occupy the Zimbabwean plateau and their intrusion marked the initial stages of land expropriation by the settler minority group. [3] The Pioneer Column penetrated

---

[1] The examples of Charles Goldie in West Africa, William McKinnon in East Africa.

[2] I. R., "White Miners in Historical Perspective: Southern Rhodesia, 1890 – 1953", *Journal of Southern African Studies*, vol. 3, No. 2,1977.

[3] B. N. Floyd, "Land Apportionment in Southern Rhodesia", *Geographical Review*, vol. 52, No. 4, 1962, pp. 566 – 582. Noteworthy, prior to the Pioneer Column's intrusion, many concession seekers had penetrated the colony. Most prominent among these was John Moffat who signed concessions with the Ndebele king Lobengula. For more information, see: S. J. Ndlovu-Gatsheni, "Mapping Cultural and Colonial Encounters 1880s – 1930s," in B. Raftopoulos and A. Mlambo (eds), *Becoming Zimbabwe: A History from the Pre-colonial Period to 2008*, Harare, Weaver Press, 2009, pp. 44 – 47.

the colony and raised the Union Jack flag in Mashonaland in 1890 and this signified the beginning of colonial occupation, and thence the colony became known as Southern Rhodesia. These events set in motion nearly a century of clashes between the settlers and the indigenous Zimbabweans. The colony was home to a number of black indigenous ethnic groups, among them the Shona and the Ndebele. The Ndebele had arrived in Zimbabwe in the late 1830s after migrating from South Africa after civil wars of the Mfecane which had been prompted by Tshaka. [1] The Ndebele, under the leadership of Mzilikazi, settled on the South-western parts of Zimbabwe, a region that came to be known as Matebeleland. [2] The Ndebele became the first group to clash with the Pioneer Column culminating in the Anglo-Ndebele resistance of 1893. [3] Further land dispersals of indigenous groups by the Column resulted in more clashes. Colonial rule was firmly established through acquisition of land and the domination and dispersal of indigenous peoples from their ancestral lands. The new colonial mindset thus transformed communal land tenure to private ownership through purchase, "a bewildering tenurial concept to the tribal Matebele and Mashona". [4] In the process, the colonial administration resettled Africans on unproductive lands in reserves on the basis of the 1894 Land Commission and the immediate responses were the 1896 rebellions. [5]

---

[1] For more information on mfecane see, L. Vail, "The Political Economy of East-Central Africa," in D. Birmingham and P. M. Martin (eds.), *History of Central Africa*, Volume 2, London, Longman, 1986, p. 201; G. Mazarire, "Reflections on Pre-colonial Zimbabwe, c850 – 1880s," in B. Raftopoulos and A. Mlambo (eds), *Becoming Zimbabwe: A History from the Pre-colonial Period to 2008*, Harare, Weaver Press, 2009, p. 31.

[2] G. Mazarire, "Reflections on Pre-colonial Zimbabwe, c850 – 1880s," in B. Raftopoulos and A. Mlambo (eds), *Becoming Zimbabwe: A History from the Pre-colonial Period to 2008*, Harare, Weaver Press, 2009, p. 38.

[3] S. J. Ndlovu-Gatsheni, "Mapping Cultural and Colonial Encounters 1880s – 1930s," in B. Raftopoulos and A. Mlambo (eds), *Becoming Zimbabwe: A History from the Pre-colonial Period to 2008*, Harare, Weaver Press, 2009, pp. 39 – 74.

[4] B. N. Floyd, Land Apportionment in Southern Rhodesia, *Geographical Review*, vol. 52, No. 4, 1962, p. 572.

[5] *Ibid*. See also, M. Bratton, "Settler State, Guerrilla War and Rural Underdevelopment in Rhodesia", *Issue: A Journal of Opinion*, vol. 9, no. 1/2, 1979.

The indigenous ethnic groups made futile attempts to resist white racialist policy and the Europeans had firmly established themselves by 1900. From here, the BSAC began to develop a dualised society in the colony consisting of a segregated African sector that largely existed on the periphery of the economy and the white sector that dominated the socio-economic and political spaces.

Building a colonial economy

Within a few years of colonial occupation, the envisaged base upon which the Southern Rhodesian economy would be built-gold mining-had proved elusive. It turned out the colony's gold mining potential had been overestimated: gold deposits on the Zimbabwean plateau were by far dwarfed by those on the Rand. [1] With these realities, the BSAC then shifted attention to the development of white capitalist agriculture and the encouragement of white immigration to facilitate the success of the new thrust. [2] However, even the white capitalist agricultural sector was initially bedevilled by many challenges during the early years. Scholars such as Ian Phimister, J. K Rennie, D. J Murray and Victor Machingaidze have demonstrated that the sector suffered many technical, financial and environmental problems. [3]

---

[1] For more information on how the failure to find vast amounts of gold influenced the BSAC to change its attitude see, I. R. Phimister, "The Structure and Development of the Southern Rhodesian Base Mineral Industry: From 1907 to the Great Depression", A. M. Hawkins et al, (eds.), *The Rhodesian Journal of Economics*; *The Quarterly Journal of the Rhodesian Economic Society*, vol. 9, No. 2 June, 1975, p. 79.

[2] V. Machingaidze, 'The development of settler capitalist agriculture in Southern Rhodesia with particular reference to the role of the state, 1908 - 1939', PhD Thesis, University of London, 1980; P. Mosley, *The settler economies: studies in the economic history of Kenya and Southern Rhodesia*, Cambridge, Cambridge University Press, 1963.

[3] I. R. Phimister, "Zimbabwe the path of capitalist development," in D. Birmingham, P. M. Martin (eds.), *History of Central Africa*, Volume 2, Longman, London, 1986, pp. 251 - 290; J. K. Rennie, "White Farmers, Black Tenants and landlord Legislation: South Rhodesia: 1890 - 1930", *Journal of Southern African Studies*, vol. 15, no. 1,1978, pp. 86 - 98; J. K. Rennie, "White Farmers and Labour Tenants: The Formation of Tenant Legislation in Southern and Eastern Africa in the Early Colonial Period, With Particular Reference to the Southern Rhodesia Private Locations Ordinance (1908)", (Not Dated) https://core. ac. uk/download/pdf/8766693. pdf? repositoryId=99, (转下页)

Writing on labour tenancy, Rennie reveals how white agriculture consisted of two farming groups: poor white farmers on the one hand and relatively better capitalised farmers on the other. [1] The major challenge for undercapitalised farmers was securing cheap labour and it was for this reason that labour tenancy was used from the 1890s to secure a ready pool of cheap African labour. Labour tenancy was later couched within the Private Locations Ordinance (PLO) of 1908, where Africans who did not vacate land earmarked for white settlement were forced to provide labour to the owner without wages, in exchange for the "right" to squat on the land. [2] Labour tenancy created a viable alternative for Africans as they retained their access to land that previously belonged to them as opposed to complete eviction to unproductive reserves.

Besides labour tenancy more measures were introduced to disrupt African agriculture. These measures included further sequestration of African land, the imposition of various taxes such as the poll and hut taxes and the enactment of punitive labour laws such as the Masters and Servants Act of 1901. [3] Along-side these was the formation in 1903 Rhodesia Native Labour Bureau which was notorious for its harsh methods of conscripting African labour to serve white economic interests. [4] Robin Palmer argues that the colonial state successfully undercut African peasant production and simultaneously created a ready pool of cheap labour for white farmers. [5] While these measures served white agriculture, labour remained one of the

---

（接上页）accessed 01 September 2019; D. J. Murray, Governmental Systems in Southern Rhodesia, Oxford, Clarendon Press, 1970, pp. 77 - 93; V. Machingaidze, "The development of settler capitalist agriculture in Southern Rhodesia with particular reference to the role of the state, 1908 - 1939".

[1] J. K. Rennie, "White Farmers, Black Tenants and landlord Legislation: South Rhodesia: 1890 - 1930", p. 86.

[2] Ibid, p. 87.

[3] B. Paton, Labour Export Policy In The Development Of Southern Africa, London, Macmillan Press, 1995, pp. 107 - 133.

[4] Ibid.

[5] R. Palmer, Land and Racial Domination in Rhodesia, Berkeley, University of California Press, 1977, p. 83.

biggest problems for the achievement of the policy thrust. This emanated from the fact that while black land dispossession had occurred, peasant agriculture proved somewhat resilient with Africans effectively competing on the agricultural market. [1]

On the other hand, Africans detested white employment because the recruitment processes and working conditions were highly punitive. [2] Diseases such as dysentery, influenza, tuberculosis scurvy and pneumonia were common among African workers. [3] This meant that Africans continued to evade wage employment through successful peasant agriculture. This in many way frustrated attempts by the white section of the colony to establish successful white agrarian capitalism. Regardless, settler agriculture profited from government intervention and developed commercial agriculture based on export products such as tobacco, maize, tea, coffee and beef which anchored the colonial agrarian economy. Naturally, under segregationist policies, blacks were restricted from growing such crops. The state provided technical and financial support at the production level while also helping to find markets for white farmers, and this was part of the Colonial Pact whose main principle was the provision of raw materials for the development of British industries. [4]

Similar systems existed in the mining sector. The BSAC possessed the colony's mineral rights exploration of gold and base metal deposits and

[1] P. Mosley, *The settler economies: studies in the economic history of Kenya and Southern Rhodesia*. Also see R. Palmer and N. Parsons, (eds), *The Roots of Rural Poverty in Central and Southern Africa*, London, Heinemann, 1977.

[2] D. Johnson, "Settler Farmers and Coerced African Labour in Southern Rhodesia, 1936 – 46", *The Journal of African History*, vol. 33, no. 1,1992, pp. 111 – 128.

[3] I. R. Phimister, "Zimbabwe the path of capitalist development", in D. Birmingham, P. M. Martin (eds.), *History of Central Africa*, Volume 2, Longman, 1986, p. 261.

[4] The Colonial Pact was a policy set by the Imperial British government and existed primarily for the purpose of securing raw material exports from Britain's colonies. The Pact effectively stifled efforts to beneficiate raw material exports by colonies. See A. S Mlambo, E. S. Pangeti, I. Phimister, *Zimbabwe: A History of Manufacturing 1890 – 1995*, University of Zimbabwe, 2000. See also A. S. Mlambo, "From the Second World War To UDI, 1940 – 65", p. 81.

allowed exploration by both small scale miners and a few big foreign owned companies. [1] The BSAC accrued profits through royalties from these companies. [2] The development of monopoly capitalism was especially evident in the base metal sector where foreign owned companies controlled virtually all production processes. [3] Colonial policy was thus premised on the advancement of imperial ideology which served the needs of industrial Europe, while whites in the colony became paternalistically responsible for Africans by driving them to the fringes and subordinating their roles. [4] By the First World War, Southern Rhodesia was in a position to serve its metropole. Indeed, the Allied war effort was boosted by Rhodesia's contribution through raw materials and soldiers. [5] However, despite the BSAC's success in establishing colonial rule and discharging its mandate, by 1923, contradictions within the colonial society had become evident. White settlers grew increasingly sentimental and felt that their interests were being side-lined and those of foreign capital were being favoured by the BSAC. [6] After deliberations with the British government, a settler government took over governance in 1923 and the BSAC relinquished its administrative role in the colony. [7] However, before long, the Great Depression struck in 1929 with adverse effects on the nascent settler economy which was already on an

[1] I. R. Phimister, 'History of mining in Southern Rhodesia to 1953', PhD Thesis, University of Rhodesia, 1975.

[2] I. R. Phimister, "Capital and Class in Zimbabwe 1890 – 1948", *Henderson Seminar Paper*, no. 30, University Of Zimbabwe Department Of History, 1960, p. 5.

[3] I. R. Phimister, "The Chrome Trust: The Creation of an International Cartel, 1908 – 38", *Business History* 38, no. 1,1996.

[4] D. Jeater, 'Imagining Africans: Scholarship, Fantasy, and Science in Colonial Administration, 1920s Southern Rhodesia', *International Journal of African Historical Studies*, vol. 38, no. 1,2005, p. 2.

[5] A. S. Mlambo, "From the Second World War To UDI, 1940 – 65", p. 78.

[6] For more information See; I. R. Phimister, "Zimbabwe the path of capitalist development", in D. Birmingham, P. M. Martin (eds.), *History of Central Africa*, Volume 2, Longman, 1986, pp. 265 – 270.

[7] N. B. Bushu, *The Politics and Economics of Training Skilled White Mine Workers in Southern Rhodesia's Mining Industry, 1923 – 1948*, B. A. Honours, Dissertation, Economic History Department 2016, pp. 1 – 25.

uneasy foundation as agriculture particularly was facing challenges. [1] National incomes fell by nearly 5 million pounds in the years 1929 to 1931 as commodity prices fell. [2] The 1930s decade therefore witnessed the passing of a series of legislative interventions meant to cushion the settler economy and concomitantly dislodging African peasant competitiveness. These acts included the Land Apportionment Act of 1930, Maize Control Act of 1931 (amended in 1934) and the Market Stabilisation Act of 1936 which were all meant to subsidise white farmers and gave them an edge over African peasants. [3] The Acts were set along with the establishments of various commodity control boards in all major agricultural industries along the same lines as the Cocoa Boards in West Africa.

African agricultural continued to evince signs of resilience, however. Terrence Ranger has demonstrated how Africans were organised and capable of responding positively to harsh policies which were etched against them by the white minority government. [4] Pius S. Nyambara reveals the resistance and resilience of Africans to colonial injustices which practice produced affluent peasants in Rhodesdale Farm in Salisbury who prospered, referring to their situation as "wonderful". [5] These scholars represent a strand in the historiography of Southern Rhodesia which deviates from the victimhood paradigm offered by Palmer who had earlier noted that through various apparatus the state was able to dislodge African peasant agriculture and create a ready pool of cheap African labour. Besides cushioning settler agriculture, legislative intervention during the 1930s aimed at further curtailing African peasant agriculture and pushing Africans on to the wage labour market. [6]

---

[1] I. R. Phimister, "Zimbabwe the path of capitalist development", pp. 271 – 274.

[2] *Ibid*, pp. 274 – 277.

[3] R. Palmer, *Land and racial domination in Rhodesia*, p. 16.

[4] T. O. Ranger, *Peasant Consciousness and Guerrilla War in Zimbabwe: A Comparative Study*, London: James Currey, 1985, p. 284.

[5] P. S. Nyambara, "That Place was Wonderful! African Tenants on Rhodesdale Estate, Colonial Zimbabwe, c. 1900 – 1952", *The International Journal of African Historical Studies*, vol. 38, No. 2, 2005.

[6] S. J. Ndlovu-Gatsheni, "Mapping Cultural and Colonial Encounters 1880s – 1930s", p. 67.

When African agricultural productivity fell with a consequent increase in rural poverty, the settler government in turn blamed what it deemed poor farming methods for this decline. [1] This, in turn, led to a shift in policy by the state as the colonial government took to emphasise conservation in African areas, ignorant of the fact that the decline in African productivity was a direct result of legislation and market mechanisms which were rigged against them. The ideological stance on the purpose of conservation in colonial policy featured in the colonial historiography in what has commonly become known as the Beinart-Phimister debate. Beinart's interpretation was that it was an official ideology which had its roots in conservationism. Contra-Beinart, Phimister argues that conservationism was a "minor facet of purely economically inspired changes in the political economy of the country". [2] Further, he maintains that conservationist policies were not first experimented with or used with respect to colonial settler agriculture as Beinart proposes. Rather, Phimister argues, anti-erosion works remained voluntary for white farmers during the 1920s and 1930s. [3] Phimister has shown that in Southern Rhodesia, ideas and prescriptions associated with conservationist thinking were first put into practice in relation to peasant agriculture, not settler farming. [4] In this view, Phimister sides with Joann McGregor who views the implementation of conservation policies in Southern Rhodesia as premised on segregationist politics. [5] Therefore, the introduction of conservation policies was viewed from the perspective of racially motivated tools meant to impoverish African peasants. Along with conservation policies, the Industrial Conciliation Act of 1934 also reinforced white

[1] S. J. Ndlovu-Gatsheni, "Mapping Cultural and Colonial Encounters 1880s–1930s", p. 67.

[2] B. Helmut, *African Peasants, Colonial Bureaucrats and Conservation in Colonial Zimbabwe; An Unpolitical Aspect of Agricultural Development*, Hannover; Im Juli, 1989, p. 52.

[3] I. R. Phimister, 'Discourse and the Discipline of Historical Context: Conservationism and Ideas about development in Southern Rhodesia 1930–1950', *Journal of Southern African Studies*, vol. 12, no. 2 1986, pp. 263–275.

[4] *Ibid*.

[5] J. Mcgregor, "Conservation, Control and Ecological Change: The Politics and Ecology of Colonial Conservation in Shurugwi, Zimbabwe", *Environmental History*, vol. 1, no. 3, 1995, pp. 257–279.

superiority and subjugated black interests. [1] Blacks were forbidden to form trade unions or participate in any form of collective bargaining. Therefore, the conditions of Africans continued to deteriorate as the colonial government increasingly became a tool for inducing and maintaining African poverty.

The Second World War and its Aftermath

The Second World War provided a platform for Southern Rhodesia to expand her manufacturing base. [2] The war brought with it a heightened sense of the need to gain self-sufficiency as production in the European industries came to a grinding halt with the commencement of the Second World War. Both local and foreign investment came together to stimulate the development of Southern Rhodesian manufacturing industry. [3] Various sections of the manufacturing sector sprang to life and Southern Rhodesia was transformed from being heavily depended on agriculture and mining to a diversified economy with an expanding manufacturing industrial sector. [4] Agriculture also witnessed a significant boom with the need to supply grain for the War effort. The boom in agriculture owed much to the role played by the government in securing much needed labour. [5] The shortage of labour had led the Southern Rhodesian government to engage in a tripartite labour agreement in 1936 with Northern Rhodesia and Nyasaland with the aim of

---

[1] A. S. Mlambo, "From the Second World War To UDI, 1940 – 65", in B. Raftopoulos and A. Mlambo (eds), *Becoming Zimbabwe: A History from the Pre-colonial Period to 2008*, Harare, Weaver Press, 2009, p. 81.

[2] *Ibid.*, p. 76.

[3] See A. S. Mlambo, E. S Pangeti, I. Phimister, Zimbabwe: A History of Manufacturing 1890 – 1995, University of Zimbabwe, 2000.

[4] N. Samasuwo, "Food Production and War supplies Rhodesia's beef industry during the Second World War, 1939 – 1945", *Journal of Southern African Studies*, vol 29, No, 2,2003, p. 67.

[5] D. Johnson, "Settler Farmers and Coerced African Labour in Southern Rhodesia, 1936 – 46", pp. 111 – 128.

securing migrant labour particularly from Nyasaland which was considered a labour reservoir. [1] Notwithstanding these efforts, the labour problem had persisted. The war provided a platform for the government to issue compulsory labour ordinances with significant pressure from white farmers. [2] The result was forced conscription of Africa labour which resulted in an expansion in grain output. As both agriculture and manufacturing expanded, they benefitted from a steady European market. For instance, Southern Rhodesia's beef, textile, footwear, iron and steel industries witnessed tremendous growth during the Second World War. [3] The base mineral sector was stimulated demand in the armament and aviation industries. [4] Chrome and copper production expanded while gold production however witnessed a significant decline. [5] The decline in gold production was prompted by the high cost of black labour once the supply slackened after the Depression. After the war, the number of small scale miners continued to decline from 1 477 operational mines in 1940 to 732 in 1945. [6] The post war period further reinforced white superiority as the number of European immigrants increased. [7] The new migrants infused well into the racially divided colony as they took to expand the sectors which were considered the preserve of whites such as cotton and tobacco farming through the further displacement of Africans. [8]

---

[1] B. Paton, *Labour Export Policy In The Development Of Southern Africa*, pp. 107 – 133.

[2] D. Johnson, "Settler Farmers and Coerced African Labour in Southern Rhodesia, 1936 – 46", p. 119.

[3] N. Samasuwo, "Food Production and War supplies Rhodesia's beef industry during the Second World War, 1939 – 1945", p. 67.

[4] B. Ngwenya, "The rise and fall of copper mining at Mhangura c1957 – 2000", MA Thesis, Economic History Department, University of Zimbabwe, 2007; T. Madimu, "Farmers, Miners And The State In Colonial Zimbabwe (Southern Rhodesia), C. 1895 – 1961", PhD thesis, 2017, Stellenbosch University; I. R. Dumett, "Africa's Strategic Minerals During the Second World War", *The Journal of African History*, vol. 26, No. 4, 1985.

[5] D. J. Murray, *The Governmental Systems In Southern Rhodesia*, p. 149.

[6] I. R. Phimister, "Zimbabwe the path of capitalist development", p. 280. On European participation in gold mining in the post-World War Two period see, I. R. Phimster, *An Economic and Social History of Zimbabwe 1890 – 1948: Capital Accumulation and Class Struggle*, London: Longman, 1988, p. 100.

[7] A. S. Mlambo, "From the Second World War To UDI, 1940 – 65", p. 76.

[8] *Ibid*.

One of the most far reaching legacies of the Second World War was increased rural-urban migration among Africans. As secondary industries expanded as a result of import-substitution industrialisation, the need for a more permanent labour in urban areas increased. The conditions and circumstances of their employment was governed by the Industrial Conciliation Act of 1934 which legislated for a racially segregatory system on the labour Market. As living and working conditions for Africans worsened, a spate of strikes was witnessed with the most famous being the Railway Strike of 1945 and the General Strike of 1948 which was ruthlessly crushed by the minority government. [1] However, the winds of change rode on these post war sentiments as Africans were increasingly gaining a sense of racial injustice as well as a nationalist consciousness. The government stood firm against this and the perception of white superiority, or rather white Rhodesian superiority further expanded with the establishment of the Federation of Rhodesia and Nyasaland in 1953. This was notwithstanding the idea that Federation was to be premised on racial partnership. [2]

Nyasaland, Southern Rhodesia and Northern Rhodesia came together to create a large economic entity that would compete with South Africa by harnessing its economic resources including labour thereby creating a more powerful super structure. However, what the Federation achieved was a far cry from the stated goals. Although the Southern Rhodesian government had been forced to review the Industrial Conciliation Act in 1959 which allowed black workers to form and join trade unions, the conditions of black workers under Federation did not resemble any form of racial partnership. [3] Instead of creating racial partnership, Federation extended white supremacy, more specifically Southern Rhodesia's white supremacy. Southern Rhodesian

[1] T. H. Mothibe, "African Workers' Militancy as a Basis for Post-War Nationalism in Colonial Zimbabwe, 1945－1953", *Trans African Journal of History*, vol. 23,1994, p. 158.

[2] For more information on the road to the creation of the Federation See, A. S. Mlambo, "From the Second World War To UDI, 1940－65", pp. 86－90.

[3] A. S. Mlambo, "From the Second World War To UDI, 1940－65", p. 103.

benefited most through the expansion of large manufacturing industries. Prior to Federation, Southern Rhodesian industries grew from 299 in 1939 to 724 in 1952. ① The removal of all tariff barriers amongst the constituent territories of the Federation meant that Southern Rhodesian manufactured goods now entered Nyasaland and Northern Rhodesia duty free which benefitted the infant industries. Southern Rhodesian industries also benefitted from the hydropower plant at the newly constructed Kariba dam wall which increased electricity generation. ② As the Federation collapsed in 1963, Southern Rhodesia emerged more economically powerful than her two co-federates. ③ Moreover, the northern territories also served as useful labour reservoirs for Southern Rhodesia's mines, farms and manufacturing sector.

UDI and the Road to Liberation

The year 1965 marked a significant flag point in the history of Southern Rhodesia. In November, Prime Minister Ian Smith declared the Unilateral Declaration of Independence which signified an antipathy between Southern Rhodesia and her mother country, Britain. ④ In response to the broken ties, Britain imposed sanctions on the colony in order to force the white minority government to concede to black majority rule. In a bid to maintain its autonomy in the face of international scorn, the colony embarked on sanctions bursting measures. These included the development of import

---

① A. S. Mlambo, "From the Second World War To UDI, 1940 – 65", p. 103.

② A. Cohen, "Voice and Vision": The Federation of Rhodesia and Nyasaland's Public Relations Campaign in Britain: 1960 – 1963, *Historia*, vol. 54, No. 2, 2009, pp. 113 – 132.

③ For more information on the reasons for the collapse of the Federation see, A. S. Mlambo, "From the Second World War To UDI, 1940 – 65", pp. 92 – 93.

④ One of the reasons for the collapse of the Federation was the growing agitation among blacks. The Southern Rhodesian government felt that the idea of a white colony was increasingly under threat from occurrences in other British colonies such as Ghana where the British government had advocated black majority governance. The Rhodesian Front party led by Ian Smith insisted on white rule leading to a deterioration in relations with Britain and Smith's declaration of independence. See, A. S. Mlambo, "From the Second World War to UDI, 1940 – 65", pp. 110 – 112.

substitution industries which registered tremendous growth. For example, manufacturing growth registered an average of 12 per cent per annum and gross fixed capital formation grew by 524 per cent. [1] Therefore, even in the face of international pressure, the colonial mind-set continued to reign supreme in the colony. While the above developments were occurring on the economic front, on the political front the nationalist movement was gaining momentum. Although a section of African peasantry remained resolute in the face of repressive land and agrarian policies, the majority of Africans were disenchanted by the unjust and racial segregation. "[2] The land issue together with became the rallying for the liberation struggle. [3] Nationalist leaders such as, Joshua Nkomo, Josiah Tongogara and Hebert Chitepo, among others used the land issue, among others, as a platform to mobilise support for the struggle. Nationalist parties in the name of Zimbabwe African National Union Patriotic Front and Zimbabwe African People's Union, in turn found sympathy from the socialist bloc and countries like Russia, Cuba and China worked to assist the liberation movement. After nearly a decade of covert and overt action, self-rule was achieved in 1980 and independent Zimbabwe was born from an intense struggle against white supremacy. However, the war had devastating effects on the economy with a slump in agriculture and manufacturing. [4] The young nation was therefore established on a shaky foundation.

A note on Zimbabwean historiography: Gaps and strengths

The historiography on colonial Zimbabwe has taken both Eurocentric

---

[1] J. Mtisi, M. Nyakudya, T. Barnes, "social and economic developments during the udi period", in B. Raftopoulos and A. Mlambo (eds), *Becoming Zimbabwe: A History from the Pre-colonial Period to 2008*, Harare, Weaver Press, 2009, p133. See also Pangeti, "the state and manufacturing industry", p. 110.

[2] B. N. Floyd, Land Apportionment in Southern Rhodesia, p. 566.

[3] L. M. Sachikonye, From 'Growth with Equity' to 'Fast-Track' Reform: Zimbabwe's Land Question', *Review of African Political Economy*, vol. 30, no. 96, 2003, pp. 227 – 240.

[4] J. Mtisi, M. Nyakudya, T. Barnes, "social and economic developments during the UDI period," pp. 136 – 140.

and Afrocentric approaches. The Eurocentric approach is influenced by racial sentiments which are prominent in the works of scholars like William Barber and Lewis Gann. [1] These scholars view colonialism as a blessing for the African continent, drawing from notions of a 'primitive and backward' pre-colonial Africa. William Barber on his part views agriculture in parts of Africa including Southern Rhodesia as inherently underdeveloped prior to colonial occupation. [2] In Duignan's view European conquest which ushered in an "agricultural revolution". [3] The Afrocentric approach countered this historiography which David Chanaiwa, labelled colonialist historiography. Chanaiwa maintains that such a view of pre-colonial and colonial Africa was conjured up to rationalise and legitimise the burdens and atrocities of colonisation and was, "primarily written to rationalise invasions, massacres and predatoriness". [4] Chanaiwa further highlights that colonialists "not only needed historians, but also a distinct historical folklore of their own". [5] On this basis, the objectivity of such a body of knowledge came under scrutiny from so called revisionist scholars who brought up a critique from an Afrocentric perspective. Embodied in Afrocentric literature, beginning at the end of the Second World War, African historiographies took this curative stance towards redressing the gross misrepresentation of pre-colonial and colonial African history. Scholars like Ian Robert Phimister, Giovanni Arrighi, and later, Victor Machingaidze Brian Raftopoulos and Alois Mlambo, among others also contributed to the Afrocentric revisionist perspective on the socio-economic

---

[1] W. Barber, *The Economy of British Central Africa*, London, Athlone Press, 1961; L. H. Gann, *A History of Southern Rhodesia*, London, Chatto and Windus, 1965.

[2] W. Barber, *The Economy of British Central Africa*, p. 93.

[3] P. Duignan, "Review of Land and Racial Domination in Rhodesia by Robin Palmer", *African Economic History*, vol. 2, no. 6, 1978, pp. 197 – 200.

[4] D. Chanaiwa, 'Historiographical traditions of Southern Africa', *Paper prepared for the international Conference on the Historiography of Southern Africa*, 1976, p. 12.

[5] *Ibid*, p. 14.

history of colonial Zimbabwe. [1] One such scholar who distinctly stood for the development of African economic thought basing on a critique of the Eurocentric perception is R. G Mtetwa. Mtetwa's work on the "cattle complex" sought to defuse the common notion among white settlers that Africans viewed cattle not in their economic sense, but rather from a mystical view point. [2] In his work, Mtetwa unambiguously stated that "there has been nothing mystical about cattle (among Africans): they have been first and foremost an economic asset and all the socio-religious attitudes held by Africans are based on their economic value". [3] Also writing on livestock regimes, scholars like Wesley Mwatwara and Godfrey Hove have further demonstrated African enterprise and expertise in raising livestock and that it was the colonial mind set which sought to disrupt successful African cattle regimes. [4] Indeed, Afrocentric scholars have interrogated the rationale of occupation and have revealed its repressive side. This has become the basis of multiple studies on the development of colonial economic thought which clearly sought to advance the interests of white settlers at the expense of Africans. Cited works by scholars such as Phimister, Machingaidze and more

---

[1] I. R Phimster, *An Economic and Social History of Zimbabwe* 1890 – 1948: *Capital Accumulation and Class Struggle*, London: Longman, 1988; I. R. Phimister, "Rethinking the Reserves: Southern Rhodesia's Land Husbandry Act Reviewed", *Journal of Southern African Studies*, vol. 19, No. 2, 1993, pp. 225 – 239; G. Arrighi, *The Political Economy of Rhodesia*, Mouton, The Hague, 1967, B. Raftopoulos and A. Mlambo (eds), *Becoming Zimbabwe: A History from the Pre-colonial Period to 2008*, Harare, Weaver Press, 2009.

[2] The term "cattle complex" was coined by Melville Herskovits while working on east and Southern African societies' relationships with cattle. Herskovits concluded that Africans had a strong attachment to cattle which influenced a general reluctance to slaughter except for ritual purposes. In this work Herskovits sought to reinforce the common perception among whites during the colonial period that Africans were void of economic rationale because they held on to cattle based on sentiment rather than economic logic.

[3] R. M. G. Mtetwa. "Myth or reality?: The cattle complex with reference to Rhodesia", *Zambezia*, vol. 1, 1978, p 23; I. R. Phimister, "Meat and Monopolies: Beef Cattle in Southern Rhodesia, 1890 – 1938", *Journal of African History*, vol. 19, no. 3, 1978;

[4] W. Mwatwara, "A history of state veterinary services and African livestock regimes in colonial Zimbabwe, c. 1896 – 1980", Phd thesis, Stellenbosch University, 2014; G. Hove, "The State, Farmers and Dairy Farming in Colonial Zimbabwe (Southern Rhodesia), c. 1890 – 1951", Phd thesis, Stellenbosch University, 2015.

recently Kudakwashe Chitofiri have demonstrated that colonial occupation by the British South Africa Company was based on its profit *motif*. [1] These works have highlighted how the pursuit of profit by the Company and subsequent settler governments disenfranchised Africans and relegated them to become minor appendages to the white economy. This is quite pronounced in cited works that focus on the development of settler agriculture, among them works by Arrighi, Machingaidze and Murray. These works have set the foundation for many contemporary works on colonial agrarian development from scholars like Mwatwara, Hove, Nyambara and Taringana among many. These scholars have continued to probe at gaps in this historiography. For instance, Taringana uses coffee to demonstrate the skew in colonial policy as it favoured white cash crop production at the expense of African subsistence agriculture. [2]

Phimister and Charles Van Onselen have covered the development of mining, capturing the roles of the state and capital in shaping mining policy. [3] Works by Brian Ngwenya and Tapiwa Madimu have focussed on the development of the base metal sectors focussing on the role of the colonial state and private capital together with the labour dynamics within the sector. [4] The labour dynamics of the colony are extensively covered by Bill Parton who emphasises the central role of the labour question in dealing with the colony's development. [5] Work by David Johnson, a contemporary scholar, also focuses on colonial labour policy shaping perspectives on the

[1] K. Chitofiri, "Hopes and Expectations: the Relationship between the British South Africa Company Directors and Shareholders, 1890 to 1923", MA thesis, Department of Economic history University of Zimbabwe, 2007.

[2] T. Taringana, "Coffee Production in Zimbabwe, 1980 – 2015", PhD Thesis, University of Zimbabwe, 2019.

[3] C. Van Onselen. , *Chibharo African Mine Labour in Southern Rhodesia 1900 – 1933*, London: Pluto Press, 1976.

[4] N. B. Bushu, "The Politics And Economics Of Training Skilled White Mine Workers In Southern Rhodesia's Mining Industry, 1923 – 1948 ", BA Honours, Dissertation, Economic History Department, 2016.

[5] See cited work.

role played by the government in shaping the labour policy of the colony particularly the development on agriculture and mining. While mining, agriculture and labour have received wide scholarly attention, the manufacturing sector has received comparatively much less attention. However, Alois Mlambo and Evelyn Pangeti have written on the development of the manufacturing sector since the inception of colonial rule. [1] Rural development in relation to the expansion of manufacturing has not been explored, however. This is mainly because African voices have hardly received much attention. This is notwithstanding works by Phimister, Pius Nyambara, Terence Ranger, and Lloyd Sachikonye who have attempted to give agency to Africans. Phimister saliently deals with African consciousness to problems emanating from segregation policies by the white minority government and that they were not passive victims and the liberation war was well orchestrated and well thought out. [2] However, African voices have been muzzled mainly because of the prejudices of colonial archives which have largely marginalised African responses and initiatives. Women's experiences during the colonial period have also not been fairly covered. Only Elizabeth Schmidt, Teresa Barnes, and Diana Jeater have done so with considerable depth. [3] Elizabeth Schmidt particularly points to "a dearth of gendered histories". [4] Until recently, researches by scholars like Kate Law and Ushehwedu Kufakurinani have begun to re-insert the social

---

[1] See A. S. Mlambo, E. S. Pangeti, I. Phimister, *Zimbabwe: A History of Manufacturing 1890 - 1995*, University of Zimbabwe, 2000.

[2] I. R, Phimister, "Rethinking the Reserves: Southern Rhodesia's Land Husbandry Act Reviewed," *Journal of Southern African Studies*, vol. 19, No. 2,1993, pp. 225 - 239.

[3] E. Schmidt, *Peasants, Traders, and Wives: Shona Women in the History of Zimbabwe, 1870 - 1939*, London, Heinemann Educational Books, 1992; D. Jeater, *Marriage, Perversion, and Power: The Construction of Moral Discourse in Southern Rhodesia, 1894 - 1930*, Oxford, Clarendon Press, 1993; T. Barnes, *"We Women Worked So Hard": Gender, Urbanization, and Social Reproduction in Colonial Harare, Zimbabwe, 1930 - 56*, Portsmouth, Heinemann, 1999.

[4] E. Schmidt, *Peasants, Traders, and Wives: Shona Women in the History of Zimbabwe, 1870 - 1939*, London, Heinemann Educational Books, 1992.

histories of men and women within colonial societies. [1] There has also been growing research on the business history of Africans demonstrating how, even in the face of colonial oppression, Africans still managed to prosper. In this regard, the works of Michael O. West and Tawanda Chambwe, in particular, are quite revealing. [2] The essays in this collection also straddle on relatively novel areas of study such as settler institutions and gender in labour colonial markets. The collection also revisits older themes, such as labour, cash crop production, settler land policy, African worker consciousness among many but using novel case studies.

Conclusion: A note on this special issue

This issue arose for a long relationship with Liu Weicai who has been visiting Southern Africa for a while. Exchanges between Weicai and the Department of Economic History have seen the latter taking up the request to work on a special issue on Zimbabwean socio-economic history which is accessible to Chinese students and scholars. The issue explores varying micro-dynamics of Zimbabwean colonial socio-economic history. It moves away from broad thematic focus on macro-developments in Southern Rhodesia and takes advantage of several archival researches done in the Department which focused on specific case studies. We hope this issue will accommodate individuals interested in having some appreciation of a spectrum of specific themes on Zimbabwe's colonial socio-economic history. Focusing on various case studies, the issue covers themes that range from gender, labour, manufacturing to agriculture, among others, which demonstrate the complex

---

[1] K. Law, Gendering the Settler State: White Women, Race, Liberalism and Empire in Rhodesia, 1950 –1980, London, Routledge, 2016; U. Kufakurinani, *Elasticity in Domesticity: White Women in Rhodesian Zimbabwe, 1890 to 1980*, Brill Publishers, Netherlands, 2019.

[2] M. O. West, *The Rise of an African Middle Class: Colonial Zimbabwe*, Indiana University Press, Bloomington, 2002; Tawanda V. Chambwe, "A History Of African Entrepreneurship In Southern Rhodesia, 1944 – 1979", PhD Thesis, University of the Free State, Faculty of Humanities, 2020.

nature of Zimbabwe's colonial history. Contributors to this issue are largely young upcoming scholars trained as Economic Historians in the Department of Economic History at the University of Zimbabwe.

Gender and the Colonial Labour Market: Women Clerks in the Public Service of Rhodesia, 1939 – 1960s

Ushehwedu Kufakurinani

Abstract

Gender and imperial studies are a recent development in scholarship. There has been growing interest in re-enacting the history of colonial / imperial / white women in the colonies understanding the nature and impact of their roles. Despite this growth, there remain several grey areas on the historical experiences of white women in the colonies. For instance, we know very little about the experiences of these women within the colonial labour market. The colonial public service, for example, was one of the greatest employers of white women's labour and, in the Southern Rhodesian case, archival documents exist that show how women's labour power was appropriated and exploited. Using this rich archival documentation, this paper makes a qualitative examination of a number of dynamics surrounding white women's participation in the labour market which, to all intents and purposes, assaulted the dominant domestic ideology that ideally confined women to domestic spaces. The changing market forces triggered by such events as the 1st and 2nd World Wars forced the colonial patriarchal system to make concessions to women's 'invasion' of public spaces in unprecedented volumes. This invasion, however, remained entrenched in a domestic ideology reminding women of their normative roles. This is why, for example, it took over 60 *years for married white women to be legally accepted into full employment in 1971, otherwise they were expected to either stop work or be employed as temporary full time. Even then, it took longer for society to adjust to the new legal parameters. The paper also examines debates that intensified from the 1950s about women taking up careers as opposed to housewifery. Using the case study of the public service of Southern Rhodesia, the paper will also analyse the changing conditions of service and women's efforts to negotiate and contest gender inequalities and gender biased labour practices.*

Key words: Gender, labour market, public service, clerks and typists, marriage bar

Introduction

The study examines the experiences of white women in the public service of Southern Rhodesia with specific reference to clerical administrators. In many ways these were in the periphery of Rhodesian employment. Not only did they receive relatively lower wages and salaries, but they experienced far more inferior conditions of service as compared to other employees in the public service. Beginning from the First World War, the clerical administration had been increasingly dominated by white women. The archival records demonstrate that clerical administration was a lowly regarded profession with conditions of service that limited women's advancement and relegated them to a largely repetitive work environment. Gender ideology also played a critical role in shaping the experiences of white women and disadvantaging them at various frontiers. From the onset, the prejudices against the education of women in both the metropole and the colony, among other things, meant that there were few women qualified for the professional and managerial levels. The colonial labour market was clearly gendered allowing for conditions of service that were skewed in favour of men. Ending the analysis here would, however, be incomplete. Even amongst women employees, the colonial state extended different conditions of service. Married women, for example, experienced the so-called marriage bar by which they had different conditions of service to their single women counterparts. Despite these differences, I argue, women's nature of employment in the public service was greatly shaped by the domestic ideology, hence the belief that a career for them was optional, what was deemed ideal for them was their domestication in the home frontier. I also demonstrate that white women clerks and typists were not passive recipients to the subordination and gender imbalances that existed in the public service. Women protested, in both their individual and collective capacities, about the poor and unfair conditions of service. These protests can be dated to as early as the First World War. However, in the post Second World War era, women intensified their campaigns for equality and justice in the Public Service.

In Southern Rhodesia, white women in the public service were concentrated in the administrative and clerical division. This group "embraced typists, shorthand typists (including writers), clerks (including registry clerks) and telephone operators". [1] Table 1 below demonstrates statistics of one year, which give some impression of the proportion of women's occupations in the Service. The administrative and clerical division constituted about 42 per cent of the women in the Service. Though these statistics capture a single period, they reflect on the general trend throughout the colonial period.

Table 1   Distribution of European women in the Public Service, 1951 – 1952

Divisions of the Public Service	Number of women
Administrative and clerical division	1,125
Professional and Technical division	
a) Professional Branch	16
b) Technical Branch	48

---

[1] T. S. Chegwidden, Survey of the Public Services of Rhodesia 1952.

Divisions of the Public Service	Number of women
General division	57
Qualified Nurses, Masseuses, Dieticians …	460
Student Nurses	192
Teachers	765
Total	2,663

Source: T. S. Chegwidden, Survey of the Public Services of Rhodesia, 1951 – 1952

The duties of women clerks and typists were not confined to shorthand or typing work; some were employed as record clerks and there were found dotted in every department of the government. The 1951 census established that the Government offered employment to nearly 3,100 Europeans of which 2,663 were women.

The evidence from the archives demonstrates that the state, through its various statutory instruments, perpetuated unfair and poor working conditions for white women. Poorer conditions of service for women helped to buttress the gender stereotypes that women were inferior to men. The salary disparities, sex-stereotypes and many injustices experienced by women in the Public Service, served to remind them of their subordination to men. This patriarchal ideology had its roots in Europe and it spread to Southern Africa.

When convenient, the state found it economic to employ white women instead of men in certain jobs because of their lower rates of pay. The recommendation of the Bagshawe Committee on Lady Clerks in 1917 is quite revealing. The committee stated that, "certain forms of the clerical work … such as the record work of some offices could be carried out with greater *efficiency and economy* by suitable lady clerks. "[1] Salaries for women were poorer than men's hence the former were economic to employ. In this sense,

---

[1] National Archives Of Zimbabwe A3/7/23 Lady Clerks in Civil Service, Increase in Salaries, Bagshawe Committee on Lady Clerks, 23 March 1917.

"ladies [were] a great commercial asset to the government. "[1] Given the financial advantage that came with employing women, it is not surprising that when campaigns for parity were at their height in the 1960s, there were concerns in the Government over the financial repercussions of implementing this principle. [2]

The paper looks at the period between 1939 and 1960. The year 1939 was a watershed as the Second World War triggered unprecedented participation of women in the labour market. The available sources make it difficult to speak about the post – 1960 period. Much of what is documented and available reflect on the experiences of women employees up to the 1960s. There is little reason to think that there may have been a drastic change in the ideology and policies from 1960s to independence in 1980. This paper draws on archival material such as correspondence by the state and women's organisations, commissions of inquiry, reports and newspapers. Evidence from newspaper sources was also used. These sources reflected on the state policies and ideologies, the perspectives of the women themselves and various other stakeholders. The aspect of positionality in a research such as this cannot be underestimated. As a young male black researcher there clearly was a limitation as to how much I could extract from white women interviewees. Experiences in the workplace such as sexual harassment, for example, could be difficult to share.

Until recently, white women have been glaringly absent in the historiography of Africa's past. In Zimbabwean historiography, these have made brief appearances. [3]

---

① NAZ A/3/7/23 Civil Service: Women Clerks and Typists, Letter from L. Reynolds, to V. Godbolt Acting Secretary to CSWA, 26 September 1918.

② NAZ S3279/11/109 Employment of Women Southern Rhodesia Public Service 1955 to 1965, Letter from Secretary of Internal and Justice Affairs to the Secretary to the Prime Minister and Cabinet Office 2 March 1961. It was estimated that the cost of bringing the salaries of Black women only to the same levels as their male counterparts would cost £200,000 per annum.

③ Some of the works that have been written on African women in colonial Zimbabwe include E. Schmidt, *Peasants, Traders, and Wives: Shona Women in the History of Zimbabwe, 1870 – 1939*, London, Heinemann Educational Books, 1992; D. Jeater, *Marriage, Pervasion, and Power: The Construction of Moral Discourse in Southern Rhodesia 1894 – 1930*, Oxford, Clarendon Press,（转下页）

Recent works by Kate Law[①] and Ushehwedu Kufakurinani[②] have, however, contributed to this historiography with studies that present sustained analyses of white women's roles, status and contributions to colonial Zimbabwe. Andrew Hartnack's more recent work has also helped re-insert white women in particular and white society in general into specifically Zimbabwe's post-colonial historiography. [③] There has, however, been very little on white women's participation in the colonial labour market which has remained obscured in history. Karen T. Hansen's work on white women in Northern Rhodesia is perhaps one of such few works. It looks at various aspects of white women's existence in the country including their employment. Among other things, it examines the nature and extent of white women's work noting that, "women's employment clustered in such gender-typed fields as nursing, teaching, shop assistance, and clerking". [④] Similar observations can also be made of the case of Southern Rhodesia and perhaps several other British colonies. The earlier silences on white women's histories have probably to do with the fact that these women were part of the privileged racial classes and, therefore, were seen as willing accomplices in the oppression of the African population. However, the exclusion of white women in African historiography only serves to distort colonial contours by missing out some of the critical puzzles that shaped colonial ideologies on various aspects such as gender. This paper not only builds on gender and empire historiography but specifically draws on the experiences of seemingly obscure elements of white

(接上页)1993; and T. Barnes, *"We Women Worked so Hard"*: *Gender, Urbanization, and Social Reproduction in Colonial Harare, Zimbabwe, 1930 - 56*, Portsmouth, Heinemann, 1999.

① K. Law, *Gendering the Settler State*: *White Women, race, Liberalism and Empire in Rhodesia, 1950 - 1980*, London, Routledge Taylor and Francis group, 2016.

② U. Kufakurinani, *Elasticity in Domesticity*: *White Women in Rhodesian Zimbabwe, 1890 to 1980*, Netherlands, Brill Publishers, 2019.

③ A. Hartnack, *Ordered Estates*: *Welfare, Power and Materialism on Zimbabwe's (Once White) Highveld*, Harare, Weaver Press, 2016.

④ K. T. Hansen, "White Women in Changing World: Employment Voluntary Work, and Sex in Post-World War II Northern Rhodesia", in Nupur Chaudhuri and M. Strobel (eds), *Western Women and Imperialism*: *Complicity and Resistance*, Indiana University Press, Indianapolis, 1992, p. 253.

women's experiences in the colonial labour market.

Changing Labour Demands for Women
in the Public Service, 1939 – 1960s

The Second World War as well as the post-war economic and political environment all presented insatiable demand for women labour. [1] In the Government Service, (and this includes the Police and Defence Services) white women were in demand, as they were needed to replace men that had gone to the war front. [2] Indeed, developments in the Defence Service help to illuminate the labour situation in the Government Service in general and the Public Service in particular. Writing on women in the Defence Service, King notes that until the Second World War, both the Defence Forces and the Police were exclusively male domains. [3] With the coming of the war, women were increasingly in demand in this section of the Government Service. In 1941, a correspondence on white women labour in the Defence Service summed up the desperate labour situation in this part of the Government service describing it as, "real, urgent and unlikely to diminish."[4] This also led to cutthroat competition between the Defence and Public services.

The post-war era up to the mid-sixties also witnessed increased demand for white women labour in the Public Service. The immediate post-war industrial boom meant an increased demand for labour to fill up in the emerging and expanding sectors of the economy. This boom also affected the region in general, which was also increasingly in need of labour, foreign and local, from both sexes. In 1955, for instance, the Public Service of South

---

[1] See U. Kufakurinani and P. S. Nyambara, "Reconfiguring Domesticity? White Women and the Second World War", *Historia*, 60, No. 2, 2015, pp. 132 – 159.

[2] Ibid.

[3] M. King, "Serving in Uniform: Women in Rhodesia Defence Forces and the Police, 1939 – 1980", BA Honours Dissertation, History Department, University of Zimbabwe, 2000. p. 78.

[4] NAZ S726 W13/1/1 – 15/1/1 Women Power Policy 1940 – 1945, Correspondence on Women Power Policy from Defence House Headquarters, 17 November 1941.

Africa's male clerical vacancies alone numbered 2200 yet the most that was likely to be filled was about 600. [1] The establishment of the Federation of Rhodesia and Nyasaland in 1953 saw the creation of the Federal Public Service, whose headquarters were in Southern Rhodesia. This also brought cutthroat competition for labour to Southern Rhodesia's doorsteps. The territorial Public Service had to be competent enough to match the conditions of service in the Federal Service.

The coming of Unilateral Declaration of Independence (UDI) in 1965 brought in new dimensions to the employment of white women in the Service. The economic blockade that came with UDI had immediate negative impact on the employment of women in the Service. The closing down of some industries and the streamlining of some departments because of the sanctions increased labour supply and consequently reduced its demand. It is in the light of such developments that the Rhodesian Government proposed in 1966 to dismiss working wives from the Civil Service to make way for people who had lost jobs because of sanctions or for school leavers. [2] It is not clear how far the State took up this proposal, but it demonstrates how married women were always the sacrificial lambs in times of crises. What can be confirmed though is that during the UDI, morning-only jobs were increasingly difficult to come by. Wormarld recalled, "morning-only jobs for women were gold, every woman wanted to have those jobs. " [3] This facility had given the married women an opportunity to earn themselves some money without much compromise to their domestic responsibilities.

---

① *The Rhodesia Herald*, 27 January 1955. The researcher was not able to obtain figures for female clerks.

② *The Rhodesia Herald*, 11 June 1966.

③ Interview with Elizabeth Wormarld, 17 April 2007. She was a qualified secretary employ at some point in the Public Service as a Secretary in different departments. On marriage, she quit work to attend to her domestic family responsibilities. Unfortunately, she was not sure about her dates of first employment in the Public Service but gave late 1960s and early 1970s as estimates.

Conditions of Service

The conditions of service for white women in the Service help to illustrate on the gender stereotypes at the workplace. Women had inferior conditions of service to men's and several justifications were put forward. Salaries were lower, promotions paper-thin and conditions generally poor. This situation was not peculiar to Southern Rhodesia. Writing on Northern Rhodesia, Karen T. Hansen observed that, "most employed white women were remunerated at worse terms than white men and had fewer options for advancement. "[1] Married women faced worse in their conditions of service hence their experiences are discussed separately from the general conditions of service for white women in the Service.

It is interesting to note how social prejudices against women shaped the type of work they took up in the Public Service. In Southern Rhodesia these prejudices were culturally embedded with their origins in the industrialised nations and more specifically in the metropole, the United Kingdom. For C. Walker "gender biologism rationalised the channeling of women into certain sex-stereotyped areas of work ... and justified lower wages for female workers. "[2] Separate spheres ideology or sex-stereotypes influenced women's destination of employment in the Service, that is, the type of employment they were to take up. In the post-Second World War era, clerical jobs were inundated with women and very few men took up these jobs. In fact, during this era, "men generally scorned office work of this nature as feminine. "[3] Few white women, if any, found themselves in higher echelons of management. Men learnt typing only when they had to. For instance, in the Meteorological Department both men and women had to learn the typing

[1] Hansen, "White Women in Changing World", p. 255.

[2] C. Walker, "The Women's Suffrage Movement: The Politics of Gender, Race and Class" in C. Walker (ed.), *Women and Gender in South Africa to 1945*, James Currey, London, 1990, p. 319.

[3] Interview with Elizabeth Wormald, Marlborough, 17 April 2007.

skills because weather forecasts would need to be sent by telefax. ①

The gender prejudice against white women saw them being relegated to the "routine" works of the departments, which were seen as suitable for them. This thinking had its roots official perceptions on what constituted feminine work. When the Public service was in its infancy, for example, the Committee on Lady Clerks observed that a great part of the work in the Junior Service was "routine" and "mechanical", "requiring for its efficiency very little *initiative* or *knowledge*."② It then recommended that such work be done by women. This mentality bred and perpetuated the separate sphere ideology. The Public Service took up these recommendations making it part of government policy to employ women in what were seen as inferior positions in the Service, which in most cases had no prospects of promotion especially to administrative positions.

Sex-stereotypes in the employment of women and the consequent feminisation of the clerical jobs had become engraved in Government labour policy by 1939. The feminisation of the clerical jobs involved the gradual replacement of men by women in office work. This process was speeded up during the First and Second World Wars as women were given greater opportunities to demonstrate and prove their ability when men left for the war front. Women were considered unsuitable for promotion. Theirs was the routine work of typing and book keeping, among other office duties. It is no coincidence that women's work in the homes also had a routine element. The routine office work resembled continuity from and extension of the domestic spaces. ③

---

① Interview with Adele Hamilton Ritchie, Marlborough, 17 April 2007. Adele worked in the Meteorological department and like several other white women of the day had trained in secretarial courses such as typing. She started her employment in the Service 1968 and ended around 1972 when she got married. She letter re-employed in the better paying banking sector.

② NAZ A/3/7/23, Civil Service; Women Clerks and Typists, G. Ade Report Submitted by the Committee on Lady Clerks and Typists 11 April 1917 (emphasis added).

③ See recommendation by Colin E. Duff in NAZ S246/645, Conditions of Service Department Committee 1917 - 1931, Letter from Colin E. Duff, Secretary of Department of the Colonial State to the Secretary Department of Agriculture, 16 August 1927.

In 1952, the Chegwidden Commission also recommended continued feminisation of the clerical jobs. The Commissioners wrote, "We think the Service should continue to offer opportunities for women in clerical and manipulative occupations. "[1] By the 1960's, clerical office work was avowedly a female domain. [2] Women did not always enjoy the routine clerical jobs. Wormarld who spent a greater part of her career as a secretary, referred to this kind of work as, "monotonous and boring. "[3] Notably, when the Civil Service employed women this did not necessarily mean an abandonment of their domestic responsibilities. In fact, it meant increased burden. One female employee, writing to the editor of *The Rhodesia Herald* lamented, "Believe me, it is not a joke to run a home and a job successfully. "[4]

Remuneration for women was always lower than men's and this was an accepted phenomenon in the industrialized societies. [5] In Southern Rhodesia, the roots of this practice can be located in Europe. Writing on the experiences of women in Europe before the 20th century, Anderson and Zinsser, note that, "women traditionally accepted one half to two thirds the money paid to man for the same job. "[6] These trends were transferred to Southern Rhodesia. As Edone Petheram recalls, "at that stage we accepted it. We were not aggravated by the fact that men earned more than us. "[7] As already noted, this is not surprising as these women had been socialised to accept the gender imbalances as normal.

Lower salaries for women were rationalised on various grounds. A letter to the editor of *The Rhodesia Herald* of 2 February 1955 by one Olivia Twist

---

[1] T. S. Chegwidden, Survey of the Public Services of Rhodesia 1951 – 1952.

[2] Interview with Elizabeth Wormarld, Marlborough, 17 April 2007.

[3] *Ibid*

[4] *The Rhodesia Herald*, 8 February 1955.

[5] B. Anderson and J. P. Zinsser, *A History of Their Own: Women in Europe from Prehistory to the Present*, Vol. II, London, Penguin Books, 1988.

[6] Anderson and Zinsser, *A History of Their Own*, p. 248.

[7] Interview with Edone Petheram, Marlborough, 17 April 2007.

captures some of the justifications that were made for paying women lower salaries. Part of this letter read, "The employer's defence has always been that female staff have always been unstable because the young ones leave to marry, or if they remain after marriage are frequently absent for domestic reasons, or throw up their jobs altogether. [1] While admitting that this was the general behaviour of women, Twist however, felt that it was simply, "an excuse, not a reason for paying all women so much less than men. "[2]

For single women, lower salaries were also rationalised on the grounds that they had only themselves to support. For married women, lower salaries were rationalised on the grounds that they had husbands to support them. Thus, for women it was a catch-22 situation, married or unmarried, they were still exposed to lower salaries. An article in *The Record* of 4 February 1957 confirms these trends. It read, "domestic circumstances also played a part in the assessment of the wages since usually a woman had only herself to support whereas the men ⋯ looked forward to having a home and family. "[3] Similar justifications were made in the Federal Public Service. In 1958, the Federal Information Department argued that, "the additional one-sixth paid to the male teacher helps him to maintain the family. "[4] The rationale was that the woman was part of this family and thus she did not need a higher salary, as the husband would maintain her and the rest of the family.

The Paterson Report of 1961 was peculiar for its 'liberal' approach to issues of white women employment in the Service, notwithstanding, it also rationalised lower salaries for women in lower grades on two major grounds. The First read:

In the lowest grades in the salary scales, there is an external

---

[1] *The Rhodesia Herald*, 2 February 1955.

[2] Ibid.

[3] *The Record*, 4 February 1957.

[4] NAZ S3279/11/109 Employment of Women in Southern Rhodesia Public Service 1955 to 1965; Press Statement by the Federal Information Department, Opportunities for women in Federal Public Service.

necessity for differential between men and women. In the cultural pattern that holds in Rhodesia, whether it be among Europeans or Africans, the commitments of say a man are greater than those of a woman. [1]

Paterson restricted his comments to men and women who had no dependents. For those women in the higher grades, the Report recommended parity in the conditions of service. However, as Wormarld recollects there were few women that ever reached these grades. [2] Qualifications and ability were disregarded in setting up the rates of pay for women and men.

The second justification made by the Report was submerged in high-sounding sociological interpretations. The justification read:

... at these lower grades in the Service, where there is the highest concentration of women, most are young and most have their eye on marriage, which comes upon them either by their failure to resist some bio-chemical urge or by accident. These external, cultural differences would normally be recognized by a positive marginal element, but in a country which cannot afford a positive marginal element; there can only be a negative element, that is to say, there should be, at these lower grades, a differential between male and female salaries. [3]

In essence, lower salaries fueled the patriarchal system as they would emphasise and constantly remind women of their subordinate role and position within Rhodesian society. As Wormarld remarked, "the system was

---

[1] T. T. Paterson, Commission of Enquiry into the organisation and development of Southern Rhodesia Public Service 1st Report 1961.

[2] Interview with Elizabeth Wormarld, Marlborough, 17 April 2007.

[3] Paterson, Commission of Enquiry into the organisation and development of Southern Rhodesia Public Service.

in such a way that it kept women constantly down, definitely low in a way. "① In any case, the lower salaries acted as a disincentive to the extent that few women ever stayed in the service to experience the higher grades. Lower salaries for women also existed in the private sector. Olivia Twist, who was in the private sector, wrote in 1955, "I know of many cases, including my own, where we do similar work for half the salary and it costs us just as much to live decently as the single man or the married one whose wife earns as well.

Despite some changes over time, the grading structure for women in the Service failed to content its women employees and ultimately the needs of the employer as the Service was consequently loosing out on its human resources. According to the evidence on women's grading system obtained by the 1939 Godlonton Commission, promotions were slow; insufficient distinction was made between officers with special qualifications and those who had indifferent or no qualification and between fully trained shorthand-typists and clerks with little or no training. Except in appointments to the Senior Grade, promotion was based on sheer Seniority and there was little scope of encouragement for the efficient officer. ② It is thus not surprising that most women never stayed long enough to realise the promotions to the highest grades.

The Godlonton Commission noted that the promotions in the so-called Senior Grade were "a negligible factor. "③ In its assessment of the promotion avenues for women clerks in the Service, the Commission observed that there was "a lack of any incentive and indifference and stagnation [were] frequently... present. "④ It therefore discouraged the emphasis on seniority in the grading system as it worked as a disincentive. According to the commission, "... if promotion from one grade to another is by merit with

① Interview with Elizabeth Wormarld, Marlborough, 17 April 2007.
② Godlonton, Report of the Commission of Enquiry into Promotions in the Civil Service 1939.
③ Ibid.
④ Ibid

due regard to seniority there will be reasonable prospects of more rapid advancement for the efficient officer. "[1] These observations and recommendations were not seriously considered as the Public Service continued to give white women a raw deal in terms of promotions in the Service.

The Chegwidden Report 1951 - 52 on the Augmented Public Service Board also noted the perpetual impediments to the promotion of women in the Service. [2] In 1952, promotion to the Senior Grade was conditional upon prior appointment to the Special Scale or possession of a qualification, which would render the officer eligible for such appointment. These qualifications were as follows: a) a pass in section A or B of the Intermediate Examinations of the Chartered Secretaries or b) a pass in one of the many other exams which were prescribed or c) a speed of not less than 130 words per minute in shorthand and 45 words per minute in typing or d) in the case of an appointment to a post of verbatim shorthand writing, a speed of not less than 180 words per minute or e) in the case of an appointment to a post of verbatim palantype operator, a speed of not less 180 words per minute. [3]

The Report considered only the qualifications mentioned in (d) and (e) as essential for the promotion of women clerks to the Senior Grade. As for the other grades, the Report recommended promotions to be made on merit and noted that no qualification exams seemed necessary. [4] In a way, this report recommended relaxation on the qualifications for the advancement of women in the Service. However, these recommendations did not entail any real improvement in the promotion prospects for women into positions of administration or greater administrative responsibility.

The state was slow in its response to women's cause with regards to their promotion avenues. It was in 1955 that the State awoke to a serious labour

[1] Godlonton, Report of the Commission of Enquiry into Promotions in the Civil Service 1939.
[2] Chegwidden, Survey of the Public Services of Rhodesia 1951 - 1952.
[3] Ibid.
[4] Ibid.

situation with regards to experienced clerks and typists. The entrance of the Federal Public Service into the scene decisively disturbed the labour market. In that year, Cabinet suggested that "at a suitable time" further considerations be made to improve the prospects for the employment of women in the Public Service for more responsible positions than were currently open to them under the existing regulations. [1] One would think the Colonial State was now initiating better prospects for women advancement in the Service. However, the "suitable time" never seemed to come. The suggestion by Cabinet remained lip service at most, as the grading system continued to reflect exclusion of women in administrative positions. In 1961, six years after the suggestion by Cabinet, the Women's Section of the Administrative and Clerical Branch of the Public Servant's Association described the existing grading structure of the women's section as "most unwieldy and unrealistic [causing] much discontent in this service because of the many anomalies."[2]

Regulations with regards to temporary and Fixed Establishment (permanent employment) were dynamic and they differed between those of married and single women. The general perception was that women would not want to make a career in the Service because their primary obligation lay with the family. As such, married women in particular were not accepted into permanent employment until 1971 when the state abolished the marriage bar. Even then, however, this concession by the Public Service had conditions attached which reminded women of their gender defined roles and subordination to men. Permanent employees, unlike temporary ones, enjoyed security in terms of termination of employment; they enjoyed

---

[1] NAZ S3279/11/109, Employment of Women in Southern Rhodesia Public Service 1955 – 1965, Letter from G. B. Clarke Secretary to the Cabinet to the Secretary for Justice, Internal Affairs, and Housing 15 March 1936.

[2] T. T. Paterson, Commission of Enquiry into the organisation and development of Southern Rhodesia Public Service 1st Report 1961, Recommendations from the Women's Section of the Administrative and clerical Branch of the Public Servant's Association, Appendix A2.

holiday grants and above all pension allowances on retirement. [1]

The prejudice against the employment of married women was deeply engraved in Rhodesian society and reflected on the extension of women's domesticity into the work place. In 1964, one Mr. K. L. Morris wrote to Hardwick, the Secretary for Public Service Board in complaint of the position of married women, "I think it is very unfair for married women to have these secretary and personal stenographer jobs when they have husbands working for them and are not in need of the extra money." [2] Even some women believed that married women had a commitment to their family and husbands and in fact were not supposed to be employed at all. [3] Show us some evidence. For example, writing in 1944, the Federation of Women Institutes in Southern Rhodesia's (FWISR) Convener for Social Service, Mary G. Mackenzie, in her contribution to *VUKA* discouraged women's continued employment after the war adding that, "a mother who is only with her children at bed time is evading one of her greatest responsibilities in life-the day to day shaping of the child's character." [4]

The bias of the Public Service against married women had its basis. As *The New Rhodesia* wrote in 1948, "when women first started careers, they nearly always gave them up on marriage." [5] Hamilton Ritchie's summary of the lifestyles of white women is also quite revealing. She said, "we worked, got married, got pregnant, quit work and that was it." [6] While this summary may seem reductionist, it gives a general picture of the behaviour of women on marriage. They quit work! Admittedly, this too was a product of social

---

[1] T. T. Paterson, Commission of Enquiry into the organisation and development of Southern Rhodesia Public Service 1st Report 1961, Recommendations from the Women's Section of the Administrative and clerical Branch of the Public Servant's Association, Appendix A2.

[2] NAZ S3454/32/4, Recruitment to the Government Service: Local Recruitment 1948 – 1964, Letter from K. L. Morris to Mr. Hardwick, Secretary of the Public Service Board dated 11/02/1964.

[3] *The Rhodesian Herald*, 6 March 1930.

[4] "WI. Notes: Social Services Versus the federation", *VUKA*, Vol. 2, No. 2 (October 1944), p. 67.

[5] *The New Rhodesia*, 15 October 1948.

[6] Interview with Hamilton Ritchie, 17 April 2007.

pressure which encouraged women to leave work upon marriage.

Negotiation and Confrontation

As this section will demonstrate, white women in the Service challenged gender disparities in many ways. Campaigns for parity were, however, intense and more widespread in the post-Second World War period. Unfair conditions of service became the focus of scrutiny. White women challenged the system first in their individual capacity and second through their representative and collective organisations such as the Women's Section of the Administrative and Clerical Branch of the Public Servant's Association (hereafter called the Women's Section or simply the Section). [1] As individuals, women would simply resign when fed up by conditions of service. At times women would unleash their frustration through the media.

Several factors help explain the sudden intensity of women's campaigns for parity from the 1950's. Developments outside Southern Rhodesia played a significant role. For example, Britain extended parity to its Civil servants in 1955 and hoped to have raised the pay for "most women Civil Servants by degrees until it equaled that of men by 1960. "[2] Commenting on this development, Miss Eva Wilkins Chairwoman of the Civil Service Woman Association (CSWA), admitted that opinion in the Federation of Rhodesia and Nyasaland was "quite strongly influenced" by events in Britain. [3] Within the Federation itself, Nyasaland was first to take up the principle of "equal pay for the same job" before Southern Rhodesia. [4] Such developments probably inspired white women in the Southern Rhodesia Public Service to

---

[1] The Public Service Association was representative body made up of public servants and worked more or less like a trade union.

[2] *The Rhodesia Herald*, 27 June 1955.

[3] *Ibid*.

[4] NAZ S3279/11/109, Employment of women in Southern Rhodesia Public Service 1955 – 1965, Letter from Secretary of Justice and Internal affairs to the Secretary to the Prime Minister and Cabinet, 2 March 1961.

battle for equality.

The determination for white women to have equality in the Service also had a racial twist. *The Record* of 4 February 1957 noted, that "it is a natural consequence of the conference resolution of 1956 that Africans entering the Civil Service should be paid the same salary as a European that the woman officers should also desire equal pay. "[1] If Africans would be entered in the Service on the same salary as Europeans, this would mean that the salaries for white women would consequently be lower than the African's. As the Women's Branch of the Administrative and Clerical Association of Southern Rhodesia acknowledged, "no normal woman would be prepared to compete with non-Europeans on a lower salary than the African is receiving. "[2]

It is important to note that campaigns for parity did not specify whether this was being done for the interests of white women per se or there were also being done with black women in mind. What is clear however is that these campaigns would ultimately affect the black women as well. This explains why in 1961 there were fears that extension of parity to white women would have a negative impact on State revenues, as this would mean increasing salaries for black women as well to match their male counterparts. The estimate for such a move was put at £200,000 pounds per month. [3]

Women could easily register their discontent by leaving the Public Service and taking up employment in a better paying job. In the early 1950s, the Chegwidden report noted that married women were shunning the Public Service and taking up employment in the private sector. [4] The situation does not seem to have changed at least until the eve of UDI. In 1964, for instance, P. Dunn, Secretary to the Public Service Board lamented, "we

[1] *The Record*, 4 February 1957.
[2] NAZ S3279/11/109, Employment of women in Southern Rhodesia Public Service 1955 – 1965, letter from Secretary of Justice and Internal affairs to the Secretary to the Prime Minister and Cabinet, 2 March 1961.
[3] NAZ S3279/11/109, Employment of Women in Southern Rhodesia Public Service 1955 – 1965, Cabinet Memorandum from Minister of the Treasury, 17 August 1961.
[4] Chegwidden, Survey of the Public Services of Rhodesia.

have a continued turnover of females leaving for better pasture. Only this morning Education Department conveyed their concern at the resignation of a good female accounts clerk who had obtained a job at £10 per month more. "[1] As already noted, this situation changed with the coming of UDI.

In the 1950s the issue of salary parity between men and women in the British Civil Service was topical. Miss Wilkin, the Chairwoman of CSWA, however gave the impression that women in Southern Rhodesia were not yet clamoring for equal pay for equal work. *The Rhodesian Herald* of 27 June 1955 reported Wilkin's position as follows, "Southern Rhodesian's women Civil Servants are now concerned at present with getting the opportunity to do jobs now done by men, than with pressing for equal pay for men and women in the Service. "[2] For her the pressing issue was occupational segregation and women now wanted to get equal employment opportunities without being segregated on grounds of gender. Of course, this position was not representative of the attitudes of other white women in the Service.

If CSWA did not openly come up to represent women on the question of parity in the Service, they were other representative bodies, which did. In 1957, the Public Service Association (PSA) executive council (apparently constituting male members only) agreed that women should be given opportunity for advancement and be awarded complete parity in all respects in the Service, whatever the department or type of work with the sole exception of the Native Department. The documents I came across do not explain this exception. The executive council also agreed that parity should be given to the women on the existing men's salaries. [3] The principle was presented to the Public Service Board, which also agreed to it. [4] However, this was just the beginning of a battle that was to intensify in the 1960s. It is

---

[1] NAZ S3454/32/4 Recruitment to the Government Service: Local recruitment 1948 – 1964, Minute Sheet M8,7 July 1964.

[2] *The Rhodesia Herald*, 27 June 1955.

[3] *The Record*, October 1957. The Public Service Association was a representative body for the Civil Servants established in 1919 as a result of dissatisfaction with the Service.

[4] *Ibid.*

telling that a male dominated executive council made recommendations to advance women without and indeed they were many men who supported eliminating discrimination against women. While this should be acknowledged, the reality is that it would have to take much more than just men agreeing the principle of women's advancement to bring change. Patriarchy is a system and goes beyond individual men and what they may say. This is why it took forever for the principle to be implemented.

The Southern Rhodesia Administrative and Clerical Branch of the PSA in particular, continued to champion the cause for parity in the Service. In a memorandum to the Paterson Commission of 1961 this Branch wrote:

> The rate for the job is the paramount point for consideration here. If a job is worth certain salary, then the person holding down that job should receive that salary, irrespective of the incumbent's sex or colour. [1]

In addition to gender, the Branch gave importance to race. There was little else said about the racial issue. More emphasis was made on the gender issue where the Branch noted that if an individual was unable to hold down a position satisfactorily because of outside factors such as family or social ties, then this individual was not to be employed in the job. In this way, the Branch was challenging the justifications used to pay women lower salaries than men.

The Women's Section also castigated the Government for its casual approach to women's plight concerning parity of salaries. They felt that they deserved to get a "voice" from Government yet for three years (1957 - 1960) the State was silent and nothing fruitful came out. The State used as one of its excuses to implementing parity that the Federal Services were yet to do so. Frustrated by such delaying gimmicks, the Women's Section wrote:

---

[1] T. T. Paterson, Commission of Enquiry into the organisation and development of Southern Rhodesia Public Service 1st Report 196, the Southern Rhodesia Administrative and Clerical Branch of the PSA, Appendix A1.

This constant "waiting" for Federal Government is a source of irritation to all territorial civil Servants, and this Section cannot understand why the Southern Rhodesia Servants should be bound by Federal Government views. [1]

The Section was bitter about the Government's delaying tactics and failure to resolve women's concerns once and for all. This bitterness was probably made worse by the fact that in the same Federation, the Nyasaland Government had already started implementing the principle of "equal pay for the same rate of work" without waiting for the Federal Government.

Some women groups also spoke against the salary disparities in the Service. The Women's Section was vigorous in its criticism of the salary disparities. Recommendations submitted by the Association to the Paterson Commission are quite revealing. The Women Section wrote:

Women feel strongly more than ever that the qualified women should receive parity with her male counterpart in the Service, not only the same salary scales but the same conditions of service throughout the qualified scales. [2]

In the same submission, the Section also pointed out that "the women of the service as a whole are very concerned with the questions of parity and feel that it is perhaps one of the most important issues that should be discussed. "[3] If in 1952 the Chegwidden Commission failed to notice "any general desire on the part of the women staff generally that equality of pay should be

---

[1] T. T. Paterson, Commission of Enquiry into the organisation and development of Southern Rhodesia Public Service 1st Report 1961, Recommendations from the Women's Section of the Administrative and clerical Branch of the Public Servant's Association, Appendix A2.

[2] Ibid.

[3] Ibid.

introduced"① in 1961, this desire was glaringly noticeable.

The prejudice held against married women was also challenged. As early as 1946, women themselves were challenging the temporary employment of married women. Temporary employment for married women entailed a loss in benefits that were enjoyed by permanent employment. In an annual congress of FWISR in 1946, it was proposed that, "the Government should recognise the principle of permanent employment for married women with academic and specialised qualifications. "② The Chegwidden Report, however, gives the impression that white women did not really want to see this "marriage bar" removed. It concluded that, "there [was] no popular demand amongst married women Civil Servants for the abolition of the marriage bar. "③ Given the resolution made by FWISR, the conclusion made by the Chegwidden Commission should be treated cautiously. Perhaps this disparity is because the consultations by either party where not as wide and comprehensive to be conclusive.

It is not clear how the Commission came to its conclusion. There is, however, no doubt that some women may have been comfortable with temporary employment as this would have given more flexibility in their domestic obligations. The Chegwidden Commission notes that married women did not "desire to assume the obligations which would be necessary collorary of permanent and pensionable employment. "④ The Commission also argued that married women preferred, for example, to transfer from one centre to another with their husbands, to be free to take their holidays when their husbands are on leave, and to relinquish their employment at short notice for domestic reasons. ⑤ The question that immediately comes to mind

---

① Chegwidden, "Survey of the Public Services of Rhodesia".
② NAZ S824/198/2 Federation of Women's Institutes, Federation of Women's Institutes of Southern Rhodesia, 20 August to 21 August 1946.
③ Chegwidden, Survey of the Public Services of Rhodesia.
④ Ibid.
⑤ Ibid.

is: how representative were these observations? The representative nature of this commission is indeed questionable. In 1961, women clearly spoke out clearly against what was being termed "marriage bar" and displayed interest in its removal.

In the 1960s, white women were challenging the mentality that married women were to be employed temporarily to suit their domestic responsibilities. The Women's Section wrote:

> The obligations of a married woman whose husband is supporting her and her family rest first and for most with her husband and family, and should she seek employment with the Government, then it follows that she must abide by the conditions of service as laid down for all government employees. They should be no special concession for this type of employee to receive unpaid leave (as at present) so that her leave may coincide with her husband-this is discriminatory and there is nothing to balance this up for the woman who has no husband. [1]

White women in the Service were discontent about the marriage bar, which perpetuated discrimination and the patriarchal ideology of subornation of women to men.

The Women's Section found the whole system of temporary employment unjust and abhorrable. As already noted, married women were employed temporarily in permanent posts for indefinite periods. There were cases of women who served the Government for anything from 15 – 18 or more years, but still received no concessions in the way of holiday grants or pension funds. [2] Bitter about such injustice, the Section wrote to the Paterson Commission:

---

[1] T. T. Paterson, Commission of Enquiry into the organisation and development of Southern Rhodesia Public Service 1st Report 1961, Recommendations from the Women's Section of the Administrative and clerical Branch of the Public Servant's Association, Appendix A2.

[2] Ibid.

Not by any stretch of imagination can an employee be considered "temporary" with 10,15 or 20 years or more continuous service with the Government, and such cases should be considered for permanent conditions of employment.... The idea for the government is that all staff should be permanent employees. ①

The Section was thus seeking sweeping reforms that would overhaul the employment system of white women in the Service. Indeed, "time [had] come for this injustice to cease. "②

The sex-stereotypes, which were engraved in the service, were also criticized as discriminatory and unfounded. Sex-stereotypes were a result of certain perceptions about women's ability or lack therein. Women in Southern Rhodesia challenged sex-stereotypes in the Public Service. Realising, for example, that if Rhodesian girls did not take up nursing they could only specialise in shorthand typing, the FWISR in 1947 passed a resolution that, "a technical school for girls be opened to give girls a wider range of careers to choose from when they come to earn their leaving. "③ The resolution was, however, turned down by the state arguing that, "a population the size of Johannesburg would be needed to justify such a school. "④ In essence, the State did not see itself striking a major benefit from this proposal hence its cold shoulder.

In 1961, the Women's Section also challenged the sex-stereotypes in the Service. The Section was bitter about the exclusion of women from certain grades of the service especially of greater responsibility. It registered women's discontent as follows:

---

① T. T. Paterson, Commission of Enquiry into the organisation and development of Southern Rhodesia Public Service 1st Report 1961, Recommendations from the Women's Section of the Administrative and clerical Branch of the Public Servant's Association, Appendix A2.

② *The Rhodesia Herald*, 2 February 1955.

③ *The New Rhodesia*, 18 November 1948.

④ *Ibid*.

The Women's Section view with concern that no provision for women has been made on the executive grade in the latest Service's Board Regulations···. When this was under discussion, the Women's Section had been given to understand that provision would be made for women in this grade. It must be noted that they are numerous female accountants clerks in the Government Service .... We should submit that women should not be debarred from this grade [the executive grade] merely from the sex point of view, and in reverse the male should not be debarred from entering the Service with typing, shorthand of machine operating qualifications ... [1]

The Section was challenging the mentality that women were ideal for what the Chegwidden Report called "clerical and manipulative occupations"[2] of the Service while men were destined for administrative and managerial posts. It was also challenging the narrow avenues of advancement for women into more responsible posts.

By and large, the battle against gender disparities and poor conditions of service for women was far from being won by the end of the 1960s. Though grading structures for women were continuously changing, promotion avenues remained skewed as white women were excluded in posts of administrative responsibilities. For married women, it was only in 1971 that concessions for their permanent employment in the Service were made, as the marriage bar was officially lifted and, in theory, married women could be permanently employed. Even then, however, the reality was that women continued to get married and proceed to either leave work or to take up temporary posts. [3]

---

[1] T. T. Paterson, Commission of Enquiry into the Organisation and development of Southern Rhodesia Public Service 1st Report 1961, Recommendations from the Women's Section of the Administrative and clerical Branch of the Public Servant's Association, Appendix A2.

[2] Chegwidden, Survey of the Public Services of Rhodesia.

[3] For details on the nature of the concession made to married women for their permanent employment in the Public Service, see Godwin and Hancock, 'Rhodesians Never Die', p. 23.

There are several factors that account for the relegation of white women to the periphery of the public service. As already been noted, not every woman was behind the cause for equality or justice for women in the Service. Many women subscribed to the status quo. While we must be cautious and even question the representative nature of the Chegwidden Commission Report we cannot out rightly dismiss its findings. In 1952, the Commission reported that it was unable to "discern any general desire on the part of the women staff generally that equality of pay should be introduced. "[1] Miss Edone Pethoram recalled, "At that stage we women accepted the disparity; we were brought up to it. We were not aggravated by the fact that men earned more than us. "[2] The attitudes displayed by these women are not surprising. As Pethoram succinctly puts it, the women had been socialised into these injustices and many naturally absorbed them as the norm. With quite a number of women still accepting the existing traditions, the success of women's cause in the service was to be compromised.

One big blow to the success of women's cries for better prospects in the Service emanated from the fact that men were the ones who occupied the policy-making positions in Government. Wormarld summarized this situation. She said, "there were all men in the [higher] positions, there were no women. So if you were having problems you had to present it to a man and hopefully they would take your case through. "[3] A male dominated system had little sympathy with women concerns sometimes not deliberately, but simply because men did not experience the same with women and as such men were least qualified to represent the interests of women.

Some men also remained conservative. *The Record* of 4 February 1957 noted that representatives of the Administrative and Clerical Association were not all completely behind the proposals of full equality for women

---

① Chegwidden, Survey of the Public Services of Rhodesia.
② Interview with Edone Pethoram, Marlborough, 17 April 2007.
③ Interview with Elizabeth Wormarld, Marlborough, 17 April 2007.

regarding salaries. [1] D. H. Spafford, for instance, considered that such a step would also tend to discourage marriage and stated that traditionally the salary of a male officer was greater than that of a woman. [2] It is not clear how parity would discourage marriage. J. I. Money, another representative, "expressed concern that by obtaining equality possibly women officers would suffer since in the majority of cases the head of department would prefer to select a male rather than a female to fill a vacant post. "[3] Thus different men opposed the proposals for equality on various grounds.

The Colonial State's inconsistence and double standards also compromised the success of women in fighting for improved and satisfactory conditions of service. In 1955, for example, the State realised that it was losing out on experienced and qualified women because of its bias against the permanent employment of married women. The Federation, the United Kingdom and other Governments for instance were making special arrangements for the employment of married women. [4] In the light of these developments, Cabinet proposed in 1955 "giving married women some better prospects for permanent employment. "[5] The idea was to make more efficient use of the services from married women who were prepared to stay in the Service. [6] In 1958, however, the Public Service Board advised Mr. M. K. B. Brookes, Secretary of Justice and Internal Affairs, that it had deferred "consideration of the appointment of married women to the Fixed Establishment pending definite information from the Interim Federal Service Commission on the policy to be adopted in the Federal Service. "[7] In 1959,

---

① *The Record*, 4 February 1955.
② *Ibid.*
③ *Ibid.*
④ NAZ S3279/11/109, Employment of Women in Southern Rhodesia Public Service 1955 – 1965, Letter to the Prime Minister 13 February 1959.
⑤ *Ibid.*
⑥ *Ibid.*
⑦ NAZ S3279/11/109, Employment of Women in Southern Rhodesia Public Service 1955 – 1965, Letter from M. K. Brookes Secretary for Justice and Internal Affairs to the Secretary to the Prime Minister and Cabinet Office, 29 October 1958.

the Prime Minister commenting on the same issue wrote, "… at the present time when there is a certain amount of unemployment, you may not wish to have this question actively pursued. "[1] Thus the issue of permanent employment for married women had to wait until it was most convenient.

The Colonial State seemed to deliberately delay dealing with pertinent issues related to women's conditions of service. In 1961, the Women's Branch of the Administrative and Clerical Branch submitted to the Government a memorandum in which they proposed salary parity between men and women in the Service. In response to these proposals, the Government "agreed to parity of pay between man and women based on equal work and responsibility provided that the typing grade was kept entirely separate. "[2] Two points can be made on the Government's response. First, many women were to get a raw deal from this arrangement because they were in the typing grade which was to be kept "entirely separate. " Second, the State only agreed to this principle but never applied it. The decision on parity was also conveniently referred to Nyasaland and the Federal Government, as "it was possible that their conditions of service would be affected. "[3] The Federal Government was not yet implementing this policy and, on these grounds, Southern Rhodesia suspended the implementation of equal pay for equal work. This was just buying time. Nyasaland had since started implementing the policy despite the fact that the Federal Government had not. [4] The Southern Rhodesia Government conveniently dismissed the path taken by Nyasaland and followed developments in the Federation.

---

[1] NAZ S3279/11/109, Employment of Women in Southern Rhodesia Public Service 1955 – 1965, Letter from M. K. Brookes Secretary for Justice and Internal Affairs to the Secretary to the Prime Minister and Cabinet Office, 29 October 1958.

[2] NAZ S3279/11/109, Employment of Women in Southern Rhodesia Public Service 1955 – 1965, Letter from Secretary of Justice and Internal affairs to the Secretary to the Prime Minister and Cabinet, 2 March 1961.

[3] Ibid.

[4] NAZ S3279/11/109, Employment of women in Southern Rhodesia Public Service 1955 – 1965, Letter from Secretary of Justice and Internal affairs to the Secretary to the Prime Minister and Cabinet, 2 March 1961.

Conclusion

The plight of white women clerks in the Service can be appreciated in the context of the perceptions that settler society had of the roles and position of women. Primarily, Rhodesian society considered white women as housewives whose entrance into formal employment, in this case the Public Service, was optional and not vital. It was only for the men that a career was vital. [①] This thinking, among others, shaped the conditions of service for women not only in the Public Service but in commerce and industry as well. In the Public Service, white women were concentrated in clerical administration, a work space that was in the periphery of the labour market. Their conditions of service reflected on the dominant domestic ideology which had been extended from the home space. In the work place, just as in the home, women were to occupy subordinated positions and take up repetitive and confined work. In the Public Service, women continued to fight for better prospects in but with little concessions from the Government.

The paper contributes to growing discourses on gender and empire which or seek insert white/colonial women into discussions of empire. While scholarship has been interested in the political and social processes shaping white women's experiences, roles and status, this paper adds a dimension of the colonial labour market. The paper demonstrates not only how the labour market was a product of social processes hinged on the nature of the gender terrain, but also a product of the economic processes. It very much demonstrates the interplay, if not conspiracy of patriarchy and capital in relegating women to the periphery of the labour market.

[①] NAZ S3279/11/109, Employment of Women in Southern Rhodesia Public Service 1955 – 1965, Press Statement made by the Federal Information Department dated 15/10/58. The exact Statement is captured in the title of the work. Though the statement was made in reference to the Federal Public Service, this thinking was prevalent in Southern Rhodesia and it affected the employment of women in the Southern Rhodesia Public Service in a big way throughout the colonial period.

Water and Power at Play: the Federal Power Board and the Politics of Hydro-Electricity on the Kariba Dam, 1950s to 1960s

Massiline Ruvingo

Abstract

   This article examines the management of the hydro-electricity project at the Kariba Dam within the context of the political economy of the Central African Federation. First, it traces the origins of the Board, delineating the economic and political factors played a critical role in the conception of both the hydro-electricity project and the board itself. Second, the article examines the operations of the Board during the 1950s and early 1960s, demonstrating that although the Board was supposedly apolitical, it inevitably became entangled in the politics of the Federation, but this did not severely affect its ability to discharge its mandate. Indeed, through cooperation by all territories involved, the hydro-electricity project worked relatively smoothly. Finally, the paper discusses the politics of the dissolution of the Federation and the extent to which it affected the FPD. It argues that the Board successfully navigated the politics of the day with the result that the project outlived the Federation under which it had been conceived. This study has contributed to at least two themes on Africa's colonial past; namely the Federation experience and colonial hydro-politics. In this way, the article makes a modest contribution to existing knowledge on the political economy of the management *of water and power resources in colonial Africa, especially among countries that shared resources. More generally, using the FPB and its management of power generation, the article engages and seeks to make a contribution to the historiography around the Central African Federation.*

Key Words: Hydro-electricity, Kariba, Federal Power Board, Southern Rhodesia, Northern Rhodesia, Federation.

Introduction

This article examines the operations of the Federal Power Board (FPB) from its inception in 1956 to its dissolution in December 1963 as it managed the power supplies to Southern Rhodesia (Zimbabwe) for its industrial development in the post 1945 period. [1] It does this within the context of the economics and politics of the Central African Federation. Established in 1953, the Federation was a loose ten-year union comprising the British colonies of Northern Rhodesia, Southern Rhodesia and Nyasaland (now Zambia, Zimbabwe and Malawi). [2] Under this arrangement, Southern Rhodesia would be the industrial hub while the two northern territories of Northern Rhodesia and Nyasaland would offer minerals, particularly copper and labour respectively. In theory, the Federation was supposed to benefit all three territories, but in practice, Southern Rhodesia reaped the most benefits by using copper and labour resources for its industrial development. Moreover, the Federation of Rhodesia and Nyasaland also sought to advance racial co-operation, but the envisaged partnership between blacks and whites

---

[1] Southern Rhodesian industry was developing fast as it supplied European countries with war needs, such as food and train ground for British air force.

[2] "Kariba Dam Zambia and Zimbabwe", Final Report prepared for World Commission on Dams, https://cpb-us-el.wpmucdn.com/share.nanjingschool.com/dist/1/43/files/2013/05/World_Commission_on_Dams_2000_Case_Study_Kariba_Dam_Final_Report_November_2000-2etc5lv.pdf, accessed 09 September 2019, p. 7.

failed, and this continued to haunt the Federation until its dissolution. [1]
Within this context, this article explores the institutional history of the FPB
and the development of the hydro-electric project of the Kariba Dam.

Moreover, this paper explores the issues that emerged during the
dissolution process and the factors that influenced developments during the
process. The dissolution was complicated by a number of factors, among
which was the independence of Northern Rhodesia at a time when the white
supremacist government in Southern Rhodesia was entrenching its power. [2]
Indeed, for this and other reasons, from the onset the Federation faced
threats from African nationalists and resentment from northern territories
due to racial inequalities. [3] Given the stakes that Rhodesia and Zambia held
in the project, the dissolution process proved to be sensitive. In this article I
demonstrate that the Kariba case is an interesting lens through which the
management of inter-state water bodies may be analysed within peculiar
socio-economic and political contexts. Apart from the hydro-politics, the
dam project had an estimated debt of 74. 5 million Pounds and it was hoped to
keep the final cost at approximately 78 million Pounds, all of which needed
deliberations on how to manage in the post-Federation era. [4] Using primary
data, especially reports by committees, correspondence between British
Government, Southern Rhodesia and Zambia, newspaper cuttings, minutes
of meetings and parliamentary debates both from the territories and the
Federation, the study argues that the relatively smooth flow of the dissolution
process with regards to the Kariba Dam owed much to the mechanics of the

---

[1] C. G. Gooseburg, "The Federation of Rhodesia and Nyasaland: Problems of Democratic Government",
The Annals of the American Academy of Political and Social Science, Vol. 306, (Jul. , 1956),
p. 98.

[2] *Ibid*.

[3] For a detailed history of African Nationalist see N. Sithole, African Nationalism (Oxford: Oxford
University Press, 1968), R. I. Rotberg, The case of Nationalism in Central Africa: The making of
Malawi and Zambia 1873 – 1964 (Cambridge: Harvard University Press, 1965) and I. Henderson,
"The origins of Nationalism in East and Central Africa: The case of Zambia", *Journal of African
History* Vol. xi, No. 4(1970), pp. 591 – 603.

[4] NAZ F116/587/ Paper No. 10: Federal Governmental Loan. p. 1.

dissolution itself and the role played by different governments. Indeed, the lack of major conflicts over the Kariba Dam when compared to other water bodies in the world has a lot to do with how this was handled during the dissolution process.

The Federation aimed to provide a bigger market and a wider pool for African labour in the territories involved, opportunities that territorial governments on their own were not capable of achieving. Southern Rhodesia would benefit from the copper exports in Northern Rhodesia, as the earnings were used to develop federal projects. These projects included the long-planned Reserve Bank, a new university, a Federal Broadcasting Corporation, the Federal Security Intelligence Bureau and the Kariba Dam Project, which were the hegemonic foundations of sovereignty and state power for a new Central African dominion "too big to fail". [1] Referring to the Kariba Dam, the hydroelectric project signified a great success for the Federal government as it called for the utilisation of resources outside the proficiency of territorial government of Southern Rhodesia, which went beyond the mere generation of electricity to meet the Federation's energy requirements. As a brain child of the Federation, the Kariba Dam project was a complicated issue when it came to dissolution. For instance, there were critical questions such as which of the three territorial government was to own the dam and what rights would be bestowed on the territorial governments over the dam.

Discoursing hydro-politics and the politics of Federation

This study is informed by the works of Isaacman and Isaacman which provides context of colonial development of dams and its deleterious

---

[1] R. P. Kay, "The Geopolitics of Dependent Development in Central Africa: Race, Class and the Reciprocal Blockade", *Commonwealth & Comparative Politics* Vol. 49, No. 3, July 2011, p. 410.

consequences. ① Massive dams symbolised progress of the humanity from a life ruled by nature and superstition to a one where nature is ruled by science. ② In the colonial period, dams were regarded as symbols of modernity and state power. Dams were also constructed to address issues of electricity in Africa. For instance, the Cahora Bassa was constructed to cement security alliance between the Portuguese colonial state (Mozambique) and South Africa by supplying electricity to South Africa. The Kariba Dam was specifically built to address issues of power supply to the Federation of Rhodesia and Nyasaland.

Apart from the works of Isaacman and Isaacman, Maseko has written on the development of electricity in Zimbabwe from 1936 to 1970. ③ Power generation has been developed to meet electrical demand for industrial (particularly in mines and in both heavy and light industry) and domestic use. Maseko discusses the transition from thermal (archaic) power to hydro-electricity (advanced), giving reason why the latter was preferred over the former and also adding why at times both forms of electricity were adopted. ④ Although Maseko discusses the FPB, there is only a handful of information regarding the FPB. Moses Chikowero writes on electrification and power politics in Bulawayo, looking at when public electricity supplies became available in Bulawayo as early as 1897 and subsequently developed to become

---

① A. F. Isaacman and B. S. Isaacman, *Dams Displacement, and the Delusion of Development: Cahora Bassa and its Legacies in Mozambique, 1965 - 2007*, University of KwaZulu-Natal Press, 2014, p. 8.

② *Ibid.*

③ D. Maseko, "The development and impact of the electricity industry in Zimbabwe 1936 - 1970", MA Thesis, Economic History Department, University of Zimbabwe, 1988.

④ See Maseko David, "The development and impact of the electricity industry in Zimbabwe 1936 - 1970", MA Thesis, Economic History Department, University of Zimbabwe, 1988; M. M. Makonnen and A. Y. Hoekstra, The water footprint of electricity from hydropower, Value of Water Research Report Series No. 51, UNESCO-IHE, Delft, the Netherlands, (2011); Tafadzwa Makonese, "Renewable energy in Zimbabwe", https://www.researchgate.net/publication/304021888; Moses Chikowero Moses Chikowero, "Subalternating Currents: Electrification and Power Politics in Bulawayo, Colonial Zimbabwe, 1894 - 1939," *Journal of Southern African Studies*, Vol. 33, No. 2(2007), p. 287.

the major source of power and lighting for industries and homes by the 1930s. [1] He demonstrates that electrification was a parochial project that advanced the interests of white settler residents to the almost total exclusion of Africans. [2] This article builds upon these studies, but seeks to add onto these voices by paying particular attention to the Kariba hydro-electric project. That is looking at the functions and operations of FPB in managing the hydro-electric project at Kariba Dam.

Writing on the effects of the creation of the dam on the Tonga people, [3] Peter Makaye concurs with Isaacman and Isaacman particularly on some of the negative effects of the construction of the Kariba dam. It is argued that the construction experiences some chaotic evictions of around 57,000 Gwembe Tonga people north and south of the Zambesi River. [4] Elizabeth Colson echoes similar observation underscoring the deleterious effect on the social lives of those that were displaced. [5] Kariba Dam construction began with the end of the Second World War in 1945 and the drive for industrial development, which followed the end of the war. The Dam did 'tame' the Zambezi but not the 'moods of violence' of the people and after years of growing unrest, the Federation broke apart in 1963. [6]

Tischler uses the Kariba Dam scheme as a microcosm of the discourses and politics of development in understanding state building of a multi-racial nation. [7] The Federation crumbled while Kariba endured economically and

[1] Chikowero, "Subalternating Currents: Electrification and Power Politics in Bulawayo, Colonial Zimbabwe, 1894–1939", p. 287.

[2] Ibid.

[3] P. Makaye, "The Economic and Social consequences of the creation of Lake Kariba upon the Tonga people with particular reference to the Zimbabwean Tonga 1955 – 1994", BA Hons Dissertation, Economic History Department, University of Zimbabwe, 1995.

[4] Tischler, Light and Power for a multiracial Nation: The Kariba Dam Scheme in Central African Federation. p. 2.

[5] E. Colson, The Social consequences of Resettlement, The Impact of the Kariba Resettlement Upon the Gwembe Tonga, Manchester: Manchester University Press, 1971.

[6] Ibid.

[7] Ibid, p. 3.

ideologically and this symbolises the incompleteness of decolonisation and points to continuities and deep entanglements between the colonial and postcolonial eras. ① David Hughes has shown how the reservoir was also used by Southern Rhodesia's settlers to construct a sense of belonging in Africa. Through Kariba, Hughes argues, Europeans in Africaintegrated themselves more deeply than ever into Africa's environment. ② This study builds upon these works by offering a nuanced discussion of the history of the FPB and the hydro-electric project on Kariba Dam, an area that has not yet been studied comprehensively.

This study also benefits from literature on the Federation of Rhodesia and Nyasaland itself. Michael Collins posits that the Federation was an ambivalent move towards decolonisation as well as a means of securing imperial control. ③ The Federation faced great resistance from the Africans. African nationalism and majority rule was a pragmatic response to changing political realities, a recognition of the bankruptcy of the Federal experiment and, in part, an attempt to safeguard the interests of Africa interests. ④ Tischler is of the view that the Central African Federation was "formed against fierce African opposition" contributing to it being "a fragile union between NR, Nyasaland, and SR with its strong settler community."⑤ A. S. Mlambo also documents the wide spread "African opposition throughout its [Federation] ten years of existence from 1953 to 1963, with the staunchest opposition coming from two northern territories where nationalists were

---

① E. Colson, *The Social consequences of Resettlement*, *The Impact of the Kariba Resettlement Upon the Gwembe Tonga*, Manchester: Manchester University Press, 1971, p. 6.
② D. M. Hughes, *Whiteness in Zimbabwe: Race, landscape, and the problem of Belonging*, Palgrave: McMillan, 2010, p. xiiii.
③ Decolonisation and the "Federal Moment", Diplomacy and statecraft. p. 22.
④ Butler, "Business and British Decolonisation: Sir Ronald Prain, the Mining Industry and the Central African Federation", p. 477.
⑤ Tischler, *Light and Power for a multiracial Nation: The Kariba Dam Scheme in Central African Federation*. p. 2.

angry at the fact that their views had not been solicited. "[1] These works offer important contextual contexts from which an examination of the FPB may be done.

T. Nyamunda and B. Chibhamu, in separate works, make reference to the dissolution processes. [2] Nyamunda discusses the financial handling of the dissolution processes by the Rhodesian Government while Chibhamu refers to dissolution processes in the sphere of pensions. Central to the Federal dissolution process was the transference of currency, banking and exchange control functions which would be suitably adapted to individual territorial economies. [3] Chibhamu refers to dissolution processes in the area of pensions, he narrates how assets were transferred from federal ownership to Central African Pensions, that is, territorial ownership. [4] Exploring the functions of FPB and examines how the dissolution process handled the Kariba Dam project, this article adds yet another dimension to studies on the delicacies associated with the dissolution of the Federation.

Kariba Hydropolitics and the Federal Power Board, 1950s – 1963

The Federal Power Board was established after the formation of the Federation to manage the hydroelectric scheme and the politics of the Kariba Dam. The Federal Power Board was responsible for managing the Hydro-politics of Kariba Dam, a critical source of hydroelectricity for the Federation. The Kariba

---

[1] A. S. Mlambo, "From World War to the UDI 1940 – 1965" Alois S. Mlambo in B. Raftopoulos and A. S. Mlambo (eds) Becoming Zimbabwe: A History from Pre-colonial Period to 2008, Zimbabwe: Weaver Press, 2009, p. 89.

[2] T. Nyamunda, "Financing Rebellion: The Rhodesian State, Financial Policy and exchange control 1962 – 1979", University of Free State: South Africa, 2015 and Ben-junior Chibhamu, "The pension fund system in Southern Rhodesian with special reference to the government 1900 – 1965", BA Special Hons in Economic History, University of Zimbabwe, 2016.

[3] Nyamunda, "Financing Rebellion: The Rhodesian State, Financial Policy and exchange control 1962 – 1979", p. 70.

[4] Chibhamu, "The pension fund system in Southern Rhodesian with special reference to the government 1900 – 1965".

project was designed as a power scheme for the Central African Federation (CAF) and irrigation was regarded an auxiliary benefit. [1] The construction of Kariba Dam did not only involve Federal territories but also other riparian territories that used water from the Zambezi river and negotiations had to be made with the Portuguese government and South African Government to avoid conflict over the use of the Zambezi waters. Portuguese authorities in Mozambique had planned the construction of an irrigation scheme at Cahora Bassa which would require greater flow from the Zambezi. [2] South Africa was involved because of its control of Namibia which has the Caprivi Strip. The construction of the Kariba Dam began in 1955 and was to be constructed in stages. Its construction was projected to end in 1968. The success of the hydro-electric project owed much to the institutions that were put in place to manage hydroelectricity and the politics around it.

This section explores the functions and operations of the Federal Power Board during the Federal period from 1953 to 1963. Some of the functions of the Board included loan acquisition and repayment to the lenders who had made construction of the dam project possible as well as negotiating with other countries over the use of the Kariba Dam. Second, I examine how Kariba Dam as a water body was managed with particular reference to the hydro-politics of the Kariba Dam and how the Board also managed the Kariba Dam to ensure "equitable" use and "reasonable" sharing of the Zambezi waters. The manner in which issues to do with hydro-electricity were handled confirms the observation that the Federation itself benefited Southern Rhodesia the most.

The Kariba Dam Project was a product of, among other things, international agreements on the use of Zambezi waters, loan agreements with lenders, huge surveys and debates on the control over the waters of Lake Kariba. Territories negotiated agreements on the use of Zambezi waters prior

---

[1] NAZ F116/587/6 Dissolution Papers: Federal Power Board, control over the waters of Lake Kariba, p. 1.

[2] Ibid, p. 3.

to the construction of the Kariba Dam project and during the construction of the Kariba Dam. Meetings were made with different countries as early as 1949. The following year separate negotiations were also made with both the Portuguese Government and the South African Government. This was before the Federation.

Prior to the FPB there were other institutions/frameworks that were implemented to manage hydro-electric projects. The Kariba Dam project was itself not the first hydro-electric scheme to be attempted. Before the Kariba Dam project there was the Kafue hydro-electric project under the Federal Hydro-Electric Board (FHEB) which handed over all its research to the FPB. This subsection traces some of these shifts and changes and other developments resulting in the establishment of the FPB.

In 1949, a meeting was held in Johannesburg to discuss development projects in general on the Zambezi River. South Africa, Nyasaland, Bechuanaland and both Rhodesias were present. The Federal Government, however, later side-lined South Africa which was considered not directly affected by the Kariba Project as this would not have direct effects on South African interests. [1] Negotiations continued the following year in 1950 with other riparian states to be affected by the establishment of the Kariba Dam. The conference was held in Salisbury to discuss prospects of exploiting the Zambezi waters. [2] Representatives from Southern Rhodesia, Nyasaland, Portugal, Central African Council and the Inter-territorial Hydro-electric power commission agreed that irrigation needs of Mozambique must be met. [3] Angola was also considered to ensure that her needs were met as well. [4] The delegates agreed that the riparian states should benefit from the construction of the hydro-electric project on the Zambezi. [5] In November of the same

---

[1] NAZ F116/587/6, Paper no. 8: International agreements about the use of the waters of the Zambezi negotiated in connection with the Kariba hydro-electric project (nd), p. 4.

[2] *Ibid*, p. 1.

[3] *Ibid*.

[4] *Ibid*.

[5] *Ibid*, p. 2.

year, the Portuguese Government and the British Government agreed to the resolutions of the conference on behalf of their colonies. [1] The above-mentioned negotiations and agreements were only the beginning of mutual understanding between the territories.

Financial obligation was one of the responsibilities of the FPB therefore, it had to consider cost cutting by altering some clauses of the 1950 agreement. The FPB made alterations to some aspects of the previous agreement (to financially compensate Mozambique due to loss caused by disturbances in the flow of the River) as part of the agreement was found to compensate Mozambique costly and inconvenient and would substantially delay the filling of the Dam. [2] The Kariba Dam project was financed from a number of local and international sources, including the World Bank, which provided a sum of $80 million in 1956. [3] The Federal Government also borrowed money from the International Bank for Reconstruction and Development (IBRD) and the International Bank which was repayable in instalments ending in 1973. [4]

The construction of the Kariba Dam was also a source of debates in the Federal Parliament. The debates, among other things, centred on the dual role which the Kariba waters could play. Despite the fact that irrigation could jeopardise electrical generation, considerations for irrigation were made. Water was not to be abstracted in such a way that it would inhibit the installation of the second power station as international repercussions could ensue. It must be noted that Mozambique was also considering constructing an irrigation scheme at Cahora Bassa which would require greater flow of water from the Kariba. [5] Territories had to be in agreement in connection with schemes which used water from Lake Kariba. And as such a

------

[1] NAZ F116/587/6, Paper no. 8: International agreements about the use of the waters of the Zambezi negotiated in connection with the Kariba hydro-electric project (nd), p. 2.

[2] Ibid, p. 3.

[3] World Commission Dams, p. 9.

[4] NAZ F116/587/6, Paper no. 10: Federal government: Loan no. 4 (nd), p. 1.

[5] NAZ F116/587/6, paper no. 9: control over the waters of lake Kariba, (nd), p. 1.

memorandum prepared by the Ministry of Power pointed out that water from the Zambezi into Lake Kariba would be utilised for power production. The hydro-electric project would be crippled if less water was available than the quantities for which the scheme was planned to be developed. [1] Water abstraction would impair electric production therefore the issue of dual role had to be traded carefully.

Prior to the formation of the FPB, there was the Federal Hydro-electric Board (FHB) which was established in terms of the Hydro-electric Power Act 1954 to further the development of the Kariba and Kafue schemes. In 1956 FHB was disbanded to make way for FPB which operated under the Electricity Act until 1961 when the Lake Kariba Waters Act was enacted. The Zambezi River Authority gives an insightful summary of the FPB as follows:

> In June 1954 the Hydro-Electric Power Act was passed which provided for the establishment of the Federal Hydro-Electric Board charged with the function of Coordinating the generation and supply of electricity within the Federation. In May 1956 the Federal Power Board was established pursuant to the enactment of the Electricity Act. This was a reconstitution of the Federal Hydro-Electric Board. The new Board was vested with the power to construct dams and power stations, to transmit electric power and sell same to Electricity undertakings. A hydrological data collection organization operating in each territory was also established. [2]

The above quote succinctly summarises the institutional shifts that occurred during the Federal period as well as some of the legislative

---

[1] NAZ F116/587/6, Paper no. 25: Agreements between governments in connection with schemes which use water from lake Kariba (nd), p. 1.

[2] "Welcome to Zambezi River Authority", (nd) https://bghes. org/hydro-electric-schemes/ accessed 07 September 2019.

frameworks that were in place.

According to the World Commission for Dams (WCD), the Kariba gorge was considered a favourable site by federal protagonists who "saw the Kariba Dam and its associated lake as a prestigious symbol of the political and economic links that they were attempting to forge between the two territories [Southern and northern Rhodesia]."[1] Initially, the Kafue project had received support even from Southern Rhodesia "largely on grounds of reduced costs and speed with which it could be constructed."[2] It was also believed that this would benefit the Copperbelt and the Federation at large. An application for a World Bank loan for Kafue was made. However, in spite of all this, "Kariba was still considered by some in the Federation as a more favourable site, whilst the potential at Kafue was seen to have been overestimated".[3]

The Federal-Hydroelectric Board took over the Inter-territorial Power Commission in May, 1954 to further the development of both the Kafue and Kariba schemes. Experts were consulted to resolve the argument for Kariba versus Kafue. After examining the two projects, the experts advised in favour of the larger Kariba scheme. Construction at Kariba started later in 1955. Not surprisingly those in Northern Rhodesia felt short changed and complained but this did not change anything. The following year the World Bank stepped in with finance. Interestingly, a substantial amount of the funding came from the copper mines "which were in dire need of cheap power".[4] The Kafue scheme was not the only scheme abandoned in favour of Kariba at that time even irrigation and fishery potential of Kariba of the Zambezi downstream of Kariba was ignored for the expensive Kariba scheme

[1] "Welcome to Zambezi River Authority", (nd) https://bghes. org/hydro-electric-schemes/ accessed 07 September 2019.
[2] "Kariba Dam Zambia and Zimbabwe", Final Report prepared for World Commission on Dams World, p. xv.
[3] Ibid.
[4] Ibid.

despite the fact that it would take longer to construct. [1]

When the FPB came into being in May, 1956, it was directed by the Minister of Power to arrange for safe keeping the results for the work done in connection of the Hydro-electric scheme on the Kafue River and to continue hydro-electrical investigations. [2] In retrospect, it can be supposed that, "had the Federation continued the planned Kafue and Kariba Hydro-electric schemes could have been run jointly to conserve water in Kariba at times when power station at Kafue was capable of meeting the electric load, and a common hydrological pattern would have developed for both rivers." [3]

Functions and Operations of the Federal Power Board and the Kariba Dam

The FPB was mandated to manage the construction of the Kariba Dam and the Hydro-electric project. The Board was to ensure the smooth running of the hydro-electric project and the hydro-politics of the Kariba Dam, that is, the generation, transmission and distribution of electricity to Federal territories. Kariba Dam was constructed in two stages, with the total cost of stage one being approximated at 78 million Pounds. [4] The FPB had regulatory powers over the use of Kariba Dam waters. The first obligation was financial obligation of loan repayment to both external and internal lenders out of revenue earned from the supply of electricity to raise and expand the capital base, and social obligations to its workers. Electricity was for industrial

[1] "Kariba Dam Zambia and Zimbabwe", Final Report prepared for World Commission on Dams World, p. xv.

[2] NAZ F116/587/6, Paper no. 17: Kafue Paper on investigation undertaken (15/10/63), p. 1 (Hydro-Electric scheme was managed by the Federal Hydro-Electric Board, which was established in 1954 and was succeeded by the FPB, 1956).

[3] "Kariba Dam Zambia and Zimbabwe", Final Report prepared for World Commission on Dams Chalo, p. 7.

[4] NAZ F116/587/6, Paper no. 20 Working party: Kariba system, reply to committee "B" Questionnaire: 2 (b) Proposed extension the existing system Kariba stage 2 breakdown of cost between Northern Rhodesia and Southern Rhodesia (16/09/63).

consumption to consumers such as Rhodesia Congo Boarder Power Corporation (R. C. B. P. C) and for household purposes. Followed by the construction of stage two in terms of its operations and functions, the FPB was regulated by three pieces of legislation, that is, the Audit and Exchequer Act (1954), Electricity Act (1956), and Lake Kariba Waters Act (1961) and terms of the Loan agreement with the International Bank. [1]

The constitution of the FPB was determined by an already existing Electricity Act which framed the administrative powers of Federal Power Board. The Federal Government had regulatory powers over FPB. [2] The Act stipulated the membership of the FPB and empowered the Federal Minister of Power to appoint members of FPB. The Federal Government activities benefited Southern Rhodesia the most, due to Southern Rhodesia having greater legislative and political control of the Federal apparatus, owing to more political representation in Federal parliament. [3]

The Board operated as independently as it could away from political influence. Members of parliament were forbidden from becoming members of FPB to ensure that the Board was free from political influence at the same time separating politics and business. Its mandate was to serve territories with the bulk of the electricity. [4] Basically, the Electricity Act gave the Board, "a large measure of autonomy in order to allow it to operate as independently as possible, with the ultimate aim of allowing complete independence for an established electricity industry. "[5] In light of the above, the FPB, at least theoretically, was to establish an electrical industry that was free from politically influence.

Despite the fact that FPB was apolitical, the Electricity Act enabled the

---

[1] NAZ F116/587/6, Dissolution Papers: Federal Power Board, control over the waters of Lake Kariba.

[2] NAZ F116/587/6, Paper no. 24 Existing Legislation Affecting the Federal Power Board (nd), p. 1.

[3] C. A. Chakanyuka and R. T. Zibani, "Did the Central African Federation benefit Southern Rhodesia more than other constituent territories? An examination of the political economy of regionalism in colonial Sothern Africa, 1953 – 1963".

[4] NAZ F116/587/6, Paper no. 24: Existing legislation affecting the FPB (nd), p. 1.

[5] *Ibid.*

Minister, after discussions with the Board to influence "general directions in the national interest for exercising its powers, duties and functions."[①] However, national interest at times would conflict with the International Bank concept of launching an economic and viable and independent electricity industry divorced from political influence[②]. For instance, in territories where electricity was supplied by FPB especially in Southern Rhodesia, economic interests would not be on rapport with International Bank initiation of an independent electrical industry.[③] Therefore, it was necessary to ensure that future legislation did not conflict with that concept but would give the Minister some form of power in accordance with the Act.[④] At the end, the FPB was to make profits to ensure continuation of the Kariba Dam project. It would complete the construction of stage one and raise funds for second stage construction.

The Federal Power Board was mandated to supply electricity to Federal territories for domestic and industrial consumption despite the fact that it was sometimes incapacitated to supply enough energy to the Rhodesia Congo Boarder Power Corporation (R. C. B. P. C) in Northern Rhodesia so much that the corporation imported energy from Miniere or U. M. H. K (Union Miniere du Hat-Katanga (French name literally translated as Mining Union of upper Katanga) in Congo. The FPB charged varying tariffs to varying categories of its consumers. As already noted, the FPB was expected to be a viable economic unity accumulating revenue surpluses "sufficient to finance not less than half the cost of future development."[⑤] Future development referred largely to the second stage of the Kariba Dam and it was hoped that this would be possible without "borrowing sums amounting to more than half

---

① NAZ F116/587/6, Paper no. 24: Existing legislation affecting the FPB (nd), p. 5.
② *Ibid*, p. 1.
③ *Ibid*.
④ *Ibid*.
⑤ NAZ F116/587/6, Paper no. 12 the Board's financial obligations and their effect on the price of electricity, p. 1.

the cost of such development. "① In an agreement with World Bank, FPB was accorded power to set its electricity tariffs. This was emphasised in one of the clauses that stated that, "the board shall at all times carry on its operations and maintain its financial position in accordance with sound financial and public utility facilities practices. "② All it meant was the Board was to engage in profitable activities that would aid its capital expenditure.

The FPB was responsible for deliberating on issues of circuit expansion to carter for the huge demand of electricity. In this light discussions around the expansion of Kariba-Kitwe circuit were held. Kariba-Kitwe expansion of transmission lines would take 330kv circuit between Kariba and Kitwe and this was intended to be part of the second stage of the Kariba. ③ In an annexure to discussions on the second Kariba Kitwe line transmission, it was noted that the FPB would make an estimated profit of over 2.5 million pounds in the period from around mid-1965 to mid-1973 which was "about 6% per annum net return after paying all annual charges on the estimated capital cost of the second Kariba-Kitwe circuit. "④ It was also estimated that the expansion of the Kariba-Kitwe lines would also help the Corporation save an estimated 3 million during the same period as it would stop importing electricity from the Union Miniere. ⑤

Ultimately, the saving to the Corporation and profit to the Board would be about 5.6 million Pounds which represented a net return on capital expenditure of about 14% per annum. ⑥ Indeed the expansion of the Kariba-Kitwe line would prove to be an economically convenient for the two territories. However, the lack of further evidence on the project suggests that this was aborted, most likely because of the dissolution of the Federation

---

① NAZ F116/587/6, Paper no. 12 the Board's financial obligations and their effect on the price of electricity, p. 1.
② Ibid.
③ NAZ F116/587/6, annexure II note on second Kariba-Kitwe Transmission line, p. 1.
④ Ibid, p. 6.
⑤ Ibid.
⑥ Ibid.

in 1963 which saw Northern Rhodesia and Southern Rhodesia developing along different political trajectories. For instance, Northern Rhodesia became an independent African nation as Zambia while Southern Rhodesia saw the greater entrenchment of white minority rule with the Unilateral Declaration of Independence in 1965.

The Board could also interconnect thermal power stations. Additional facilities for the supply of bulk electricity was essential therefore, investigations in any area for new or additional facilities for co-ordination or co-operation were a necessity to existing electricity undertakings.[1] The Electricity Act stipulated that the Board could interconnect thermal power stations on a national grid serving both Rhodesias.[2] The Federal Power Board through R. C. B. P. C had to generate enough electricity in order to supply reliable and secure electricity to mines in Northern Rhodesia and Congo by interconnecting separately run thermal power stations in mining areas.

If the FPB had capacity, it would have preferred to monopolise the supply of electricity in the Federation. Electricity consumers in the Federation had to consult the Board first in any transactions that involved accessing electricity outside the Federation. R. C. B. P. C, for instance, did not only purchase power from FPB but also from Union Miniere (U. M. H. K), however, once FPB gained capacity to cover the demand by the Corporation, the latter would have to stop purchasing electricity from U. M. H. K. This was not only for financial returns that would help raise surplus for further developments but also for "the avoidance of reliance on a foreign country for an important part of the Federations electrical supply requirements. "[3] In its final recommendation, the proposal for the Kariba-Kitwe expansion was to be placed "before the Federal Power and the Board of the Corporation for approval. "[4] If approved, the Board was to approach

----

[1] Existing legislation affecting the FPB, p. 2.
[2] Ibid.
[3] NAZ F116/587/6, annexure t note on second Kariba-Kitwe Transmission line, p. 6.
[4] Ibid, p. 7.

the Federal Government with a view to exploring the possibility of raising necessary capital. ①

In 1961 the Lake Kariba Act was enacted to specifically guide the operations of the FPB in relationship to using the waters of Lake Kariba. The Act gave autonomous power to the Federal Board over use of waters of Lake Kariba, with the Minister of Power in the Federal Government having the overall say over issues concerning specifically the use of waters of Lake Kariba. ② The FPB answered to the Minister of Power as the Act in one of its clauses stipulated that:

> It shall be lawful for the Minister for any of the purposes of undesignated works by order to impose prohibitions of or restrictions or conditions (including payment charges) on the use, diversification or abstraction of water in Lake Kariba; Provided that nothing contained in such order shall apply to the taking or use of water for domestic purposes, including watering of cattle or other stock, by persons who by custom or usage take to use water from lake Kariba for such purposes. ③

The Minister was at the helm of the FPB and some of his duties were to prohibit or control access of any persons to the designated works. ④ Designated works referred to the Kafue and Kariba gorge (hydro-electric project and irrigation works), Shire valley (controlling the out flow of Lake Nyasa, for irrigation and land reclamation, or for generation of hydro-electric power) and Sabi valley (construction of water works and irrigation works for control, storage and use of water in the Sabi River) as stipulated in

---

① NAZ F116/587/6, annexure t note on second Kariba-Kitwe Transmission line, p. 7.
② NAZ F116/587/6, Paper no. 26: Bill (nd), p. 1.
③ Ibid, p. 2.
④ Designated works referred meant irrigation and water works at the Kariba gorge specified in the schedule to the Major Irrigation and Water works (Designation) Order, 1954.

Major water and Irrigation works (Designation) Order, 1954. ① The Minister approved use of water for any designated works by issuing a certificate as evidence. This included irrigation, eradication, prevention or control of the growth of weed in the lake to construction of booms, piers, fences, piles or anchorages within Lake Kariba. Failure to comply with the Act would lead to a fine 200 Pounds or risk imprisonment. ② All this was put in place to ensure smooth operation at Kariba Dam. The Board had the overall power to do anything with the water provided the water would not be raised above 1 605 or lower it below 1 560 feet above sea level at Beira. Normal level would be 1 590 feet above sea level at Beira. ③ The Federal Power Board assumed responsibility for the loan repayment, and any other designation that was not generation of hydro-electricity was to contribute toward capital investment. ④

The flow of water within the Zambezi was disturbed due to the construction of the Dam placing FPB in a tricky situation that needed to be handled carefully to minimise conflict. As part of its operations, the FPB had to present proposals for changes to be made before implementing them to ensure co-operation among the territories to be affected. For instance, disturbance of the natural water flow due to the construction of the Dam had a potential to cause conflict among the riparian states involved with the Zambezi River. The FPB made proposals on how water would be controlled through flood control. This involved consulting Southern Rhodesia, Northern Rhodesia and Mozambique for their cooperation.

The concerned authorities of territories had to be engaged so as to get their support on the changes that would affect them as far as flood control was concerned. The territories had various interests and concerns. Southern

---

① NAZ F16/587/6, Annexure "B" to paper No. 9: Major Water and Irrigation Works (Designation) Order, 1954.

② NAZ F116/587/6, Paper no. 26: Bill (nd), p. 1.

③ Ibid.

④ NAZ F116/587/6, Paper no. 18: Present position as regards the Kariba township with brief resume of past negotiations and information relating to land at Kariba. Ministry of power letter, no. C. 1015/5/83 of 12th August, 1963. (15/09/63), p. 1.

Rhodesia, on the one hand, wanted the flow to follow the pre-Kariba regime. [1] Both Northern Rhodesia and Mozambique believed that the proposed method would affect their industries. For Northern Rhodesia, "a drawdown each year [would] adversely affect the fishing industry and the annual drawdown [had] therefore [to] be limited. "[2] For Mozambique, large variations in discharge would cause the same difficulties for agriculture as in the areas of Northern Rhodesia downstream of the Dam. High rates of discharge during the flood season would introduce a risk of damage, particularly to the economically important sugar crop. Therefore, action had to be taken to cater for the interest of Northern Rhodesia and Mozambique.

Nevertheless, the Board's proposals for the spilling in the dry season were acceptable with the reservation that special agreements over discharges were necessary during periods when major works were being constructed on the Zambezi in Mozambique. [3] Ultimately, downstream populations had to adapt their agricultural programmes to a changed river regime. [4] The Board proceeded with its proposals after tabling them to the territories, notwithstanding some of the concerns raised by the territories. This confirms the domination of Southern Rhodesia and its interests in the affairs of the federation.

The level of Kariba continuously required flood control by discharging water through the spillway sluice gates. It should be noted that "The Scheme was designed as a power scheme and not as a flood control scheme, but because of the vast lake formed it would require a measure of flood control. "[5] A combined scheme would have been more costly and taken longer to construct and for this reason spillage discharge was not incorporated into

---

[1] NAZ F116/587/6, Annexure II: Opening of spillway Gates. Long-term proposals for future operation pg. 2 (nd) "pre-Kariba regime" referred to the natural flow of the Zambezi before the construction of the Kariba Dam at the Kariba gorge.

[2] Ibid.

[3] Ibid.

[4] Ibid.

[5] Ibid.

the design of the Dam. [1] This had challenges of poor flood control system and spillage discharge was, "open to criticism by those concerned with the lake and river" who only saw the "effects of discharge without knowing the basic causes. "[2] It was the responsibility of the Board to ensure that necessary discharge was to provide maximum benefit to all riparian states[3] by improving the flow of water in the dry season in the river downstream of Kariba.

FPB had lease agreements with Southern Rhodesia Government, some of its operations required land from both Southern Rhodesia and Northern Rhodesia. This land was granted through a lease to "accommodate and protect the Board's works and installations, to accommodate the Board's employees, and to provide enough land for sporting and recreational facilities for such employees. "[4] The Southern Rhodesia government had power over the buildings and could take the buildings whenever it deemed necessary and compensate the Board. [5] In the event of termination the lease agreement stipulated that, "Within one year from the date of termination of this lease the Board shall remove or cause to be removed all buildings, erections or improvements not taken over or sold or let…and shall leave the land upon which the same were situated in clean, tidy, and sanitary condition. "[6] These conditions were altered in 1961 as Southern Rhodesia government required shoreline land that had been leased to the Board for other developments and the Board agreed to hand back areas of the shoreline it no longer needed. [7] It was also agreed that the Board would be granted a lease for eight years from

---

[1] NAZ F116/587/6, Annexure II: Opening of spillway Gates. Long-term proposals for future operation pg. 2 (nd) "pre-Kariba regime" referred to the natural flow of the Zambezi before the construction of the Kariba Dam at the Kariba gorge.

[2] Ibid, p. 1.

[3] Ibid, p. 2.

[4] NAZ F116/587/6, Paper no. 18: Present position as regards the Kariba township with brief resume of past negotiations and information relating to land at Kariba. Ministry of power letter, no. C. 1015/5/83 of 12th August, 1963. (15/09/63), p. 1.

[5] Ibid.

[6] Ibid.

[7] Ibid, p. 3.

first April, 1963, with an option for renewal. ① These were some of agreements taken by FPB to facilitate smooth running of events.

The Dissolution of the Federation: From Federal Power Board to Central African Corporation

In this section I turn to how the issue of hydro-electricity and the Kariba Dam was handled in the face of dissolution of the Federation, when the issues to be resolved in their complexity and the extent of agreement achieved in a short time was remarkable. ② The machinery for bringing about speedy and orderly dissolution of the Federation was set up in June of 1963 at a conference held in Victoria Falls. ③ At that conference it was decided that, if possible, dissolution be done by 31ˢᵗ December, 1963. ④ Dissolution was inevitable given the circumstances [failure of racial co-operation] and the sooner it was done the better for the three territories. The three territories had to go their separate ways. ⑤ This section discusses the prospects and fears of the dissolution process and secondly, it also discusses the general experience of the dissolution process. Apart from the Kariba Dam, the Federal Public Service, Federal Pensions schemes, airways, and railways were also among other federal projects affected by mechanics and measures put in place to manage the dissolution experience. My focus, however, is on the Kariba Dam. Pressing issues that existed on the eve of the dissolution of the Kariba Dam project included loan repayment to both external and internal lenders, the need for a new power board and new authority, prospective arbitrator, and

---

① NAZ F116/587/6, Paper no. 18: Present position as regards the Kariba township with brief resume of past negotiations and information relating to land at Kariba. Ministry of power letter, no. C. 1015/5/83 of 12ᵗʰ August, 1963. (15/09/63), p. 3.

② https://api. parliament. uk/historic-hansard/commons/1963/dec/17/federation-of-rhodesia-and-nyasaland accessed 04, May 2019.

③ Ibid.

④ Ibid.

⑤ Ibid.

how construction of the second stage was to be completed after dissolution.

Prior to dissolution, the Federal Government had made efforts to build foundations of inter-territorial co-operation for projects that could not be dissolved in the event of disintegration of the Federation. For example, on the Kariba Dam, the FPB was one such foundation that allowed for inter-territorial cooperation. In the post-dissolution era, the FPB still had the obligation of loan repayment to both external and internal lenders and stage two of Kariba was still to be constructed. There was the threat of the project discontinuing and this section helps understand why, in spite of dissolution, the territories were able to recognise the importance of continued collaboration and the Kariba Dam hydro-electric project was still completed as a project to benefit two former federation territories.

Committees A and B were set up to bring about smooth process of dissolution. According to T. Nyamunda, the two inter-territorial committees managed the business of dissolving the Federation and liquidating some of its shared assets, and setting up a platform for cooperation until the business was concluded at the set deadlines for the various processes. [1] The functions of Committee A was to preside "over the reversion of Federal functions such as the public service, judiciary, and recommend on matters relating to Federal assets and public debt. "[2] Committee B "worked out possible areas of future cooperation in matters relating to the Kariba Dam, air, power, transport and railways. "[3] With regards to the Kariba Dam project, the committee discussed the issues of loan repayment to both internal and external lenders, the future FPB, and construction of the second stage of Kariba with minimum changes as possible. The question of irrigation potential was regarded as trivial to be considered. It was resolved that neither government would remove water from lake Kariba without prior consultation with the FPB. FPB

---

[1] Nyamunda, "Financing Rebellion: The Rhodesian State, Financial Policy and exchange control 1962 – 1979", University of Free State: South Africa, 2015, p. 70.

[2] Ibid, p. 71.

[3] Ibid.

would continue to operate up until the dissolution process was completed and give way for the new power board that had to be in operation immediately after the dissolution for effective continuation of the hydro-electric project.

An inter-Territorial order was regarded as a wise and far-sighted approach to a future which did not discard the undoubted success of the past. [1] According to Part 111 of the order, Kariba Hydro-electric scheme would continue to be operated and developed as a unity under the joint ownership or control of Northern and Southern Rhodesia, and these two territories would enter into an inter-Governmental agreement. [2] The same order also covered the setting up and prescribed the functions of a Higher Authority for Electric power composed of two Ministers from each of the two territories. [3] A new Corporation to be known as Central African Power Corporation would be established with the same functions, duties, and powers as the FPB. [4] Provisions for all the assets and liabilities of the existing FPB would pass to the new Corporation upon the dissolution of the Federation. [5]

The Kariba system was to continue to be operated and fully developed as a single entity under the joint ownership of Southern Rhodesia and Northern Rhodesia under a new power board. [6] This would allow the two governments to honour the obligations incurred to those who lent 74. 5 million Pounds to allow the project to be a success. This would also allow the two Governments to repay the loan in accordance with the terms of the loan agreements in a manner which involved the smallest possible departures from the original arrangements. [7] Southern Rhodesia questioned the effectiveness of the new proposed board after dissolution. It expressed doubt if the new board would

---

[1] https://api. parliament. uk/historic-hansard/commons/1963/dec/17/federation-of-rhodesia-and-nyasaland, accessed 10 September 2019.
[2] Ibid.
[3] Ibid. The higher Authority was to replace the Minister of Power.
[4] Ibid.
[5] Ibid.
[6] NAZ F116/587/1, Dissolution papers: Kariba First report of the Committee on inter-territorial Questions, 19 September 1963, p. 1.
[7] Ibid.

not risk territorial sovereignty of the two states and possibly prejudicing development plans especially if the two Governments were to pursue divergent economic policies. ① To avoid different economic policies in connection with the hydro-electric project, it was resolved that Southern Rhodesia would not establish electric projects that would compete against Kariba. ② The two territories would be free to seek other alternatives for power if the power generation at Kariba failed to meet their demand. ③

A new Power Board was the only way forward with separate but identical territorial legislation to replace the Electricity Act (EA) of 1956. Sufficient time was needed to reconsider certain clauses of the EA and the Audit and Exchequer Act (AEA) to fit the new conditions of its revenue and expenditure, if any. The FPB was exempted by EA and AEA from requiring ministerial approval to manage its revenue and expenditure and also that it could set its own tariffs which was also a pre-condition by International Bank for its loan agreement. Approximately 90% of FPB's revenue was devoted to servicing loans or accumulation to finance development. ④ The accumulation of surpluses was geared towards financing the construction of the second stage of Kariba hydro-electric project. Part of stage two was to be brought forward by completing the second transmission line to Kitwe. The assumption was that there should be little difference on how the board's funds would be used. ⑤ After intense deliberations, it was later agreed that the new board should continue with the autonomy of determining its own tariffs.

Committee B recommended that the Central African Power Corporation be set up to replace the existing FPB, with the same powers and functions. ⑥

---

① NAZ F116/587/6, Dissolution of the Federation Committee "B" Record of the Fourth meeting held on Tuesday, 20th August, 1963, p. 1.

② Ibid.

③ Ibid.

④ NAZ F116/587/6, Dissolution of the Federation Committee "B": Record of the twenty fourth meeting of Committee "B" held on Monday, 16 September, 1963.

⑤ The Federal power board loan from C. D. C.

⑥ Ibid, p. 2.

Each government was to nominate its representatives to be deputy chair and would act in rotation. Members of territorial legislature were not eligible but civil servants. The Board still had to be a non-political body with commercial and administrative functions. ① The new board would continue to practice the functions and obligations of old board's powers of interconnection. For the time being the new Corporation was not to undertake any additional expense to further activities on agency basis as Higher Authority may approve. It was agreed that an inter-governmental agreement was to be signed in Lusaka on either the 25th or 26th of September 1963.

The Agreement would have to provide for coordinated operation for continued development of Kariba until it was completed as originally planned by FPB. The new board was also permitted to construct and operate a plant in both territories while both governments would need to agree not to develop other major stations or enter into agreements for major power purchases to supply power which could be obtained more economically from Kariba. There was need for arbitration in the event of failure of agreement in Higher Authority or in the event of disagreements between the two Governments on any matter arising on the Inter-Governmental Agreement. ②

There was also to be a Higher Authority whose functions had to be similar to those exercised by the Ministry of Power under the Electricity Act, 1956. ③ The new Authority was to be formed to replace the Minister of Power. Southern Rhodesia and Northern Rhodesia agreed to change ownership but not the legal function of the former minister. The Higher Authority would require statutory powers and would almost have to certainly have Ministers from both territories jointly running the new authority. It would make rules providing for which members of New Board should hold office and their conditions such as remuneration and pension.

---

① The Federal power board loan from C. D. C, p. 2.
② NAZ F116/587/6, Dissolution of the Federation Committee "B": Record of the twenty fourth meeting of Committee "B" held on Monday, 16 September, 1963, p. 5.
③ Ibid, p. 2.

The New Board was to inherit its predecessor's financial obligation and it was highly unlikely that the lenders were ready to contemplate more than the minimum prescribed versions of the standing loan agreements. [1] Guarantees would need to be replaced by something equivalent as the Federal Government was the former guarantor of loans and territorial governments had to be new guarantors. In Sir Alegernon Rumbold's view, both IB and United Kingdom Governments were to expect Federal Government guarantees to be taken by territorial governments as this would be the nearest possible thing to the original security provided to the lenders. [2] Territories had no choice but to comply with the new arrangement as failure to comply would result in compromised future relations with the International Bank. Lack of co-operation on the part of territories would jeopardise future prospects of acquiring loans for stage 2 development. [3] The New Power Board had to come to an agreement with lenders to come into a relationship with territorial governments supplying suitable guarantees. It was proposed that an agreement would be entered into by lenders with Central African Power Corporation before dissolution of the FPB to become effective on the transfer of assets and liabilities of the Board to the Central African Power Corporation. [4] If lenders were to enter into an agreement with CAPC then CAPC would have to be in existence before 31st December 1963. [5] There was to be no gap between dissolution of Federation and the date on which guarantees of territorial governments would become effective. It was all a question of timing whether this would be possible before dissolution. This, however, depended on territorial clarification on guarantees and the lender

---

[1] NAZ F116/587/6, Dissolution of the Federation Committee "B": Record of the twenty fourth meeting of Committee "B" held on Monday, 16 September, 1963.

[2] NAZ F116/587/6, Dissolution of the Federation Committee "B": Record of the forty-ninth meeting held at 2. 15 on Monday, 11 October, 1963.

[3] NAZ F116/587/6, Dissolution of the Federation Committee "B": Record of the fourth meeting of Committee "B" held on Tuesday, 20th August, 1963.

[4] NAZ F116/587/6, Memorandum: Kariba Legislation proposed dissolution.

[5] Ibid.

being informed in time.

Loan repayment to both external and internal lenders was one of the major issues that committee B dealt with and the loan amounted to 74.6 million Pounds. The external lenders were the International Bank (IB), Commonwealth Development Corporation (CDC) and Commonwealth Development Financial Company (CDFC). [1] After several consultations with the lenders, the chair of working parties, Sir Alegernon Rumbold was sure that the lenders were quite clear as to the issues and the pressure of timetable committee B was working under. [2] A meeting was held in Washington between members of Board of IB, chancellors of the Exchequer and governor of Bank of England (BE). In this meeting, IB made it clear that they were ready to negotiate about Kariba on the basis of Federal Government guarantee was being replaced by a separate guarantee from Southern Rhodesia and Northern Rhodesia governments guaranteeing half of International Bank loan. Responsibilities for Federal Government liabilities had to be borne equally by Southern Rhodesia and Northern Rhodesia governments. Indeed,

In 1956 an assurance had been given by Federal Government to the International Bank that if at any time the Federal Power Board should be unable to meet its obligations to lenders other than the Federal Government, that Government would temporarily waive its right to receive payments of principal and interest in respect of its loan to the Board, to such an extent as would enable that Body to meet its other obligations. That position would have to be taken over by Territorial Governments. [3]

---

[1] NAZ F116/587/6, Memorandum: Kariba Legislation proposed dissolution, p. 3.

[2] NAZ F116/587/6, Dissolution of the Federation Committee "B": Record of the thirty-sixth meeting of Committee "B" held on Monday, 30 September, 1963.

[3] NAZ F116/587/6, Dissolution of the Federation Committee "B": Record of the 23rd meeting of Committee "B" held on Monday, 16th September, 1963.

In the above context, dissolution was now causing confusion as Federal representatives were now disregarding the issue of priority payments of external loans over local loans as payments from Federal Government were slower than those from Federal Government to external lenders. ① And this would complicate any attempt to transfer Federal Government's liabilities to the new Power Corporation. ② As such, it was clear that the Committee wanted to reach an agreement on the new organisation without departing from the existing realities. ③ At another meeting with CDC and CDFC, the two requested for an increase interest rate on their loan or possible compensation by a lump sum payment if governments would not agree to joint guarantees but territorial representatives refused. ④ Representatives of governments of SR and NR agreed that CAPC should pay a negotiating fee to CDFC of 5000 pounds and not more than 7000 pounds to CDC. ⑤

More so, loan repayment to internal lenders such as the Copper mining companies (20 million) and BSAC (4 million), Standard Bank (2 million) and Barclays D. C. O (2 million) was equally important to external loan and negotiations had to done. Federal Government was to give FPB a loan of not more than 6 million pounds for the completion of stage 1 but the loan was not called for instead the Board used 3. 4 million pounds from revenue. ⑥ Copper mining companies assumed that each government would meet its obligations in its own currency and raised the possibility of one or other currency being devalued in relation to sterling. ⑦ They also stated that in terms of the loan

---

① NAZ F116/587/6, Dissolution of the Federation Committee "B": Record of the twelfth meeting of Committee "B" held on Friday, 30th August, 1963.

② Ibid.

③ Ibid.

④ NAZ F116/587/6, Dissolution of the Federation Committee "B": Informal Record of the twenty-fifth meeting at 8. 45 am on Monday, 4th November, 1963.

⑤ NAZ F116/587/6, Dissolution of the Federation Committee "B": Record of the eighty-sixth meeting of Committee "B" held at 8. 45 am on Monday, 11th November, 1963.

⑥ NAZ F116/587/6, Dissolution of the Federation Committee "B": Record of the thirty-sixth meeting of Committee "B" held on Monday, 30 September, 1963.

⑦ Ibid.

agreement Federal Government should have established a sinking fund and presumed that territorial governments would do likewise. [1] The British South Africa Company in the view of changed circumstances loans were to be renegotiated, with all the lenders treated alike and all loans covered by negotiable securities. [2] The BSAC accepted the committees' proposals concerning Kariba loans.

After lengthy negotiations all parties were on board with the proposals and agreements that it brought relief to everyone involved. Both countries were happy with the results. It was even recorded in the *Rhodesian Herald* of October 1963 that, "the announcement that the Governments of Southern Rhodesia and Northern Rhodesia will operate and develop as a single entity, was most welcome. The chaos that would have resulted from a decision to divide Kariba into two parts, even if this were practicable, was avoided and the people of both countries looked forward to the establishment of Central African Power Corporation and to its smooth working. "[3] It had taken not only great persuasive powers but also extreme tact to get the two territories to work towards the agreement. [4] The announcement that FPB was to be administered by a corporation and a Higher Authority representative from both Governments was a welcome sign of continuing partnership between the two Rhodesias after the dissolution of Federation. [5] Kariba Dam and the hydro-electric project was not likely to inspire any serious differences of opinion. However, what was to cause friction was jealous but even then, it had to be submerged in national interest: both sides would want to appoint the chair of the new body and both would want its headquarters. These were minor problems that were not allowed to impede the harmonious running of

---

[1] NAZ F116/587/6, Dissolution of the Federation Committee "B": Record of the 26th meeting of Committee "B" held on Tuesday, 17th September, 1963.
[2] Ibid.
[3] NAZ F116/587/6, *Rhodesia Herald*: Kariba 25/10/63 To secretary of committee "B" Federal Assembly.
[4] Ibid.
[5] *Rhodesian herald*, 26/10/63.

the corporation. ① For instance, employees of the FPB would not suffer as a result of change over.

In the end, the general feeling was that of satisfaction, for instance, the Secretary of State for Commonwealth Relations and for Colonies, Mr Duncan Sandy was satisfied with the reports of inter-governmental committees in which all territories unanimously agreed to the recommendations. ② The three territories were able to continue common services [federal projects] and work together despite the dissolution and hoped that, "as time passes these territories, whose interest are interwoven", would gradually on their own will, come closer together. ③ However, on the other hand he was disappointed that a final seal was put on failure of multi-racial partnership in Central Africa. ④

The Duke of Devonshire applauded the committees that were set up following the Victoria falls Conference as they were tasked with a great burden such that the problems, they were called upon to resolve were multiple, complex and difficult to handle. ⑤ The Duke paid a warm tribute to all Central African Governments, particularly the Federal Government, for displaying throughout the whole process a spirit of realistic co-operation and compromise. He also thanked the officials of all governments concerned who carried forward with the greatest urgency the detailed work which formed the necessary preliminaries to inter-Government agreement on the subjects covered. ⑥ The Federation was successfully dissolved in 1963 and control of generation of power and its transmission continued to be operated and was fully developed as a single system under joint ownership and control of the

① *Rhodesian herald*, 26/10/63.
② https://api. parliament. uk/historic-hansard/commons/1963/dec/17/federation-of-rhodesia-and-nyasaland accessed 21 September 2019.
③ Ibid.
④ Ibid.
⑤ https://api. parliament. uk/historic-hansard/commons/1963/dec/17/federation-of-rhodesia-and-nyasaland accessed 21 September 2019. The source does not mention the name of the Duke of Devonshire.
⑥ Ibid.

two Governments of Northern and Southern Rhodesia under the Central African Power Corporation (CAPC) which was established in the same year.

Conclusion

This study has contributed to at least two themes on Africa's colonial past namely the Federation experience and colonial hydro-politics. The Kariba Dam has been used as a lens to unpack these themes. This study has demonstrated how the Kariba dam was managed and exploited for hydro-electricity from Federation to the dissolution. That the Federation crumbled while Kariba endured symbolises continuities and deep entanglements between the colonial and postcolonial eras.

This discussion has also contributed to our understanding of the dissolution of the Federation with particular reference to the Kariba Dam Scheme while there is already literature on dissolution of the financial sector and the pensions. The study explored the functions of FPB and how the dissolution process handled on the Kariba Dam project. This work is not a final word on the Kariba experience during the Federation and into the dissolution. There is room, for example, to investigate further the legislative framework that governed FPB. Indeed, the successor of the FPB would also offer interesting area of research.

Labour History of African Municipal Workers in Colonial Harare: 1945 – 1979

Blessing Dhliwayo and Eric Kushinga Makombe

Abstract

This article examines the working conditions of Salisbury African municipal workers from 1945 to 1979. The conditions pertaining to workers' job environment, such as leave privileges, pension, health and welfare provisions will be analysed. The work aims to look at the responses made by the municipal workers to the working conditions within the municipality. Salisbury Municipal African workers responded through strikes, participating in the informal sector, joining unions, supplemented their wages through farming, borrowing, pilfering and by simply changing jobs. Labour history in Zimbabwe has been researched by different scholars and their arguments help one to understand the intricacies of African workers and their working conditions from different employers and capitalist sectors. African workers encountered different problems with different white colonial employers. This article examines these labour issues within the Salisbury City Council. Methodologically, the article makes use of qualitative research techniques with Salisbury as the case study. Several sources were used to obtain data for this study. These sources include reports, oral interviews, books, and internet sources.

Key words: Working conditions, welfare, labour, trade unions, workers compensation

Introduction

This article examines the working conditions of African municipal workers in colonial Harare (then called Salisbury). The workers' job environment, leave privileges, pension, health, and welfare provisions will be analysed. The article also looks at the responses made by the municipal workers to the working conditions within the municipality. Salisbury's Municipal African workers responded through strikes, participating in the informal sector, joining unions, supplementing their wages through farming, borrowing, pilfering, and simply changing jobs. Several scholars have contributed to the historiography on the labour history of Zimbabwe and have furthered the understanding of the intricacy of the plight of African workers in the colonial capitalist economy. This article contributes to that historiography by examining responses by African workers expanding the scope of agency given to Africans in the face of racial policies in the workplace using the case of Salisbury Municipal African workers. African daily challenges varied greatly depending on the individual's job, location, and employer. Therefore, African workers responded differently to their diverse problems, opportunities, and challenges. Hence, the study of the working conditions of African workers in the Municipality of Salisbury adds new knowledge to that which exists in Zimbabwean labour history. This article focuses on the period after the Second World War in 1945 to 1979. The period marked the expansions of the Municipality of Salisbury in terms of both population and industrial development which increased the number of African municipal workers employed in Salisbury. The study ends in 1979, on the eve of independence and the end of racial discrimination and harsh forms of exploitation from the white minority at the City Council.

The city of Salisbury became a colonial municipality in 1897. Like any other institution in colonial Zimbabwe, the expansion of the city was at its peak during and immediately after the Second World War. The employment of Africans was at its peak during the Second World War due to the expansion of the city in terms of population. [1] Salisbury Municipal workers like African workers during the colonial period suffered discrimination, seclusion, and were exposed to harsh forms of exploitation. The terms and conditions under which Africans were recruited to the City Council meant that Africans were exposed to poor working conditions and poor welfare benefits. The state-imposed legislations facilitated the exploitation of the African workforce in the Municipality of Salisbury. For instance, the job colour bar set by the Industrial Conciliation Act of 1934, meant that Europeans were given first preferences to white-collar jobs within the Municipality. [2] The state also imposed taxes aimed at providing the Municipality and other capitalist sectors with a pool of Africans to exploit.

Methodologically, the article uses a qualitative research approach. According to Marshall and Rossman qualitative research is "pragmatic, interpretative, and grounded in lived experiences of the people. "[3] This approach helped in understanding the working conditions of Salisbury African Municipal workers through an examination of their life experiences. The research used primary archival sources, which included reports from the Director of Native Administration, as well as those from the Department of Native Affairs which helped to substantiate facts about leave privileges and other benefits offered to Africans. Furthermore, reports from the Treasurer helped to analyse wage disparities between the Europeans and Africans. Colonial newspapers, such as *African Weekly*, helped to shape perspective on the common position regarding the condition of African workers. Oral interviews were conducted to provide information on the experiences of both men and women within the municipality during the colonial period. Primary

---

① T. H. Mothibe, 'African Workers' Militancy as a Basis for Post-War Nationalism in Colonial Zimbabwe, 1945 – 1953', *Trans African Journal of History*, Vol. 23,1994, p. 157.

② NAZ Annual Report from NADA Vol. 20 – 26 1943 – 49, p. 39.

③ C. Marshall and G. B. Rossman, *Designing Qualitative Article*, Thousand Islands, Sage Publications, 1999, p. 12.

sources were complemented by secondary sources in the form of books which helped situate this study within the existing historiography on African workers and their working conditions.

Overall, this article uses data analysis techniques. According to Shamoo and Resnik data analyses methodically applies measurable or coherent methods to portray and outline, condense and recap, and assess information. [1] Most data from primary sources were both descriptive and narrative while data from secondary sources were analytical. Thus, distinguishing common designs of information and analysing them made it less demanding to attain the article's goals.

Zimbabwe's Labour Historiography: An Overview

Zimbabwe's labour historiography has over the years tried to give material reality to two broad imperatives: to write on the history of the labour movement and to also capture the 'history from below'. Hence we identify a duality of labour and social history in the historiography. The influence of leading Marxist historians and doyens of Zimbabwe's labour history, Charles Van Onselen and Ian Phimister's works of the 1970s and 1980s, is the rather obvious starting point. [2] Their scholarship was superb and their impact on subsequent historiography immense. Bill Freund regards Van Onselen's *Chibaro* as one of the greatest contributions to the historiography of African labour. [3] Phimister and Van Onselen made the rather novel

[1] A. E. Shamoo and B. R. Resnik, *Responsible Conduct of Article*, New Delhi, Oxford University Press, 2003, p. 34.

[2] Charles Van Onselen, *Chibaro: African Mine Labour in Southern Rhodesia*, London: 1976; Charles Van Onselen and Ian Phimister, *Studies in the History of African Mine labour in Colonial Zimbabwe*, Gwelo: 1978; Phimister, I. R. *An Economic and Social History of Zimbabwe*, 1890 - 1948: *Capital Accumulation and Class Struggle*, London: Longman, 1988.

[3] Chibaro laid bare the mining industry's cost structure and its fundamental imperative of cost minimisation; the often appalling consequences of this imperative for African workers' wages and living conditions; how, given these remarkably unpleasant conditions, labour was mobilized; how, once at the mines, this labour was controlled and disciplined; and how, in the face of all this, workers nonetheless fought back. See: Bill Freund, *The African Worker*, Cambridge, 1988.

discovery of uncovering and theorising about sources on African social life in the mine compounds that had hitherto been lying dormant in the National Archives of Zimbabwe. However, the political economy approach ultimately proved inadequate for an analysis of the African urban situation. Marxist writers shared an excessively economistic bias that underplayed the non-material aspects of the lives of workers.

Labour historiography in the 1980s and 1990s witnessed the emergence of works by scholar-activists such as Brain Raftopoulos and Lloyd Sachikonye who had a distinct socio-political goal of making Zimbabwean workers aware of their *own* history. [1] In one article Raftopoulos examines the nexus of nationalism and labour in the period between 1945 and 1965. [2] He observes that in the period he was studying, Zimbabwean labour began to move with international currents, in terms of general political and social ideology and specifically on strike action. The 1948 General Strike has been the subject of immense scrutiny by many Zimbabwean Scholars and expatriates studying Zimbabwe and many agree that this was something of a coming of age moment. [3] Tefetso Mothibe, for instance, illustrates the reasons that caused unrest among African workers during and after the Second World War. [4] This unrest was exacerbated by post-war inflation and led to the growth of African militancy culminating in both the 1945 Railway Strike and 1948 General Strike. The radical analysis proffered by Ratftopoulos, Mothibe, and others

---

[1] Raftopoulos, B. , and I. Phimister, ed. 1997. *Keep on knocking : A History of the Labour Movement in Zimbabwe : 1900 – 97*. Harare: Baobab Books; Raftopoulos, B. , and L. Sachikonye, ed. 2001. *Striking back : The labour movement and the post-colonial state in Zimbabwe 1980 – 2000*. Harare: Weaver Press.

[2] Raftopoulos, B. 1995. "Nationalism and labour in Salisbury 1953 – 1965", *Journal of Southern African Studies* 21: 79 – 95.

[3] Michael O. West, *The Rise of an African Middle Class : Colonial Zimbabwe, 1890 – 1965*, Indiana University Press, Bloomington: 2002; Raftopoulos, B. , and I. Phimister. 2000. "Kana Sora ratswa ngaritswe": African nationalists and black workers: The 1948 general strike in colonial Zimbabwe". *Journal of Historical Sociology* 13: 289 – 323; Michael O. West, "Ndabaningi Sithole, Garfield Todd and the Dadaya school strike of 1947". *Journal of Southern African Studies*, 18/2,1992: 297 – 316.

[4] T. H. Mothibe, "African Workers' Militancy as a Basis for Post-War Nationalism in Colonial Zimbabwe, 1945 – 1953", *Trans African Journal of History*, Vol. 23,1994, p. 158.

served as a springboard for what was to become throughout the 1990s and beyond, a series of wide-ranging and thorough-going critiques of authoritarian nationalism.

The 1990s period and beyond also witnessed the emergence of other works by sociologists on labour and proletarianisation connected with urbanisation. These studies ushered in new socio-historical investigations of cities that stressed first class and then culture and gave some definition to certain previous studies. [1] Teresa Barnes uses the lens of social reproduction to avoid the pitfalls of earlier studies that celebrated the agency of 'remarkable' (often-elite) women while ignoring the important constraints on 'ordinary' women in the urban space. [2] These works through situating women in the workspaces also go some way in challenging the androcentric discourse that had for a long-time dominated Zimbabwe's labour historiography.

David Johnson's monograph on Zimbabwean labour during the Second World War interprets the war years as a crucial watershed. [3] Johnson connects two major bodies of research in modern African history: the development of an early colonial economy and labour regime, and the rise of post-war political and labour activism. However, Johnson's contributions on the impact of urban wartime policies, and perhaps on the process of secondary industrialisation are not thoroughly developed. It is only in the sixth and final chapter that Johnson's work jumps to the urban areas to outline post-war African political and labour activism. This is a rather abrupt transition in that the preceding chapters deal largely with settler farmer politics and rural labour.

---

[1] Some examples include an excellent collection on urban colonial history by Brian Raftopoulos & Tsuneo Yoshikuni, eds. , *Sites of Struggle: Essays in Zimbabwe's Urban History* (Harare: Weaver Press, 1999).

[2] Teresa Barnes, *"We Women Worked So Hard": Gender, Labour, and Social Reproduction in Colonial Harare, Zimbabwe, 1930 - 1956*, Portsmouth, NH: 1999.

[3] David Johnson, *World War II and the Scramble for Labour in Colonial Zimbabwe, 1939 - 1948*, Harare: University of Zimbabwe Publications, 2000.

There are several other works anchored on the established traditions of political economy and social history located in the Economic History Department at the University of Zimbabwe that, unfortunately, remain unpublished. We have chosen to include some of these works in our review to bring attention to these dissertations and theses. Matthew Mataruka's focus is on Mutare's African municipal workers. [1] He highlights the general working conditions and the racially charged environment in that workplace. Africans were deprived of their right to work benefits, bonuses, pension, and leave privileges. Mataruka also illustrates the changes that came with Zimbabwe's independence in 1980 by comparing the colonial and post-colonial periods. However, Mataruka's dissertation does not effectively illustrate how Africans responded to their unpleasant working environment during the colonial period.

Rorisang Siziba discusses the work conditions of ranch workers from 1965 to 1980 using a case study of the Gwanda district. [2] He notes that ranch workers suffered poor working conditions and poor wages. Siziba opines that conditions faced by ranch workers were worsened by their isolation and limited socialisation. Richard Mtisi's work focuses on the socio-economic conditions of agricultural labourers in Trelawney and Banket. [3] Mtisi argues that although Zimbabwe's independence led to a wide range of changes, African workers on commercial farms did not experience a total break from their pre-independence circumstances. Similarly, Noel Ndumeya discusses the working conditions of citrus plantations workers with specific reference to Mazowe Citrus Estate. [4] Ndumeya does well to show the seasonal variations of labour demand requirements which differed depending on the stages of

---

[1] M. Mataruka, "A history of Mutare African Municipal Workers: 1945 – 1994", BA Hons Dissertation, University of Zimbabwe, 1995, p. 10.

[2] R. Siziba, "Labour conditions on Ranches: A case of the Gwanda District: 1965 – 1980", Dissertation, University of Zimbabwe, 1995, p. 19.

[3] R. Mtisi, "Working and Living conditions on commercial farms: The case of Trelawney and Banket: 1980 – 1998", M. A. Thesis, University of Zimbabwe, 1998, p. 15.

[4] N. Ndumeya, "Labour Conditions on Citrus Plantations in Mazowe District: With Specific Reference to Mazowe Citrus Estate, 1980 – 1999", Dissertation, University of Zimbabwe, 1999, p. 20.

tree growth. Ndumeya asserts that the wages received by the workers did not reflect the work done, meaning that the workers' welfare was always compromised. The author also illustrates that although farm labourers' children were able to access education and health facilities, the lack of adequate accommodation posed a serious challenge.

Our article, therefore, constitutes a broadening of the labour historiography through the inclusion of previously silenced or forgotten voices or perspectives. As we stated in the introduction, we incorporate interviews of African municipal workers to capture the granular lived experiences of these workers while, at the same time, we move away from a master narrative of all African worker experiences during colonialism. Put differently, we situate a section of the African workforce into the discussion about the growth of the African labour movement that had hitherto been unexplored by the works cited above. Our contribution, in a small way, also situates rural-urban linkages in labour activism which have remained largely unexplored in Zimbabwe's labour historiography.

Salisbury's Labour Recruitment Policies

The Salisbury City Council (SCC) benefited from state-imposed policies for its recruitment system, for instance, poll, dog, and head taxes among others. These policies meant Africans had to pay tax in cash and Africans were left with the little option than to look for employment. [1] Furthermore, the state provided subsidy loans to white settler producers, paying better prices to white settlers and also removing Africans from better infrastructure necessary for African commodity production. [2] All these policies were

---

[1] L. Malaba, "Supply, Control and Organization of African Labour in Rhodesia", *Review of African Political Economy*, No. 18, 1980, p. 11.

[2] E. K. Makombe, "Agricultural Commodity Pricing Policy in Colonial Zimbabwe with Particular Reference to the Settler Maize Industry: 1950 - 1980", MA Dissertation, University of Zimbabwe, 2005.

important in providing a pool of labour not only needed by the Salisbury Municipality but all capitalist sectors in Southern Rhodesia. [1]

The pool of manpower from which the City Council employed its workforce comprised of skilled, semi-skilled, and unskilled workers. From the standpoint of the City Council, the relevant skills were acquired through formal training from technical and apprenticeship institutions. Africans who had failed to access these institutions were recruited to low posts with low wages. Those who had the necessary training and had completed apprenticeship were guaranteed relatively better-paying jobs in the municipality. However, the majority of Africans recruited by the SCC were unskilled workers and were mainly employed to do manual work. Consequently, the majority of Africans recruited by the municipality were the least paid workers. In 1945 the wages given to a European worker ranged from £600 to £3800 annually depending on the experience of the individual. This was ten times the wages received by African workers. [2] Comparatively, the few Africans who were engaged in white-collar jobs had their wages deliberated on first and the commencing wages ranged from £150 to £300. [3] This clearly shows the unfairness of the recruitment system used by the Salisbury Municipality.

According to Luke Malaba, "skill is an aptitude developed from and during labour activity, a result of the combination of practice and theory

---

[1] Giovanni Arrighi identified land alienation, the creation of labour reserves and so on as vital initial mechanisms assisting the birth of capitalism, but their essence, as Duncan Clarke insisted, never came to an end. Clarke maintains that in their ultimate incarnation such policies included influx control mechanisms and a wide variety of other forms of control contained in policies of labour stabilisation. All of these devices had 'one common central effect, viz, the creation and maintenance of a cheap labour system, the basis of which was the supply of labour power below the cost of its own reproduction, and the objective of which was to provide through the transfer of value for the primitive accumulation of capital under conditions of settler colonialism. See: Clarke D. G., *Contract Workers and Underdevelopment in Rhodesia*, Gwelo, Mambo Press, 1974; Arrighi, G. (1973): "Labour Supplies in Historical Perspective: A Study of the Proletarianisation of the African Peasantry in Rhodesia", in Arrighi & Saul (eds.): *Essays on the Political Economy of Africa*, Monthly Review Press.

[2] NAZ LG68/5/, Annual Report of the City Treasurer, 1945.

[3] Ibid.

within defined social conditions". [1] So, even though Africans were engaged as unskilled workers, the long periods of continuous work they undertook eventually made them acquire some dexterity and aptitude. This partly explains why long-serving Africans were ultimately engaged to do jobs formally reserved for semi-skilled and skilled white workers within the municipality such as welding, painting, plastering, bricklaying, and glazing. In the same vein one informant, B. Chidazembe first worked as a general worker in 1963, but he was promoted to become a truck driver in 1974. [2] However, although Africans were motivated to acquire these semi-skilled and skilled jobs, they were not paid the wages previously given to former incumbents. That explains certain partiality and the lack of employment equity within the Salisbury Municipality recruitment system.

The City Council used different methods when recruiting Africans. For instance, hiring from direct applications from Africans themselves or enrolling from kith and kin of long-serving or trusted African employees and, last, through public employment agencies like the Rhodesia Native Labour Supply Commission (RNLSC). All these methods were pursued in the recruitment methods used by the City Council. The number of workers waiting to be hired or seeking work with the Salisbury Municipality was at its peak during the Second World War up until the late 1940s due to economic difficulties in the rural reserves. [3] The poverty-stricken Africans were willing to apply for work and sell their labour at wages lower than subsistence levels. Another of our informants, Tawengwa Mhembere, who was employed by the municipality in 1968, was adamant that working in town was much easier compared to work done in rural areas. [4]

---

[1] L. Malaba, "Supply, Control and Organization of African Labour in Rhodesia", *Review of African Political Economy*, No. 18, 1980, p. 13.

[2] Interview with B. Chidazembe by Honest Koke, 18/02/17.

[3] T. H. Mothibe, "African Workers' Militancy as a Basis for Post-War Nationalism in Colonial Zimbabwe, 1945 - 1953", *Trans African Journal of History*, Vol. 23, 1994, p. 160.

[4] Interview with Tawengwa Mhembere by Joseph Seda, 12/12/1991.

African employees in the City Council acted as recruitment agents by reaching out to their kith and kin to come and join them. For instance, Mutesva was recruited as a builder by his friend, L. Bakause, from the same rural reserve of Murehwa in 1970. Others, however, used established social networks and associations. This meant that whenever job opportunities arose within the municipality, social networks and associations would help spread the word to other unemployed Africans in the city. Another informant, C. Kachikuni, who was engaged as a painter, confirmed this as he remembered that when he came to Harare in the late 1960s, it took him only a week before finding work with the City Council. He credited his social networks and associations which he praised for providing him with information about possible job vacancies. [1] Hence, unemployed Africans benefited through already employed Africans who acted as informal recruitment agents.

The RNLSC was the public labour recruitment agent used by the City Council in recruiting its workforce. The post-Second World War years were characterised by a continuous increase in the indigenous African workforce and a relative decrease in foreign employees. The RNLSC was formed in 1946 to regulate manpower supply and it represented several employers which included the SCC. [2] L. Bakause conceded that when he was employed at the City Council in 1964 as a builder, some of his long-serving migrant workmates at the City Council had been recruited by the RNLSC. [3] These migrant workers were conscripted from Northern Rhodesia (now Zambia), Nyasaland (now Malawi), and Portuguese East Africa (now Mozambique). Hence, the City Council relied on the RNLSC for both its local and migrant workforce recruitment.

The Salisbury Municipality also used the grading in their recruitment like any other local authority in colonial Zimbabwe. The grading system was

---

① Interview with E. Kachikuni by Joseph Seda, 01/03/1992.

② L. Malaba, "Supply, Control and Organization of African Labour in Rhodesia'" *Review of African Political Economy*, No. 18, 1980, p. 14.

③ Interview with Bakause, Secretary at the Harare Municipal Workers' Union offices, 01/03/2018.

meant to determine someone's wages, exceptional privileges, position, and influence in the SCC. From 1945 to 1979, the prevailing grades were from one up to seven consisting of skilled, semi-skilled, and unskilled workers. The first and highest grade consisted of City Council delegates including Chief Officers, the Town Clerk, and the Mayor. [1] The second grade covered other heads of departments which included the City Treasurer, the City Engineer, the Medical Officer of Health, the Director of Native Administration, and their deputies. [2] The third grade absorbed those professionals employed on a fixed salary including secretaries, typists, and other professionals of the administrative roles in the council. [3] The fourth grade to the sixth grade consisted of other races apart from Africans and Europeans who were employed as foremen, inspectors, and drivers. The seventh and last grade was made up of labourers and most of them, if not all, were Africans. Africans were further divided into a wage cluster which ranged from notch one up to notch six. The first notch was the least paid and it consisted of street cleaners, grass, and tree cutters. [4] The sixth and highest-paid notch comprised of beer hall workers and municipal police force among others.

The recruitment and employment of local female labour also increased in the period under study. This is because the SCC viewed women as a ready source of low-cost unskilled workers who were ready to replace migrant workers. The SCC also wanted to use female labourers as a bargaining chip to bring down the local males' wage demands. In 1953 there were fifty-seven locally employed women by the City Council compared to just twenty-eight in 1945. [5] The use of female employees was advantageous to the SCC since wages paid to female workers were lower than those paid to their male

---

[1] NAZ LG 68/8, Annual Report from the City Treasurer, 1970.
[2] Ibid.
[3] Ibid.
[4] Ibid.
[5] NAZ LG 68/5/4, Annual Report from City Treasurer, 1953.

counterparts. For instance, Gogo Muchipi who was employed by the City council as a general worker in 1971 remembered that her wages were lower when compared to her husband's wage yet they were both employed by the City Council as general workers. [1] In the country as a whole, females of any age received three quotas of the minimum wage given to men doing the same work because of what Joyce Kazembe has characterised as a "dubious breadwinner concept". [2] Put differently, female wages were regarded as a subsidy for male wages.

The SCC was made up of different departments. These departments provided services to both the residents of Salisbury and to transient visitors who included those who came to the city from the countryside to sell their farm produce and also to the tourists. The major departments consisted of the Town Clerk's Department, City Engineer's Department, City Architects Department, City Treasurer's Department, Department of African Native Affairs, and the Health Department. [3] Certain departments that required special training such as the Town Clerk Department, City Architect Department, and the City Treasurer's Department had fewer Africans than departments like the Department of Native Administration, the City Engineers Department, and the Health Department where more Africans were recruited. For instance, in 1958, the City Engineers Department alone employed 1 331 Africans. [4] This was more than double the number employed by those departments which required special training.

The Working Conditions of African Municipal Workers

The labour policies designed by the colonial government kept African

---

① Interview with Gogo Muchipi, 20/08/2018.
② See: J. Kazembe, "The Women Issue", in Mandaza, I. (ed.), *Zimbabwe: The Political Economy of Transition*, Dakar: CODESRIA, 1986.
③ NAZ LG68/5/, Annual Report from the City Treasury, 1958.
④ Ibid.

wages low. This extended to the Municipality of Salisbury. For instance, in 1947, the wages of unskilled European municipal workers employed as supervisors ranged from £300 up to £600 annually. In comparison, unskilled African municipal workers earned from £2 to £4 per month. [1] According to the Department of Statistics, to maintain a normal healthy life, a single Urban African worker in Rhodesia needed £4 monthly, while a married worker with two children needed £10 a month. [2] This meant that African municipal workers were paid well below their minimum efficiency level. The City Council had already fixed a theoretical minimum standard on which health and life could be maintained. [3] These fixed wages rarely increased in the event of changes in the cost of living. African wages, therefore, did not include any allowances for rent and transport and this left many African municipal workers in an unsatisfactory position. Besides wages, the other issue that impacted on the African's work environment was about rations. Food rations received by Africans were way below Africans' need and the result was decreased efficiency. In 1950, Africans were given food rations of one and a half pounds of meat a week which was way below average.

Africans did not worry about wages or food rations alone, they were also concerned about the supervisors who led and commanded them at different worksites and departments. Their supervisors used inflammatory language filled with hatred towards Africans. Sekuru Kwazawayana remembered that while he was employed by the municipality in the late 1950s as a cleaner the use of hate speech by supervisors was commonplace and that those workers who were not used to this leadership were forced to leave the job. [4] In the same vein, B. Marozva confirmed that his experiences were very difficult more so during the initial days when he was employed in 1960 as a builder by

---

[1] *African Weekly*, 29 August 1947.
[2] Ibid.
[3] Ibid.
[4] Interview with Sekuru Kwazawayana, 21/08/2018.

the municipality. [1] He added that the supervisors used hateful words and sometimes insulted workers. However, with time, he yielded to this brashness and instead chose to focus on working for the good of his family. Some however left their jobs altogether because they distasted the insults from such overseers.

The 1948 report by the Manager of the Municipal Compound recounted that African workers left the municipality not only because of low wages but because of the personality of the overseer who loved to treat Africans as slaves. [2] Thus increasing wages alone did not necessarily translate to increased efficiency within the municipality. R. Mukombe, who was employed by the city council as a cleaner in 1969, remembered that whenever he worked under a friendlier supervisor this would make his work much easier. [3] He also argued that insults demoralised workers and that alone affected their efficiency at work. [4]

From 1950 up to 1959, the poor working environment did not change which affected many African municipal workers. Worse still, in 1959, the City Council's Employment Regulations directed Africans working in the public sector to gather in one place during paydays, while Europeans accessed their wages through banks. [5] The Officer in Charge of managing the pay parade would call the name of the worker and the wages were counted at the table while everyone was watching. Besides being degrading, the system lacked accountability since there was no information regarding the hours worked at a specified rate of pay and even the amount due. [6] This was a major source of discontent among African municipal workers in Salisbury. Africans felt stigmatised by the payment method since other races received

---

[1] Interview with B. Marozva, 21/08/2018.

[2] *African Weekly*, 5 July 1948.

[3] Interview with R. Mukombe, 22/08/2018.

[4] Ibid.

[5] NAZ LG69/2/ Annual Report from the City Treasurer, 1959.

[6] Ibid.

their wages through banks or pay packets. The complaints by Africans were frustrated by the continuous resistance from the municipality to change the regulation. The Employment Regulations were only changed in 1973 following the intervention of the Salisbury African Municipal Workers Union (SAMWU). Following the change, African workers were paid through the pay packet instead of a pay parade. [1] This was one of the achievements made by the union at the time.

Another grievance arose out of the use of canteens. While European municipal workers used canteens for all their meals while on duty, Africans used empty containers of paint to prepare their meals. [2] These empty containers were taken from council warehouses after they had finished painting municipal premises. The containers were then used as pots for cooking food while the lids of these containers were used as plates. [3] Worse still, Africans did not have canteens of their own or designated meal-breaks. They prepared their food while on duty, be it during the construction of roads or repairing municipal premises. [4] The effect of using these empty containers was not only stomach aches but a sense of being stigmatised as well. Racial discrimination was further worsened by the fact that Africans used different lavatories and anyone found using European lavatories would be punished or even fired. [5] Therefore, the work environment in the municipality was so racialised that, even though some Africans performed the same job with Europeans, different eating places and lavatories ensured that Europeans and Africans did not mix.

Maturuka argues that Africans were deprived of administrative posts solely because of discriminatory labour policies. [6] For instance, when the

---

[1] NAZ LG 93/ 150, Council Meetings, 1973.
[2] Interview with Mr Mutesva, Administrator Harare Municipal Workers Union on 01/03/2018.
[3] Ibid.
[4] Interview with R. Mukombe, 22/08/2018.
[5] Ibid.
[6] M. Mataruka, "A History of Mutare African Municipal Workers: 1945 - 1994", Dissertation, University of Zimbabwe, 1995, p. 8.

advert for the post of Medical Doctor arose in 1946, the number of African qualified doctors was only 12 in the region south of the Zambezi with a population of around 10 million Africans. [1] The number of African doctors was few because of the difficulties encountered in entering medical school. Africans were, therefore, underrepresented in the higher posts in the municipality. This was a consequence of both a lack of requisite academic qualifications and discriminatory labour policies. However, even when Africans had the required qualifications they were still lowly paid. The *Bantu Mirror* captured the story of a K. Dube, who had graduated in Johannesburg in 1947 and was appointed as a welfare worker for Harari Township on a commencing salary of £160. [2] Needless to say, Dube's wage was much lower than that of Europeans carrying out a similar job.

African municipal workers were agitated by these conditions. In 1948, the Director of the Municipal Native Administration admitted that the shortage of African workers was caused by the prevailing wages. [3] On top of poor wages, African workers were poorly fed, treated poorly and they were also housed poorly. [4] The accommodation provided by the municipality was unsatisfactory. The SCC's double-storey hostels or dormitories were built in 1948. [5] Though these double-storey buildings were touted as self-contained hostels, in reality, the conditions were unbearable. About 2 500 single municipal workers lived in a single hostel and there were signs of overcrowding. [6] The majority of rooms in a hostel accommodated five men on steel beds. There was one very large room that was used as a dormitory for about 250 men. In essence, Africans lived in a constant state of neglect under white paternalism.

① *African Weekly*, 29 May 1946.
② *Bantu Mirror*, 7 June 1947.
③ *African Weekly*, 1 May 1948.
④ Ibid.
⑤ Valerie Moller, "Migrant Labour in Harare Hostels", *Zambezia*, 5/2,1977.
⑥ *Bantu Mirror*, 12 May 1948.

Wage Patterns and Rations of African Municipal workers

As noted earlier, the municipality used a grading system in paying both its European and African employees. However, wage disparities were alarming in the municipality as they were in Rhodesia as a whole. The council perpetuated racial inequality following the colonial government's policy. Africans engaged in administrative and other higher positions would sometimes work outside the council's premises and they qualified for field allowances. However, these allowances oscillated very much in their European counterparts' favour since they were already promulgated by the City Council's Employment Regulations of 1957 which regulated Africans wages upon employment. [1] For conferences and meetings attended by both Europeans and Africans outside the municipal limits, Africans were given half the allowance given to Europeans. For instance, in 1957 Europeans received £8 per 24 hours attended while Africans received half of that allowance. [2] Even on food allowances, the case was the same. There is no doubt that this impacted the well-being of Africans. This was the context within which Africans spearheaded resistance through strikes, participation in informal employment, and partook side jobs.

Over and above the wage and allowance disparities, the wages given to Africans were well below the poverty datum line of £4 a month. In addition to that Africans employed by the SCC were paid well below what other workers from different employers received. For instance, in 1957, the monthly wages of Africans employed by building contractors were £7. 16 a month including accommodation, allowance for rations, and fuel. [3] The council's minimum wage paid to workers in the same category was £4. 15, 6d

---

[1] *Bantu Mirror*, 21 September 1957.

[2] Ibid.

[3] NAZ LG93/ 145 Council meetings, 1957, p. 147.

a month including accommodation, allowances for rations, and fuel. [1] The need to provide services at a minimum cost led to the exploitation of Africans despite the colonial government sometimes condemning the low levels of pay. In 1953, the council even protested against the government's decision to extend the Native Labour Boards Act (NLBA) to local authorities. [2] The NLBA was aimed at making the Native Labour Board responsible for determining the rates of pay and terms of employment for the council's African employees.

Municipal wages differed depending on access to food rations. In 1949, those who received cash wages only received £3. 14s. 6d while those who received cash wages and food rations got £3. 4s. 5d. Those who received both cash and accommodation got £3. 6d and finally those who received cash, food, and accommodation received £2. 3s. 9d a month. [3] However, the wage increases awarded to workers were not commensurate with the increase of both housing and food costs and other increases in the cost of living. Many African municipal workers were left in the most unsatisfactory of positions. In 1948, the Howman Commission recommended that a minimum wage of £ 10 per month be imposed, which would have applied to all African workers, men, women, and juveniles in urban and commonage areas, with food and accommodation provided by the employer. [4] However, the council's minimum rate of pay ignored the cost of living, the type of work undertaken, and whether a worker was married or not. Conversely, minimum rates of pay for European workers were based on information relating to the cost of living and work undertaken.

While most African municipal workers received food rations, the majority of ration scales were inadequate in relation to the work undertaken. The food supplied lacked variety and, in quantity, it was lower than the

---

① NAZ LG93/ 145 Council meetings, 1957, p. 147.
② Ibid.
③ NAZ LG70/8, Annual Report from the City Treasurer, 1949.
④ *African Weekly*, 30 April 1949.

general minimum requirement. [1] Married African workers did not receive family rations as well. The inadequate feeding of African municipal workers led to poor work performance which, in turn, led to low-level efficiency. [2] There were calls for increasing rations for Africans but the municipality turned a deaf ear. The Director of Native Administration authoritatively claimed that an African male worker should have a daily consumption of between 4 000 and 5 000 calories with full wages. [3] However, the Salisbury Municipality ration scales showed an average daily consumption of little more than half the recommended calories. As a consequence of this inadequate feeding, many African workers found it necessary to spend a substantial portion of their meagre wages on food. The feeding habits of these municipal workers who received only cash wages left a good deal to be desired and malnutrition undoubtedly existed.

Pension Schemes, Leave Privileges and Workers' Compensation Benefits

Pensions were not common, but possible, for African workers provided the worker was a member of the municipal pension fund. [4] The City Council funded the Salisbury Municipal Pension Fund (SMPF) which provided municipal workers with a pension upon reaching the pensionable age. Given the sum paid to the SMPF, the pension amount received by Africans was very little. The guidelines used by municipal workers to access pensions were adopted from government regulations set by the government public service. [5] The liable pensionable ages for municipal workers were set at 55 and 60 years

---

① NAZ Annual Report from NADA Vol 20 - 26 1943 - 49 p. 39.
② Ibid.
③ Ibid.
④ NAZ LG191/11/3, Reports from Salisbury Municipal Pension Fund, 1949.
⑤ B. Chibhamu, "The pension fund system in Southern Rhodesian with special reference to the government 1900 - 1965", BA Dissertation, University of Zimbabwe, 2016, p. 38.

for both men and women. ① The retirement ages were set by the public service and included workers in local government.

Africans who failed to be part of the SMPF owing to low wages or those who were unwilling to join the fund fell under the gratuity scheme. The gratuity scheme was a token of appreciation for work done and this was given upon retirement. Following the adoption of the Employment Regulations of 1975, Salisbury African municipal workers who had at least 12 years of continuous services were eligible to gratuities upon retirement. The municipality gave a gratuity of £1 for each year of service. Such gratuities were paid by the Native Commissioner on condition that the workers concerned returned to their rural villages and did not seek further employment in Salisbury. ② The payment of the gratuity was also subject to a certificate of consent from the head of the department under which the employee had discharged his or her duties.

Leave privileges were determined by the experience and number of years the worker had provided to the council. However, the Employment Regulations of 1945 outlined that leave for an African worker was not a right to be claimed. Leave was determined by the wage group or notch in which an African worker belonged to. The first group consisted of those who received substantive salaries of more than £5 monthly. ③ Since leave privileges were not a right, African workers in this category qualified for vacation leave of up to 30 days but only after they had completed 3 years or more of continuous service. ④ The second group was for Africans whose salaries were between £2 and £5 monthly. These workers received up to 28 days of vacation leave. ⑤ The third and final group was for Africans who received wages not exceeding

---

① NAZ LG191/11/3, Reports from Salisbury Municipal Pension Fund, 1949.

② Ibid.

③ NAZ LG191/12/7/102/2/5, Salisbury Municipal Undertaking Employment Regulations, 1945.

④ Ibid.

⑤ Ibid.

£2 and these received up to 21 - days' vacation leave. [1] Besides the stipulation that only those workers with 3 years of continuous service to the municipality qualified for leave privileges, African workers who opted to take up their leave days would have their wages cut. In comparison, Europeans received their vacation leave annually, and even while on vocational leave they received their salaries in full. Even when a European and a African were performing the same or similar profession they differed on these leave privileges. These differences in leave regulations fortified the racial discrimination that Africans faced in colonial Zimbabwe.

The formation of the Federation of Rhodesia and Nyasaland in 1953, helped in relaxing the leave conditions for Africans. [2] Africans were now able to access leave privileges annually as was done by their European counterparts. Further, from 1953 onwards sick leave with full pay for Africans was also approved. [3] While Europeans could take sick leave for up to 21 days on full pay for each year of service this could easily be increased to 84 days. However, Africans could only take sick leave on full pay for just 15 days with a maximum permissible period of 21 days but this would be on half-pay. [4] Though there were similarities between these leave regulations, Africans still received fewer days and would earn half their pay if they exceeded 15 days. Though vacation and sick leave were granted to both races, the same cannot be said for study leave. This was regarded as special leave only reserved for Europeans even within the liberal façade that the colonisers tried to advance following the Federation of Rhodesia and Nyasaland.

Workmen's compensation was important in the whole Rhodesian economy. [5] It was the employer's mandate to compensate workers for

---

[1] NAZ LG191/12/7/102/2/5, Salisbury Municipal Undertaking Employment Regulations, 1945.

[2] These measures coincided with the colonial state's efforts of trying to build a liberal justification for the Federation of Rhodesia and Nyasaland.

[3] NAZ LG68/2/3 Annual Medical Report, 1953.

[4] NAZ LG 68/5/4 Annual Report from City Treasurer, 1953.

[5] See: R. Murinda, "Factory Health and Safety legislation in colonial Zimbabwe 1930 to 1970", MA Thesis, Economic History Department, University of Zimbabwe, 2005.

inconveniences and injuries incurred while on duty. The legislation which promoted these type of claim was propounded as far back as 1912. [1] The legislation conceded that a worker had to be compensated by the employer if he or she sustained injuries at work. Within the SCC both European and African workers were eligible for compensation but at different levels based on one's race. African workers who sustained injuries were compensated up to 75% of their wages while European workers were able to access their full salaries after sustaining injuries at work. [2] Some of our informants did concede that in case of injuries at work the municipality did take responsibility for their health bills. R. Chizarura, who worked as a builder for the SCC, remembered that some of his workmates were injured while they were repairing municipal premises in Harari (now Mbare) Township in 1970. Fortunately, all of them were compensated and the costs of their health bills were covered by the municipality. [3]

African Municipal Workers' Responses

According to Mothibe, the Second World War came as a disguised blessing for the economic development of colonial Zimbabwe. [4] The expansion of the Rhodesian economy led to the expansion of cities and towns, and Salisbury was no exception. The number of Africans employed by the Salisbury Municipality during the war increased owing to the economic boom. In general, the boom was reflected in the expansion of the city. However, the post-war years were characterised by inflation and financial difficulties which affected African municipal workers. The rising cost of

---

[1] C. Chiratidzo, "Workers compensation in colonial Rhodesia with particular reference to African workers", Article Thesis, University of Zimbabwe, 1985, p. 10.

[2] NAZ LG 68/5/4 Annual Report from City Treasurer, 1953.

[3] Interview with R. Chizarura, 22/08/2018.

[4] T. H. Mothibe, "African Workers' Militancy as a Basis for Post-War Nationalism in Colonial Zimbabwe, 1945 – 1953", *Trans African Journal of History*, Vol. 23, 1994, p. 160.

living due to financial difficulties coupled with poor treatment increased the discontentment among African workers.

One of the most common reactions used by Africans to their poor working conditions was industrial action. African grievances increased as fiscal austerity and inflation worsened especially during the post-war period. The first African workers' strike took place in form of the 1945 Railway strike, where railway workers were agitating against poor wages and poor working conditions. [1] Although Salisbury African municipal workers did not participate during the 1945 strike, the strike inspired them positively. [2] The strike attested to many African municipal workers that they were capable of transforming their sorrowful situation through striking. Also, the strike showed that unity was important in achieving better working conditions in the workplace since it gave them bargaining power.

The 1945 Railway strike and the 1948 General strike gave birth to African trade unionism. For instance, as early as 1946, the white-dominated union, the Salisbury Municipal Employees' Association (SMEA) was even advocating for the formation of an African Municipal employees' union. [3] This was because SMEA was concerned about the poor working conditions of Africans in the municipality and thought that an African employees' union would help to improve the working environment. [4] However, the SCC contemptuously alleged that Africans would abuse such rights by carrying out unauthorised strikes that were against the interest of the municipality. [5] Hence, they denied Africans the right to unionise. Even the colonial government had mixed views regarding the recognition of African trade unions. Some legislators who purported to have experience of Africans derisively maintained that many Africans were not yet at the stage where they

---

[1] T. H. Mothibe, "African Workers' Militancy as a Basis for Post-War Nationalism in Colonial Zimbabwe, 1945 - 1953", *Trans African Journal of History*, Vol. 23,1994, p. 160.

[2] Ibid.

[3] NAZ LG191/11/215 Proposed Municipal Native Employees' Association, 1947.

[4] Ibid.

[5] NAZ LG93/60 Council meetings, 1945.

were able to understand the principles of trade unionism. ① Hence, they believed that it was practically difficult to recognise such a trade union as the sole mouthpiece of African workers.

The 1948 General strike presented Salisbury's African municipal workers with a chance to express their discontent. ② The 1948 General Strike started in Bulawayo and spread throughout colonial Zimbabwe. Meagre wages, poor working environment, and poor living conditions were among the chief reasons that ignited the strike. However, the situation in Salisbury's Municipality was more complex than that of other African employees from other municipalities and employers. Salisbury had relatively few local Africans working for the municipality and in 1948 the migrant workforce dominated the municipality. About 70% of Salisbury's municipal workforce was dominated by migrant workers that came from Nyasaland, Northern Rhodesia, and elsewhere. ③ It was difficult for these migrant workers to strike since striking was perceived to be a rebellion which attracted punishment such as deportation. As a result, very few African municipal workers participated during the 1948 General strike.

The strike brought tangible benefits for African municipal workers nonetheless since wages were increased and the municipality promised to improve working conditions for African workers. For instance, in 1949, several council meetings were held focusing on improving African municipal workers' working conditions and wages. ④ This led to a wage increase for African municipal workers to cover the cost of living allowance. The effected increase was 60 shillings annually. ⑤ The wage increase was meant to avoid future industrial action similar to the 1948 strike.

---

① *African Weekly*, 30 April 1949.
② Raftopoulos, B. 1995. "Nationalism and labour in Salisbury 1953 – 1965", *Journal of Southern African Studies* 21: 84.
③ Ibid p. 233.
④ NAZ LG93/140 Council meetings, 1949.
⑤ NAZ LG69/1/ Annual Report of the City Treasurer, 1950.

The years from 1950 up to the end of the Federation of Rhodesia and Nyasaland in 1963 were relatively positive for African workers in terms of welfare and working conditions. The formation of the Federation of Rhodesia and Nyasaland in 1953 led to the further expansion of the city in terms of population, infrastructure, and budget since Salisbury also doubled as the federal capital. ① Strike action however persisted during the Federation period which reflected some of the unresolved African workers' grievances but these were much smaller in terms of scale. Several strikes also took place after the declaration of the Unilateral Declaration of Independence (UDI) in 1965 by Ian Smith due to the economic hardship which affected the full functioning of the municipality. ② The government's reluctance to amend the 1934 Industrial Conciliation Act on numerous occasions in 1967, 1971 and 1973 also spurred numerous strikes from 1972 up to 1979. However, these strikes failed to yield the much-needed results in terms of working conditions and wages.

Most Salisbury Municipality's councillors opposed unionisation of African municipal workers and even condemned other African trade unions. A few voices from SMEA and the local government ministry, nonetheless, sympathised with Africans and wanted African trade unions to be encouraged and recognised as the sole mouthpiece of African employees. ③ Trade unions in Southern Rhodesia were fully recognised in 1959 through an amendment of the Industrial Conciliation Act. ④ Despite this, the SCC did not immediately reciprocate until 1962 when SAMWU was formed.

In 1960, only five African unions were fully registered and had the appropriate certificates. Most of the trade unions in colonial Zimbabwe did not have registration certificates from the authorities. However, the support

---

① *Bantu Mirror*, 12 April 1967.

② Ibid.

③ Ibid.

④ T. H. Mothibe, "African Workers' Militancy as a Basis for Post-War Nationalism in Colonial Zimbabwe, 1945 - 1953", *Trans African Journal of History*, Vol. 23, 1994, p. 157.

and willingness to assist by both SMEA and the Salisbury Municipal Professional Officers Association (SMPOA) helped towards the setting up of SAMWU in 1962. [1] According to R. Riddell, SAMWU became one of the effective unions in colonial Zimbabwe in terms of negotiating a rate of pay for its members, and also in bettering the working environment in general. [2] However, the activities of the union were greatly affected by the stubborn standpoint taken by the SCC. The increase in wages, for example, was by a little margin, and still, the Europeans were paid more than Africans despite carrying out the same trade.

Overall, the formation of SAMWU was a positive achievement for Africans towards a better working environment. These changes were evidenced by improved working conditions and African welfare. Gogo Chitoro observed a similar change in her working conditions and wages. The informant reiterated that when she worked for the City Council as a general worker in the 1960s, her working conditions were poor and so were the wages. [3] However, in the 1970s her working conditions and even treatment by supervisors were friendlier than the years when she first got employed. [4] This reflected some of the changes brought about following the formation of SAMWU.

Survival Strategies

African municipal workers resorted to several survival strategies to supplement their meagre wages. Some workers borrowed from their kith and kin who were in better-paying jobs as a measure to improve their poor remuneration. Giving evidence before the National Native Labour Board

[1] R. Riddle, "The Salisbury Municipal Workers' Union: A case study", *Rhodesian Journal of Economics*, Vol. 1, No. 7, 1973, p. 26.
[2] Ibid.
[3] Interview with Gogo Chitoro, 23/08/2018.
[4] Ibid.

(NNLB) in 1948, several African municipal workers conceded that they borrowed money every month to make ends meet. For instance, a refuse cart driver bemoaned that after 17 years of service he was earning 75 shillings a month, and yet he was married with two children but received no rations for his family. [1] His living expenses were well over £5 a month. When asked how he bridged the gap he responded that he borrowed from friends. [2] Also, a compound policeman at the municipal quarry who joined the municipal staff in the early 1940s testified that he was receiving just 30 shillings monthly. [3] But he was also married and had two children to support. His monthly expense exceeded £5. When asked how he survived, he responded that he also borrowed from friends. [4] This strategy was usually associated with usury but these workers had little choice because of the meagre salaries they received.

As stated earlier, African wages in the SCC were well below what other Africans in similar trades but employed elsewhere received. For instance, the monthly wages of African and ancillary workers from other building contractors ranged from £7.16 to £9.00 which included allowances for rations and fuel. [5] The Salisbury Municipality's minimum wage paid to African workers in this category was £4.15 including the allowances for rations and fuel. [6] In the evidence presented before the NNLB in 1948, several African municipal workers disclosed that many African workers, especially the locals, had left the municipality looking for better-paying jobs in other institutions and companies. [7] The SCC recorded a labour turnover of 84 percent and 78.3 percent in 1959 and 1960 respectively. [8] In the same

---

[1] *African Weekly*, 7 May 1948.
[2] Ibid.
[3] NAZ Annual Report from NADA Vol. 20 - 26, 1943 - 49, p. 48.
[4] Ibid.
[5] NAZ LG93/ 145 Council meetings, 1957, p. 115.
[6] Ibid.
[7] *African Weekly*, 7 May 1948.
[8] Report of the Director of Native Administration: 1959 - 1960, 32.

vein, Sekuru Banda who was engaged by the SCC as a driver in 1973 confirmed that several of his friends left their jobs in the municipality to find better-paying jobs elsewhere. ① Valerie Moller estimates that, even by 1973, one in four jobs held by hostel dwellers (i. e. generally the worst paid) changed each year. ② This clearly shows that Salisbury Municipality's working conditions were much poorer when compared with other institutions and companies in colonial Zimbabwe. This explains the way African municipal workers reacted by leaving the municipality for other better-paying institutions and companies.

Social networks and associations were comprised of friends, relatives, and sometimes people from different home villages. These associations bound African workers in town together normally under an older-timer with more urban-life experience. They were not only important in providing information about better-paying jobs, accommodation, and other issues, but they were also important in organising thrift and help in case of death. ③ These associations responded to some socio-economic challenges faced by municipal workers and other African workers from different companies and institutions. Naturi Pilali who was employed by the SCC as a painter between 1972 and 1980 recounted that he belonged to a burial society. He added that such associations were important as they helped to bury relatives, give financial, emotional, and material support when called upon. ④ Also, Peter Rusike who was employed as a clerk from 1974 to 1976 by the SCC confirmed that he belonged to several homeboy associations and burial societies during his working days and he credited their role in shaping his life. ⑤ These social networks and associations were formed as a response to socio-economic

---

① Interview with Sekuru Banda, 21/08/2018.
② Moller, "Harare Hostels", 146.
③ K. Manganga, "A historical study of industrial ethnicity in urban colonial Zimbabwe and its contemporary transitions: The case of African Harare, c. 1890 – 1980", PhD thesis, Stellenbosch, 2014, p. 100.
④ Interview with Naturi Pilali by Susan Ziki, 12/02/2017.
⑤ Interview with Peter Rusike by Honest Koke, 02/02/16.

pressures faced by African municipal workers.

A few African municipal workers also participated in some illicit or unlawful activities that included theft, gambling, and, to a lesser extent, prostitution as a way to supplement their meagre wages. Several informants confirmed that as a last resort unscrupulous means were taken when African workers needed to survive. For instance, Mukombe who was employed by the municipality as a cleaner in 1969 stated that gambling was part of his life during his working days in the municipality together with some of his workmates. [1] L. Mutesva who was employed by the municipality as a builder in 1970 observed a similar pattern and also confessed to have moon-lighted by taking up some odd jobs outside his normal working hours. He even fingered some of his former female workmates as sex workers who spent some nights with rich white men in the downtown areas of Salisbury. [2] All these were measures aimed at supplementing family incomes.

Salisbury Municipal African workers also participated in informal employment outside of their formal working hours. Some men and women practised as traditional doctors while others were herbalists. In 1957 the Harari Musika Market had 15 *herbalists* plying their trade. [3] However, operationally the herbal stalls at the market were owned by traders rather than African traditional herbalists and functioned as 'herbal pharmacies' or as dispensaries of herbal medicines and preparations. [4] They sold their herbal medicines either directly to consumers or to township herbalists-cum-traditional doctors who worked under the radar of state surveillance within their homesteads or rented lodgings. Although these activities provided health care to the urban populace, they were also an important source of income for these workers and this was important in supplementing the family

---

[1] Interview with R. Mukombe, 22/08/2018.

[2] Interview with Mr Mutesva, Administrator Harare Municipal Workers Union on 01/03/2018.

[3] Report of the Director of Native Administration: 1956 - 1957,118.

[4] See: Pamela Reynolds, "The training of Traditional healers in Mashonaland", in Murray Last and G. L. Chavunduka, eds., *The Professionalisation of African Medicine*, Manchester: Manchester University Press and International African Institute, 1986.

income. K. Mware who was engaged by SCC as a general worker in 1972 revealed that he got his health care services from his workmate within the municipality, Kamombe, who practised as a traditional doctor. [1]

Besides traditional healing, beer brewing also made the list of several activities African municipal workers participated in to supplement their poor salaries. In its 1958 report, the Department of African Administration admitted that "prior to the opening in June 1954, of the Council's new Native beer brewery, the amount of Native beer available was totally inadequate and so to supplement supplies; the illegal brewing of *skokiaan* was widely indulged in by the African community". [2] Thus, *skokiaan* brewing was, largely, the direct result of uneconomic wages paid to the Africans in the council's employ who optimised on the shortages of their preferred beer types. [3]

Many of the local African municipal workers who maintained a rural home also took part in farming activities. Among other things, they grew maize and other grains and they also participated in cattle rearing. [4] These economic activities were essential in supplementing not just poor wages but also their dietary requirements. Since maize was the staple food for most Africans, its cultivation helped reduce the expenditure needed to buy maize. In some cases, they produced maize surplus and green produce which were then sent to the local market (*Musika*). All these efforts lessened the burden on wages, and yet at the same time, it increased family income aimed at covering all family expenses including food and other expenses. [5]

Some Salisbury African municipal workers who gave evidence before the

---

[1] Interview with K. Mware, 23/08/2018.

[2] Report of the Director of Native Administration: 1957 – 1958, 113 – 114.

[3] *Skokiaan* brew was made from a mixture of yeast, maize meal and sugar to start with but such ingredients as methylated spirits, and tobacco were also added to increase its "punch". It is believed that the process was invented in Johannesburg and hence the name is also derived from Johannesburg.

[4] T. H. Mothibe, "African Workers' Militancy as a Basis for Post-War Nationalism in Colonial Zimbabwe, 1945 – 1953", *Trans African Journal of History*, Vol. 23, 1994, p. 160.

[5] Interview with Bakause, Secretary at the Harare Municipal Workers' Union offices, 01/03/2018.

NNLB in 1948, declared that rural farming was indispensable to their continued stay in the cities. [1] A boss-boy at the municipality claimed that he was earning £2.45 a month and yet he was married with four children but received no rations for his family. [2] His living expenses were well over £5 a month. When solicited how he bridged the gap he reiterated that rural farming was crucial for his survival. [3] Africans thus confirmed the continued importance of rural livelihoods subsidising urban work. Bakause asserted that when he worked for the municipality he would buy farming inputs each time he visited his rural home for use when farming. [4] He added that farming helped to reduce some of the expenses of buying food and it provided his family with the much needed nutritional needs which would have been affected by the low wages he received. [5] Mutesva also reinforced that rural farming at his rural home in Murehwa helped reduce his food expenses for the family. [6] Hence, rural farming was a source of income for some municipal workers in supplementing their wages and helped maintain a healthy life.

Conclusion

This article has captured the working experiences of Salisbury municipal workers and their reaction to their working conditions. Africans faced difficult experiences during their working days in the municipality. Without ruling out some conviviality in the workspace many African municipal workers were however not happy due to the treatment they received from the City Council, low wages, inadequate food rations among a host of grievances. The article defined the nature and conditions of African

---

[1] *African Weekly*, 7 May 1948.
[2] Ibid.
[3] Ibid.
[4] Interview with Bakause, Secretary at the Harare Municipal Workers' Union offices, 01/03/2018.
[5] Ibid.
[6] Interview with Mr Mutesva, Administrator Harare Municipal Workers Union on 01/03/2018.

municipal workers between 1945 and 1979 to reveal the sorrowful state of affairs. Although Africans were able to access leave privileges and pension schemes, in most cases these privileges were limited and the rate of payment was different from their workmates of European descent. However, the African workers displayed an incredible amount of agency as they employed several strategies in response to their oppression under the Salisbury Municipality. For instance, they responded through strikes, unionising, supplementing their wages through farming, borrowing and simply changing jobs. The Salisbury African municipal workers participated in the 1948 General strike to let their voices be heard. The strike birthed African unionism and SAMWU was formed in 1962. The union tried to address Africans' grievances but with little success. That notwithstanding, Africans were already using different survival strategies to supplement their meagre wages. Pilfering became a common habit in the municipality. Some workers simply left the municipality for better-paying jobs elsewhere. The article concludes that, because of their poor working environment, African municipal workers used different measures to let their voices be heard and also resorted to various measures to survive in the city.

Agrarian Capitalism and Labour Dynamics in Rhodesian Coffee Plantations C. 1900 – 1980

Takesure Taringana

Abstract

　　This paper reconnoitres the labour dynamics involved in the evolution of the coffee industry in colonial Zimbabwe from c. 1900 – 1980. It unpacks the interrelationship of forces that shaped the labour ecology in the coffee plantations. The paper argues that the labour relations that obtained in the coffee plantations were a function of a long process of the State's efforts to consolidate economic opportunities for white settlers at the expense of the Africans. Coffee plantation labour configurations were a cumulative process of the massive transfer of productive resources from the hands of the Africans to the European settlers. This was aimed at strengthening the socio-economic and political position of settlers for the basic goal of developing Southern Rhodesia as a settler country. In this case, the alienation of land in particular and the distribution of other factors of production, mainly capital, was designed to push Africans into the realm of poverty from which they would be forced to seek employment in the European sector. Sequestration of African land in the Eastern Highlands created a situation where Africans, who were forced into the unproductive reserves in the low-veld, had to seek employment in coffee plantations, forcing them to underwrite the creation of a white men's country by providing cheap labour. The paper also examines other micro-factors affecting labour supply in the coffee plantations and efforts by plantation owners to stabilise labour over time.

Introduction

The expansion of coffee production, particularly from 1962 to 1980 resulted in a corresponding increase in labour demands in the plantations. Both farmers and the state connived to ensure consistent labour supply into the plantations through various legal tools and cohesive measures. Labour supply trends in Rhodesian coffee plantations were largely shaped by the general structure of colonial Zimbabwean political economy. The evolution of agrarian capitalism in colonial Zimbabwe created an economic dualism characterised by the white sector on the one hand and the African sector on the other. The need for transfer of labour from the African to the white-managed economy raised issues of importance on the interaction between these two sectors. It also generated some institutional mechanisms that became the linchpin of the white settler colonial system. The model of colonial economic development for Southern Rhodesia was the 'settler frontier' of Kenya and South Africa rather than the "trader's frontier" characteristic of most West African countries. [1] Based on this model, Southern Rhodesia's officialdoms aspired to put all factors of production, labour, land and capital under the direct control of the whites. These were deliberately transferred from the indigenous African economies to create the much-hyped dynamism and prosperity of the whites. Generally, this stalled the capacity of African economies to transform themselves into rival centres of market production. This inspired a colonial scheme in which African development would be subordinated to that of whites and initiated a process of *depeasantisation* designed to force as many Africans to the labour market as possible. The state resorted to numerous methods of procuring labour for various European enterprises and these were couched in various legal

---

[1] See A. Mlambo, "Building a Whiteman's Country: Aspects of White Immigration into Rhodesia up to World War 2", *Zambezia*, vol. 25, no. 2, 1998, pp. 123 – 46.

apparatus. Among these were forced labour, taxation and land sequestration. [1] These processes had a fundamental bearing on the nature of labour supply to the coffee plantations.

Deployment of factors of production and the configuration of labour patterns

Labour supply trends in the coffee plantations in colonial Zimbabwe can be understood within the context of a two-tier economic system founded largely on land alienation by the white minority. The exploitation of African labour was a cumulative result of the land sequestration policies of succeeding colonial Zimbabwean governments. The imposition of a capitalistic form of development in the form of coffee plantations steadily restructured and disrupted the 'traditional' African society, a process which eventually led to the emergence of cheap labour "reserves" in the areas that surrounded the coffee plantations. All government policies in shaping the distribution of the factors of production had a direct bearing on the labour supply scenario and, in part, deliberately intended to create pools of cheap labour supply. Essentially, a regular supply of cheap labour was the hallmark for capital accumulation in colonial Zimbabwean commercial agriculture. [2]

During the earliest years in the development of white settler agriculture in the Melsetter district, labour tenancy mainly defined labour relations in

---

[1] For more on labour processes in colonial Zimbabwe in general, see C. van Onselen, *Chibharo: Africa Mine Labour in Southern Rhodesia, 1900 – 1933*, Johannesburg, Ravan Pr, 1976; D. B. Ndlela, *Dualism in the Rhodesian Colonial Economy*, University of Lund, Student-literature, 1981; G. Arrighi, "Labour supplies in Historical Perspectives: A Study of the Proletarianisation of the African Peasantry in Rhodesia", in G. Arrighi and J. S Saul, *Essays on the Political Economy of Africa*, London, Monthly Review Press, 1973; I. Phimister, *An Economic and Social History of Zimbabwe, 1890 – 1948: Capital Accumulation and Class Struggle*, New York, Longman, 1988; J. K. Rennie, "White Farmers, Black Tenants and landlord Legislation: South Rhodesia: 1890 – 1930", *Journal of Southern African Studies*, vol. 15, no. 1, 1978, pp. 86 – 98.

[2] D. G. Clarke, *Agricultural and Plantation Workers in Rhodesia: A Report on Conditions of Labour and Subsistence*, Salisbury, Mambo Press, 1977, p. 16.

coffee-producing farms. As Rennie put it, labour tenancy was a form of serfdom which developed where undercapitalised white settler farmers took land for agriculture. [①] White settler farmers who alienated land also took control of the people occupying that land. Labour tenancy was later couched within the Private Land Ordinance (PLO) of 1908, where Africans who did not vacate land earmarked for white settlement were forced to provide labour to the owner without wages, for the "right" to squat on the land. [②] From the occupation of Gazaland, white settlers admitted to using tenant labour on their lands. As C. Moody put it, "those who do gang work have to do it for the right of squatting on my farms," while another farmer affirmed that "hoeing mealies, was performed for nothing but the right of staying on my farm."[③] While labour tenancy was abolished in the wake of the Land Apportionment Act of 1930, the Chipinga-Melsetter area was given a grace period to extend it for another 10 years. [④] Moyana attributes this to the level of undercapitalisation of most settlers of Afrikaner origins who settled in that area. [⑤] In 1935, the Chipinga Native Commissioner had this to write to the Chief Native Commissioner:

I have to say that with few exceptions, the natives working for the Europeans in this district are tenants of the farmers for whom they work and that they work for them without wages for more or less fixed periods in lieu of paying rent for the land they occupy and use. [⑥]

---

① Rennie, "White Farmers, Black Tenants and landlord legislation: South Rhodesia: 1890 – 1930", p. 86.

② Ibid, p. 87.

③ NAZ: DM2/8/1, Minutes of a Meeting held at Kenilworth, Melsetter, September 10th 1895.

④ Rennie, "White Farmers, Black Tenants and Landlord Legislation: South Rhodesia: 1890 – 1930", p. 98.

⑤ Moyana, *The Political Economy of Land in Zimbabwe*, p. 119.

⑥ NAZ: S235/356, Correspondence from the NC Chipinga to the Chief Native Commissioner, 13 August, 1935.

In this context, labour tenancy on most farms in Gazaland became one of the basic forms of capital accumulation for farmers in that region. This scenario, however gradually changed during the late 1940s when most farmers became stable.

Meanwhile, the occupation of Gazaland initiated a process of land alienation and this forced Africans into "reserves" which were located in the dry low veld for African habitation. This process immensely impacted on the nature of labour supply that obtained in coffee-producing areas. In Gazaland, seven "reserves" were created that is, Ingorima North, Ingorima South, Mutambara, Mutema, Muusha, Sengwezi and Musikavanhu. Reserves were also created in Honde Valley, Inyanga and Vumba areas. Save for "reserves" in the latter and the Sengwezi, Ingorima South and part of Musikavanhu, which were on the Highveld, most of them were unfit for human settlement and crop production. [1] To make matters worse, the 1915 Native Reserves Commission recommended the surrender of Sengwezi reserve and Africans living in that area were relocated to a newly created Ndanga "reserve" in the drier Sabi valley. [2] The conditions of the "reserves" were appalling. Meredith, the District Commissioner, acknowledged this in 1925 when he described the "reserved" areas as useless as they "consisted of either mountain precipices or of the low lying Sabi region where the heat was unbearable and where for every four years Africans faced serious food shortages as a result of drought."[3]

These conditions were typical of the "reserves" that were to surround the coffee plantations. Mutema and Musikavanhu reserves, for example, received an average rainfall of 17.89 inches between 1932 and 1952. This was typical of an area which could not support agriculture for basic living. Much cultivation took place on inferior soils which were extremely weak and could not sustain crop production that corresponded with population increase. As a result of these unbearable conditions for Africans in the "reserves", the District Commissioner was forced to suspend collection of taxes in these areas

---

[1] Moyana, *The Political Economy of Land in Zimbabwe*, p. 112.

[2] *Ibid*, p. 113.

[3] *Ibid*.

from 1935. [1] The Native Commissioner argued that "Africans in the valley had lived a precarious existence because of the droughts and scarcity of food, a situation that forced them to obtain their food away from their home areas. "[2] The discretion for demarcating African "reserves" was basically the unproductivity of the area. An example of this is the rationale behind the creation of Umtasa North Reserve which the Assistant Director of Land Settlement described as:

> Consist[ing] of a steep gorge with the Hondi River flowing through it and that this portion at least is quite unsuitable for European occupation. Further that Natives are thickly scattered throughout the area and that the climate is intensely hot and probably malarious. In view of these factors, and of the remoteness of the land from the market and railway, I suggest that there is no objection to its reservation. [3]

As coffee plantations expanded in the mid-1960s, labour supply to the Eastern Districts was generated out of the steadily impoverished African peasant sector. The creation of an internal labour supply from increasingly poor African "reserves" was the linchpin of colonial labour policy. The mobility of labour from adjoining "reserves" to the coffee plantations was, therefore, a natural consequence of the development of capitalist agriculture in the country. The general scenario captures P. C. W. Gutkind et al's assessment of the major features of labour exploitation in colonial economies. They argue that the precondition to a situation where African labour was subordinated to the capitalist mode of production was that the primary means of production-land, had to be wrestled away from the Africans. [4] Through the same process, the dispossessed Africans had to submit their labour-power

---

① Moyana, *The Political Economy of Land in Zimbabwe*, p. 118.
② *Ibid.*
③ Phimister, *A Social and Economic History of Zimbabwe, 1890 – 1948*, p. 66.
④ P. C. W. Gutkind et al (eds), *African Labour History*, London, Sage publications, 1978, p. 7.

to the directives of agrarian capitalism. [1]

Africans living in highlands "reserves" met their own match of developments that were skewed towards their *proletarianisation*. Despite the potential of the land to support crop production, the areas soon became overcrowded and land became very scarce. Increased population pressure in the African land area combined with soil erosion led to low productivity. The general trend was that most family members were forced to look for work in the coffee plantations. Government also checked African access to capital through bank loans as the Land and Agricultural Bank did not offer loans to Africans; save for a loan scheme for the African Purchase Areas. [2] Loans for Africans in the Tribal Trust Lands (TTLs) only started in the 1960s. [3] Nevertheless, these loans were too meagre and were designed in a manner that Africans would not compete with white settlers but rather supplement European agriculture through the provision of cheap labour. As S. Sticher argues, the extension of capitalism to the "Third World" necessitated the creation of a "Third World" working class. It also follows that the penetration of agrarian capitalism in parts of colonial Zimbabwe resulted in the emergence of a rural agrarian proletariat. [4] In this case, colonial land and credit policies and the development of the coffee industry resulted in changes that led to the emergence of an impoverished rural working class.

Elimination of a class of African coffee planters

Another feature that shaped labour supply trends in the coffee plantations was the deliberate elimination of potential African coffee planters. Coffee

---

[1] P. C. W. Gutkind et al (eds), *African Labour History*, London, Sage publications, 1978, p. 7.

[2] D. B. Ndela, *Dualism in the Rhodesian Colonial Economy*, p. 14.

[3] Ibid.

[4] S. Sticher, "The Formation of a Working Class in Kenya", in R. Sandbrook and R. Cohen (eds), *The Development of an African Working Class, Studies in Class Formation and Action*, London, Longman, 1975, p. 21.

production in Southern Rhodesia was considered a preserve for the European settlers. [1] Africans were supposed to contribute to this endeavour through the provision of labour. Understandably, some enterprising Africans, especially on the Highveld, particularly in Honde Valley, ventured into coffee production. [2] However, African coffee potential was thwarted through discriminate access to capital, which made it difficult for them to sustain economic commercial coffee establishments. This development was carefully coiled within a fundamental policy that guaranteed white dominance and African poverty, a feature designed to ensure an adequate supply of cheap African labour to all capitalist establishments in the country.

European coffee farmers and government officials hardly entertained the idea that Africans could be groomed to be established coffee farmers. Farmers' common view was that, "the most significant needs of this country are European population and wealth based on permanent crops, these advances cannot be carried out by the African population. "[3] White settlers in Rhodesia re-echoed the sentiments of their fellow German settlers in Tanganyika who argued that, "we don't need black capitalists, we need black workers. "[4] This thinking in the coffee sector became pronounced in the mid – 1960s when a few African coffee planters emerged in the Honde Valley, Ingorima South and part of Musikavanhu. European planters claimed that the poorly looked-after African coffee plots would be breeding grounds for pests and diseases that would later destroy European coffee establishments. [5] Moreover, white farmers argued that the export of ill-prepared African coffee would damage the reputation of Rhodesian coffee quality which could result in Rhodesia losing her stake in the international coffee markets. This was clearly pronounced by J. E. Marzorati, Chairman of the Rhodesian Coffee

---

[1] "Coffee Settlement Schemes", *The Rhodesian Farmer*, vol. 8, no. 23, April 1965, p. 34.
[2] Ibid.
[3] Ibid.
[4] J. Iliffe, *A Modern History of Tanganyika*, Cambridge: Cambridge University Press, 1979, p. 155.
[5] "Coffee Settlement Schemes", *The Rhodesian Farmer*, vol. 8, no. 23, April 1965, p. 34.

Growers Cooperative, when he stated in 1965 that, "we are in the dark regarding the government's policy towards African coffee growers, but clearly, they are jeopardizing the high national standards we are striving for. "[1]

European planters also claimed that ownership of a few coffee trees by most Africans surrounding large coffee plantations gave them a good cover for theft from their European neighbours. While these dissenting voices were, in part, true, they were mainly designed to thwart the emergence of a class of African coffee planters in order to restrict most Africans to the provision of labour to the coffee plantations. Enigmatically, the CGA used the public platform to show that it was prepared to promote both African and European coffee-growing ventures. [2] Practically, however, the discriminatory nature of the distribution of the factors of production-land and capital-pushed most Africans off the coffee business and left them with limited options dominated by selling the third factor, labour. This political economy of exclusion exhibited continued vestiges of the process of primitive accumulation which has been further defined by F. Cooper as, "not the mere amassing of resources [but also] the effective exclusion of access to the means of production of an entire class. "[3]

In colonial Zimbabwe, much like Kenya, the major aim of European settlers was to create a white nation based on a permanent settlement. Rhodesian officials worked on the conjecture that the future of Rhodesia lay in white immigration and the expansion of settler agriculture. This was made possible by the favourable climatic conditions conducive for white settlement. On this basis, high-value crop ventures like coffee production were considered European ventures for one basic reason. They provided the much sought after economic opportunities for the white settlers in a bid to attract more settler

---

[1] *Rhodesia Herald*, 8 June 1965, "African grown coffee may jeopardize Standards sought".

[2] NAZ: RC, Ministry of Agriculture, Box 81922, File, 1233/f3, Coffee Production vol. 5, Coffee Grown by Africans, 1964.

[3] F. Cooper, "The State and Agricultural Labour: Zanzibar after Slavery", in D. C. Hindson, *Working Papers in Southern African Studies*, vol. 3, p. 1.

immigrants from Europe so as to create a strong white state at the heart of Central Africa. In this respect, the exclusion of Africans from the mainline economic activities, particularly coffee production, was in part determined to strengthen the socio-economic and political dominance of the white settlers. [1] By restricting the African population to poverty, this would, in turn, force the same to look for wage employment in European capitalist establishments, like, coffee plantations. The coffee industry, therefore, is representative of the organic formation of the entire Rhodesian political economy as far as the distribution of labour was concerned in that capitalist agricultural system.

Nature of work and labour costs in coffee plantations

Coffee production encompassed various related tasks that required labour either on a seasonal or regular basis. For this reason, farmers employed two types of labour: permanent and casual/seasonal labour. In the initial development phase of a coffee plantation, permanent labour was mainly responsible for general and preparation work like clearing land, digging holes for the trees, planting, fertilizer application and nursery construction and maintenance. [2] As the coffee plantation aged, permanent labour became more engaged in general plantation maintenance work such as fertilising, spraying, pruning, irrigation, coffee processing, grading and packing. [3]

Casual labour was required in tasks such as weeding around coffee trees, filling of seedling pots and harvesting. Seasonal tasks were mainly done by women and children. These tasks constituted the largest category of unskilled jobs. The nature of work undertaken in the plantations, therefore, largely defined the nature of stratification that obtained in the same. Most of these part-time workers were drawn from the compounds that were created as a labour

[1] Leys, *European Politics in Southern Rhodesia*, p. 33.
[2] W. V. Lacey, "An Estimate of Coffee Production Costs on a Fifty Acre Basis", Ministry of Agriculture, 1964.
[3] Clowes and Hills, *Coffee Handbook*, p. 164.

stabilisation strategy. Male labourers were mainly employed as supervisors, security guards, drivers, sprayers and builders. They also engaged in more technical jobs like mechanics and coffee processing mill operations. These tasks constituted what could roughly be referred to as the semi-skilled and skilled tasks at least in the context of a plantation set-up. These tasks were less seasonal and, therefore, required a more stable labour base.

The labour requirements of coffee plantations were determined by various factors, chief among them being the size of the plantation, age of the crop, and the length of the ripening season. These factors also defined the seasonal nature of labour intake for various tasks in the plantations. Establishing a coffee plantation, for example, required large quantities of labour to perform menial work such as clearing land, stumping and establishing the required infrastructure. [1] Pioneering plantations needed a lot of attention on weeding, mulching, pruning, irrigation and application of fertilisers. These different tasks were largely seasonal. Weeding and mulching were normally done during the rainy season while irrigation was undertaken during the dry season. Developed coffee plantations demanded labour, particularly during the harvesting stage which spanned from March to September. These facts testify to the industry being a labour-intensive sector. Coffee production required an average of one labourer to one-and-half acres of young coffee establishments and one labourer to two acres of mature coffee. [2] Younger coffee plantations had higher labour requirements compared to mature ones due to higher preparatory headwork in the former. Initially, coffee plantations in the region comprised of coffee trees in different stages of development at any given time. As a result, there was need for a regular supply of labour at all times. Nevertheless, labour

---

[1] NAZ: RC, Ministry of Agriculture, Box 81922, File 1233/f3: Tenant Settler Coffee Unit Analysis; Explanatory notes on Schedules, 1965.

[2] NAZ: RC, Ministry of Agriculture, Box 81922, File 1233/f3: W. V Lacey, Analysis of Estimated Capital Requirements for Settler Tenant Coffee Units in the Chipinga Melsetter Area, Economics and Markets Branch, Ministry of Agriculture, 6 October, 1964.

requirements differed from plantation to plantation, depending on the location of the plantation and level of farm mechanisation.

Even if mature coffee plantations' labour demands were largely seasonal, there was a regular labour demand in the Eastern Districts because of the variety of crops that coffee planters handled. Most coffee planters ventured into tea and macadamia production on the same estate or adjacent plantations. This was considered as a safety measure against unfavourable price fluctuations if they were to occur, an undertaking recommended by P. J. Broadway, a Coffee Advisor in Kenya when he wrote:

> I am sure that there will be less attendant risks if a scheme could be worked out whereby coffee is grown in say 25 – 50 acre units attached to a mixed farm. There are many farmers in Kenya who produce the best quality coffee from such small acreages. I think it is also pertinent that since it takes a minimum of 4 to 5 years for a unit of coffee to get established, the price of the produce in the world market might well change or even drop over this period, and any farmer who is solely dependent on such a crop might stand to lose everything he had. [1]

Diversity of production was hence considered as a safeguard against the possibility of future slumps in coffee prices and no coffee planter, therefore, depended on coffee alone. Tea, in particular, is a crop that requires all year round labour supply. As a result, labour continuously alternated between coffee, tea and macadamia plantations all year round, depending on the peak labour needs of each crop.

The labour requirements for coffee plantations and the wages given to the workers determined the total labour costs of the coffee business. From 1965, wages for permanent labourers were fixed at £3 8s 0d, plus food, in

---

[1] NAZ: RC, Ministry of Agriculture, Box 81922, File 1233/f3, Coffee Production vol. 5; letter from P. J. Broadway to Bill, 01 October 1964.

the form of rations and housing which made a total average of up to £5 8s 0d per labourer. This roughly translated to an average of £60 0s 0d per annum per labourer. [1] Wages for workers were very low considering the fact that they included rations and housing. This was but a smokescreen behind which to justify the low wages given to the workers. Most coffee plantations like Elizabethville, San Michele, New Castle, Smalldeel and others had an average area of ten acres each of maize which was employed as rations, thereby reducing labour costs. [2] Therefore, the net wages for the permanent labourers per month was an average of £3 per worker. [3]

Casual labourers were normally paid on a daily basis on the scale of their measurable work output. For example, harvesting pay-out was pegged at 6d per 10 lb. tin. A picker was generally expected to garner a minimum of three tins a day. [4] This was worked with the understanding that 1 ton of clean processed green coffee was equivalent to 4,800 lb. of coffee cherry. [5] As a way of minimising labour costs, an average of two-thirds of coffee in the Eastern Districts was picked under contract conditions and the balance was worked by permanent labours. Coffee farmers, notably Boswell Brown and H. Fennel, argued that labour costs could be best reduced by applying more casual labour and attempts at mechanisation. [6] Operations like filling seedling pots were at a cost which varied from 6d to 1s per 100 pots and weeding rates were pegged at an average of 9d per row. [7]

---

[1] NAZ: RC, Ministry of Agriculture, Box 81922, File 1233/f3, Coffee Production, vol. 5, Coffee Growing Industry, 1968.

[2] NAZ: RC, Ministry of Agriculture, Box 81922, File, 1233/f3, Coffee Settlement Scheme, vol. 1, Labour Costs, 1965

[3] Ibid.

[4] Ibid.

[5] Ibid.

[6] NAZ: RC, Ministry of Agriculture, Box 81922, File, 1233/f3, Minutes of a meeting to consider the cost of establishing a coffee unit, 22 September 1964.

[7] NAZ: RC, Ministry of Agriculture, Box 81922, File, 1233/f3: W. V Lacey, Analysis of Estimated Capital Requirements for Settler Tenant Coffee Units in the Chipinga Melsetter Area, Economics and Markets Branch, Ministry of Agriculture, 6 October 1964.

The ticket system was the dominant method used by plantation owners to keep the record of a labourer's work and the amount they were supposed to get over a period of a week, fortnight or month, depending on a plantation's pay schedule. This system was used chiefly for contract workers who were paid according to their proven work output. For example, the amount of coffee harvested, area weeded, number of pots filled and so on and the amount each would garner was tendered against each date. The total amount was then calculated and paid to them at set dates. However, the ticket system was subjected to some abuse ranging from rigged scales, dishonest mathematics and harsh punitive measures. Mistakes such as branch breaking and picking unripe cherries were punishable by tendering a lower amount on the workers' ticket than would be anticipated. [1] Table 1 is an expression of the labour requirements and cost based on a 50 acre coffee unit.

Table 1   Labour costs for a 50 acre coffee unit from year 1 – 6

Year	1	2	3	4	5	6
Acres	25	50	50	50	50	50
Permanent labour force	6	10	12	12	15	18
Permanent wages at £48/labourer/ annum[2]	£288	£480	£576	£576	£720	£864
Casual labour: Clearing	£75	£75	—	—	—	—
Cultivation	£15	£30	£30	£30	£30	£30
Striping and harvesting	—	—	£58	£151	£210	£233
Total labour costs	£378	£585	£665	£757	£960	£1 127

Source: NAZ: RC, Ministry of Agriculture, Box 81922, File, 1233/f3, Tenant Settler Coffee Unit Analysis Explanatory Note.

The information Table 1 testifies to the fact that casual labour was a vital constituent of the coffee plantation economy. The more the plantations

---

[1] Interview with Mrs Madhubeko, Madhuku, 15 December 2013. See S. C Rubert, *A Most Promising Weed: A History of Tobacco Farming and Labour in Colonial Zimbabwe*, 1890 – 1945, Ohio, University Centre for International Studies, 1998, for such abuses in the tobacco industry.

[2] This figure does not take into account housing and rations, this explains why it differs with the average total amount of £60 referred to above.

matured, the more they became productive and the more casual labour was demanded. The amount of cash outlays for casual labour was very minimal, yet the labourers performed the largest part of coffee plantation tasks. Casual labour was, therefore, an essential aspect in bankrolling the expansion of agrarian capitalism in the coffee plantation set up.

Stabilisation of labour on coffee plantations

The totality of coffee production in the country pointed to the need for a regular supply of labour. Consequently, planters made moves to stabilise labour supply. Stabilisation of labour in the plantations embraced the notion that a plantation was not only a system of economic production but also a community and a system of social reproduction. For a guaranteed consistent supply of labour, a more settled and family-based labour supply had to be created. The desire to stabilise labour on a family basis ensued from the benefits of improved productivity accrued from the use of experienced pickers. A seasonal labour force, which brought in new people season in season out, could become more of a liability in the development of agrarian capitalism. Stabilisation, in this case, entailed the integration of the entire family unit into plantation labour. As one planter noted, "what we are really aiming at in the long run is family participation-the husband, the wife and children all working on the plantation. "[1] This was largely done through the provision of social services such as housing, education and health services.

Coffee plantations adopted the compound system as a means to have control over labour. The provision of housing on coffee plantations reduced incentives for labour to dessert in favour of neighbouring plantations. Compounds in the plantations were organised on a two-tier system that reflected the degree of *proletarianisation*. There were dormitories for single labourers who usually came to the plantations during peak seasons like

[1] *Sunday Mail*, 23 June 1974.

harvesting. These were semi-*proletarianised* labourers who had strong links with the reserve economy and, therefore, seasonally migrated to the coffee plantations from their rural homes. Most of them had small pieces of land in the reserves, where they grew food staples. Moreover, many also tried to gain some income through self-employment in economic activities such as mat and basket making, beer brewing, tailoring, carpentry and all sorts of small-scale trading. [1] Still, plantation wage labour formed an essential element of these people's livelihood.

Highly *proletarianised* labourers employed on a permanent basis constituted the core of the coffee plantations workforce. [2] These labourers lived on the estate in dormitories for married couples as families and were largely dependent on the farm owner, a dependency that embraced all aspects of life. They had largely one main means of reproduction at their disposal, namely, their labour-power. Although they had access to a small piece of land on the farm, the owner who "gave" them the land decided which crops they were allowed to grow and when they could plant or harvest. No cash crops were allowed as this would lead to economic independence that would jeopardise labour supply. Therefore, only food crops were allowed. Other sources of income were often not accessible because these households were in most cases not allowed to perform income-generating activities elsewhere. Small plots parcelled to workers by planters were in a way used to justify the plantations' low wage system as it helped reduce the employer's need to pay out more cash to meet food costs. The provision of small pieces of land turned out to be a cheap way of catering for the plantation workforce's food requirements. [3]

The compound system and the provision of small pieces of land as a

---

① Interview with J. Pahla, former coffee plantation employee, Madhuku, 28 December, 2013.

② In Southern Rhodesian coffee plantations, like in most settler economies, the degree of *proletarianisation* was not as "complete" as that experienced by workers in the metropolitan countries during the industrial revolution. However, the creation of a working class as it were, was a major social transformation worthy recognising and the degrees of attachment to the plantation differed.

③ Clarke, *Agricultural and Plantation Workers in Rhodesia: A Report on Conditions of Labour and Subsistence*, p. 52.

means of stabilising labour on the plantations created a quasi-feudal relationship between coffee planters and the African labourers.[1] This relationship was expressive of the total control of the worker by his/her employer. As the degree of *proletarianisation* increased so did the umbilical cord of dependency of the labourers on their employers. As Clarke notes, loss of job meant loss of the right to tenure, loss of basic subsistence and a high degree of insecurity.[2] The compound system, therefore, created a strong interconnectedness of the employee's job and everything to do with his social welfare, for example, rudimentary health services, education and food rations. This relationship reflected the subtle continual operations of the Private Location Ordinance (PLO) of 1908 which gave planters, a farmer-employer-landlord authority over the entire workforce in the compounds.[3] The "feudal paternalistic system", as Clarke describes it, which existed in the compound's landholding systems created a scene in which the output of the land was considered to be part of payment for plantation workforce. The general set up resulted in higher levels of dependency of the workers on the planters, giving the farm owner the advantages of cheap labour and low-cost production. The whole set up sums what S. C. Rubert describes as "'a system of benevolent paternal autocracy' designed to regulate both the quantity and quality of work and ensure that labour stayed on."[4]

Coffee plantation owners also capitalised on the use of women and child labour which was cheaper than conventional male labour. Women were generally paid half of what their male counterparts were rewarded.[5] Plantation owners tended to employ more women and children as casual

---

[1] Clarke, *Agricultural and Plantation Workers in Rhodesia: A Report on Conditions of Labour and Subsistence*, p. 16.

[2] *Ibid.*

[3] Rennie, "White Farmers, Black Tenants and landlord legislation: South Rhodesia: 1890 – 1930", p. 87.

[4] S. C. Rubert, *A Most Promising Weed: A History of Tobacco Farming and Labour in Colonial Zimbabwe, 1890 – 1945*, p. 89.

[5] Interview with M. Hlabano, a former coffee plantation employee, Chipinge, 18 December 2013.

workers during labour demand peak seasons. Stabilisation of labour on the plantations on a family basis gave the planters an added advantage of utilising ultra-cheap female and juvenile labour. Although there were some permanent female labourers in coffee plantations, child and female labour was largely seasonal and on a contract basis. As Clarke notes, coffee planters benefited from the juvenile labour supply which was made available to the employer at low marginal costs without, for example, additional investment in housing. In the long run, the juvenile labourers would become permanent staff of the same plantations, giving planters a guaranteed supply of labour used in the plantation work. [1] For the purposes of cutting costs, most coffee planters tended to keep a small number of permanent male labourers and a large pool of casual labourers.

The use of cheap juvenile labour, in particular, expresses the central *modus operandi* of the colonial state, which was, capital accumulation through cost minimisation and profit maximisation. Cheap juvenile labour was important to the profit margins of all white farmers in Southern Rhodesia and white farmers looked to the state for assistance in accessing child labour. [2] One of the legal tools used by farmers to access cheap child labour was the Masters and Servants Act of 1901 which "allowed" parents and /or guardians to contract for the services of a child or to "apprentice the child to a 'proper' person until the child was 18 years. "[3] Since the Master and Servants Act did not make provisions for a minimum wage, generally wages given to juveniles were much lower than those given to their parents. In this case, the adoption of the compound system by coffee farmers and the Master and Servants Act provided unrestricted access to child labour by exploiting the pre-capitalistic family labour systems in African societies.

The provision of educational services through the establishment of estate

---

[1] Clarke, *Agricultural and Plantation Workers in Rhodesia*, p. 72.

[2] B. Grier, "The Political Economy if Child Labour In Colonial Zimbabwe, 1890 – 1930", *Journal of Southern African Studies*, Vol. 20, No. 1, 1994, p. 28.

[3] *Ibid.*

schools was a step geared towards labour stability in the plantations. Admittedly, education was not part of plantation culture. It was neither technically necessary. As the coffee export economy expanded, there was a growing requirement of unskilled and low paid labour. Many of the African labourers were illiterate and for the farmers, the purpose for them being in the plantations was to labour, not to learn. Any kind of formal education was perceived by the planters to represent a threat to the supply of labour. Nevertheless, as a result of the desire to stabilise labour on the plantations, it was thought necessary to use established farm schools as baits for mainly juvenile labour. Examples of these schools include New Year's Gift, Ratelshoek, Zona and Jersey, among others. Most of these schools only offered education at primary level and in the case of Ratelshoek, education was provided up to Grade Two. As the headmaster of Ratelshoek indicated, children worked in the morning and went to school in the afternoon. [1] For the African workers and their children, education was a means to a better future. The provision of estate schools attracted most African youth in the reserves as that was another way of earning an education apart from mission schools that were established in the region. Albeit, most farms received little support from the government and because of that, many farm children faced a situation in which they received only a very low standard of education. As one former employee recalled:

> The lives of farmworkers revolved around the farm compound and most of the children became farm labourers as well. With limited exposure to the world around them, equal education and carrier opportunities were limited for the blacks. The system was designed to restrict them to the provision of labour in the coffee and tea plantations. [2]

---

[1] *Sunday Mail*, 23 June 1974.

[2] Interview with J. Manono, former coffee plantation employee, Madhuku, 30 December 2013.

This background restricted them to the plantation low wage system and assured the farmers of a future generation of workers. ① The methods of labour stabilisation in coffee plantations were crafted in such a way to minimise costs and maximise profits for the coffee plantation capitalist economy. The extraction of labour value from the Africans was one key pillar of the process of the development of agrarian capitalism in colonial Zimbabwe.

Wages and conditions of service

Wages for African labourers in coffee plantations like in other agricultural sectors remained very low throughout. In 1971, the bulk of permanent workers received a monthly salary of less than $ 12, roughly less than £6 including rations and housing. ② This was not very different from a cash wage of £5 8s 0d paid out in the 1920s. This figure further declined to less than $ 10 in 1975, and no significant improvements were made up to 1980. ③ This issue was compounded by the farm store credit system which ensured that most of the meagre wages the worker got were ploughed back into the farmer's pocket. Farmworkers were compelled to purchase their groceries and other goods from farm stores on credit. The mark-up on goods obtained at the farm was exorbitant and farmers attributed this discrepancy to the cost of transport. ④ O. Munyarari further captured this exploitative scenario:

On Fridays, Chipinge [Chipinga] town was littered with white

---

① Clarke, *Agricultural and Plantation Workers in Rhodesia: A Report on Conditions of Labour and Subsistence*, p. 120.

② *Rhodesia Herald*, 5 May 1971. Rhodesia dollarized in 1970 and the exchange rate was pegged at £1 equalling $ 2.

③ *The Financial Gazette*, May 24 1985.

④ Interview with O. Munyarari, former 'boss-boy' in coffee plantations, 26 December 2013.

farmers in khaki shorts, shirts and farmer-shoes, stocking up on supplies in the company of their black servants. The system had complete control over the farmworkers who were allowed to buy items on credit thereby producing a dependency syndrome. This meant that the meagre wages ended up back in the white farmer's pocket after deductions owed for the purchase of goodies on credit. This cycle of poverty and general illiteracy among farmworkers prevented them from progressing socially and economically and would haunt them into the future. [1]

The system that obtained on the coffee plantations, therefore, allowed for further accumulation of profits by farmers at the expense of workers, whose conditions of service remained unattended throughout the period under review.

Attempts by the Minister of Labour, A. E. Abrahamson, to introduce a minimum wage for farmworkers in the late 1960s were resisted by the Rhodesian National Farmers Union (RNFU). This was believed to set in motion a situation for the continued increase of farm wages to the detriment of farmers. [2] Some of the reasons presented by coffee farmers to stop efforts at improving workers' wages were that; high profits were needed to ensure that reinvestment levels were maintained. To ensure high profitability, wages were, therefore, to be kept low. It was also argued that the low wage structure would improve the competitiveness of all export-based agricultural sectors. [3] Workers were, therefore, forced to bear the cost of obtaining high profits to underwrite the prosperity of the industry.

Even under these circumstances, it was very difficult for agricultural workers in general to bargain for better wages. The main constraint was the legal framework within which the agricultural industry operated. The

---

[1] Interview with O. Munyarari, former 'boss-boy' in coffee plantations, 26 December 2013.
[2] Clarke, *Agricultural and Plantation Workers in Rhodesia: A Report on Conditions of Labour and Subsistence*, p. 61.
[3] *Ibid*, p. 64.

industry remained within the confines of the Master and Servants Act which governed farm labour relations according to the patronising assumption that the white farmer knew what was best for his workers. Under this act, there was no minimum wage and workers' collective bargaining was not sanctioned. [1] This piece of legislation was only scraped off in 1979. [2] The 1959 amendment to the Industrial Conciliation Act (ICA) of 1934 only incorporated African industrial workers and deliberately left out agricultural workers. The generality of African agricultural workers could not be represented by any legally registered trade union and did not have any legal basis to advance unionism. While the establishment of the Agricultural and Plantation Workers Union (APWU) in 1964 was a step in the right direction, the organisation was weak and 'illegal' as it was paradoxically registered as an "Unregistered Trade Union". [3]

White farmers were, therefore, determined to prevent the growth of agricultural unionism to ensure that the demand for labour was met without impediments. This position was clearly articulated in 1963 by C. G. Tracey, chairman of the RNFU when he said, "we are categorically opposed to the development of trade unionism, minimum wages and all that implies for agriculture [sic]. "[4] This was further reiterated a decade later by L. T. Molan, who replaced Tracy as chairman of the RNFU when he maintained, "I would like to turn to another warning sign which has very serious implications, that is the threat of trade unionism, you can rest assured that an agricultural trade union will not get official recognition. "[5] Consequently,

① Clarke, *Agricultural and Plantation Workers in Rhodesia: A Report on Conditions of Labour and Subsistence*, p. 173.

② B. Rutherford, "The Forgotten Fifth: Farm Workers in Zimbabwe", *Southern African Report Archive*, vol. 9, no. 4, 1994, p. 30.

③ Clarke, *Agricultural and Plantation Workers in Rhodesia: A Report on Conditions of Labour and Subsistence*, p. 189.

④ RNFU proceedings, 20th Annual Congress, June 1963.

⑤ L. T. Molan, Labour committee Chairman's address to "Labour and Productivity Days, Labour Supply and Demand warning Signs, Salisbury, 1973.

workers in the coffee plantations did not have a legal platform to advance demands for improved wages.

The level of dependency of the farmworker to the farmer made it very difficult for workers to be involved in union activities. Social controls of the worker through the provision of piecemeal housing and other rudimentary services made farms not easily penetrable by union activists. This is evidenced by the obstructions imposed on the Secretary General of the APWU, P. J Mpofu, who was on several occasions barred from entering most farms in parts of Mashonaland and the Eastern Districts in particular finally leading to his detention in 1973. [1] Further, as the Second Chimurenga (liberation war) intensified, so did security concerns and farmers strongly controlled entry into compounds. As a result of this weak unionisation, there were no improvements to the conditions of workers in coffee plantations.

Despite an increase in coffee price from 1973 to 1980, African workers in the plantations did not enjoy the coffee bonanza as their wages remained considerably low while working and living conditions also did not improve. One of the major reasons forwarded by the coffee planters to justify their reluctance to improve the wages of their workers was that the increases of coffee prices were matched by increases in the general costs of production and increasing workers' wages would push planters out of business. [2] It was also put that security threat posed to the plantations by the Liberation war resulted in many planters devoting much of their investment to farm security. [3] In this case, ordinary farm labourers became the sacrifice from which coffee planters managed to cut production costs. Yet it can be argued that generally with or without increased costs of production, and with or without the security threat, plantation workers in southern Rhodesia were the most exploited type of labour in the country.

---

[1] Clarke, *Agricultural and Plantation Workers in Rhodesia: A Report on Conditions of Labour and Subsistence*, p. 191.

[2] Coffee Growers Association News Letter, 26, November, 1979.

[3] *Ibid.*

Conclusion

The labour supply scenario in the coffee plantations in colonial Zimbabwe epitomises trends in the general political economy of the country. The configuration of labour supply was achieved through various policy and legal mechanisms designed to restrict the African to the realms of poverty, from which he/she was forced to contribute to the advance of settler farmers by the provision of cheap labour. Like in many other agricultural sectors, the low wage system was the pulse of the coffee sector's body economic. This typified the entire Rhodesian colonial economy whose profitability came to depend significantly on abundant supplies of cheap labour. [1] The whole process exhibited the continual operations of the fundamentals of primitive accumulation on the part of agrarian capitalists throughout the colonial period. The state turned a blind eye to workers' conditions in the plantations as it supported white farmers' right to civilized life. Farmers, therefore, benefited from farm poverty as they made receipts of profits from a low wage system. [2] Labour was critical to ensure that coffee of appropriate quantity and quality was produced. However, the crop had to be marketed to make the required incomes in line with the objectives of the state.

---

[1] Phimister, *An economic and Social History of Zimbabwe 1890 – 1948: Capital Accumulation and Class Struggle*, p. 23.

[2] Clarke, *Agricultural and Plantation Workers in Rhodesia: A Report on Conditions of Labour and Subsistence*, p. 11.

Colonial Zimbabwe and Technical Training: White Miner's Training Institutions in Historical Perspective, 1923 – 1948

Nyasha Blessed Bushu

Abstract

This paper historicises the establishment Southern Rhodesia's first formal miners' training schools. The study is situated within the context of a tug of war between international capitalist interests and settler ambitions of establishing a "white man's country." In 1890, international capital represented by the British South Africa Company had been driven to Southern Rhodesia by the prospects of discovering a Second Rand, thereby setting the colony on the path to development pivoting on mining. Engraved in the Company's policy was a profit motif based on cost minimisation and profit maximization. This became one of the many platforms that the Company resisted the establishment of a School of mines such as that which existed on the Rand in South Africa. White Rhodesian settlers fiercely opposed this stance as they saw an opportunity for the colony's white youths to obtain formal training within such an institution. Using primary archival material, this paper therefore feeds into existing historiography on Southern Rhodesia's mining industry by further emphasising the deleterious nature of the Company's influence on the Southern Rhodesian economy. While it also gives agency to the settler constituency by highlighting its efforts to overturn the negative and *overbearing influences of foreign capital up to 1948, the paper argues and maintains that the desire for profit by international capital had an enormous bearing on colonial policy. Consequently, in cases where a choice had to be made between the desires of the colonial government and those of capital, the latter often won the day. In this context, colonialism presented itself primarily in its aggressive capitalist sense rather than based on racism and sentiment.*

Key words: International big mining capital, Profit motif, School of Mines

Introduction

The establishment of the mining industry in Southern Rhodesia presented many challenges for the British South Africa Company (BSAC). The Company had been driven to explore the colony by the prospect of discovering vast amounts of gold deposits therefore establishing a Second Rand. [1] However, such hopes were shattered when it was discovered that the colony's gold reserved had been overestimated. The Company thus reverted to granting out royalties to other companies for gold prospecting and the exploration of other minerals such as base metals. [2] This in turn meant that the Company did not halt in its endeavor to establish Southern Rhodesia as an economic sphere from which it could extract profit. This meant that the Company's involvement in the colony's economic exploits was rather relaxed

---

[1] Phimister extensively discusses this preoccupation on gold mining. See, I. R. Phimister, "The Structure and Development of the Southern Rhodesian Base Mineral Industry: From 1907 to the Great Depression", p. 79. See also, I. R. , "White Miners in Historical Perspective: Southern Rhodesia, 1890 – 1953", *Journal of Southern African Studies*, Vol. 3, No. 2 1977; I. R. Phimister, "Capital And Class In Zimbabwe 1890 – 1948," *Henderson Seminar Paper*, No, * 30 University Of Zimbabwe Department Of History, 1960; I. R. Phimister, "The Making of Colonial Zimbabwe: Compromise of the Settler State, 1923 – 1929", *African Studies Seminar Paper*, University of Witwatersrand, African studies institute. 1983.

[2] *Ibid.*

as it mandated other organs to extract surplus on its behalf. The sum total of the Company's approach was enshrined in what scholars have described as the profit *motif* which amounted to a profit extracting exercise. Indeed, the period of Company rule from 1890 to 1923, became synonymous with profit minimisation and profit maximisation as the BSAC sought to extract surplus from economic activities in the colony. The context of profit maximization became one of the grounds on which the Company turned a blind eye to the establishment of any formal training for white miners. This was indeed coupled with the fact that the colony's mining sector, particularly gold mining, had developed largely based on rudimentary small operations which required little mechanisation and less sophisticated extraction modes. [1] This was also abetted by profitability constraints which prompted the extensive use of cheap African labour.

Notwithstanding these realities, white racialist sentiment lobbied for the penetration of white skilled miners into the mining sector after 1923 and these grew after the achievement of Responsible Government status in 1923. At the insistence of the settler constituency which had vested interests in agriculture and mining, the BSAC had relinquished its administrative hold on the colony. However, while the administrative hold was released into the hands of the settlers, certain elements of the Rhodesian economy remained in the hands of private capital. The mining sector was one of these sectors which were priceless to foreign interests. As a consequence, while the BSAC relinquished its administrative hold, mineral rights continued to be held in its hands. This meant that the trajectory of mining policy continued to be governed from beyond the borders of Southern Rhodesia.

Hence, while settlers embarked on multiple policy shifts to suit them in their endeavors to create a white man's country, foreign interests continued to deter them. For example, ambitions to establish formal training for white

---

[1] Phimister, "History of mining in Southern Rhodesia to 1953", PhD Thesis, University of Rhodesia, 1975, p. 100.

youths were continuously frustrated from 1923 onwards. The settler government continued to meander in the face of multiple collisions with foreign capital interests which resisted the establishment of a school of mines on the basis that the colony was deemed not to have been on a sound footing for such a venture by international capital interests which intended to extract surplus without unnecessary costs on its part.

However, agitated into seeking political action which coincided with the relinquishing of mineral rights by the BSAC in 1933, the settlers pushed the government into establishing the first miners' training school in Bulawayo in 1935. The second was established in Gwelo in the colony's Midlands province in 1945, much against the wishes of capital. These power dynamics led both schools to appear like anomalies and misplaced by 1948 with the unceremonious closure of the school at Gwelo. This paper therefore examines the power excesses of big international mining capital and the power it wielded which was able to greatly alter mining policy. The study contributes to existing historiography on the complex nature of colonial relations between capital and the state.

Historiographical Considerations

The existing historiography on Southern Rhodesia's colonial mining does not directly capture factors leading to the establishment of training schools for whites. Ian Robert Phimister, Charles Van Onselen, Giovanni Arrighi and Murray write about skilled labour on Southern Rhodesian mines, but do not pay particular reference to the efforts by the colonial authorities to establish mining training institutions in Southern Rhodesia, and the dynamics that characterised them. [1] This literature focuses on the peculiarities of the

---

[1] C. Van Onselen, "The Role of Collabourators in the Rhodesian Mining Industry 1900 – 1935", *African Affairs*, Vol. 72, No. 289. 1973; C. Van Onselen, *Chibharo African Mine Labour in Southern Rhodesia 1900 – 1933*, London, Pluto Press, 1976; G. Arrighi, , *The Political Economy Of Rhodesia*, The Hague: Mouton, 1967; Murray, *The Governmental Systems In Southern Rhodesia*, Oxford, Claredon Press, 1970.

colony's mining sector, chief among them profitability constraints which led
to the constant desire by mining capital to make use of cheap African labour
as a cost effective strategy. African labour was compelled into service
through a number of punitive measures which have come to be enshrined in
Southern Rhodesia's historiography as primitive accumulation. [1] According to
Phimister, white workers whether skilled or unskilled had always occupied a
position of vulnerability in a "... condition of fundamental insecurity... "[2]
Notwithstanding this limitation, Murray's publication chronicles the political
relations that inspired the need to establish training for the whites from the
time of the Responsible Government. Murray situates these developments
within a political context. He, however, does not make a detailed account of
the very core of issues and the factors leading to the establishment of the
schools or their functions. Although he makes a hint on how training was a
"cherished scheme" for the small workers, his work does not explain the set
of dynamics which shaped their establishment. Overall, the focus of the
literature above gives context to this study. This paper is a modest attempt at
a chronological narrative of the factors surrounding the establishment of
training institutions and the subsequent failure to attract the intended
beneficiaries up to 1948. The paper employs primary sources from the
National Archives of Zimbabwe in the form of correspondence, reports,
memoranda and legislative debates to give a refined appreciation of the
political economy surrounding the establishment of formal training for white
miners. The paper therefore contributes to historiography on colonial power
dynamics between state and capital. Particularly it demonstrates how the
white government contradicted with capital in its efforts to improve
aspirations of white settlers by establishing training for whites at the expense
of profit which provoked the full wrath of international mining capital.

---

[1] C. Van Onselen, *Chibharo African Mine Labour in Southern Rhodesia 1900 – 1933*, London, Pluto
Press, 1976; J. K. Rennie, "White Farmers, Black Tenants and landlord Legislation: South Rhodesia:
1890 – 1930", *Journal of Southern African Studies* vol. 15, no. 1, 1978, pp. 86 – 98.

[2] Phimister, "White Miners in Historical Perspective: Southern Rhodesia, 1890 – 1953", p. 187.

Skills in the Early Years of Mining

Southern Rhodesia's mining industry took off on a gaiety platform compared to operations on the Rand. This in turn affected the desire for technically skilled personnel at the beginning of mining operations. Most glaringly, in the initial stages of the establishment of mining, operations on the colony were primarily carried out by small undercapitalised personal enterprises. [1] Some features of their operations negatively impacted employment and training of skilled white miners. Firstly, many small workers were already skilled because they had originally been employed on large mines on the Rand before acquiring their own properties in Rhodesia. [2] Secondly, it was not uncommon for one small worker to possess skills as a timber man, engineer and black smith. [3] Moreover, they operated with less sophisticated machinery which did not require specialised hands to operate. [4] In this instance, it was common for miners to rely solely on operations using picks and shovels. Where operations were more sophisticated and required skilled labour especially on big mines, Phimister notes that, "... because the operation of the mines depended on certain skilled occupations, the companies had been obliged to attract the necessary skilled workers through offers of high wages. "[5] In any case, Phimister notes that skilled white labour

---

[1] Murray, p. 126.

[2] Phimister, *History of mining in Southern Rhodesia to 1953*, p. 193.

[3] *Ibid*, p. 100.

[4] Phimister notes that small workers operated often with, "small crushing plant, often only two stamp in capacity and normal no greater than 5, an equally small cyanide plant 9 if employed at all, a boiler and a pump. " Phimister, *History of mining in Southern Rhodesia to 1953*, p. 100. The lack of technical sophistication was not limited to gold mining but also to mica mining. See, Phimister, "The Structure and Development of the Southern Rhodesian Base Mineral Industry-From 1907 to the Great Depression", *The Rhodesian Journal of Economics*; *The Quarterly Journal of the Rhodesian Economic Society*, vol. 9, No. 2 June, 1975.

[5] Phimister, "White Miners in Historical Perspective: Southern Rhodesia, 1890 – 1953", p. 198.

was often in excess on the big mines even when it was imported. [1] Southern Rhodesia's mine labour policy was also largely influenced by the "profitability constraints" and the British South Africa Company's desire to reap large profits from the colony. [2] This influenced a policy which largely side-lined skilled white mine labour in favour of a predominantly unskilled and semi-skilled African labour force. Phimister notes in certain instances, "... some mines were even run entirely by Africans. "[3] It was no secret that white skilled labour was expensive to employ due to "... unduly high wages paid to artisans ... "[4] Van Onselen notes that, given the precarious state of the industry, employment of skilled European personnel was not practicable. [5] African labour was a cheap alternative, a factor which alienated both skilled and unskilled whites from the mining industry. In line with this cost cutting approach, miners undertook to train Africans on the job. Up to 1920, the Minister of Mines stated quite firmly in Parliament that, "... especially on the small mines natives who had been taught how to work hauling machines were an extremely safe class drivers and appreciated the responsibility of their work. "[6] In 1921, the Chief Native Officer was tasked to provide regulations which would equip African workers with mining terminology in vernacular to be distributed among the African employees in form of cards. [7] On the job training for Africans with relevant and sufficient skills "certified" them to work with no certification from a formal school. It became quite

---

[1] Phimister, "White Miners in Historical Perspective: Southern Rhodesia, 1890 - 1953", p. 189.

[2] See Phimister "White Miners in Historical Perspective: Southern Rhodesia, 1890 - 1953", p. 191, "As Our mining position is of course totally different from yours [on the Rand]. Our mines are very much scattered, and thought his produces its own separate difficulties, it does militate against the force of white trade unionism. More use can be, and is, made of skilled natives here than your white gentry on the Rand will allow. "

[3] Phimister, *An Economic and Social History of Zimbabwe 1890 - 1948: Capital Accumulation and Class Struggle*, London, Longman, 1988, p. 49.

[4] Debates of the Legislative Assembly, Vol. 14, 7 May 1935, p. 504.

[5] Van Onselen, "The Role of Collaborators in the Rhodesian Mining Industry, p. 402.

[6] Debates of the Legislative Assembly, 28 June 1920, p. 1319.

[7] *Ibid*, p. 1323.

evident that where profit was concerned, capital was willing to set aside racialist sentiment by opting to employ and train Africans as a cost cutting measure. Indeed, it was the case with the profit orientation enshrined by the BSAC the colony's governing authority that when it came to the retaining what it had invested in the colony, the Company never compromised on ways which ensured maximisation of profit. [1] Ultimately this practice became quite ubiquitous among miners across the colony.

However, various sections of the Rhodesian settler population had expressed desire for training institutions to be established in the colony for various industries. In 1922, H. B Thomas, who was on the Committee of the Unemployment Agency, pointed to the necessity of "training youths technically."[2] The Chamber of Commerce echoed the same sentiment and saw the need to call all sectors of the colony to attention over, "... the important question of technical or vocational training."[3] The response by the Chamber of Mines which was the governing authority over mines however resisted this by arguing that such an undertaking would have been premature and ill-advised. [4] The Chamber of Mines had an influential position but, "... the particular interests which it sought to safe guard involved a largely negative approach to issues."[5] What had perturbed the settlers and white small scale miners was the continuous awarding of skilled mining jobs to whites from the Rand because the local folk were left without certificates as those from the Rand possessed. [6] What existed was a stalemate regarding the issue of white skills but the Chamber of mines which represented the interests of the BSAC

① K. Chitofiri, 'Hopes and Expectations: The Relationship between the British South Africa Company Directors and Shareholders, 1890 to 1923', M. A thesis Department of Economic history University of Zimbabwe. 2007, p. 7.

② NAZ S/ GI22. The School, Bulawayo Technical School Magazine, Vol. 1 1929. No. 2. May, 1930, p. 5.

③ Ibid.

④ NAZ S/CH 13 Chamber of Mines Incorporated; Annual Report 1928.

⑤ Murray, p. 126.

⑥ NAZ S480/103. Mine-Issue of certificates to mine captains 1924 – 1926. Letter to the Secretary of Mines from Durrant, a prospective miner, 1926.

continued to resist such an undertaking to establish formal training for whites.

Mining Labour and Responsible Government 1923

The attainment of Responsible Government did not entail a sudden transition from Chartered Company to absolute settler economic dominance. The irony of Responsible Government status was that Southern Rhodesia's mineral rights and other businesses were not locally owned, "As well as possessing the colony's mineral rights and railways system, both of which enjoyed imperial protection through the constitution's reserved clauses, the BSA Company had fingers, occasionally a whole hand, in many companies. "[1] In fact, "shortly before surrendering its administrative powers, the Chartered Company tightened its already powerful grip on Southern Rhodesia's coal deposits…"[2], Moreover, the economy continued to be dominated by individuals such as Sir Davis who was regarded by Phimister as "powerful enough to make or break the Rhodesian economy. "[3] Inevitably this meant that economic policy was still heavily tilted in favour of foreign interests at the expense of settlers. Armed with the ability to dictate mining policy, the mining industry took a trajectory that brew discontent among local white settlers. What made this turn of events retrogressive to general development and other aspects which included the issue of providing training was that the government could not challenge the position of the Company.

Phimister notes that, "On the few occasions that the settler government was moved to challenge the entrenched position of international capital, it came off worst. "[4] This, "economic dependence on foreign capital instead

[1] Phimster, *An Economic and Social History of Zimbabwe*, p. 118.

[2] *Ibid*, p. 122.

[3] *Ibid*, p. 119.

[4] Phimster, "The Structure and Development of the Southern Rhodesian Base Mineral Industry: From 1907 to the Great Depression", *The Rhodesian Journal of Economics*; *The Quarterly Journal of the Rhodesian Economic Society*, vol. 9, No. 2 June, 1975, p. 119.

forced the settlers' government to adopt middle of the road policies compromising between the interests of the national bourgeoisie and white workers … "[1] This became part of the conundrum that government had to contend with, a dilemma which continued to widen the cleavage between government and settlers. As far as training was concerned, adoption of, "middle of the road policies", manifested in a delay in instituting any form of training for the generality of industry. This is despite the fact that in 1924, the Colonial Secretary had expressed the utmost desire for youths to be trained. Speaking in the House of Assembly in 1924 he stated that, "I have in my notes here, one crying want in the country there was no school were trade was being taught. "[2] For mining, in the same year, Moffat as Minister of Mines had proposed 1000 Pounds for experimental classes for mining to be held. [3] Again, in 1926, Moffat initiated a program which would, "introduce mining subjects in schools. "[4] These were, however, half-hearted attempts at providing training. There were still no talks of a school which would effectively deal with training for all sectors of industry as had been prescribed by the Colonial Secretary.

The neglect of mining training manifested itself in the fact that in 1927, when Bulawayo Technical College which was the first major vocational training centre was established, it was established without training for mining, a sure sign that the question of whether it was the right time for such a move was still hovering. [5] The Chamber of Mines, on behalf of foreign owned companies, had a perceived negative attitude when consulted over the issue of training. The negative orientation reached an extent whereby the Chamber felt that the colony was not yet ready to issue even Mine Captain's

[1] G. Arrighi, *The Political Economy Of Rhodesia*, The Hague: Mouton, 1967, p. 30.
[2] Debates of the Legislative Assembly, Vol. 1 – 2,7 July 1924, p. 725.
[3] NAZ S/CH 1, Chamber of Mines Incorporated; Memorandum to Prime Minister Moffat, 1924.
[4] NAZ S254/2233 – 4, Correspondance from secretary of Mines to the Minister of Mines, 1928.
[5] NAZ S/CH 09, "Bulawayo School Of Mines", *The Chamber of Mines Journal*, Vol. 29, No. 4,1987, pp. 37 – 39.

certificates. [1] Some white miners were livid at this because in the few instances when whites were needed on the mines, although there were Rhodesians with sufficient capabilities, jobs were constantly being given to men from the Rand because they possessed training certificates. [2] In 1926, Durrant, an individual miner, noted that when whites applied for a Mine Captains certificate, "... they were siphoned to another country and when they got there they were refused the certificate on the basis that they were from Southern. "[3] Furthermore, in 1928 the Chamber stood against a school for mining and was of the opinion that the idea was, "premature and should a school be started the number of pupils would be very small. "[4] This reflected what appeared to be neglect by the Chamber and the " *pro-settler* ", government with regards to addressing the creation of a professional class of skilled white mine workers. It was ironic that a government that was meant to serve the desires of the settlers which it represented continued to be out-witted by foreign capital.

Turn of the political tide

General dissatisfaction in the mining industry led white small scale miners to begin exertions to out-stage extraneous domination. The immediate stroke came as government was planning to grant mining concessions to big companies in the Hartley district which was dominated by small workers. At this stage, small workers were already frustrated by government's continued open expression of its helplessness to their plight. For instance when, in 1931, the Minister of Mines noted that, "there is not a man in Rhodesia whatever his trade or occupation may be who does not want to help the small

---

[1] NAZ S480/103. Mine-Issue of certificates to mine captains 1924 – 1926.

[2] NAZ S480/103. Mine-Issue of certificates to mine captains 1924 – 1926. Letter to the Secretary of Mines from . Durrant, a prospective miner, 1926.

[3] *Ibid.*

[4] NAZ S/CH 13, Chamber of Mines Incorporated; Annual Report 1928.

worker in every way possible … The difficulty is how to do it. "[1] The government seemed not to have any meaningful solutions to issues raised by small producers. This resulted in them mobilising in defence of their concerns, resulting in a historic meeting at Gatooma in July 1931. [2] At the meeting, the topic of training was raised and the small workers pursued the issue more and even accused the government of dragging its feet when it came to the issue of establishing a school of mines.

The small workers thus stood firmly for white supremacy as far as skills were concerned and Murray posits that the issue of the training scheme was one well "cherished" by the small workers. [3] In addition, Murray notes that, "even at the expense of increasing production costs the small workers were willing to secure improved conditions of Europeans on the mines and that they were at the centres of white racialist feeling. "[4] This became evident as the question was crucial to them and indeed played centre stage at the meeting. The question however remained whether increasing mining costs was worthwhile or even acceptable enough for the scheme to be successful. The school was seen to have been the key to creating employment and increasing production on the mines. It was suggested that one of the greatest difficulties in the country was lack of opportunities whereby youths could be made fit to take part in the development of the colony's resources. [5] It was also noted that mining was the premier industry and the government had to provide the means of training the youth of the industry. [6] The small workers thought that, "The technical institute in Bulawayo could be the nucleus of a school of mines and this could be conducted in conjunction with a producing mine. "[7] Thus, it appeared that a school was indispensable to the mining

---

[1] Debates of the Legislative Assembly, Vol. 23, April 1931.

[2] Murray, p. 129.

[3] Murray, p. 126.

[4] Ibid. , p. 164.

[5] NAZ S/480/5, A Conference of Small Workers' Association. Minutes of the meeting, 1931.

[6] Ibid.

[7] Ibid.

industry but the concern of raising costs was ignored and overridden by racist
sentiment.

However, not all small workers at the meeting shared similar views.
Instead of establishing a school, some at the meeting pressed for more mining
engineers rather than opting to have themselves trained in the same
manner. [1] This came in light of the view that it had long been the norm that
whenever the small workers needed some inspection they could always call in
government engineers. [2] Regardless, the conference proposed that steps had
to be engaged to educate the youths whether a school of mines was be
established or arrangements were to be made to apprentice youths to some of
the mining companies. In spite of this resolution, and the recommendations
given, the Chamber, while indeed acknowledging the importance of
training, continued to raise concerns over estimated high costs of establishing
such a school and the anticipated low turn-out. [3] The Chamber had set a
memorandum expressing desirability of arranging for mining education but
instead of advancing the issue of a school for Rhodesia, it urged government
to enter into an agreement with the University of Witwatersrand so that it
could take on board some students from Rhodesia. [4] However, nothing was
done towards this end because of financial difficulties. [5] At this point it
seemed that the Chamber was speaking only to defend the profiteering
attitude of foreign companies by not investing in a school which would have
required huge financial investments. Although the meeting had agreed to
press for the establishment of a school, the Chamber and the big mines
remained unchallenged.

The frustrations of unresolved grievances led small workers to a path of
seeking reform through the political system. One of the major outcomes of

① NAZ S/480/5, A Conference of Small Workers' Association 1931. Minutes of the meeting, 1931.

② NAZ S/1673, Assistance to Small workers. Correspondence from the manager Falcon Mine to the
Minister of Mines, 1924.

③ NAZ S/CH 13, Chamber of Mines Incorporated; Annual Report 1928.

④ Rhodesian Herald, 18 June 1932.

⑤ Ibid.

the 1931 meeting was the formation of the Rhodesia Mining Federation (R. M. F). This organisation became a front for small worker interests and was to, "take direct action in the electoral political system". According to Phimister, "the small workers had on many occasions been irritated by the Moffat's administration's negative attitude". Consequently, small workers swung their political support in favour of the Reform Party in the 1933 election, a party which had announced that, "whilst the Rhodesian Party looks at the people through the eyes of the big financial organisations, the Reform Party looks at the big financial organisations through the eyes of the people. "[1] With this, the Reform Party clearly underlined itself as sympathising with settlers. Through the help of small workers, the party won the election and immediately bias towards settler and small worker interests.

Thus, the new government was more accommodative to small workers' interests, including the hotly debated issue of a mines training school. This was to mark a direct shift in policy, one which would put prospects of a school on sound footing. In a stroke of good fortune, the new party's rise to power coincided with the Company's relinquishing of mineral rights in 1933. [2] Therefore, government took a more definite interest in the mining industry and the small workers began "... pressing for a reconstruction of the administrative system of the sector. "[3] Consequently, among the immediate resolutions made by the new Ministry of Mines, "... a miners' training scheme was projected". [4] In 1934, he noted that, "There is also undergoing an investigation into the possibility of establishing a training School for youths. What might perhaps be termed a junior school of mines. "[5] This

---

[1] Phimister, *An Economic and Social History of Zimbabwe 1890 - 1948*, p. 179.

[2] Arrighi, p. 47. The government was able to buy the mineral rights which was in the hands of the British South Africa Company in 1933 which allowed the government to have direct control over its mineral resources for the first time.

[3] Murray, p. 146. Indeed, the small workers were increasingly getting agitated and Murray highlights that, "As the years passed the list of their goals and grievances grew longer".

[4] Murray, p. 135.

[5] Debates of the Legislative Assembly, Vol. 14, 24 April 1934, p. 504.

notwithstanding, doubts over establishing a school persisted amongst some government officials. Even officials of the Ministry of Mines, including the Minister of Mines himself were certain of the establishment of a school, citing concerns over costs. In 1934 Senior himself reported in parliament that, "... the cost might be too large for the result likely to be achieved, we thought it would be possible after further investigations to obtain the same result in another way and with much less expenditure. "[1] These concerns, however, did not deter his efforts to establish some formal means of training. The Minister of Mines then went on to set, "3000 pounds to start the Mining Training School. "[2] This reveals how the practicality of a school was cast in doubt right at inception, but the government could not back-track, in this case very much likely due to its indebtedness to the small workers.

Establishment of the first training institution

The first mines training institute at Bulawayo Technical College was duly inaugurated in 1935 as the Mining Department. The establishment of a Mining Department at the Bulawayo Technical School is directly the result of the deliberations of the Special Committee appointed by the Minister of Mines to consider the best means of affording technical and practical training for youths who wished to enter the mining industry. The Minister of mines had considered mining as the principal industry of the colony; and it had clearly been felt that Rhodesian youths taking up mining as a profession would be greatly helped in their future careers, if they were provided with technical training in mining subjects whilst the mines of the country would benefit by being able to draw upon the school as a source of junior officials. [3] The Mining Department offered theoretical and practical sides of mining

---

[1] Debates of the Legislative Assembly, Vol. 14,24 April 1934, p. 504.

[2] Debates of the Legislative Assembly, Vol. 15,23 April 1935, p. 1141.

[3] NAZ S/ GI 22. The School, Bulawayo Technical School Magazine, Vol. 1, No. 8,1935, p. 11.

operations. ① The former included geology, surveying, chemistry, mechanical and electrical engineering. The latter involved assaying, pipe fitting, track laying, drilling, surveying and timbering as well as operation of machinery.

In order to enhance the standard of learning, teaching staff at the Department was mandated to have two years mining experience from an approved mine and a degree or relevant qualification. This was coupled with a much more hands-on approach to training as opposed to learning through observation alone. Therefore, as per stakeholders' recommendations, the school was to work in conjunction with producing mines. Big mines had indicated willingness to accepting students as they had made "... a very sympathetic consideration to the scheme and made a generous gesture by agreeing to place learners as apprentices when they have completed their two years at the technical school. "② The plan was that "as many students as possible would be placed on working mines and this experience would assist them greatly to an understanding of their school work. "③ The consequence of such an undertaking was that it would have improved the degree of skills of white youths and perhaps put them at an advantage over Africans. What was perhaps perturbing at this early stage was how big mines which represented large capital interests had accepted to engage white apprentices when the idea of skilled white mine labour had been so fiercely resisted.

However, government further extended financial aid to prospective students, a procedure which was not without its own difficulties. The idea was initiated as a measure to ensure that all willing students would not be deterred by any financial difficulty. The Chamber of Mines began granting scholarships worth 180 Pounds to Bulawayo Technical College. ④ Government also extended boarding grants. The process was directly controlled by the

---

① NAZ S/ GI 22. The School, Bulawayo Technical School Magazine, Vol. 1, No. 9,1936, p. 31.

② Debates of the Legislative Assembly, Vol. 15,23 April 1935, p. 1141.

③ NAZ S/ GI 22, The School, Bulawayo Technical School Magazine, Vol. 1, No. 8,1935, p. 13.

④ NAZ S245/962, Mine Schools Pupil Maintenance Grants, letter from the Minister of Mines and Public Works to the Education Committee, 1940.

new Minister of Mines and Public Works because it was felt that "Ministerial
control was essential."[1] Ministerial control was granted after the realisation
that, in the past, the school Advisory Board had been rather inclined to
recommend grants in cases not warranting them.[2] The stance by
government, however, was not fashioned out of benevolence. At this early
stage there was beginning to show signs of low attendance at the Mining
Department. The move to offer grants was thus fashioned by the need to
prop up enrolment and ensure the success of the scheme. The questions over
sustainability raised by the Chamber of Mines and the preceding government
were thus beginning to emerge as a reality as by 1939, the Principal of
Bulawayo Technical College pointed out that the Mines Department was far
from yielding satisfactory numbers of students.[3] The reality on the ground
was that employment in the mining industry was not so lucrative at the time
compared to other industries, and mine workers were held in far much less
esteem.[4]

Moreover, mining had been dominated by already African labour which
had acquired some skills.[5] This acted to deter youths from engaging the
mining industry as a profession. The Chamber of Mines of Rhodesia
Incorporated reported in 1939 that only 50 students had been trained as
apprentices compared to South Africa that had already trained "thousands" of
apprentices at this time.[6] At this point, in Southern Rhodesia only 16
students were drafted to the larger mines to complete the second part of their
training.[7] Although it is acknowledgeable that the school in South Africa had
been opened long before the one at Bulawayo, the comparison is still relevant

---

[1] NAZ S245/962, Mine Schools Pupil Maintenance Grants, letter from the Minister of Mines and Public
    Works to the Education Committee, 1940.
[2] Ibid.
[3] NAZ S/CH 10, Chamber of mines of Rhodesia Incorporated 1939 Annual report.
[4] Murray, p. 18.
[5] Phimister, A history of mining in Southern Rhodesia, p. 234.
[6] NAZ S/CH 10, Chamber of mines of Rhodesia Incorporated 1939 Annual report.
[7] Ibid.

in pointing out intakes in Southern Rhodesia were beginning to indicate the irrationality of establishing a school. Despite frivolous and racialist sentiment, this highlighted the inadequacies that continued to haunt efforts to train the indigenous white labour in preparation for mine work. With time, big mines also began to falter on their earlier promise to take on board students from the Department. The excuse given by mine managers was that the majority of students left school at junior certificate and were therefore too young to take underground. [1] The big mines had leeway to pose such restriction because the government had not instituted any law that bound mines to strictly employ students from the school and mines still could employ miners without stipulating that workers had to pass through the school first.

Thus, of the few white students who went to the school, they did so after already having gone through several years of practical experience on the mines. [2] This was indeed evidence that formal training was just a secondary option and not a prerequisite for prospective miners. A further constraint was that mines could still employ Africans from Southern Rhodesia and the sub-region without them having had any prior instruction. In some instances, the Portuguese East Africa Organisation was even prepared to recruit unskilled African labour for the Rhodesian mines. [3] These factors totalled to make formal training appear to be a white elephant in Southern Rhodesia's mining industry.

The government continued to endeavour to make the school viable. Following resistance by most mines in Southern Rhodesia to take in apprentices from Bulawayo Technical Colleges, the Mines' Department reached an agreement with companies on the Northern Rhodesian Copperbelt to house trainees in order to equip them with relevant mining skills in 1939. The 1939 Chamber of Mines of Rhodesia stated, "It is gratifying to

[1] NAZ S/ GI 22, The School, Bulawayo Technical School Magazine, Vol. 1, No. 8,1935, p. 12.
[2] NAZ S/CH 09, "Bulawayo School Of Mines", *The Chamber of Mines Journal*, Vol. 29, No. 4,1987, p. 37.
[3] NAZ S/CH 13, Chamber of mines of Rhodesia incorporated chamber of mines report, 1937.

report during the year the large mining corporations in Northern Rhodesia
signified their willingness to cooperate and take apprentices for training. "[1]
Thus, local training through the institution continued to lose favour as
training was best served outside the colony or directly on the mines
themselves. It seemed the small workers had made a rush decision and
bundled training together their many grievances at a point when it was not
yet quite relevant.

Towards a School of Mines for Southern Rhodesia: A Response to changing politics

Notwithstanding the obvious signs that the institution in Bulawayo was
under threat, a second mine training institution: the Guinea Fowl Miners
Training School was established in 1945 which was earmarked to evolve into
the School of Mines for Southern Rhodesia of university standard, bigger
than the Department at Bulawayo. The school was again a product of
political scheming by Prime Minister Huggins' administration. By 1943, the
government's position in the electoral political system was precarious, and
Huggins sought to re-establish a basis of support. [2] The party was faced by
desertion from crucial party members who defected from the government
party who along influential figures associated with the mining companies as
well as prominent small workers were joining with others active in business
and in manufacturing industry to form a new opposition Liberal Party. [3] In
order to prop up his waning support, Huggins once again resorted to making
concessions to the small workers. Thus, in 1943, among the concessions, the
government also prepared the ground for a miners' training scheme by
appointing a committee to supervise a school at Guinea Fowl. [4] This meant

---

[1] NAZ S/CH 10, Chamber of mines of Rhodesia incorporated Annual report, 1939.
[2] Murray, p. 153.
[3] *Ibid.*
[4] *Ibid.* , p. 154.

that despite many challenges that the school in Bulawayo faced, Huggins had to continue endeavouring to have youths trained for the mining industry as had been prescribed by small workers so as to win over their votes this resulted in the formation of another school, Guinea Fowl Miner's Training School at Gwelo.

The school was therefore established in 1945 on the grounds of a rehabilitation scheme for ex-soldiers, initially to cater for training white conscripts whose training had been disrupted by the war. [1] The government argued that the school had been successful and had trained a considerable number of men in the mining industry and generally fulfilled the purpose the Government intended when the school was established. [2] However, again the issue of attendance proved to be a formidable challenge. By 1947, an insufficient number of service men were coming forward for training and it seemed then that there was no justification in continuing the school for its original purpose. [3] Training white miners was evidently proving futile as senior citizens showed general unwillingness to engage the school. In a desperate attempt to save the School from closure, the government sought immediately to shift enrolment from war veterans to Southern Rhodesia's youths. The government began contemplating on "... whether it was to be advanced to the role of the Rhodesian School of Mines on the lines of the School of Mines in the Union..." [4] This could only be done if the School was to attract sufficient numbers of youths. The Department of Mines and Public Works was thus tasked to enquire if the younger generation was keen to take up courses at the school to warrant its continued existence. [5]

---

[1] NAZ S245/1151. Guinea Fowl Miners Training School, Report by Chief Industrial Inspector, 31 May 1945. The Second World War had brought labour demands which entailed conscription of individuals who were in the process being of having vocational training; the School was thus opened in 1945 to cater for these individuals.

[2] Debates of the Legislative Assembly, Vol. 27, Part 2, 20 January 1948, p. 2586.

[3] NAZ S245/1151. Guinea Fowl Miners Training School, letter from the Chief Inspector of Schools to the Chief Education Officer, 11 February 1948.

[4] *Ibid*.

[5] *Ibid*.

Undoubtedly Huggins would have favoured the school's continuance as a way of signalling unwavering support for ideas proposed by small workers. The Minister of Mines, then tasked the Education Department to make an enquiry from the colony's schools and amongst parents, "for the purpose of ascertaining the number of boys who might be prepared to take up mining as a career and attend Guinea Fowl for training purposes."[1] Overall, the report was gloomy. Colonel Brady, who headed the Committee tasked to make the enquiry, reported in parliament that:

> The committee tried very hard to get witnesses who would be able to give them indication of any real benefit that might accrue to the industry from the establishment of this school and I don't know whether any of the members of the committee put up a really good case.[2]

Another Member of Parliament for Salisbury and member of the committee on the enquiry further indicated that there was no serious desire amongst the youth of the colony to enter the mining industry as a profession.[3] In fact, only two boys had expressed desire to enrol for mining courses at Guinea Fowl School, which was a sure cause for concern.[4] It therefore was no secret that mining was not an appealing profession yet government, because of its desperation to please the small workers, tried to find justification to keep the school open, regardless of the degree of the impracticability. Many reasons were forwarded to explain why boys were reluctant to enter the School. The Chief Education Officer reported that "it is difficult to get even a 15 year old to think clearly about careers."[5] In

[1] NAZ S245/1151. Guinea Fowl Miners Training School, letter from the Chief Inspector of Schools to the Chief Education Officer, 11 February 1948.
[2] Debates of the Legislative Assembly, Vol. 27, Part 2, 20 January 1948, p. 2587.
[3] Ibid., p. 2593.
[4] NAZ S245/1151, Letter from Chief Education Officer to the Department of Mines and Public Works, 27 November 1947.
[5] Ibid.

addition, he noted "... it would appear that mining is not at the moment offering attractions to compete with those of other occupations. "[1] In the mining industry as a whole, there was a gradual but significant decline in the number of small workers. In the post war period, the number of small workers dwindled from 3000 to 756 in the ensuing decade. [2] The proportion of employed Europeans involved in the mining industry had grown as a result of the depression and then similarly declined so that numerically those associated with the industry were less than half as important in 1956 as they had been 35 years earlier and relative to other sectors were less significant. [3] This position led to a growing unpopularity among the white youths who generally shunned employment opportunities in the industry. The report highlighted and reaffirmed the existence of an apparent negative attitude towards mining as a profession by the settlers which culminated in a stalemate. The negativity of the report notwithstanding, debate on the relevance of the school continued to rage. Some sentiment was that the continuation of the school would have been appropriate in order to alleviate the technical problems faced by the small workers. It was argued that:

> There are 290 small workings crying out for young lads better trained than they have been before who should know something about mining shaft making, timbering, electrical work, maintenance of machinery, reduction, who cannot obviously be highly skilled at all branches but have at any rate some skills and more than they have had in the past. [4]

This was premised on the idea that the amount lost by the small workers

---

① NAZ S245/1151, Letter from Chief Education Officer to the Department of Mines and Public Works, 27 November 1947.
② Murray, p. 149.
③ Murray, p. 18.
④ Debates of the Legislative Assembly, Vol. 27, Part 2,20 January 1948, p. 2589.

through lack of knowledge was high. [1] However, "It was impossible on the small mines to have either highly paid or skilled executives with neither university training, nor it is desired to have skilled artisans skilled on the same branch. "[2] From this point of view a school was not altogether irrelevant, but was supposed to be carried on with the bias towards small workers. This perception was clearly aimed at appeasing small workers and earning their votes.

However, other sections of parliament felt that evidence was conclusive and that those who wanted the school to be continued were making a sentimental decision. This opinion hinged on that those who wanted the school to continue were, "... somewhat influenced by the fact that so much money was spent that it would be a pity to close down. "[3] Unfortunately for Huggins, however, his newly appointed Minister of Mines, Davenport, crushed all hopes of continuing with the School or upgrading it to a School of Mines. Davenport had found his way to Huggins' United Party through an invitation by Huggins as a means to for him to regain political support among small workers. [141] Davenport came in the wake of numerous hiring and firing of mines ministers by Huggins and was chosen because he appeared capable to deliver the much needed support and consequently he was appointed Minister of Mines in 1946. [4] However, Davenport's appointment was "parallel" to that of his predecessor because he took measures that went against small workers' interests and removed features of their privileged position. [5] His appointment thus appeared paradoxical, and under him, "... where there was conflict between interests of small workers and those of mining companies, the latter

---

[1] Debates of the Legislative Assembly, Vol. 27, Part 2,20 January 1948, p. 2589.

[2] Ibid.

[3] Ibid.

[4] Murray notes that Huggins sought to establish support by attracting prominent members to his party. Davenport had been manager of Globe and Phoenix Mine and had been president of the Rhodesia Chamber of Mines. See p. 154.

[5] Ibid. , p. 155.

tended to be favoured. "[1] He took measures which were hostile in the eyes of the small workers and eliminated traces of what remained of the relationship between Huggins and the small workers. [2] The Minister made it clear that he favoured training to be conducted on the larger mines due to the limited plant machinery of the school. [3] Besides, he pointed out that, "the apprentices would suffer on the practical side through the limited plant and machinery at the school and the restricted size of mining operations generally which were possible at a mine such as Guinea Fowl. "[4]

Determined to salvage something, small workers proposed that the school be kept open, at least to train African boss boys. [5] Davenport acknowledged this given Africans given his alliance with big mining capital which saw African labour as the best form of labour. The chief inspector of schools noted that: . . . the proposition that native labour should be trained to give greater efficiency [had] much to be commended in it, the Minister believed that the mining industry itself is alive to this necessity and will, in its own interests take stand to see that the training of native boys is undertaken to meet modern conditions. [6] However, plans to put Africans into the school in order to keep it open were ignored along with the other proposals and the school was duly closed in 1948. Justifying his resentment for the school, Davenport declared dismissively that the 10000 pounds needed to keep the school afloat would have been best utilised buying maize for the colony. This gave Davenport the right excuse to close the school and frustrate small workers. The failure for the school to advance thus rested on the failure to

---

① Murray notes that Huggins sought to establish support by attracting prominent members to his party. Davenport had been manager of Globe and Phoenix Mine and had been president of the Rhodesia Chamber of Mines. See p. 157.

② Ibid, p. 158.

③ NAZ S245/1151, Guinea Fowl Miners Training School letter from the Chief Inspector of Schools to the Chief Education Officer, 14 February1948.

④ *Ibid*.

⑤ NAZ S245/1151, Guinea Fowl Miners Training School, letter from the Chief Inspector of Schools to the Chief Education Officer, 14 February1948.

⑥ *Ibid*.

attract a meaningful number of prospective students and conflict of interests favouring big mining capital. Davenport contributed immensely to this closure, he worked to eliminate "... the remaining vestiges of the partnership Senior had started to build up between the government and the small workers ten years before. [1] A pro-small worker administration had instituted the School; a pro-big capital Minister had worked tirelessly for its demise.

Conclusion

In conclusion, the story of the two schools for training white miners tells a story of the incompatibility between the interests of big business and racialist attitudes of the general settler community. These two fronts along the way contradicted each other leading to the birth and death of the idea of training white youths in preparation for the mine work. Overall, in the context of these power struggles, three critical points can be arrived at in trying to contextualise the factors behind the rise and immediate precarious standing of white miners' training institutions in Southern Rhodesia. Firstly, beyond 1923, the power excesses and influence of the BSA Company and other big businesses extended far beyond the issue of mineral and railway rights. In a wide range of issues, big business had a hand in shaping colonial economic policy and consequently, in the delayed establishment miners training institutions and their subsequent demise thereof. Secondly, the struggle for influence worked to make colonial policy all but ineffective in instances where racialist sentiment was involved. The case of training for white mine labour therefore also reshapes perceptions on the imperfections of colonial policy. Therefore, in such circumstances, the superstructure of colonialism may be viewed as an enigma which leads to the third point. The lines of convergence and divergence between racist sentiment and profit maximisation may appear blurred under colonialism. These two ideas

---

[1] Murray, p. 158.

coexisted yet in some instances were mutually incompatible. However，in this case the desires of capital often reigned and the whole superstructure of colonialism may be thus understood in purely economic terms.

Meteorological Services and Settler Agricultural Development: the Case of the Meteorological Service Department in Southern Rhodesia, 1897 – 1945

Trish Marjory Paida Gombe

Abstract

Numerous scholars have dealt with the development of settler agriculture in Southern Rhodesia. Yet, none of available works historicises the role of the Meteorological Service Department in the development of settler agriculture. This paper uses primary and secondary sources to demonstrate how the Meteorological Service Department became one of the most important institutions in the development of settler agriculture from 1897 to 1945. Apart from the Southern Rhodesia government's effort to develop settler agriculture using racial segregation, the Meteorological Service Department influenced the development of settler agriculture by playing a crucial role in providing information about weather and climate systems of the colony to settler farmers which allowed them to take advantage of Southern Rhodesia's climate, rainfall and temperatures. The Department also helped to minimise the damage to agricultural production caused by unfavourable and unpredictable weather conditions through studying durations of drought in the colony. This, in turn, helped the Agricultural Department to come up with solutions to *safeguard settler agriculture. The activities of the Meteorological Service Department in developing settler agriculture up to 1945, inform historians, economists and students to grasp the importance of meteorology to the agricultural economy of the country up to the present day.*

Keywords: Settler agriculture, Meteorological Service Department, Southern Rhodesia

Introduction

Meteorology is defined as "the science of the atmosphere ... embracing both weather and climate. It is concerned with the physical, dynamical and chemical state of the earth's atmosphere (and those of the planets), and with the interactions between the earth's atmosphere and the underlying surface.'[1] Meteorology is important not just for our everyday comfort and well-being, but it is crucial to the development of the economy since it has application in diverse fields such as military, transport, agriculture, construction and industry. However, despite its importance to the economy, the development and operations of the Meteorological Service Department in Zimbabwe have been overlooked by scholars of Zimbabwean history. The Meteorological Office itself has found some mention at times such as Weinmann's research[2], but even then, it is only tangentially. Interest in the area has come mainly from meteorologists.

This paper attempts to cover this gap by offering a history of the Meteorological Service Department (hereafter Met Department) and evincing how it became one of the most important institutions in the development of

---

[1] Met Office, 'What is Meteorology', http://www. metoffice. gov. uk/learning/what-is-meteorology, n. d, (accessed 20 August 2016).

[2] H. Weinmann, *Agricultural Research and Development in Southern Rhodesia: Under the Rule of The British South Africa Company*, *1890 – 1923*, Salisbury, A. W. Bardwell & Co. Pvt. Ltd, 1972, pp. 102 – 103.

settler agriculture in colonial Zimbabwe (hereinafter Southern Rhodesia).
The paper traces the origins of the Met Department and then unpacks its role
in the colonial agricultural project. The study takes off in 1897, the year
when the Met Department was established. During the same period, the
British South Africa Company (BSAC) made efforts to develop and benefit
from agriculture in the colony. Hence the Company needed knowledge of
characteristics of the colony and its meteorology. Information on this could
only be provided by experts of meteorology, thus marking the beginning of
the Department. The study ends in 1945 when there were changes to the
Department once the Second World War ended. These changes included the
restructuring of the Meteorological Service Department which allowed the
department to become more sophisticated in terms of scientific technology in
Southern Africa. The paper makes extensive use of primary sources, sourced
from the National Archives of Zimbabwe and the library of the
Meteorological Services Department. In this study, I consulted primary
sources which give first hand evidence on the relationship between the Met
Department and agricultural development.

Settler Agriculture and the Meteorological Service Department of Southern Rhodesia

The immediate reason for the British South Africa Company (BSAC) to
expand further into the interior and gain control over the area today known
as Zimbabwe was the search for gold. Machingaidze notes that as early as
1891 the BSAC directors had stated that, "As splendid as are the agricultural
prospects of the country, it is to the mineral wealth that the Directors look
for the most profitable returns. "[1] However, by 1900, the directors of the
BSAC had switched modes, "from high expectations that had characterised

---

[1] V. E. M. Machingaidze, 'The development of capitalist agriculture in Southern Rhodesia with
particular reference to the role of the state 1908 – 1939', PhD Thesis, School of Oriental African
Studies, 1980, p. 56.

the first decade of conquest to a place where it questioned the financial wisdom of its investment in the colony. "[1] The mining sector did not yield the expected boon because gold seams did not exist in the amount initially expected. [2] The slow take-off of the mining sector prompted the BSAC to diversifying the colony's economy. They realised that the future of the colony could not be based on mineral wealth. Thus, they began to encourage European settlers to focus on capitalist agriculture in the colony with the aim of transforming Southern Rhodesia into an agriculture-based settler colony.

After two decades of trial and error, settler agriculture began to expand quite rapidly in terms of output and acreage under cultivation in the 1920s. Mosley and Haviland make the case that the period of settler agricultural growth was influenced by significant policies such as White Agricultural Policy (WAP)[3], African labour and segregation policies. [4] However, they do not take into consideration that the Meteorological Service Department of Southern Rhodesia played a huge role by providing information about weather and climate systems of the colony to settler farmers which allowed them to take advantage of Southern Rhodesia's climate, rainfall and temperatures.

The Meteorological Service Department was established in 1897 when the BSAC efforts were inspired by the "Second Rand" dream. [5] However, from 1897 – 1908, the MSD did not do much to help farmers since it lacked meteorological expertise. Also, the BSAC did not do much during this period to improve the Department. This neglect can be seen in summaries of meteorological observations, which were partly incomplete due to breakage

① Ibid.

② T. Madimu, 'Farmers, miners and the state in colonial Zimbabwe (Southern Rhodesia), c. 1895 – 1961', PhD Thesis, Stellenbosch University, 2017, p. 36.

③ WAP was the reorganization of the Department of Agriculture to reflect the BSAC new agricultural thrust to promote settler agriculture.

④ P. Mosley, *The settler economies*, Cambridge, 1983, p. 45 and W. E. Haviland, "Tobacco farm organization, costs and land-use in Southern Rhodesia", *South African Journal of Economics*, vol. 21, no. 4, 1954, pp. 367 – 380.

⑤ L. H. Gann, *A History of Southern Rhodesia: Early days to 1934*, London, Chatto & Windus, 1969, p. 161.

of instruments. ① According to the BSAC Reports for 1898 - 1900, there were only seven barometric stations and three thermometric stations, whilst rainfall was recorded at nineteen centres and these stations did not do much in helping white farmers to develop during this period. ② The neglect of MSD by BSAC shows that it had only been created to study the climate of the colony and in this case the Department relied on biotic weather forecast used by indigenous Africans since it had insufficient scientific materials to use in studying climate. The BSAC saw that if it created the institution then many whites would come to the colony on the basis that MSD would assist them in developing agriculture, industries and other economic activities integrated with the knowledge of meteorology.

The hugely neglected farmers had to contend with enormous difficulties. They faced constant threats from plant pests, failed crops and diseases which struck down men and beasts because little was known about the country's meteorology and resources. For example, Afrikaans-speaking pioneers (George Dunban Moodie and Thomas Moodie) faced enormous difficulties when trying to prove the country's agricultural possibilities, before they settled at Melsetter. ③ In this area, they encountered great hardship because crops failed to germinate. George Dunban Moodie and Thomas Moodie attributed that the failure of crops owed much to the little knowledge of the country's meteorology. ④ The difficulties faced by farmers relating to meteorology also manifested when, in 1906 a wealthy Italian officer, Lieutenant Margherito Guidotti tried to launch an early group settlement in the Lomagundi District. ⑤ The new comers did everything they could to increase agricultural productivity. Nevertheless, Guidotti's project turned out

---

① History of Stations and their Records, *Climatological stations in Southern Rhodesia* [334] MSD
   Library, Harare.
② Ibid.
③ L. H. Gann, p. 163.
④ *Ibid*.
⑤ R. Blake, *A history of Rhodesia*, London, Eyre Methuen, 1977, p. 56.

to be a complete failure because the BSAC failed to acknowledge that the MSD created in 1897 had to be active in promoting the growth of agriculture. ①

The measures taken to boost settler agriculture in 1908 through WAP led to the MSD being active in boosting capitalist agriculture. In 1908, the MSD was put under the Agricultural Department. This transfer initiated a period of development that boosted capitalist agriculture. The Department organized the available data methodically and prepared the results. Special articles on cotton and maize growing and water resources were issued regularly in the climatological bulletins. ② Daily rainfall and synoptic reports started in 1922, and experimental forecasts were issued. In 1924, regular forecasts started, with bulletins submitted to the press and by telegraph to all Post offices in Southern Rhodesia. ③ These developments helped to boost capitalist agriculture because farmers now had the knowledge of the weather on a daily basis. It helped them make strategic decisions in agricultural planning as well as in avoiding fatal schemes because they now had the knowledge of the country's meteorology to determine the kind of seeds to sow relating to seasonal variations, rain and temperature.

The Meteorological Service Department and settler agriculture, 1908 – 1945

The recognition and organization of the MSD in 1908 under the Agricultural Department marked the beginning of the Department's involvement in the economy of Southern Rhodesia. The MSD functions provided information and advice for the planning and execution of weather sensitive activities such as aviation, agriculture, civil engineering, commerce and transport, resettlement programs and to undertake research into a

① R. Blake, *A history of Rhodesia*, London, Eyre Methuen, 1977, p. 56.
② History of Stations and their Records, *Climatological stations in Southern Rhodesia* [334] Meteorological Service Department Library, Harare.
③ Ibid.

number of sensitive problems. [1] The meteorology information was useful since farmers used it to improve efficiency and ensure sustainability of their farm management; to protect and ensure the continuing health of their crops, livestock and environment; to increase their yield and the market value of their crops as well as in solving problems caused by weather hazards. The meteorology information was also essential to policy makers. They used weather and climate information to ensure affordable prices for consumers and sufficient farm income for farmers; reduce the impact of agricultural practices on the environment, ensure food security and to react to potential famine situations. [2]

The MSD started in a very humble way by assisting settler farmers and the BSAC to improve agriculture. The first step that the Department of the Meteorological Services took was to provide the main physical characteristics of the country and these characteristics were later used in the enactment of the Land Apportionment Act (LAA) of 1930. The characteristics of the country were the high watershed areas, mostly between 1200 and 1500m above sea level. These stretched from Plumtree to Marandellas and to the southern and central watershed. The northern watershed laid roughly north-west to the south from Karoi to Trelawney, Salisbury and Marandellas, and to Rusape and Inyanga. Secondly, the Eastern highlands were a series of mountain ranges lying along the eastern border of Zimbabwe, and extending from the north of Inyanga to the south of Chipinga. [3] Thirdly, the area constituted the main river valleys of the Zambezi, Limpopo and Sabi. Lastly, was the northern escarpment, stretching from 40km to the north of Mount Darwin to Sipolilo. The northern slopes are steep and have an altitude of about 1000m. [4] These physical characteristics of the country were used to

---

[1] History of Stations and their Records, *Climatological stations in Southern Rhodesia* [334] Meteorological Service Department Library, Harare.

[2] Ibid.

[3] Department of Meteorological Services, *Climate Handbook of Zimbabwe 551. 582(689. 1)* Salisbury, the Government Printer, 1981, pp. 3 – 5.

[4] Department of Meteorological Services, *Climate Handbook of Zimbabwe 551. 582(689. 1)* Salisbury, the Government Printer, 1981, pp. 3 – 5.

prepare an agro ecological and climatic map, designed to show which areas were suitable for intensive or extensive farming, for cropping or ranching. [1]

The MSD also provided information about weather conditions of the country which was helpful in the development of settler agriculture, industries and aviation. The Department divided the year into three seasons, that is, the cold weather, the hot weather and the rainy season. R. A. Jubb notes that the cold weather began sometime in May and extended into August; the hot weather commenced in the middle of August, continuing until the first set of the rains, which usually occurred in the latter part of November and the rainy season varied in length from year to year, but normally covered the period from the end of November to the end of April. [2] These seasonal characteristics were used at the experimental farms created by the BSAC in assisting in the development of settler agriculture. The experimental farms established the kind of seeds to be sown in different seasons. For instance, C. L Robertson, director of the Hydrographic Branch and Meteorology, used these seasonal characteristics to experiment, prepare results and issue special articles on favourable conditions for cotton and maize growing. [3] G. Melvyn Howe noted that the knowledge of rainfall, that is, the amount, seasonal distribution, variation and effectiveness in relation to the water needs of agriculture and industry were essential to the development of schemes in the two Rhodesias. [4] He further points out that the knowledge of rainfall played a critical role in averting ill-fated schemes such as those experienced in the cultivation of cotton in the vicinity of Barberton, southern eastern Transvaal, the citrus culture in Natal, groundnuts in Tanganyika and

---

[1] Department of Meteorological Services, *Climate Handbook of Zimbabwe 551. 582(689. 1)* Salisbury, the Government Printer, 1981, p. 17.

[2] General Weather conditions in Southern Rhodesia, [70] Meteorological Services Department Library, Harare.

[3] History of Stations and their Records, *Climatological stations in Southern Rhodesia* [334] Meteorological Service Department Library, Harare.

[4] G. Melvyn Howe, 'Climates of the Rhodesias and Nyasaland: According to the Thornthwaite Classification', *Geographical Review*, vol. 43, No. 4,1953, p. 525.

sorghum in Queensland. [1] Thus, the MSD had begun to gain prominence in the agricultural sector.

Between 1906 and 1912 when settler agriculture was gaining more prominence and state support, the Department of Agriculture acknowledged that each district taken up for settlement was to have an experimental farm to assist experimental work, such as trials and selection of seeds and trials in insecticides. [2] These experimental farms had meteorological stations to collect information about the weather in order to perform their trials successfully. Not only were meteorological stations created around experimental farms but were also created in each district so that they could assist farmers and Government policy makers by providing information about current weather and climate. It is reported that there were about 48 meteorological stations established in Southern Rhodesia by the year 1935. [3]

For instance, at the Sandveld Experiment Station established in 1912 at Longila near Lochard in Matabeleland, it was reported that the experiments done during the seasons 1913/14 and 1914/15 were both unfavourable due to weather conditions. [4] Winter crops grown on the Sandveld Experiment Station in 1921 were also only partly successful due to late heavy rains and delayed planting. [5] Another example where the information of weather provided by the Met stations assisted in experimental trials is seen in the Salisbury Experiment Station. At this station it was established that maize grew well in Mashonaland because of the favourable rainfall in the area. [6] The Department of Agriculture used the information provided by Met Stations to

---

[1] G. Melvyn Howe, 'Climates of the Rhodesias and Nyasaland: According to the Thornthwaite Classification', *Geographical Review*, vol. 43, No. 4, 1953, p. 525.

[2] Agro-Met information sheets file 4, [NAZ/RG3/MET612] National Archives Zimbabwe.

[3] Agro-Met information sheets file 4, [NAZ/RG3/MET612] National Archives Zimbabwe.

[4] J. Muirhead, 'Report of results of experiments at the Government Farm, Longila, Matabeleland-season 1914 – 15', *Rhodesian Agricultural Journal*, vol. 12, 1915, pp. 807 – 810.

[5] Ibid.

[6] Investigations of the conditions favorable for rain in Southern Rhodesia, [6] Meteorological Service Department Library, Harare.

determine places where maize production thrived more. For instance, if one looks at the Table 1 below, one can draw the conclusion that Gwanda had the lowest maize production because of its climate which consists of high temperatures and low rainfall and therefore this kind of environment does not support good maize production. One would also draw conclusions that Salisbury and Bulawayo had the highest maize production because they had climatic conditions necessary for the growth of maize.

Conclusions drawn from Table 1 led to the introduction of irrigation at a small scale in order to improve crop production in areas that had low rainfall. Not only were irrigation schemes implemented in areas were rainfall was low but they were established in areas that engaged in the plantation of winter crops and also in areas where crops needed more water above the rain fed levels. In 1904, it was recorded that there were 7 083 acres of irrigated land in Southern Rhodesia. However, in light of more relevant information on weather and climate the acres of irrigated land increased by 6 415 in 1924. [1] Of this area, 1 694 acres were in Mazoe district, 788 in the Umtali district, 421 acres in Chilimanzi, 585 acres in Salisbury, 366 acres in Gwelo and 321 acres in Lomagundi. [2] The crops under irrigation were chiefly wheat, oats, barley, lucerne, tobacco, potatoes, onions, vegetables and fruit trees. [3] Among these crops, most were winter crops. In Southern Rhodesia winter rainfall was low so irrigation was crucial to increase production. Citrus growing in Mazoe Estate extensively used irrigation since citrus growing was an industry.

TABLE 1   MAIZE PRODUCTION

District	Maize Production Bags
Bulawayo	17 725
Charter	3 162

[1] H. Weinmann, p. 106.
[2] Ibid, p. 99.
[3] Ibid.

续 表

District	Maize Production Bags
Gwanda	100
Gwelo	2 468
Hartley	—
Melsetter	1 657
Salisbury	13 942
Selukwe	—
Umtali	5 653
Victoria	1 108

Source: H. Weinmann, *Agricultural Research and Development in Southern Rhodesia: Under the Rule of the British South Africa Company 1890 - 1923*, p 18.

In the 1940s, when Southern Rhodesia experienced three bad rainfall seasons, small scale irrigation schemes were increased under Alvord. [1] The irrigation schemes were mainly increased in Bulawayo, Gatooma, Gwelo, Fort Victoria, Plumtree, Darwin, Marendellas and Salisbury since they were mostly affected by the 1946 - 1949 droughts. [2] In the Rhodesia Herald one farmer noted that the irrigation schemes had helped to increase yields in the 1946 droughts. [3] The increase in irrigation schemes in Southern Rhodesia led to the formation of a Hydrological Commission and Irrigation Department. This Department ensured that the dams constructed for irrigation purposes had adequate water for the provision of irrigation and also ventured into the construction of dams in areas that needed more water. [4] The Hydrological Department used information about the weather provided by the Met Department to construct dams in areas that needed them and also to contain water in the already constructed dams. For instance, during a Hydrological Conference in September 1954, the Hydrological Department concluded that

[1] Drought 1946/47, 47/48, 48/49 in Southern Rhodesia, [220] Meteorological Service Department Library, Harare.
[2] Ibid.
[3] Hydrological Conference Victoria Falls Sept 1954, [NAZ/S2625/16/1] National Archives Zimbabwe
[4] Ibid.

in order to reduce and control losses by evaporation in small dams due to the high temperatures of Southern Rhodesia they had to use Cetyl Alcohol. ① This development greatly reduced evaporation in dams, hence more acres of land were put under irrigation. At this conference, four papers on rainfall presented by Dr Samson, Miss Lineham and Mr. Peake suggested that it would be more useful to know about rainfall in order to solve the issues of irrigation, erosion and hydro-electric potential. This shows that the Met Department played an essential role in the development of settler agriculture.

The Department of Agriculture also used Met information to conduct trials on whether the production of maize was influenced by the date of planting. The Department of Agriculture confirmed that it was an advantage to plant early, that is, from mid-November to mid-December. ② They argued that this was the appropriate time since the first rains and moderate temperatures were essential to seed germination. ③

With the knowledge of meteorology the Department of Agriculture also performed trials with cotton. Although in the report there are no records on how low the rainfall was, it is recorded that most trials with cultivated cotton showed that the crop suffered from drought and was destroyed by frost in the period between 1907 and 1910. ④ However, when H. W. Taylor was appointed to the Department as Tobacco and Cotton Specialist in 1918, a new attempt was made at giving the crop a full and fair trial. In 1919, trials were conducted on 91 farms in 12 districts, and the results of these indicated that cotton was likely to be successful at altitudes of up to 3 800 ft. above sea level. ⑤ Clearly, the altitudes had been provided by the Met Department who made an effort to study the climate of the colony. In 1922, further experiments with cotton were conducted and it was identified that the yields

---

① Hydrological Conference Victoria Falls Sept 1954, [NAZ/S2625/16/1] National Archives Zimbabwe.
② H. Weinmann, p. 35.
③ Ibid.
④ Agro-Met Information Sheets, [NAZ/RG3/MET612] National Archives of Zimbabwe.
⑤ H. Weinmann, p. 69.

and growth of cotton were affected if the amount of rain was excessive and if the amount was also low. Thus, in order to overcome this impediment the Department of Agriculture obtained information of rainfall patterns from the Met Department and established that cotton grew in areas that had altitudes of up to 3800 ft. above sea level and where the rainfall was moderate. The Department of Agriculture also established that if the area had favourable altitudes for the growth of cotton and insufficient rainfall then irrigation schemes would be established in those areas. [1]

The Met Department also provided information about temperatures to farmers. This information was relevant because high temperatures had an effect on evapo-transpiration of plants. High temperatures caused most plants to wilt whilst low temperatures caused dense evaporation. [2] An example of how temperatures affected crops can be seen in the year 1935. In 1935, Rhodesian cotton farmers complained that their crops were not growing well because of lack of sunshine. [3] In Gwebi and Melsetter crops failed to grow because of lack of sunshine. [4] In December 1935, farmers had complained that maximum temperatures were causing their seed not to germinate since the rains had not come, yet the Meteorologists were telling them to plant since rains were being expected. [5] In both cases, it can be seen that the growth of crops depended on moderate temperatures and thus accurate information of weather statistics helped farmers to come up with solutions on when to expect high or low temperatures. The Rhodesian white farmers used weather statistics so that they could come up with solutions on how to overcome the wilting of plants when the temperatures were high, and how to overcome the frosting of plants when temperatures were low. They established that they would need to increase irrigation in areas that had high

---

[1] Agro-Met Information Sheets, [NAZ/RG3/MET612] National Archives of Zimbabwe.

[2] Notes on Agricultural Meteorology file 11 (The Effect of Cloudiness on Evaporation), [NAZ/RG3/MET651] National Archives of Zimbabwe.

[3] "Hot Weather", *Rhodesia Herald*, 18 October 1935, p. 8.

[4] Ibid.

[5] "Late rains", *Rhodesia Herald*, December 1935, p. 11.

temperatures and more water had to be applied to reduce the effect of evaporation on plants. [1] They also established rudimentary forms of green houses to protect plants from high temperatures. [2]

Meteorology and the Cattle Industry

The Met Department played a critical role in the development of cattle industry. The industry was one of the most important commercial trades to European farmers. Southern Rhodesia was recognized by entrepreneurs as a potentially valuable beef country when Europeans settled in the colony. [3] Europeans tried to break into the world meat market, but they failed due to economic constraints. Phimister notes that the economic constraints included capital shortages and competition from countries that already dominated the world meat trade. [4] However, lack of meteorological knowledge was another factor which contributed to this failure to break into the world market. Naturally, Southern Rhodesia's climate was conducive for cattle keeping, but there were some weather aspects that tended to affect the survival and growth of the beasts and also milk production. [5] Thus, in order for the farmers and the Department of Agriculture to improve the cattle industry and break into the world market, they had to rely on the knowledge of weather provided by meteorologists in the colony.

Temperature and rainfall were the most important aspects of climate that influenced beef and dairy production. For example, it was discovered that high temperatures caused stress on the beasts. In order to reduce this stress the Department of Agriculture advised farmers engaged in beef production to

---

[1] Notes on Agricultural Meteorology file 11 (The Effect of Cloudiness on Evaporation), [NAZ/RG3/MET651] National Archives Zimbabwe.

[2] Ibid.

[3] I. R. Phimister, 'Meat and Monopolies: Beef Cattle in Southern Rhodesia, 1890 – 1938', *The Journal of African History*, vol. 19, no. 3,1978, p. 391.

[4] Ibid.

[5] Met series notes File no. 25, [NAZ/RG3/MET 640] National Archives Zimbabwe.

build shelters for the animals. However, due to capital constraints this was not followed and the result was the failure to break into the world market since heat stress reduced feed intake, lower birth weights and lower natural immunity making animals vulnerable to diseases. [1] It was also discovered that high temperatures affected the natural veld that was used for grazing. High temperatures caused veld fires and in turn these fires reduced the grazing areas of the beasts. [2] A solution was sought to address this problem. The solution was adopting supplementary feeding but due to capital constraints it failed.

The Department of Agriculture conducted a series of interesting and instructive cattle feeding experiments at Gwebi Agricultural College from 1915 to 1923. In the experiments, three groups of eight bullocks each were used. The first group was kept in a yard and stall fed; the second was allowed to graze during the day, but yarded at night and fed the same ration of farm produced feed as group 1; and the third group was fed on grazing and veld hay only. [3] In the experiments, stall feeding resulted in considerable weight gains. In as much as the Department of Agriculture used the knowledge of weather and climate to improve the beef industry, capital constraints meant that the farmers failed to break into the world market.

Met Department role in the formation
of the Land Apportionment Act

The LAA in Southern Rhodesia has been generally viewed by historians as a means of segregation. For example, N. H. Wilson declared that, "We [white settlers] are in this country because we represent a higher civilization,

---

[1] Met series notes File no. 25, [NAZ/RG3/MET 640] National Archives Zimbabwe.
[2] H. Weinmann, p. 129.
[3] Ibid, p. 112.

because we are better men. It is our only excuse for having taken the land. "[1] However, the division of land between Europeans and Africans in Southern Rhodesia occurred because settler farmers wanted the best areas that would support increased production of crops since most of them engaged in commercial agriculture. Thus, in order to have the best land they had to remove Africans from those areas and place them in areas that had unfavourable conditions for the promotion of agriculture. The information provided by the MSD about weather and climatic conditions of various areas in the colony played a very crucial role in the LAA because this information was used to critically ascertain areas for Europeans and Africans. Firstly, it provided maps that showed the altitudes of areas in the colony; secondly, it showed the annual temperatures of the areas and thirdly the annual rainfall.

The cartographic representation of land apportionment in 1958 reveals the complex and peculiar alignment of boundaries between the areas reserved for African settlement and those set aside for European settlement. In general, the European area included the greater part of the salubrious high veld (4000 feet and above), which forms a distinct northeast-southwest backbone of the country.[2] Considerable parts of the elevated Eastern Highlands also fell within the European area because of its wet dry savanna climate.[3] Most of the better watered parts of the country also fell within European areas since higher annual rainfall guarantee greater reliability, making agriculture and animal husbandry less hazardous than in dry areas.[4]

This overview, therefore, reveals the importance of the Met Department paying particular attention to the development of settler agriculture. It shows how the Met Department greatly helped in the development of settler

---

[1] B. Floyd, 'Land Apportionment in Southern Rhodesia', *Geographical Review*, vol. 52, no. 4,1962, p. 566.

[2] B. Floyd, 'Land Apportionment in Southern Rhodesia', *Geographical Review*, vol. 52, no. 4,1962, p. 568.

[3] *Ibid.*

[4] *Ibid.*

agriculture by providing weather and climate statistics to farmers, the
government and to the Department of Agriculture. From 1908 to 1945,
settler Agriculture developed compared to the period 1897 - 1907 because the
farmers and the Department of Agriculture were equipped with the
knowledge of meteorology that was critical to crop production in the colony.
During this period the Met Department faced challenges but it managed to
overcome them and thus making a significant impact on the development of
settler agriculture in Southern Rhodesia.

Conclusion

Many scholars have written on the development of settler agriculture in
Southern Rhodesia as a key example of it managed to successfully establish
itself with assistance from colonial policies that assured them access to land
and local wage labour. However, none of these works addresses how the
Meteorological Service Department played a crucial role in the development
of settler agriculture. Using primary and secondary sources, this article has
discussed the role of the Meteorological Service Department, noting that it
became one of the most important institutions in the development of settler
agriculture from 1897 - 1945. This paper has shown the role played by the
Meteorological Service Department to the development of settler agriculture
through the provision of information on weather and climate systems of the
colony which allowed settler farmers to take advantage of Southern
Rhodesia's climate, rainfall and temperatures. The Department provided
climate data of the colony and this information was used to draw an agro-
ecological map that showed where intensive and extensive farming could
thrive the most.

Weather forecasts provided during 1908 - 1945 assured the farmers
success. They guaranteed positive results in crop production since crop
production was greatly linked to weather conditions. The weather forecasts

were also used by experimental farms to improve crop and beef production in the country. One of the greatest achievements of the Met Department for the white settlers of the colony was the provision of climate and weather information which was used in the designing of the LAA of 1930. It also helped to minimise the damage to agricultural production caused by unfavourable and unpredictable weather conditions by studying durations of drought in the colony and this helped the Agricultural Department to come up with solutions to safeguard settler agriculture. Thus, it can be concluded that the knowledge of meteorology gained since 1897 was important to the development of settler agriculture up to 1945.

Southern Rhodesia and the Commissioner of Taxes Department During UDI: Reform and Transformation in A 'Cordoned' Economy, 1964 – 1979

Rumbidzai Chitaukire

Abstract

The paper uses the case study of the Commissioner of Taxes Department in Rhodesia which was responsible for virtually the whole tax system. It examines the efforts by the Rhodesia Commissioner of Taxes Department to maximise returns from its tax systems while under siege after the Unilateral Declaration of Independence (UDI). In 1965, Ian Smith declared UDI after the collapse of the Federation of Rhodesia and Nyasaland and this attracted sanctions from the international community. Taxation was critical as a source of revenue yet the Department was facing a lot of challenges some of which stemmed from the shift from the Federal government which necessitated adjustments in the tax system. The collapse of the Federation of Rhodesia and Nyasaland in 1963 put the Department under sudden pressure to absorb some of the functions that had been taken up by the Federal tax Department. Challenges in staff quality and quantity also haunted the Department. It thus became critical for the Rhodesian state to put its tax systems in order and execute lasting reforms. The problems of staff retention, poor revenue collection, inadequate systems and infrastructure became immediate concerns. The paper examines the experiences of the Department and the manner in which the Commissioner of Taxes

Department tried to deal with such challenges. It contributes to debates on the role of institutions and institutional reforms in the economy. Using tax reports, commission of inquiries and correspondence within government, among other archival sources, this paper demonstrates the efforts by the Commissioner of Taxes Department and its attempt to counter the challenges it faced.

Introduction

A politician once noted that, "Nothing is certain except death and taxes". [1] This echoes the importance of taxation in any given society and why it is a permanent feature in all economies worldwide. The development of any human society is largely based on taxation. In order to achieve certain developmental goals, there is need for humanity to group their resources together. Vital facilities such as education, health and national security to residents are dependent upon the ability of administrations to deliver, whilst the administrations are dependent upon funds collected from taxes to be able to deliver.

This paper therefore, examines the work of the Rhodesian Commissioner of Taxes in a "cordoned" economy between 1965 and 1980 with the country under sanctions. These sanctions forced the colonial state to institute what was arguably the most far reaching changes in the Rhodesian tax system since 1890. Tax in its various forms played a decisive role in capitalist primitive accumulation especially in the creation of labour for the new capitalist industries and grabbing land across African colonies. [2] For instance, the inducement for African participation in the colonial economy was moulded through the collection of tax. It also provided a vital basis of colonial revenue

---

① B. Hill and C. Cahill, "Taxation of European Farmers" in *EuroChoices*, Volume 6,2007. p. 45.

② M. Forstater, "Taxation and Primitive Accumulation: The Case of Colonial Africa, The Capitalist State and its Economy", *Democracy in Political Economy*, Vol. 22, p. 56,2005.

and sustained the political machinery erected by the British across their colonial empire. [1] Southern Rhodesia was part of this empire before it divorced itself from Britain through the Unilateral Declaration of Independence (UDI). Studies on colonial taxation have shown its economic role, notably its effects in forcing African men to engage in wage labour. [2]

Taxation was central to imperial ambitions to engineer 'disciplined' African subjects. Tax had an important symbolic role as a token of submission to colonial authority. [3] A collection of recent articles on different parts of Sub Saharan Africa has drawn attention towards taxation's centrality to the broader philosophy of colonialism and to the governmental organisation of African people under imperial rule. [4] Bush and Maltby for instance, while recognising taxation's economic and fiscal aspects, emphasise its purpose as a "moralising force", noting its centrality in "proper" governance and the construction of the colonial economic and political atmosphere. [5] Concurring with this notion, Foucault demonstrates the role of taxation in the development of disciplinary as opposed to sovereign power and the shaping of governable subjects in other parts of the world. [6] Thus, the prime incentive for taxation ascribed to British administrators by scholars has been their yearning to inspire, if not compel African involvement in the colonial economy, specifically through wage labour. [7] Taxation was not just an attempt to force Africans into wage labour, but also a fiscal contribution important for the accruement of revenue. It was paramount in keeping the government solvent. [8] The relevance of African taxation was eminent in political endeavours of the colonial government. An observation showed that, shrinkage in

---

[1] A. Burton, "'The Eye of Authority': 'Native' Taxation, Colonial Governance and Resistance in Inter-war Tanganyika", *Journal of Eastern African Studies*, Vol. 2, No. 1, 2008, p. 74.

[2] *Ibid.*

[3] *Ibid.*

[4] *Ibid.*

[5] B. Bush and J. Maltby cited in Burton, "The Eye of Authority", p. 74.

[6] M. Foucault cited in Burton, "The Eye of Authority", p. 75.

[7] Burton, "The Eye of Authority", p. 79.

[8] *Ibid.*

tax collected was not simply a loss of revenue but a sign of dwindling control and subsequently, a loss of respect for the Administration Authority. [1]

This paper, however, argues that in the Rhodesian case, the specific functions were also shaped by the context of U. D. I and a war economy considering the period under discussion. This political change as a result of the U. D. I, transformed the role of tax in Rhodesia. The settler government viewed itself as sovereign. After the U. D. I, the tax system implemented was to some extent reactionary to the sanctions engineered by Britain. The tax policy had several objectives which aimed at protecting and maintaining the independent settler economy. Thus, taxation within the context of the role played by the Rhodesian Commissioner of Taxes Department during the U. D. I period is examined.

The institutional capacity to cope in a besieged economic environment with particular focus on the experiences of the Commissioner of Taxes Department is established. There have been a lot of discussions among scholars on the role that institutions can play particularly in developing countries. [2] A number of scholars have proceeded to examine African economic development through lenses of the legacies of colonial institutions. [3] In this way, therefore, this study contributes to an understanding of the relations between institutions and development.

Emerging histories of late colonial Zimbabwean economic history which include Nyamunda's "Financing Rebellion..." have begun to shade light on how the Rhodesian state was able to sustain itself for 15 years when the

---

[1] Burton, "The Eye of Authority", p. 80.

[2] D. North, *Institutions, Institutional Change and Economic Performance*, Cambridge: Cambridge University Press, 1990; "The contribution of the new institutional economics to an understanding of the transition problem", WIDER Annual Lectures 1, United Nations University/WIDER (World Institute for Development Economics Research), Helsinki, 1997; and R. M. Bird et al, "Societal institutions and tax effort in developing countries", Working Paper No. 2004 - 21, CREMA, 2004.

[3] T. Mkandawire "On Tax Efforts and Colonial Heritage in Africa", *The Journal of Development Studies*, Vol. 46, No, 10, pp. 1647 - 1669, 2010; and D Acemoglu, et al, "The colonial origins of comparative development", NBER Working Paper 7771, Cambridge, MA: National Bureau of Economic Research, 2001.

British Prime Minister Harold Wilson had predicted its collapse in a matter of weeks. [1] This paper looks at the work done by the Tax Commissioner's Office from 1964 shortly after the demise of the Federation of Rhodesia and Nyasaland in 1963 in line with existing literature. It argues that the collapse of the Federation provided for the increased self-control of tax systems by Rhodesia including taking over some duties that had hitherto been the responsibility of the Federal government. The research further establishes the relevance of taxation on income and other taxable features of the economy after the imposition of economic sanctions in line with existing studies on the country's history on finance and taxation to establish a more robust and enhanced knowledge of Rhodesia's economic and more specifically fiscal history. It contributes to broader discourses on the political economy of revenue mobilisation in African countries.

This study used a qualitative method and employed a case study approach in discussing taxation during the UDI period through the lenses of the Commissioner of Taxes Department. It collaborated primary data from the National archives of Zimbabwe and secondary material. The former includes reports, legislation, and budgets and parliamentary debates which helped to reflect on government policies and practices and gave insight on the then contemporary events, discussions and realities during the time under study. The latter included books, journals and dissertations which helped historicize and theorise the study.

Writing taxation in African colonies

Works on colonial taxation can be broadly divided into two, those that discuss taxation on Africans and others which discuss taxation on white settler communities. On fewer occasions some studies have examined taxation that

---

[1] T. Nyamunda, "Financing Rebellion: The Rhodesian State, financial policy and exchange control, 1962 to 1979", Dphl, University of the Free State, 2015.

has affected both Africans and Europeans. [1] The common story when it comes to colonial taxation in Africa is that on the use of taxation for the monetisation of African economies which would in-turn push Africans into the labour market. Different taxes were imposed and this meant Africans had to enter wage labour in order to be able to meet the new monetary demands of the economy which included affording to pay the taxes. Hence, taxation was a strategy used by the whites to indirectly force or manipulate the Africans into wage labour. It was also meant to incapacitate the African and keep him at the mercy of the white man. Thus, scholarship is generally agreed that African taxation was a critical element to colonial rule and being a vital source, taxation also played a role in stimulating export production. [2] For Bas De Roo, taxation was also "a critically important nexus in which the African subject and the state produced colonial authority". [3]

However, scholars have often downplayed other roles that taxation could play. In Rhodesia for example, rates of Income Tax were cut by the government to encourage white immigration in 1969 and 1970, only to increase thereafter in 1974 as a response to the guerrilla war. [4] By and large, however, the colonial state in Africa lacked the capacity to enforce tax compliance especially among Africans. Various mechanisms were involved for survival among which were the involvement of African chiefs in tax collection and the expansion of taxation to include Europeans especially in settler societies like Southern Rhodesia.

Indeed, the significance of an efficient tax system in economic development has been outlined and acknowledged in a number of discussions and existing literature has made huge strides in the study of taxation in Africa

---

① See L. Gardner, *Taxing Colonial Africa: The Political Economy of British Imperialism*, Oxford: Oxford University Press, 2012.

② Bas De Roo, "Taxation in the Congo Free State, an exceptional case? (1885 – 1908)", *Economic History of Developing Regions*, Vol. 32, No. 2, (2017), pp. 97 – 126.

③ *Ibid*, pp. 97 – 126.

④ L. Harris, "The Tax System from U. D. I to Independence", Economic Symposium, Salisbury, 8 – 10 September, 1980, Vol. 2, paper 29, pp. 7 – 8.

during colonial rule. Conklin for instance, illustrates the significance of taxation in colonial economies with particular focus on colonial Africa. He points to the fact that taxation was justified in early colonial Africa for several reasons which included "upgrading the 'native' by making him contribute to common expenses". [1] This and a number of other works on taxation in colonial Africa pay much attention to the impact of taxation on the "newly colonised" African societies. This paper however, examines the processes that helped develop and improve tax systems. The tax systems affected both the colonisers and the colonised.

To illustrate the significance of taxation in colonial economies, Gardner observes that taxation and "concerns about the budget shaped public policy at every level. "[2] Taxation also played traditional roles which include raising government revenue, distribution of resources, protecting local industries and financing development inter alia. Murray shows that initial colonial administrative revenue was collected from African taxation. [3] Tax was also used as a means of survival by Europeans and an impoverishing burden for Africans in Rhodesia for example during the Great Depression in the early 1930s. [4]

Forstarter's work also adds to the list of works illustrating the relevance of taxation in colonial capitalist states. He points out that, "From a Marxist view point... Taxation has been greatly significant in capitalism even as primitive accumulation···and public cohesion for local colonisers, especially in the creation of labour for their industries. "[5] Thus, existing work on colonial taxation focuses on the oppressive nature of the early introduction of capitalism to Africans. In the same vein, a number of works like Nyambara,

① A. L Conklin, *A Mission to Civilise: The Republican Idea of Empire in France and West Africa*, *1895 - 1930*, Stanford: Stanford University Press, 1997.
② Gardner, *Taxing Colonial Africa*.
③ C. S. Murray, "The Foundations of A "Native" Policy: Southern Rhodesia 1923 - 1933", PhD Thesis, Simon Frazer University, 1972, p. 2.
④ Ibid, p. 100.
⑤ Forstater, *Taxation and Primitive Accumulation: The Case of Colonial Africa*, pp. 53 - 54.

Khumalo and Mundiya`s[1] also study taxation in relation to Africans in colonial Rhodesia. Though their works focus on colonial Zimbabwe, varying in space and time, they do not look at taxation in the UDI period and the experiences of the taxing Departments themselves.

Development of Tax Systems in Southern Rhodesia before 1953

There is limitation on sources that discuss issues surrounding the formation of the Rhodesia Commissioner of Taxes Department or when the Department was established. There is however, clear evidence from works which have been written that taxation had always been part of the colonial government and certain Departments were established during the colonial era that were responsible for the collection of taxes.

Various taxes were collected from earlier days of colonial rule though at times in an informal way without institutions presiding over tax collection. As the colonial government progressed, different entities which were responsible for the collection of different taxes were established. For instance, the Income Tax Department was established in 1918 by an administration led by the British South Africa Company (BSAC). The Income Tax Department being one of the very first tax administration agencies in British Tropical Africa was established in Southern Rhodesia at the dying moments of World War I. [2] The formation of the Department was, however, not the genesis of tax collection, it only formalised a tax regime that already existed within the colony with regards to income tax. The main aim of this Department was to

---

[1] See P. Nyambara, "Land appropriation, taxation and labour migration: the underdevelopment of Nyanga district under colonial rule, 1890 – 1923", M. A. thesis, Economic History, University of Zimbabwe, 1984; M. M. Khumalo, "Taxation and African Response in the Bubi (Inyati) District in the period 1894 – 1939", B. A. Hons, University of Zimbabwe, 1985; F. Mundiya, "African Taxation in Southern Rhodesia up to 1960", B. A. Hons, University of Zimbabwe, 1985.

[2] G. Mhene, "A History of the Southern Rhodesia Income Tax Department: 1918 – 1946", BA Hons, Economic History, University of Zimbabwe, 2014.

raise revenue that was needed for the sponsoring of administration activities and to support public spending in the colony. Before the establishment of the Department, the BSAC relied on land as its major source of revenue but this had to change after the Privy Council declared all land in the colony to belong to the crown hence making it necessary to start greatly relying on tax for revenue and establish Departments that would ensure efficient tax collection and compliance. Therefore, even before the Rhodesia Commissioner of Taxes Department, tax collection had always existed even way before 1953 and a tax Department responsible for the collection of taxes had been established.

It was not only income tax that was collected in Southern Rhodesia. The tax system also included taxes imposed on gold mining companies by the state. Corporate taxes included gold premium tax and excess profits tax. As noted by scholars, the state depended heavily on gold mining revenues. [1] This demonstrates that corporate taxation was important and that such taxes provided essential funds that enabled the construction of a solid state by financing agriculture and industry as well as sponsoring the instilling of racial supremacy in Southern Rhodesia.

Other taxes that developed overtime were those imposed on Africans. These developed even in the absence of an institutional framework like a tax department. As early as 1894, a hut tax of 10s. for every adult male and 10s. more for every other wife was imposed as early as 1894. [2] This was replaced ten years later by a poll tax of 10s. upon each wife exceeding one and £1 on each male over 16. [3] One of the effects of such taxation was to indirectly force Africans into wage labour thereby ensuring that colonial capital was

---

[1] See S. Dansereau, "State, Capital and Labour: Veins, Fissures and Faults in Zimbabwe's Mining Sector" in *Labour, Capital and Society*, Vol. 33, No. 2; Ian Phimister, "The Reconstruction of the Southern Rhodesian Gold Mining Industry, 1903 - 10", *The Economic History Review*, Vol. 29, No. 3, 1976.

[2] G. Arrighi, "Labour Supplies in Historical Perspective: A Study of the Proletarianization of the African Peasantry in Rhodesia", *Journal of Development Studies*, Vol. 6, No. 3, 1970, p. 208.

[3] Ibid.

well supplied in terms of ultra-cheap labour.

After Federation the tax systems were now under the Rhodesia Commissioner of Taxes Department. The Department oversaw taxation in Rhodesia which included both individual and corporate taxes. It had before it a mammoth task of raising revenue at a time when the colony was experiencing sanctions and a war. The tax Department had the responsibility of re-organising and rationalising the tax systems after the break-up of the Federation of Rhodesia and Nyasaland. Its duty was to ensure smooth tax accumulation in the colony in order to gain revenue to finance colonial activities which included public works.

A Struggling Rhodesian Commissioner of Taxes Department

The Commissioner of Taxes Department faced a plethora of challenges emanating, in part, from the complications of dissolution of the Federation of Rhodesia and Nyasaland. As mentioned earlier, taxation was central to governing revenue collection and sustenance of state operations. However, there was change in the tax system with the change of the government because the joint taxation that had been there was only appropriate for the Federation. Therefore, demise of the CAF meant the collapse of some aspects of the tax system and new systems had to be adopted to cater for Rhodesia's new political establishment. Federal collapse and the need to change the tax system gave rise to some challenges for the Rhodesian Commissioner of Taxes Department as it had to adapt to the new systems in order to cater for the new and ever increasing demands under UDI government. The Department also faced other challenges besides the ones posed by the CAF demise and the extent to which the Department was able to achieve its mandate is discussed as well as the challenges it faced. The paper argues that these challenges compromised the proper functioning of the Department's duties making it largely inefficient in terms of revenue collection and reaching maximum tax potential.

As mentioned earlier, a joint taxation system catered for Federal Tax collection. The joint tax system integrated both the Federal tax and territorial tax systems. The CAF demise led to a shift towards a new tax system exclusive to Rhodesia. The dissolution of the Federation by Order in Council No. 2085 of 1963, witnessed the creation of a Liquidating Agency whose duties included the functions of the Federal Commissioner of Taxes to levy and collect all taxes from Nyasaland, Northern and Southern Rhodesia. [1] The Agency temporarily lasted until 31March 1965. Its duties especially included the collection of Federal surcharges. [2]

However, by 1965, perhaps owing to significant cuts from a Federal budget to a smaller local one, the Department faced financial challenges especially in operational expenses. This was worsened by a huge task of assessing and fairly allocating 1964 taxes from trade done across the three territories that constituted the federation, Northern Rhodesia, Southern Rhodesia and Nyasaland. [3] There was increased double taxation in Rhodesia after the collapse of the Federation, whereby the income from the same source was mistakenly taxed twice, by the Federal Tax Department just before the collapse of the Federation and by the new government which had not realised it had already been taxed, before translating into net income. This challenge exerted more pressure on the limited and less experienced staff dealing with such issues. [4] Thus, the collapse of the Federation brought to the fore challenges which threatened tax collection for the Rhodesian Commissioner of Taxes Department.

Since 1965, the major tax offices has been in Salisbury, Bulawayo, Gwelo and Umtali while field officers has been located in Fort Victoria,

---

[1] G. Arrighi, "Labour Supplies in Historical Perspective: A Study of the Proletarianization of the African Peasantry in Rhodesia", *Journal of Development Studies*, Vol. 6, No. 3, 1970, p. 208.

[2] A surcharge referred to extra taxes which would owe from the previous years.

[3] The First Report of the Commissioner of Taxes, January 1964 to June 1965, p. 6.

[4] Second Report of the Commissioner of Taxes, June 1966, p. 4.

Gatooma, Karoi, Marandellas, Que-que, Rusape, Sinoa and the support for the collection of taxes was given by the Ministry of Posts. [1] Tax collecting and assessing offices were located across the country to ensure smooth tax accumulation country wide. Regardless, there was still "unsatisfactory security for the cash collected by the itinerant in rural areas until they could bank it". [2] Thus, security for collected taxes was highly limited for the daily tax collector in the field during this era. This also risked limitation of revenue collected due to lack of transparency and security for the field work tax collector.

Tax collection and assessment challenges were magnified by the increased number of people leaving Rhodesia after the demise of the Federation probably due to company closures and withdrawals especially of Head Quarters. This was true especially when people had to be compelled to pay their taxes on/before departure. [3] During the Federation the payment of taxes on/before departure had not been a territorial responsibility. The end of Federation brought greater responsibility and huge volumes that needed attention. By the end of 1965 debtors amounted to 1.3 million pounds. [4] From 1965, challenges were more visible in the monitoring of personal Tax and Stamp Duties. [5] The reduction of collected revenue endangered the strength of the economy as it meant potentially reduced national revenue whose main source was taxation.

A number of other difficulties became ripple effects on the Department's financial constraints resulting from fiscal reductions after the Federation's collapse. According to the Commissioner of Taxes Report of June 1965, the Department was seriously understaffed, unattractive to qualified workers and it faced challenges of retaining professional existing staff. [6] Almost half of

---

[1] The Second Report of the Commissioner of Taxes, 30 June 1966, presented to Parliament 1967, p. 8.
[2] Ibid.
[3] Ibid, p. 9.
[4] Ibid.
[5] Ibid.
[6] First Report of the Commissioner of Taxes, p. 6.

the assessing staff was made up of temporary clerical officers, the majority of whom lacked experience yet the Department was 20% under capacity. [1] This was largely due to poor salaries as compared to other more attractive employers in commerce who attracted young qualified workers some of whom would have gained experience from the Department. [2] Thus, the Department 's tax administration and collection was incapacitated from the initial phases of the UDI, making the first eighteen months after the collapse of the Federation "extremely difficult. "[3]

The Overseas Territories Income Officer in London dealt with Rhodesian pensioners residing in the United Kingdom. [4] Owing to the economic sanctions imposed on Rhodesia, in 1965 the work done by the Overseas Territories Income Tax Office in London was transferred to the Bulawayo assessing office. [5] This increased the work and burden of the country`s Department of taxation. It put pressure on the limited professional labour available in the tax office as those with more than 4 years experience of assessing tax were scarce yet an assessor was considered fully trained after a five year field experience. [6]

Labour shortage was a huge challenge particularly the specific people responsible for tax collection. The Department failed to recruit permanent employees for that section. This was largely due to the financial strains faced by the Department making it offer low wages which could not sustain the lives of the workers hence, the workers started leaving. The sanctions imposed on the Rhodesian economy had also scared away labour in Rhodesia as people started seeing a bleak future for Rhodesia therefore, making them see no reason to keep staying in a "doomed" economy leading to labour migration to neighbouring countries like South Africa.

---

[1] First Report of the Commissioner of Taxes, pp. 4 – 5.

[2] Ibid, p. 6.

[3] Ibid.

[4] Ibid, June 1965, p. 14.

[5] Second Report, p. 10.

[6] Report of the Commissioner of Taxes, June 1967, presented to Parliament 1968, p. 3.

Due to these labour shortages, backlogs of un-assessed taxes had risen from £859 in June 1966 to 1452 in June 1967. Schatchil the Rhodesian Chief Tax Commissioner noted that, the figure "would have been extensively worse if assessing standards were not sacrificed to increase output. "[1] The Senior Inspector of Taxes' reports were most disturbing regarding the sub-standard work done by the tax assessing staff who lacked experience leading to loss of revenue. For instance, by 1967, collected personal tax had decreased by 160 910 pounds. [2] The situation persisted and by 1968, 77% of the workers in the assessing office had less than 2 years experience, while the remainder largely comprised senior staff. [3] There was serious concern over the persisting experienced worker flight to more remunerative employment after gaining training and experience from the Department. [4] The volume of work kept increasing together with backlog of un-assessed cases. This increased the burden on the Senior Inspector of Taxes Head Office which was responsible for checking the overall accuracy and uniformity of assessment and enforcement within the Department. [5] Evidently, this presented a need to expand the Department's auditing branch.

The Department was enlarged in 1969 to include the collection of direct and indirect tax, taking over from the Department of Customs and Excise on the 1st of July. [6] However, the added responsibilities of the Department ignored the much needed expansion of labour force. For example, by 1970, only 38% of tax assessors were fully trained for their job. [7] Sletcher, the Tax Commissioner in 1970, emphasised the lack of professional labour to be a product of poor wages compared to commerce, accounting and law. [8] A

---

[1] Report of the Commissioner of Taxes, June 1967, presented to Parliament 1968, p. 3.
[2] Ibid, p. 8.
[3] Report of the Commissioner of Taxes, June 1968, presented to Parliament 1969, p. 4.
[4] Report of the Commissioner of Taxes, June 1969, presented to Parliament 1970, p. 4.
[5] Ibid.
[6] Report of the Commissioner of Taxes, June 1970, presented to Parliament 1971, p. 3.
[7] Ibid, p. 7.
[8] Ibid.

similar remark had been made in the 1965 Report of the Commissioner of Taxes; hence job aversion in the Department of taxes would most probably be cured by increased wages to act as incentives for experienced and qualified workers to take up employment in the Department. The collecting branch's work was also increased in 1970 due to the takeover of sales tax which increased their collection to nearly 25 million pounds more than the previous year. [1] This resembled the growing significance of the branch as well as the ever increasing workload.

In 1971, 148 workers across the Department's grades were recruited while 140 resigned during the same year. [2] This pointed to an alarming staff turnover and an additional burden to train new recruits to fill in the gaps. The Sales Tax Department, for example, continued to be dominated by temporary labour, the stamps duty branch was understaffed and tax collecting was generally lacking permanent labour. [3] Staff turnover was a cause of serious concern attacking the Department as a whole and there was no improvement in retaining experienced employees. By 1972, offices in Gwelo were the most dependent on temporary labour in tax collection. [4] The continued failure to attract, train and maintain experienced workers distorted the work of the Rhodesian Tax Department.

Another problem which compromised the success of the Rhodesian Tax Department was the ratio disparity between direct and indirect taxation which was also a major concern for the Rhodesian government. The Department relied more on direct taxation which did not make sense because it automatically meant the exemption of Africans from paying taxes and put the burden on the whites because they made up the larger part of the working class. This is because most of the Africans were not in wage labour hence they had no income to be taxed yet Africans were the greater population.

---

[1] Report of the Commissioner of Taxes, June 1970, presented to Parliament 1971, p. 13.
[2] Report of the Commissioner of Taxes, June 1971, presented to Parliament 1972, p. 4.
[3] Ibid.
[4] Report of the Commissioner of Taxes, June 1972, presented to Parliament 1973, p. 3.

Besides creating an unequal distribution in the contribution between direct and indirect taxation it made it impossible for the Department to reach its full tax potential hence the need to shift towards indirect taxation in order to strike a balance and create a wider tax base to increase the amount of revenue collected.

Regardless of attempts to make improvements in the Department and make it more attractive for employees, by 1965 these attempts were highly unsatisfactory. A recruiting campaign in South Africa and overseas costing £ 1070 was extremely disappointing as only 2 appointments out of 26 enquiries were made. [1] This could have been a result of the sanctions imposed which made people predict a bleak future for Rhodesia in a short period of time making attempts to get employees futile. The instability associated with the liberation struggle also had a negative impact on white skilled labour. Besides those assumptions, the generally relative low wages offered by the Department as compared to other sectors contributed to the ineffectiveness of these campaigns hence the Department had to do something about it first in order to successfully recruit employees.

Increased levels of shortfalls and penalties in the early 1970s resembled a great deal of trader misunderstanding of the sales tax legislation and certain deliberate omission by operators leading to underpayments. [2] The Rhodesian Tax Department largely aided in the accountability of taxes which would not have been paid due to failure of keeping proper tax records and contemplated tax evasion schemes. [3] As remedy, the Department published a booklet titled "Traders' guide to sales tax." This was intended to enlighten traders on the law, in order to reduce avoidable shortfalls and penalties in the future. [4] The branch profits tax complemented the non-resident shareholders tax as it taxed

---

[1] First Report of the Commissioner of Taxes, 1965, p. 6.
[2] Report of the Commissioner of Taxes, June, 1973, p. 6.
[3] Ibid.
[4] Ibid.

profits leaving the country by way of dividends. [1] Income tax increased by 21million pounds compared to the previous year. [2]

Tax System in Relation to Africans

As already hinted above, one of the challenges that the Department faced was in the manner they integrated Africans in the tax system. In 1974, only 1.1% of individual's liability for income tax was accounted for by Africans. [3] Income Tax was only paid by African elites, largely a merchant class. [4] The Prescribed Areas Tax was paid by the Africans at a rate of $ 2 per annum per adult male to the village head. The village head received 10% commission tax which was mainly collected from Tribal Trust Lands from rural Africans for the financing of development in their respective areas. [5] However, due to the migratory tendencies brought about by the post U. D. I industrial development, many were now considered urban dwellers rather than rural dwellers and village heads found themselves in a dilemma. [6] This disrupted the accumulation of revenue to finance rural areas since the development of respective areas lay on the basis of self-financing. Migration of Africans into urban areas mainly to work in industries contributed to limited financial capacity for development in rural areas. On the whole, African aggregate contribution to the tax base increased rather than declined. For example, their contribution rose from $ 101 068 in 1967, $ 376 540 in 1970 and had reached $ 508 583 by 1972. [7]

The "illegal" Rhodesian government also operated under a segregationist

[1] Report of the Commissioner of Taxes, June, 1973, p. 7.
[2] Ibid.
[3] Harris, "The Tax System from U. D. I to Independence", p. 8.
[4] Ibid, p. 9.
[5] Ibid. p. 10.
[6] Ibid. p. 11.
[7] Report of the Commissioner of Taxes, June, 1972, p. 5.

tax policy, based on a principal of apartheid in public finance. ① The tax system was designed to ensure that whites enjoyed services financed by their taxes and Africans also received services financed by their own taxes. ② White owned farms and industries were indulged with tax concessions for investment and improvement. These included low tax on foreign investors to attract foreign skilled labour while Africans received in principle no public assistance. ③ Hence segregationist tendencies are noted in the Department's tax systems which ensured development and improvement on facilities in White areas in the name of self-financing. This could have been a deliberate attempt to elevate the settler community and give them a better competitive advantage over Africans. This was hinged on the government's overall policy of making Rhodesia a "white man's country". African areas were left largely to their own devices and greatly incapacitated save for cosmetic interventions in the 1970s which were made under the banner of community development.

In Search of increased revenue

Due to the increase in government spending after the intensification of the war against nationalists in the mid-1970s, the proportion financed by borrowing rose to nearly one-third as taxation could not be increased to the same extent. ④ In the first decade of UDI, capital and current expenditure of both local and national government, accounted for almost a third of the Gross National Product fluctuating between 28 and 32% . ⑤ The central government borrowed to a relatively small extent until 1976. ⑥ Harris argues that though the government also relied on rents, fees and interests, over 80%

---

① Harris, "The Tax System from U. D. I to Independence", p. 6.
② Ibid.
③ Ibid.
④ Ibid, p. 2.
⑤ Ibid.
⑥ Ibid, p. 6.

was accounted for by direct taxation. [1]

Direct taxes were levied from income and profits directly paid as lump sum per person and on company profits, branch profits and non-residential shareholders tax and prescribed areas tax paid by Africans. [2] Indirect tax included small taxes paid on goods and services when they are bought and sold, for example, customs duties. [3] Between the years 1964/65 and 1972/73, taxes and profits ranged from 52% and 57% of the Central Government's total tax revenue but in 1975/76 it rose to a peak of 70%. [4] The ratio of direct to indirect taxation worried the government and there was need to reduce direct taxation for the sake of investment and economic growth. For instance, in a budget speech on 18 July 1968, the Finance Minister noted that, "My own view... is that of further movement from direct to indirect taxation to spread and realise the country's full tax potential to encourage investment and economic growth. "[5] Harris saw this as part of a policy to ensure that Africans who paid little income/profits tax but bought goods bearing indirect tax, were involved. [6] As will be shown in later the discussion, this was not entirely successful.

In many Western countries, a progressive income tax was an important tool for reducing income inequality. But, in Rhodesia racial separation and Central government taxes defined authority. These segregationist tendencies were spread across varying geographical areas and poor local authorities depended on their own resources while rich towns kept theirs. [7] Consequently, there was no redistribution of resources even through government taxation.

---

[1] Harris, "The Tax System from U. D. I to Independence", p. 6.

[2] Ibid, p. 3.

[3] Ibid.

[4] Harris, "The Tax System from U. D. I to Independence", p. 4.

[5] 1968 Parliamentary Debates cited in Harris, "The Tax System from U. D. I to Independence", paper 29, p. 4.

[6] Ibid, p. 4.

[7] Ibid, p. 5.

Indirect taxes of goods, for example, sales tax as percentage of goods price increased from $5^1/_3\%$ in 1969 to 15% in 1977 through a failed programme of shifting from direct to indirect tax which saw an increase in both kinds of taxes. [1] Sales tax affected the larger combined population. The main source of tax revenue financing the central government grants for African areas was the Prescribed Areas Tax. [2] The second major source was from levies raised by the African Development Fund from levying African produce from the Tribal Trust Lands, that is, tax from peasants' sales income. [3] Tax and levies from African beer sales played crucial roles in financing current and capital expenditure in African townships for example, in 1976/7 Bulawayo. [4] Local government revenue was raised from levies on African Beer from particular townships. This worked in Salisbury for instance through rents, transport and housing from 1973 the levies were channelled to development of Tribal Trust Lands not just areas of origin alone. [5] In comparison, white councils paid for expenditure by property tax like in the United Kingdom. [6] According to Notcutt and Latham, "The contribution of the individual native to the state in the form of tax" was "the price which he pays for security and good government, for communications, education, agricultural and veterinary activities, medical attention, in fact for all the advantages of an orderly and progressive society". [7] A similar situation is apparent in the study of Rhodesian tax collection distribution and use in social service provision which was governed by racial divisions.

Looking at the complex tax system, it can be noted that although the

---

[1] 1968 Parliamentary Debates cited in Harris, "The Tax System from U. D. I to Independence", paper 29, p. 11.
[2] Harris, "The Tax System from U. D. I to Independence", p. 16.
[3] Ibid, p. 16.
[4] Ibid, p. 19.
[5] Ibid, p. 19.
[6] Ibid, p. 20.
[7] L. A. Notcutt and G. C. Latham cited in, A. Burton, "'The Eye of Authority': 'Native' Taxation, Colonial Governance and Resistance in Inter-war Tanganyika", *Journal of Eastern African Studies*, Vol. 2, No. 1,2008, p. 80.

Commissioner of Taxes Department enforced these taxes in order for Rhodesia to reach its full tax capacity or potential, it was highly segregating on the part of the Africans. These taxes were meant to ensure the benefit and enjoyment of the settlers who could afford to pay the taxes while impoverishing the Africans in the name of "self-financing." Hence, the segregationist tax system during the UDI was not only aimed at enabling Rhodesia to reach its full tax potential but also to diminish the African.

This sums up an account of the experiences, challenges in particular, of the Rhodesia Commissioner of Taxes Department. The collapse of the C. A. F placed insurmountable pressure on the Department as it had to take up work that had previously been done by the Federal Tax Department. A shift from the joint taxation system to a new one which would cater for Rhodesia only also proved to be challenging. Furthermore, poor salaries made the retention of staff almost impossible and experienced workers were on the loose. The Department faced recruitment problems leaving large volumes of work to the not only few but also inexperienced workers. These challenges amongst others became a threat to the capacity of the Department to reach its full tax potential hence a need to address them.

Navigating the Challenges: Reform and transformation

The colonial state implemented various reforms to the tax systems so as to effectively deliver and do more for a colonial state under siege. The changes within the tax system made by the Department were more specifically intended at countering the challenges it was facing and improving its services. New tax systems such as the P. A. Y. E were implemented and these raised the government's capacity to increase revenue. The Department imposed stricter measures in its tax system to ensure more reliable and consistent payment of taxes. Mechanisms to maintain, improve and retain staff within the Tax Department were engineered. Training schools were set up and staff training commenced in order to counter the challenge of lack of professionally trained, skilled and knowledgeable workers. As a way of countering flight risks by workers, salary improvements were made. In the final analysis, the study observes that the Department was not entirely able to retain well trained staff. Although the staff development schemes and increase in salaries had improved the situation, there remained a continued thirst for experienced labour and, at some point, the Department began to reverse its gains when its wages were yet again overtaken by competitors.

In order to realize and understand why it was important that the Department fix their tax systems and find solutions to their challenges there is need to bring out the importance of tax in an economy. The following paragraphs will help contextualize the importance of tax hence, the need for the Department to improve its efficiency and increase revenue collection. Taxation as a domain of political economy is very important to understanding the nature of a state. Skocpol argues that, "a state's means of raising and deploying financial resources tells us more than could any single factor about its existing and immediate potential capacities to create or strengthen state organisations, to employ personnel, to co-opt political support, to subsidize economic enterprises and to fund social programmes."[1] It is in this context that we should appreciate the realisation by the Commissioner of Taxes Department of the need to improve and revise its tax systems in order to reach its full tax potential to gain financial resources to enable smooth flow of Rhodesia's economy, politics and society.

Revenue performance depends on the degree of coercion involved in tax enforcement.[2] From a fiscal point of view, the state collects taxes and allocates them in order to fulfil three functions in the economy: allocation,

---

[1] T. Skocpol cited in, R. T. Orock and O. T. Mbuagbo, "'Why government should not collect taxes': grand corruption in government and citizens' views on taxation in Cameroon", *Review of African Political Economy*, Vol. 39, No. 133, 2012, p. 479.

[2] O. Fjeldstad, "Taxation, Coercion and Donors: Local Government Tax Enforcement in Tanzania", *The Journal of Modern African Studies*, Vol. 39, No. 2, 2001, p. 289.

distribution and stabilization. ① Furthermore, the organization of a country's economy significantly influences taxation. It is for example, administratively inexpensive and much easier to tax major industrial activities than peasant agriculture. Such differences in economic structure should inform tax policy making, based on reasonable valuations of the potential for increased taxation. ② Farmer and Lyal consider power to tax as one of the most basic and jealously guarded prerogatives of the state to assure state revenues. ③ Based on the social contract, the government may use tax revenues for financing public goods or different transfers that citizen tax payers desire. ④ It is this importance of tax which made it necessary to find solutions to the various challenges that the Department was facing.

As part of its efforts to come up with informed solutions, the colonial state also instituted commissions of inquiry which came up with detailed reports with recommendations. For example, as a way of cost minimization and to improve efficiency as well as for the convenience of its customers, recommendations were made by one of the Department's reports. The 1972 Report, for instance, recommended the need to house the Salisbury collecting office and three assessment offices in a single building for economic reasons and for public convenience. ⑤ This would be convenient on the part of the Department itself in terms of rentals and people needing its services.

As already hinted, one of the reforms was the introduction of the Pay As You Earn (PAYE) system. This is a system of income tax withholding that requires employers to deduct income tax and sometimes, the employee portion of social benefit taxes from each pay check delivered to employees. It

---

① M. Mutascu, "Taxation and Dermocracy", *Journal of Economic Policy Reform*, Vol. 14, No. 4, 2011, p. 343.

② O. Therkildsen, "Understanding Taxation in Poor African Countries: A Critical Review of Selected Perspectives", *Forum for Development studies*, Vol. 28, No. 1, 2011, p. 101.

③ P. Farmer and R. Lyal cited in, M. Mutascu, "Taxation and Dermocracy", *Journal of Economic Policy Reform*, Vol. 14, No. 4, 2011, p. 343.

④ M. Mutascu, "Taxation and Dermocracy", p. 343.

⑤ Report of the Commissioner of Taxes, 30 June 1973, Presented to Parliament 1974, p. 9.

is different from income tax in that the system is a method of paying Income Tax on remuneration whereas income tax is the tribute paid to the government on monetary proceeds of an individual. On PAYE, the employer deducts tax from the employee's salaries or pension earnings before paying them net salary or pension. The PAYE system was introduced on the First of April 1966. The aim of the PAYE system was to benefit the country by facilitating a steady constant flow of revenue to the government. [1] It aimed at enabling the employee to spread tax payment over 12 months rather than the annual assessment payable within thirty days. The system owed greatly to the employer's cooperation. [2]

Precautionary measures were employed to ensure compliance with the new tax system. For example, an employer would become personally liable for payment of any P. A. Y. E that he failed to deduct with an 18% penalty and an $8^1/_3\%$ interest per annum from the first day it would have been overdue. [3] Employers were also cautioned against failing to register as an employer and any other failure to comply with any demands imposed by the tax commissioner in regards to the new and other tax systems. [4] The PAYE tax was to be paid by anyone classified as an employee or any individual to whom remuneration was paid. [5] It is apparent from this evidence that the government was extremely strict in its tax system. Income tax started being paid on similar bases used in many advanced Western countries after the introduction of the PAYE system. [6] Through such exercises, Rhodesia therefore, proved innovative in its tax system and this contributed to the survival of the economy in the face of sanctions. The non-cumulative system of PAYE tax collection adopted in Rhodesia proved satisfactory and

---

[1] NAZ, RG-P/TAX 3, Employer's guide to the Pay As You Earn System of tax collection, 1970, p. i.
[2] Ibid.
[3] Employer's guide to the Pay As You Earn System of tax collection, 1970, p. 9.
[4] Ibid, p. 12.
[5] Ibid, p. 1.
[6] Harris, 'The Tax System from U. D. I to Independence', p. 7.

presented administrative advantages over more complicated systems in other countries. [1] Regardless of the difficulties resulting from the new currency, the PAYE system in itself continued relatively smooth. [2]

Due to the twin effects of economic sanctions and the liberation struggle, and possibly other factors, there was a reduction in taxable income in a number of sectors. [3] These would, without doubt reduce the level of total annual tax collected. However, this was compensated by collections made from PAYE based on monthly income for the year ended June 1968. The average income was higher than expected in face of economic sanctions leading to a rather negligible drop in total revenue collected. [4] Contrary to common anticipation, the amount of Income Tax, Super Tax and undistributed profits, the June report of the Commissioner of Taxes noted that tax had increased by £120 816. [5] These trends, on the contrary, somehow implied absence of hurt on Rhodesia in terms of taxation which was surprising considering it was an economy under economic sanctions. As a result, PAYE taxation became the national revenue acquiring priority in the Rhodesia Tax Department while Stamp Duty was of second significance. [6] This was based on the amount of revenue obtained from these means of tax. Thus, Rhodesia was to some extent shielded from the full impact of economic sanctions by the PAYE system.

A number of measures were also put in place as part of an effort to improve the quality and number of employees in the Department. For example, an Assessors Training School was set up in February 1965 training 17 officers by June through three month courses. It was essential in giving the staff good grounding in all income tax work providing them with better

---

[1] Report of the Commissioner of Taxes, June 1971, p. 8.
[2] Report of the Commissioner of Taxes, June 1970, p. 11.
[3] Report of the Commissioner of Taxes, June 1968, p. 4.
[4] Ibid.
[5] Ibid, p. 7.
[6] Ibid, p. 9.

understanding of practical difficulties facing tax payers. [1] By 1971, the methods of staff training were maintained as on job training, training courses at the Head Office and full time training at polytechnics. [2] Staff training was inspired by the amount of work and staff available but full time training at polytechnics had a major drawback of completely taking away staff from work. [3]

A number of taxation articles were published to increase public awareness on issues of national taxation for a clearer understanding of the tax system. [4] A review by the Inspectorate of the Public Service Board in March 1966 noted improvements in the Department for example, salaries. These improvements were aimed at refining the incentive for working in the Department and to upgrade quality of staff to satisfactory levels. [5] The Assessor's school continued and managed to train another 19 officers in 1966. [6] In 1967 the school trained 22 candidates; it now provided visits to commercial, farming, industrial and mining areas for practical training showing every sign of improvement in the making of expert tax officers. [7] However, a number of years were expected to lapse before the proficiency of the Department's staff became even reasonably satisfactory.

There was the introduction of a £575 salary which rose to £780 in one year after passing the Department's lower examination, to £1320 if one passed the Department's higher examination. [8] Though not as successful as intended, the salary improvements yielded some level of success. Three investigation officers were appointed on 3 year contracts in July 1966 and by

---

[1] First Report of the Commissioner of Taxes, 1965, p. 14.
[2] Report of the Commissioner of Taxes, June 1971, p. 12.
[3] Ibid.
[4] First Report of the Commissioner of Taxes, 1965, p. 16.
[5] Second Report of the Commissioner of Taxes, June 1966, p. 4.
[6] Ibid, p. 10.
[7] Report of the Commissioner of Taxes, June 1967, p. 11.
[8] Second Report of the Commissioner of Taxes, June 1966, p. 6.

the end of the year, 39 tax cases were investigated to the collection of £11 175. [1] Between June 1965 and June 1966, £2 429 923 of personal tax had been collected. [2] But, the 1966 Commissioner of Taxes' report recognised the need and advised for proper pension fund legislation with a register to control investment policy and movement of finance.

By the end of 1969, net Personal Tax collected by the Department amounted to 111 584 pounds above the previous year. [3] This showed every sign of upward development resulting in the recruitment of 12 more members of staff during that year. [4] However, the assessing Department faced loss of experienced personnel largely to retirements on medical grounds among senior investigation officers. Replacement of such mature skilled workers was not easy. Regardless, they managed to investigate and collect 78 069 pounds worth of revenue that year. [5] The Department successfully continued with their policy of centralised training at the Assessor's Training School in Salisbury. A technical college was set up in Bulawayo during the year ended 30 June 1969 which managed to train 24 students from all over the country. [6] Though such employee development schemes yielded positive results, they still failed to quench the continued thirst for experienced workers.

In 1968, the assessing staff had increased by 12 people who filled 12 out of 16 vacant posts necessitated by the increasing volume of work. [7] Perhaps this successful recruitment may have been also part of the fruits of the 1966 salary improvements. By 1969 the Department was clearly enjoying improved numbers in recruitment especially school leavers. Regardless of cost, the Department needed experience among employees, this was a satisfactory achievement as attracting school leavers had been a difficult task in the past

------

[1] Second Report of the Commissioner of Taxes, June 1966, p. 10.
[2] Ibid, p. 8.
[3] Report of the Commissioner of Taxes, June 1969, p. 6.
[4] Ibid, p. 3.
[5] Ibid.
[6] Ibid, p. 10.
[7] Report of the Commissioner of Taxes, June 1968, p. 3.

number of years. [1]

There was a relatively horrible turn of events due to the relapse in the Department's ability to retain well trained staff. Regardless of the 1971 salary increase to match other fields like commerce, by 1973 these "increased" salaries had been by far, overtaken again. [2] This suggests that the Department was generally underpaying compared to other fields and serious considerations and improvements would have helped avoid several challenges affecting the Department especially in retaining staff. This was complemented by a general persisting lack of tax clerks country wide except for Bulawayo alone. [3] Substantial turnover of staff re-crippled the Department's work especially in Salisbury but Bulawayo, Gwelo and Umtali remained relatively satisfactory. [4] There was, however, visible revenue accumulation to the national treasury due to increased work by the tax investigation branch.

The training of the Department's staff continued but the proportion of trained employees remained unsatisfactory. To attract suitable recruits, the Department introduced a selective staff training scheme. This was done under government expense in Salisbury and Bulawayo Polytechnics to prepare staff for the Intermediate Examination of the Chattered School of Secretaries. [5] Those privileged with the programme were obliged to serve the Department for three compulsory years. [6] This would satisfy the increasing deficiency for professional labour which had for long haunted the Department.

The full time training of staff at polytechnics was discontinued due to time spent away from work at school. [7] This was replaced by a series of in-office training courses which would prepare one for the intermediate

---

[1] Report of the Commissioner of Taxes, June 1968, p. 4.

[2] Report of the Commissioner of Taxes, June 1973, p. 2.

[3] Ibid.

[4] Ibid, p. 4.

[5] Report of the Commissioner of Taxes, June 1970, p. 7.

[6] Ibid.

[7] Report of the Commissioner of Taxes, June 1972, p. 9.

examination of the Chattered School of Secretaries and Administrators. [1] The in-office training courses introduced in 1972 had already proven better effective than the full time polytechnic courses. [2] All these efforts were still aimed at staff development and creating a qualified workforce for the Department.

By 1971, the Department reported an overall improved position of the assessing staff. There was an increase of 2 years experienced recruits by 36% but the 2 - 5 years experienced staff continued to fall. [3] Increased pay seemed to be working as bait as shown by the increase of new recruits into the establishment. This increase in recruits was "at a satisfactory level" as it had "been conspicuously absent,"[4] before the implementation of pay increasing mechanisms within the Department. Head Office training was extended by introducing periodical refresher courses to the tune of varying grades and experiences across departmental ranks. [5]

Another intervention came in the form of shifts in the taxes themselves. For instance, between 1965 and 1979, indirect tax (sales tax) and customs and excise duties fluctuated between 24% and 32% reaching a peak of 36% in 1978/9. [6] A shift from direct to indirect taxation burdened the poor more as it made tax less reliable on income but on expenditure. [7] This is because imposing taxes on commodities made the goods much more expensive and yet most Africans were either not working or working but receiving low remuneration. With the increase in prices because of imposed taxes on commodities, people had to fork out more than they could afford in order to get basics and this further impoverished people especially the Africans. However, for the whites who owned the means of production and were

---

[1] Report of the Commissioner of Taxes, June 1972, p. 9.

[2] Report of the Commissioner of Taxes, June, 1973, p. 9.

[3] Report of the Commissioner of Taxes, June, 1971, p. 4.

[4] Ibid.

[5] Report of the Commissioner of Taxes, June, 1972, p. 9.

[6] Monthly digest.

[7] Harris, 'The Tax System from U. D. I to Independence', p. 25.

employed, a shift towards indirect taxation was not going to be as burdensome as it was to many of the local people.

However, in Rhodesia a total shift towards indirect taxation failed to benefit the state because of several reasons. One of the most critical ones being the fact that food stuffs which constituted much of the poor's expenditure were exempted from tax. [1] According to a family budget weight used by the Rhodesian Central Statistical Office, urban Africans spent between 50% and 55% of their expenditure on food stuffs while Europeans spent 21%. [2] Most of the poor people were Africans and yet they are the ones whose aggregate expenditure on foodstuffs was more by virtue of their huge population. As noted above, most food stuffs which constituted much of the poor's expenditure were exempted from tax. Hence this would not fully benefit the Tax Department.

A number of changes were also made while some practices were continued and entrenched in a bid to find the best system to service an economy under siege. For example, there were special allowances given to immigrants in income tax which were designed to maintain the supply of white skilled labour for white industry, agriculture, tourism among other trades. [3] Low rates of tax on profits made by foreign investments were also imposed with a considerable number of exemptions. [4] The 1972 and 1973 financial Laws introduced 15% tax on 60% of taxable income of profits made in Rhodesia by foreign companies and shareholders. [5] This was to keep the much needed foreign investments which were crucial to the economy. [6] Pension funds were exempt if they provided pensions for Rhodesian residents. [7] Interests to foreign creditors were exempted if they were of loans

---

[1] Harris, 'The Tax System from U. D. I to Independence', p. 25.
[2] Ibid.
[3] Harris, 'The Tax System from U. D. I to Independence', pp. 28 – 29.
[4] Ibid.
[5] Ibid.
[6] Ibid.
[7] Ibid.

for mining, banks or mortgage on lands. However, these were reversed in 1976 as profits were easily channelled out of the country disguised as interests. [1] But, exemptions on loan interests to mines remained due to the importance of foreign investment in those sectors.

The Department registered notable surplus in its collections. For instance, taxation on income or profits (income tax, super tax and undistributed profits tax) estimated $ 24,550,000 but receipted $ 28,727,666 with a $ 4,177,666 surplus on the estimate due to P. A. Y. E collections for which there were no previous figures to the estimate. [2] Tax surplus surpassed the estimated figures because employment was maintained at a higher level than expected under "the prevailing economic conditions. "[3] Higher imports and economic activity continued. There was a total of £54,628,441 in tax collected during 1967 with a surplus of £6,949,939. [4] This is evidence that the Commissioner of Taxes Department had achieved considerable success as tax collected improved and a surplus was even reached which had not been the case before.

The Customs and Excise Amendment No. 5 aimed to ensure the importation of industrial goods or raw materials duty free and to protect local industries. [5] According to Mr. Wrathall, the Minister of Finance and Rhodesian Deputy Prime Minister, "other goods were exempted from import tax for example, fire engines and surgical appliances because they were used for public service. "[6] The Customs and Excise Amendment Bill reduced duty on certain chemicals from 5% to free like other raw materials. [7] If analysed, this would serve as an advantage to the Tax Department in the future. This

---

[1] Harris, 'The Tax System from U. D. I to Independence', p. 30.
[2] Rhodesia, Comptroller and Auditor General Report, 1966 - 7 to 1967 - 8, p. 72.
[3] Ibid.
[4] Ibid.
[5] Rhodesia, Parliamentary Debates, Vol. 69, 1967, 5th to 27th September, 24th October to 7th November, J726. K2, p. 967.
[6] Ibid.
[7] Ibid, p. 894.

entailed that these raw materials and chemicals would be cheaper on the Rhodesian market because they were duty free. As a result of raw materials being cheaper, this would promote industrialisation hence creating a wider tax base for the Department. These industries would pay taxes and so would their employees. Besides the tax from these industries, commodities being produced by these industries also meant a wider tax base because taxes would be imposed on them since the government was moving towards indirect taxation. Therefore, this can be regarded as a long term solution that would ultimately increase the Rhodesia Commissioner of Taxes Department's tax potential.

Despite the repeal of a number of items in the stamp duties tariff in July 1970, the revenue collected by the Department increased by $ 55 905 amounting to an overall increase of $ 258 021 for the year. [1] This largely owed to the increase in business dealings involving dutiable instruments. [2] The Department's increased awareness campaigns increased public awareness on duty liable goods and led to the increase of goods referred to the Department for official advise. [3] Different ways were used to raise this awareness and the campaigns included the distribution of fliers. Newspaper advertisements or announcements, government commissions and direct publications were also used. Great strides were made as a result of these awareness campaigns as the amount of revenue collected actually increased. In 1971, it was reported that the Department collected around $ 13 million more revenue than previous years. [4] The Department, therefore, reached considerable heights in finding solutions to counter its challenges and its performance greatly improved.

Therefore, it can be said that the Department found mechanisms or solutions to counter the challenges it was facing which impeded it from realising its full tax potential. These included the Pay As You Earn tax system

---

[1] Report of the Commissioner of Taxes, June, 1971, p. 9.

[2] Ibid.

[3] Ibid.

[4] Ibid. p. 10.

which has been discussed above. The Department also embarked on the opening of training schools in order to improve the quality of workers and, therefore, the quality of the work done by the Department. Recruitment schemes were also put in order to increase the number of workers hence lessening the pressure on the previously few existing workers as this had been one of its challenges. Efforts were made to try and avoid flight risks of the workers. These were solutions put in place to maintain, improve and retain the workers as a measure of improving the efficiency of the Rhodesian Commissioner of Taxes Department. An attempt to shift from direct taxation to indirect taxation was also made and this was to increase the amount of revenue as they realised that direct taxation was not yielding much. As has been noted, the limited contribution of Africans towards direct taxation was partly because they were excluded from much of the better paying formal wage employment where they would have been eligible for income tax. As demonstrated, the efforts by the Department had mixed successes.

Conclusion

The work of the Rhodesian Commissioner of Taxes Department in an economy bound by sanctions between 1965 and 1980 was examined. Due to the shift from Federation to territorial administration, the Rhodesian tax system underwent alterations in its tax systems and went through many tax amendments meant to cater for the new administrative systems. These changes affected the Rhodesian population differently. The Department itself, faced many challenges in trying to achieve its mandate especially because of the change in the tax system when the government changed, the Department became overloaded with work in the midst of difficulties in recruiting qualified workers and retaining staff because of its low wages as compared to other sectors.

The demise of the Federation somehow contributed to some of the challenges later faced by the Department during the UDI. The Department also faced broader challenges which included financial strains which made it difficult to pay the workers decent wages hence making it hard to retain them. Labour shortages due to low wages, labour migration as a result of the sanctions, lack of qualified workers and all this put unimaginable pressure on the Department as the work became too much for the few available workers leading to backlogs. Such poor performance also led to the reduction of revenue collected which became another major challenge among many others. The study has shown how Africans were affected and integrated in the tax system via the Department and the challenges associated with the nature of their integration. It has been shown that in theory the tax paid by the Europeans financed development in European areas and tax paid by Africans were meant to develop African areas. However, in reality, there was little trickling in the way of African development. African integration in the tax systems was itself compromised by their limited capacity in making contributions. The reality was that African areas remained underdeveloped and revenue accrued by the Department mainly served the interests of the whites.

Challenges faced by the Department reduced its fiscal capacity and rendered it inefficient in many ways. There was therefore, the need to find solutions to these challenges to improve the Department's efficiency because as discussed earlier in this research, tax was essential in the Rhodesian political economy just as it was in other colonies and capitalist economies. It had always had an economic role and even before the U. D. I, it contributed in forcing African men to engage in wage labour. It had been a form of incentive for African participation in the colonial economy and an important source of colonial revenue.

However, while acknowledging these notions it should be noted that tax systems were modelled towards greater efficiency in the context of a challenged economy facing the twin problems of war and sanctions. After the UDI, the tax system implemented was to some extent reactionary to the sanctions engineered by the former mother country. The tax policy had several objectives which aimed at protecting and maintaining the independent settler economy. The Department also wanted to improve its quality of work and counter its challenges in order to realise its full tax potential. Long term solutions were implemented to counter some of the challenges and these included the Pay As you Earn tax system which was closely and strictly monitored to ensure tax compliance. This facilitated a steady constant flow of revenue to the government and to some extent managed to shield Rhodesia from the full impact of the economic sanctions which had been imposed on it.

The quality of staff was paramount to the efficiency of the Department and maintaining, improving and retaining staff had been one of the Department's major challenge. Training courses were put into action and an Assessors Training School was set up. This was meant to create a well-qualified and experienced workforce and this aided in the improvement of the quality of work done by the Department although a gap in qualified workers remained a constant problem over the years. Salaries were improved and this achieved great strides in the recruitment of workers as compared to years before, however, because the salaries were still low in comparison to other sectors, recruitment levels remained relatively low despite it being an improvement from the previous years.

Relative reduction in the volumes of work was realised due to the considerable increase in recruitments for example in 1968 whereby the assessing staff had increased by 12 people out of the 16 vacant posts which were available. Due to the awareness campaigns, there was increase in revenue collected. Hence, the Department reached considerable heights in its attempt to counter challenges.

On the whole, this research contributes to discourses on institutional capacity to cope in a demanding economic environment and in the face of many challenges which threaten its overall tax potential through examining the institution of the Rhodesian Commissioner of Taxes Department. It highlighted the role institutions in this case, the tax Department and institutional reforms can play in improving revenue collection which is critical to national economies. A number of scholars have proceeded to examine African economic development through lenses of the legacies of colonial institutions. There clearly are lessons to be learnt about how the state used institutions such as tax departments to survive economic and political threats.

State and Drought Management in the Matabeleland Region of Southern Rhodesia: the Case of the 1960 Drought

Chengetai Musikavanhu

Abstract

This study focuses on one of the severest and most remembered droughts that occurred in the Matabeleland region of Southern Rhodesia in 1960. The drought was countrywide, but was arguably most acute in the Gwanda, Beitbridge, Filabusi, Matobo and Plumtree Districts of Matabeleland. Due to poor climatic conditions and fragile tropical vegetation, Matabeleland is not suitable for cash and food crop cultivation. Livestock rearing and in particular cattle and goat keeping became the main economic activity among black pastoralists and white ranchers. This paper discusses the negative effects caused by the 1960 drought on the cattle industry of Southern Rhodesia such as the deaths of a large number of cattle. It also discusses other factors which affected the marketing and the pricing structures of the cattle such as effects on breeding which in turn affected the quality of the livestock. The paper shows that the situation would have been worse if it was not for the relief measures that were provided by the colonial government through the Drought Relief Committee and some by the farmers themselves. The wide-ranging measures included offering grazing facilities on crown-land and national parks, financial support from the Cold Storage Commission, loans from the Land Bank, income tax relief, supply of trucks for transportation of cattle and *feeds, provision of feeds, mass slaughtering for destocking and exportation, among others. It also shows that not all the measures were successful this being a result of poor implementation and lack of resources. This study is critical in understanding the role that governments can play to assist the agricultural sector during crisis periods and it feeds into the broader historiographies of droughts in the context of food security.*

Introduction

This paper discusses the negative effects caused by the 1960 drought to the cattle industry of Southern Rhodesia in general and Matabeleland region in particular. The drought resulted in the death of a lot of livestock, thus a reduction in the cattle population of southern Rhodesia. It also affected the marketing and the pricing structure of the cattle which affected both the farmers and the buyers such as the Cold Storage Commission (CSC). The reproductive system as well as the quality of the livestock was also affected. Thus, the paper demonstrates the importance of the relief measures that were provided by the colonial government and some by the farmers themselves. Indeed, farmers and the government had to come up with relief measures to save the cattle from the drought. The wide-ranging measures included offering grazing facilities on crownland and national parks, financial support from the Cold Storage Commission, loans from the Land Bank, income tax relief, supply of trucks for transportation of cattle and feeds, provision of feeds, mass slaughtering for destocking and exportation, among others. Some cattle were moved from the drought stricken Matabeleland region to other places like Mashonaland Central.

The paper also shows that not all the measures were successful this being. This was partly as a result of poor implementation or reluctance of farmers to adopt some of the relief measures. Studying drought relief measures is important to the Zimbabwean economy because the occurrence of droughts and its threat on food security in Southern Africa generally and Zimbabwe in particular is a topical issue. The country continues to experience drought, for example, as recent as 2016 more than a quarter of the population experienced food shortages due to drought. The drought conditions of Southern Africa are worsened by the El Nino phenomenon and this left thousands of cattle dead, reservoirs dry and crops destroyed. It is important to carry out this research on drought relief measures which can help to shade light on the measures that can be adopted to save the livestock during the occurrence of drought. The thriving of the beef industry helps to improve food security in the country and the surplus can be exported thus contributing to the reduction of the balance of trade deficit which is a major problem in Zimbabwe and Southern Africa at large.

Background to the 1960 drought

The occurrence of drought in Matabeleland can be viewed as a natural factor considering its geology and climatic conditions. Zimbabwe is divided into 5 agro-ecological regions. The first region lies in the east of the country. It is characterized by rainfall of more than 1 000 mm/year, most of which falls throughout the year, low temperatures, high altitude and steep slopes. [1] It is suitable for timber production and ideally suitable for intensive diversified agriculture and livestock production, mainly dairy farming. Common crops are tropical crops such as coffee and tea, deciduous fruits, such as bananas and apples, and horticultural crops, such as potatoes, peas and other vegetables. [2]

Region 2 is located in the middle of the north of the country. The rainfall ranges from 750 to 1 000 mm/year. It is fairly reliable, falling from

---

[1] Food and Agriculture Organisation of the United Nations Report, Rome 2006, http://www. fao. org/docrep/009/a0395e/a0395e06. htm#TopOfPage.

[2] R. Mugandani (et al), "Re-Classification of Agro-Ecological Regions of Zimbabwe in Conformity with Climate Variability and Change", African Crop Science Journal, Vol. 20, No. s2,2012, p. 365.

November to March/April and because of the reliable rainfall and generally good soils, the region is suitable for intensive cropping and livestock production. [1] It accounts for 75 – 80 percent of the area planted to crops in Zimbabwe. Crops cultivated include flue-cured tobacco, maize, cotton, wheat, soya beans, sorghum, groundnuts, seed maize and burley tobacco. [2]

Region 3 is located mainly in the mid-altitude areas of the country. It is characterized by annual rainfall of 500 – 750 mm, mid-season dry spells and high temperatures. Farmers in this natural region mainly concentrate on maize, tobacco, cotton, wheat and cattle ranching. The predominant farming system is smallholder agriculture. [3] Region 4 is located in the low-lying areas in the north and south of the country. The region receives an annual rainfall of 450 – 650 mm, characterised by severe dry spells during the rainy season, and frequent seasonal droughts. Natural Region 4 is an extensive livestock production area with some drought tolerant crops such as sorghum, millet and rapoko. Farmers also grow some short season maize varieties. [4] Region 5 covers the lowland areas below 900 m above sea level in both the north and south of the country. The rainfall is less than 650 mm/ year and highly erratic. Although the region receives reasonable rainfall in the northern part of Zimbabwe along the Zambezi River, its uneven topography and poor soils make it unsuitable for crop production. Generally, it is suitable for extensive cattle production and game-ranching. [5]

Matabeleland Province falls within ecological regions 4 and 5 with characteristically low epileptic rains of 500 mm with areas such as Beitbridge receiving an annual rainfall of 453 mm against a backdrop of annual

---

[1] Food and Agriculture Organisation of the United Nations Report, Rome 2006, http://www. fao. org/ docrep/009/a0395e/a0395e06. htm # TopOfPage.

[2] R. Mugandani (et al), "Re-Classification of Agro-Ecological Regions of Zimbabwe in Conformity with Climate Variability and Change," p. 366.

[3] Ibid.

[4] Ibid, p. 367.

[5] Food and Agriculture Organisation of the United Nations Report, Rome 2006, http://www. fao. org/ docrep/009/a0395e/a0395e06. htm # TopOfPage.

evaporation of 2 034 mm. Average temperatures of 40 ℃ in summer and 13℃ in winter are experienced in the province. High temperatures combined with low erratic rainfall result in semi-arid conditions characterized by sporadic drought periods as well as vulnerability to other meteorological hazards such as flash floods especially in low lying areas and of late violent tornado like gusty winds which usually leave trails of destruction. The common types of soils include mainly sand, gravel and clay. The most dominant tree species are the acacias and mopane. These are drought tolerant crops which have water and food storages which enable them to survive through the dry periods. The rate of deforestation is high as communities exploit Mopane for use as firewood and fencing material around their properties; homesteads, kraals, fields and other projects. Once the trees are cut down, because of poor rains they are not easily replaceable. This makes the lands vulnerable to erosion. Animals such as elephants also contribute to the destruction of vegetation in the Province. The province generally is characterised by low vegetation cover which exposes it to severe erosion. [1] Thus the occurrence of drought in this region can be understood as a geological factor.

During the 1959 – 60 farming season, the region received below average rains and this resulted in the occurrence of drought. The Chief Native Commissioner reported that 1960 was an extremely difficult year from the livestock and grazing point of view. [2] Stock losses were severe and grazing was badly denuded, particularly in the overstocked areas of Matabeleland. [3] This was supported by the Native Commissioner for Filabusi who stated that Matabeleland South experienced one of the worst seasons on record with disastrous effects on grazing, water supplies and livestock. The five most severely stricken districts of Matabeleland South that is Filabusi, Gwanda,

[1] Environmental Management Agency document, https://www. ema. co. zw/inde-x. php/ema-national-maps/61-matabeleland-south. html (accessed 26 October 2018).

[2] NAZ F229/2022/1080/2/6 Drought Relief General.

[3] NAZ 32987, Report of the Under Secretary for Native Economics and Marketing for the year ended 31/11/1960.

Matobo, Plumtree and Beitbridge lost a total of 98 999 head of cattle during the year of which 56 769 were recorded dead due to the effects of the drought. [1]

Ndlovu views drought as an act of God but concedes that it is exacerbated by human practices that impact negatively on the environment. [2] This means that drought is a natural occurrence which is worsened by human activities such as deforestation, overstocking and the emission of gases into the atmosphere which causes global warming and consequently the occurrence of drought. Chenje and Johnston note that Southern African droughts are often linked to El Nino phenomenon which is associated with the reduction of Southern Africa's rainfall. [3] In Matabeleland, the 1959 – 60 rains were late in starting and generally ended early. [4] This meant that the crops as well as the vegetation did not receive adequate rainfall hence there was no adequate grazing for the animals and there was limited food for the people. The rains also tended to come in isolated showers rather than as prolonged sinking rains and this resulted in much of the water being lost through runoff. [5] The replacement of ground water necessary to maintain pastures, streams and dams throughout the following dry season failed to take place hence streams, boreholes and dams were quick to go dry. This impacted negatively on the people and livestock of the region.

Impact of the 1960 drought
on the Matabeleland cattle farmers

As noted by Nangombe, the effects of droughts are worsened by factors

[1] NAZ 32987, Report of the Under Secretary for Native Economics and Marketing for the year ended 31/11/1960.
[2] M. Mutasa, "Zimbabwe's Drought Conindrum: Vulnerability and Coping in Buhera and Chikomba Districts", Masters Dissertation, Norwegian University of Life Sciences, 2010, p. 11.
[3] M. Chenje and Johnson P. (eds), "State of the Environment in Southern Africa," Harare, Southern African Research and Documentation Centre, 1994, p. 332.
[4] NAZ 1080/2/F6, Drought Relief, Report of the National Drought Committee 1960, p. 3.
[5] Ibid.

such as lack of strategic and comprehensive drought plans, underdeveloped infrastructure, lack of cooperation among public and private sectors and lack of people's participation in drought management planning and high rates of water wastes and pollution. [1] The cattle farmers in Matabeleland had no strategic and comprehensive drought plans thus their livestock was under threat. They had no reserves of feeds for their cattle neither did they have much capital to buy the feeds in cases of drought. [2] There was also lack of infrastructure whereby the people had not built water storage facilities such as huge dams and boreholes. Although a few dams had been built in Matabeleland at this time, they were not sufficient to see the animals throughout the drought period. Most of them were not huge and this meant that they had a low storage capacity hence they were quickly exhausted in the drought years. The people had been advised to build water storage facilities prior to the occurrence of the drought but most of the white commercial farmers were reluctant to cooperate. [3] Hence when the drought occurred, they did not have enough water. The African cattle owners did not have the capacity to build the dams or to drill boreholes. They earned very little from their subsistence hence they could not save much for the construction of water storage facilities.

The effects of the drought in Matabeleland had also been worsened by overstocking. As shown by the table below, both the Africans and the Europeans owned cattle which exceeded the carrying capacity of their farms. Oliver West, the Chief Pasture Research Officer assessed that effects of the 1960 drought were aggravated by overstocking and bad management. Despite having very large tracts of land, the white commercial farmers exceeded the carrying capacity of their farms which worsened the effects of the drought. [4]

---

[1] S. Nangombe, "Drought Conditions and Management Strategies in Zimbabwe," Meteorological Services Department, Harare, www. droughtmanaementinfo/literature/UNW-DPC-NDMP-Country-Report-Zimbabwe-2014. pdf (accessed 20 June 2018).

[2] NAZ 1080/2/F6 Report of the National Farmers Union, p. 3.

[3] *Ibid.*

[4] NAZ 1080/2/F6, Drought Relief, Report of the National Drought Committee 1960, p. 5.

African farmers were confined to the reserves were they were given small portions of land in their large numbers. Thy owned small heads of cattle, an average of 7 heads per family. [1] Despite having small heads, they exceeded the carrying capacity of their allocated areas. The colonial government was not willing to give them more land and they advised them to destock with each family expected to have less than 5 cattle. The Africans could not comply with this since they regarded livestock as their source of wealth. The Minister of Agriculture reported that the Sabi district was more than 50% overstocked by the beginning of 1960. [2] Thus when the drought occurred the little pastures that were there were exhausted quickly and the effects of the drought were aggravated.

Table 1: Quantities of overstocked livestock in the 5 Matabeleland regions

Region	Number of cattle above the carrying capacity of the Area
Gwanda	41 280
Beitbridge	15 339
Matobo	3 5814
Plumtree	22 243
Filabusi	8 455

Source: NAZ F226/1080/2/6/, National Drought Relief Committee.

This table shows the extent of overstocking in Gwanda, Beitbridge, Matobo, Plumtree and Filabusi regions of Matabeleland. The areas had the numbers of cattle shown in the table above the carrying capacity of the area. Gwanda had the highest number of cattle above its carrying capacity with 41 280 extra. Filabusi was the least overstocked with 8 455 cattle above its carrying capacity.

The 1960 drought resulted in the reversal of the trend of ever increasing cattle numbers. Before the drought the cattle for both the African and white farmers were on the increase and this resulted in overstocking. However the

---

[1] NAZ 1080/2/F6, Drought Relief, Report of the National Drought Committee 1960, p. 5.
[2] NAZ F226/1034/1112 Annual Report, Ministry of Agriculture, 1960 – 62.

recorded numbers of disposals during the year reversed this trend and the cattle population was reduced. [1]The region had vast quantities of livestock before the occurrence of the drought and, as illustrated in table 2 below, most of the areas were overstocked. However with the occurrence of drought, a huge number of cattle died due to lack of pastures and water facilities. Also large herds of cattle were moved from the Matabeleland region to other areas such as Mashonaland central were there were better grazing facilities. [2] There was also increased slaughtering for sale as well as family consumption and this also reduced the cattle population of the region. The Chief Native Commissioner reported that because of drought, stocking position at the end of 1960 was the most favourable. [3] Thus it can be said that the 1960 drought was a blessing in disguise since it managed to control the cattle expansion and reduced the cattle population to almost acceptable carrying capacity of the region. However, the report of the Secretary for Native Affairs for 1961 shows that there was a decrease in disposals for 1961 and this was due to the fact that the farmers were building up their heads which had been severely depleted by the drought. As a result holdings had resumed an upward trend. The rate of natural increase continued to decline however and for 1961 it was at 11.2% compared to 14.5 in 1959. This was a direct impact of the 1960 drought. [4]

Table 2: Effects of overstocking on the cattle industry

Region	No. of cattle held 01/01/60	Extent of overstocking	No. of cattle sold 01/01/60	Deaths during the year due to drought
Gwanda	113,066	41,280	36,542	19,793

[1] NAZ F1040/2, Economic Report by R. Anderson: Secretary to the Ministry of Agriculture dated 6 March 1962.

[2] Correspondent, "Grim farmers ready for giant £11,500 Cattle Drive", *The Rhodesia Herald*, 20 January 1960, p. 13.

[3] NAZ 12/NEM, F226, Drought Relief, The Extent of Drought 1960.

[4] NAZ 32986 Report of the Secretary for Native Affairs and Chief Native Commissioner for the year ended 31/12/1961.

续　表

Region	No. of cattle held 01/01/60	Extent of overstocking	No. of cattle sold 01/01/60	Deaths during the year due to drought
Beitbridge	68,138	15,339	18,030	3,730
Matobo	89,618	35,814	16,182	22,146
Plumtree	89,787	22,243	17,044	9,031
Filabusi	46,458	8,455	11,196	1,996

Source: NAZ F226/1080/2/6/, National Drought Relief Committee

Table 2 above shows the numbers of cattle which were held in the 5 regions of Matabeleland as at January 1960. It also shows the extent of overstocking in the regions, the number of cattle sold and the numbers of cattle which died due to the effects of the drought. It also shows that the areas which were highly overstocked had the great occurrence of the death of livestock as compared to those which were less overstocked. There was also a great reduction in the cattle population in Matabeleland as indicated by the numbers of cattle that were there in January 1960 compared to those that were there by January the following year.

The breeding of the cattle was also affected by the drought. The calving rate was reduced because of the drought. [1] This was because of the inadequate feed supplies which impacted negatively the calving of the cows. Ainslie, acting Chief Animal Husbandry Officer stipulated that the number of cows in 1960 increased by 20 000 while the number of cows decreased by 11 000, a drop in the calving percentage from 48% to 4.5%. [2] The Chief Native Commissioner assessed that the drought also affected the rate of natural increase in the African cattle population which dropped from 14.5% in 1959 to 12.8% in 1960. The rate of natural increase was the lowest since 1954 when it was on 12.3%. [3] This was a major setback to the cattle industry since

---

[1] NAZ F229/2022/1080/2/6 Drought Relief General.

[2] NAZ F229/2022/1080/2/6 Drought Relief General.

[3] NAZ 32986 Report of the Under Secretary for Native Economics and Marketing for the year ended 31/ 12/1960.

the cattle were not increasing at the rate that they used to. This also contributed to the decline in the cattle population of the region.

The value of the cattle was also affected negatively by the occurrence of the 1960 drought. The drought resulted in a drop in the value of cattle. The average realised per beast for African cattle was £14 3s 0d as compared to 1959s average of £19 14s 0d. Secretary for Native Economics and Marketing, W. H. H. Nicolle assessed that taking the average realisation per beast in 1960 as £14 13s 0d, a total of £831 401 was lost by the Africans as a result of the drought. This can be attributed to the fact that the cattle did not have sufficient feeds and this resulted in a drop in the weight of the cattle which also meant a drop in the value since the cattle were valued according to their weight. The drop in the value of cattle can also be explained by supply and demand. The supply cattle was greater than demand as many people of Matabeleland wanted to get rid of much of their cattle before they were severely affected by the drought. Thus, the market was flooded by cattle which needed to be sold resulting in the drop in prices.

Table 3: Drop in the value of cattle

Region	1959	1960	Drop in value
Gwanda	£18. 10. 1	£12. 3. 4	£6. 6. 9
Beitbridge	£15. 19. 6	£14. 0. 6	£1. 19. 0
Matobo	£19. 7. 9	£13. 1. 0	£6. 6. 9
Plumtree	£19. 0. 8	£15. 5. 5	£4. 15. 3
Filabusi	£17. 4, 1	£12. 7. 11	£4. 16. 2

Source: NAZ F229/2022/1080/2/6, Drought Relief General.

The table shows the drop in the value of cattle as a result of the 1960 drought. It shows the maximum prices of cattle paid in 1959 before the occurrence of the drought and those paid in 1960 during the drought. In Gwanda and Matobo there was a drop in the value of cattle by over £6. Plumtree and Filabusi had a drop of about £4 while Beitbridge had the least drop of £1. 19.

In as much as the drought affected all the farmers in the region. African farmers were more severely affected. This was because the Africans had small pieces of land as compared to that of the Europeans. Land legislation during the colonial period such as the Land Apportionment Act (1930) and the Native Land Husbandry Act (1951) resulted in the division of land along racial lines. The African farmers were left with small pieces of land which had poor soils and the driest in the region. In addition to this, the African farmers faced financial challenges. Most of them were communal farmers who did not have large savings as compared to their European counterparts who were largely commercial farmers and had large savings. Thus, when drought came the African farmers, on top of having the most exhausted pastures because of overpopulation and overstocking, they did not have the money to buy supplementary feeds. The Land and Agricultural Bank provided financial credits to the people of white descent only. [1] The European farmers were on a better footing because on top of having their own savings, they could easily access loans from the Land and Agricultural Bank hence they could buy supplementary feeds for their livestock.

The drought resulted in African cattle ranchers selling off their cattle. At the Dombodema Mission Farm, 4, 5 miles from Plumtree, the farm manager reported that the drought condition was so severe that almost all the people sold most their cattle. By April 1960. all the streams were almost dry and the grazing fields were nearly exhausted. The people were advised by the Native Commissioner, Mr Dawson, that they should sell their cattle when they were still in a better condition so that they would obtain profits from them. Further delays meant further deterioration of the animals. One old man in this area confirmed that he had sold all of his seven cattle by end of the year. [2] In the districts of Gwanda, Lupane and Tjolotjo, some 3 100

[1] M. Drinkwater, "Technical Development and Peasant Impoverishment: Land Use Policy in Zimbabwe's Midlands Province", *Journal of Southern African Studies*, vol. 15, no. 3, p. 301.

[2] Mr. E. D. F. Dawson, "South Nata Reserve Africans Reluctant to Sell Their Cattle", *The Bantu Mirror*, 16 April 1960, p. 1.

heads of African cattle had died by January 1960 and this amounted to a loss of £46,500 in money. [1] The Native Affairs Department noted that the losses had been the severest stab on the economies of Africans in the Reserves who had depended upon their cattle as their main source of wealth. [2]

The condition of Africans in the reserves was so critical that one reporter of the Bantu Mirror Newspaper reported in February 1960, that unless there was some relief soon in the form of heavy rains in the region, the year would be yet another year of starvation and intense suffering among the Africans living in the reserves. [3] Crops were dying and the long spell of uninterrupted heat were experienced throughout January had added to the number of cattle losses already sustained towards the end of the year 1959. The position was distressing since most Africans depended on cattle and farming for their livelihood.

In January 1960, officials from the Federal Ministry of Agriculture in collaboration with the Farmers Union, Cold Storage Commission, Intensive Conservation Areas (ICA) organisation and the Native Department made an assessment of drought conditions in Matabeleland. The condition was considered sufficiently serious to recommend the immediate implementation of special emergency measures to counteract the effects of the drought. The measures adopted related to the feeding, watering and removal of animals to areas with better grazing facilities or slaughtering of the animals. A further result of the drought was reflected in a significant increase in the numbers and percentages of the lower grades.

Considering the extent of the drought it became necessary to set up a committee in the Ministry of Agriculture to advise the government and farmers on any action to be taken and to coordinate and organise assistance. On the 21st of January 1960, a Livestock Drought Relief Committee was set

---

[1] Reporter, "Thousands of Cattle died In Matabeleland", *The Bantu Mirror*, 2 January 1960, p. 11.
[2] *Ibid*.
[3] The Correspondent, "Peculiarities of This Year's Drought", *The Bantu Mirror*, 13 February 1960, p. 4.

up in Bulawayo by the Federal government to advice on the action to be taken to meet the ill effects of the drought which were particularly severe in Matabeleland. This Committee was under the chairmanship of the Director of Conversation and Extension and was composed of representatives of the Federal and Southern Rhodesia Agriculture and Conservation Services, Native Administration, Cold Storage Commission, Rhodesia Railways and the farmers. The essentially administrative and executive character of the Committee was confirmed with the establishment of the National Drought Committee (N. D. C). It was agreed that the Bulawayo Committee should become the "Action Committee" for all drought problems. ① The Action Committee made recommendations to the N. D. C. from which the recommendations were submitted to the ministers for approval. The decisions were communicated to the N. D. C. and through it to the Action Committee. ② The main purpose of the Livestock Drought Relief Committee was to ensure that the breeding stocks of the country were maintained and that practical assistance was provided to all producers who found themselves in difficult circumstances as a result of the drought. In order to achieve its objective, the facilities of the C. S. C, Rhodesia Railways and other Federal and Territorial department were freely placed at the disposal of the Committee.

The relief measures and farmer's response

Considering the extent and effects of the 1960 drought it became necessary for the colonial state to come up with relief measures so that they could help the Matabeleland cattle ranchers. T. D Mushore notes that, the effects of drought are expected to deepen where the capacity to provide relief is very low. ③ The colonial

---

① NAZ F229/2022/1080/2/6 Drought Relief General, Report from the National Drought Relief Committee dated 19 March 1960.

② Ibid.

③ T. D. Mushore (et al), "Effectiveness of drought mitigation strategies in Bikita District, Zimbabwe", *International Journal of Environmental Protection and Policy*, vol. 1, no. 4,2013, pp. 101 - 107.

government had to reduce the impact of the drought by implementing drought relief measures. Mushore further assets that it is important to ensure that measures are in place to minimize impacts of drought on human beings and their livelihoods although the strategies also have limitations. [1] This means that the strategies are not an end in themselves thus they do not entirely solve the impact of the drought but they help to minimize it. Drought impacts and loses can be substantially reduced if authorities, individuals and communities are well prepared, ready to act and equipped with knowledge for effective drought management. Therefore, the goal of mitigation and preparedness is to reduce impacts of drought, reduce vulnerability and foster drought resilient societies. It was considered that one of the main difficulties in providing drought relief lay in deciding who was eligible for such relief and who was not. It was decided that those districts which were particularly badly affected should be officially declared as Drought Stricken Areas after being accessed and recommended by the Action Committee whose formation have been discussed in the first section. [2] The Committee was to ensure that practical assistance was provided to all producers who found themselves in difficult circumstances as a result of the drought.

The drought relief measures were provided to both the white commercial farmers and the African ranchers. There were, however, some limitations on the part of Africans to access relief. The majority of the Africans lived in the reserves or in Special Native Areas where there was limited space hence it was easy to overstock. Also the government advocated destocking of the reserves through laws such as the Native Land Husbandry Act. The African farmers did not have the capacity to stock feeds as a result of both space and the finances. They were mainly subsistence farmers who kept the livestock for their own consumption and could only sell during the times of need. The European farmers on the other hand were commercial farmers who had vast

---

① T. D. Mushore (et al), "Effectiveness of drought mitigation strategies in Bikita District, Zimbabwe", *International Journal of Environmental Protection and Policy*, vol. 1, no. 4, 2013, pp. 101 – 107.
② NAZ/1080/2/f6/, Drought Relief, Report of the National Drought Committee, 1960, p. 2.

tracts of land and owned large heads of cattle. They also had the capital and the capacity to stock feeds for their cattle. These differences had an impact on the type of relief that each group received as is going to be shown as the section proceeds.

One of the relief measures that were offered by the state was the provision of grazing facilities on Crown Land. In order to ease the grazing situation, the Southern Rhodesia government opened up large areas of Crown Land to farmers as an emergency measure in various parts of the colony. Altogether, Crown Land was allocated for use by 13 850 head of European owned cattle, 20 000 head of African owned cattle and 10 500 Cold Storage Commission cattle, mainly African owned. [1] No charges were placed for grazing these cattle but farmers were however required to pay for the establishment of boreholes in the Crown Land then recover the cost when the land was alienated. Mr Murray confirmed to this after receiving a formal confirmation that no charges was levied for grazing on Crown land. [2] In Gwanda some 2000 cattle made use of crown lands available but the Africans turned down an offer to move up to 3000 herd to the adjacent Nuanetsi District where good grazing and water were available, this despite the fact that the Native Department Fund was prepared to meet the major part of the movement costs. [3] The resistance by Africans to move their cattle was because the Africans owned few cattle which were so precious to them hence they feared that their cattle would not be returned to them when the drought was over. In Beitbridge about 3000 herd of cattle utilized nearby Crown Land. 1 470 head were moved to Nuanetsi district were relief grazing was offered for 2000 head but this total was not taken up due to reluctance of the stock owners concerned. In Matopos, about 700 head were moved to Matopos National Park were grazing was kindly made available by the Parks Board. In

---

[1] NAZ/1080/2/f6/, Drought Relief, Report of the National Drought Committee, 1960, p. 5.

[2] Mr Quinton, "250 000 Africans Must be fed if rains hold off", *The Rhodesia Herald*, 3 February 1960, p. 13.

[3] NAZ/1080/2/f6/, Drought Relief, Report of the National Drought Committee, 1960.

Filabusi 7000 heads utilized the vacant Crown Land. [1] Plumtree's condition was worsened by an outbreak of foot and mouth disease which caused the district to be placed in quarantine in July and sales were not permitted until May/June the following year. The cattle from this region could not be moved to other places because they feared the spread of the diseases to other areas.

There was also the provision of finances from the Cold storage Commission. The Cold Storage Commission had been approached by the Ministry of Agriculture and had agreed to advance the cost of railing to farmers who could not afford the railing cost. This cost would be recovered when the cattle were slaughtered. Nearly 6 000 cattle were railed to Northern Rhodesia by the Commission up to the end of June. [2] The 1960 drought was less severe in Northern Rhodesia and these were the days when the three British colonies of Southern Rhodesia, Nyasaland and Northern Rhodesia were under a Federation hence it was easier to move the cattle across these 3 territories. Thus farmers in Southern Rhodesia benefited from grazing lands in the two less affected colonies. The majority of the Africans were not comfortable railing their cattle to faraway places and so few of them did so. They did not have the money to pay for the railage neither did they have the money to pay the people who were to take care of the cattle in those places. Thus they went for other measures which did not involve the movement of the cattle to other places.

The provision of loans was another relief measure adopted by the government during this period. The need to finance the purchase of feed for cattle and putting down the additional boreholes, the government decided that loans should be readily available. It was recommended, therefore, that additional funds should be made available to the Land Bank of Southern Rhodesia to enable it to relax its rules governing amounts lent and the security required and that the rate of interest should be reduced from 7% to 3%,

---

[1] NAZ/1080/2/f6/, Drought Relief, Report of the National Drought Committee, 1960.
[2] *Ibid.*

these recommendations were accepted. ① By the end of June an amount of £400 469 had been given out in long and short term loans. Financial assistance was granted through special loans with special conditions and rates of interest. The fund was to be administered by a committee consisting of the Chairman of the National Drought Relief Committee, Chairman of the Food Advisory Committee and the Chairman of the Land Bank. Famers who had been carrying on their farming operations efficiently but who have been so seriously affected by the drought that they could not continue operations without financial assistance were eligible for the loan provided there were reasonable prospects that it would result in the rehabilitation of the farmers. ② Loans could be used to pay labour for farm operations, living expenses of the farmer and family, purchase of feeds, purchase of cattle for restocking, hire of mechanical units and for water conservation works and any other purpose approved by the Committee. Interest was to be charged at the rate of 3% per annum with no interest free periods. Period of repayment could not exceed 10 years. It could be agreed that during the first 3 – 4 years no payments needed to be made and that the interest accrued over this period be repaid over the remainder of the period for which the loan was granted. Loans could not exceed £1, 000 with some special circumstances as exceptional. ③ Most of the African farmers were not eligible to get the loans from the banks since they did not have the collateral property. ④ Thus, African farmers were limited from accessing this relief measure because of this.

There were also some finances which were provided to the farmers who were not eligible to get loans from the banks. This was given to a farmer who was not able to pay for the fodder or to obtain the fund from elsewhere. The

① NAZ/1080/2/f6/, Drought Relief, Report of the National Drought Committee, 1960.
② NAZ S2500 /1080/3, Department of Agriculture, Letter from the Secretary Department of Agriculture to the National Drought Relief Committee dated 03 August 1960.
③ Ibid.
④ Ibid.

farmer purchased the fodder and submitted the invoices together with the order form to the State Advances Recoveries office for payment. A maximum loan of £7 per 10 heads of cattle per month for purchasing of fodder was allowed. These loans were given at an interest rate of 5%. [1] This provision catered for the African farmers since there was no need for collateral. However, the maximum loan one could access was too little to cover all the expenses for the drought relief hence they continued to feel the impact of the drought.

There was also the income tax relief as a response to the drought circumstance. The incidence of drought made it necessary for many farmers to sell large proportions of their cattle, the exceptional income which made them liable to a particularly heavy rate of income tax. It was accordingly recommended that the taxable income derived by farmers from the enforced sale of cattle should, for tax purposes, be spread over a period of 3 years. [2] This concession was provided for in the Income Tax Amendment Act of 1960. The *Rhodesia Herald* reported that the Federal Treasury would give sympathetic consideration to spreading the tax burden resulting from abnormal slaughtering. [3]

The limited supply of trucks made it essential for some system of priority to be introduced. It was recommended that the railways should accept the directives of the Action Committee in the allocation of cattle trucks. Trucks were prevented from going to Northern Rhodesia were the long distance meant that trucks would not return for up to 2 weeks. [4] The railways was recommended to obtain a loan of 100 cattle trucks over the 72 already on hire from the South African Railways. The additional cost was spread over all

---

[1] NAZ F226/1080/2/F6, Matabeleland Drought Relief, The Report of the Livestock Drought Relief Committee, 15 October 1960, p. 5.

[2] NAZ/1080/2/f6/, Drought Relief, Report of the National Drought Committee, 1960.

[3] Correspondent, "Grim farmers ready for giant £11,500 Cattle Drive", *The Rhodesia Herald*, 20 January 1960, p. 13.

[4] NAZ F226/1080/2/F6, Drought Relief, The Report of the Livestock Drought Relief Committee, p. 5.

users of trucks. Other trucks were also converted to cattle trucks. [1] This helped the farmers in that they were now able to move their cattle to other places at a faster rate. However, most of the African farmers could not afford the transportation rates hence they could not move their cattle.

There was shortage of hay in Matebeleland thus the government made provisions for the hay to be available for the farmers. It was at first thought that trucks returning empty from Mashonaland could be used for the transportation of hay. Private enterprise undertook to handle the importation of Lucerne hay but the collection and handling of veld hay and maize Stover was to be undertaken by the GMB. The GMB purchased on behalf of the government, considerable quantities of hay from the less affected districts for the Matabeleland farmers. [2] The Drought Relief Committee appealed to farmers in parts of the country unaffected by the drought to help out Matabeleland farmers who were desperately short of roughage. Dairy farmers alone needed 7000 – 8000 tons of roughage to stay in production through the winter. [3] Thus, hay provision was very much needed in Matabeleland and its provision was of great help. Farmers in areas declared to be drought stricken were permitted to be allowed to buy maize from the GMB in quantities less than the usual minimum of 15 tonnes. The GMB was requested to provide maize on a lease-lend basis. [4] Since most of the African farmers could not move their cattle to other places, provision of hay was very much useful to them since they could now feed their cattle from their area of residence.

Relief borehole drilling was another measure undertaken by the state to save the Matabeleland farmers from the impact of the drought. Farmers could no longer rely on dams and streams for providing their livestock with water. Most of the dams and rivers had dried up due to the drought hence the

---

[1] NAZ F226/1080/2/F6, Drought Relief, The Report of the Livestock Drought Relief Committee, p. 5.

[2] Ibid.

[3] Mr Quinton, "250 000 Africans Must be fed if rains hold off", The Rhodesia Herald, 3 February 1960, p. 13.

[4] NAZ/1080/2/f6/ Report of the National Drought Committee, 1960.

government undertook to provide drills for drilling deeper boreholes. In order to organise the allocation of drills to areas affected by drought, it was required that farmers who were experiencing water shortages should apply immediately to their conservation officers who would assist them with their water shortage reports. New charges were launched on government drills based on the footage rate instead of an hourly charge. The basic rate was 22s 6d per foot including provision for rebates on unsuccessful boreholes. [1] The Native Development Fund made available £55,126 for the development of additional water supplies in the stricken areas and a further £11,388 for other drought measures including the provision of seed and stock feed. [2] This helped the farmers since they could now access water to feed their cattle with.

Relief slaughter was another measure which was undertaken to deal with the effects of the drought. The farmers were encouraged to slaughter their cattle when they were still in better condition hence there was an increase in the supply of slaughter cattle. Supplies of slaughter cattle in the controlled areas of Southern Rhodesia exceeded the previous year by 17 000 head. [3] Slaughtering by private butchers decreased by 3000 head while that of the CSC increased by 10 000 head. [4] In 1961, the slaughtering in controlled areas decreased by 16 439, slaughtering by CSC decreased by 18 339 while those of private butchers increased by 2 900. [5] This shows that the increase in slaughtering of cattle for the year 1960 was a reaction to the occurrence of drought. The Under Secretary for Economics and Markets assessed that the Cold Storage Commission developed enough slaughter facilities in Matabeleland to deal with any expansion in slaughter cattle in the near

---

① NAZ F226/2021/1080/2/F4 Cattle Drought Relief Committee Minutes of Meetings.
② NAZ S2521 Drought Relief Committee Report.
③ NAZ F226/ 1080/F6, Report of the Secretary of the Federal Ministry of Agriculture for the year ended 30th September 1960.
④ *Ibid.*
⑤ *Ibid.*

future. [1] The African cattle farmers responded positively to the advice to sell their cattle in the 1960 drought. The figure of 213 469 heads of African cattle sold during the 1959/60 drought was the highest recorded, the previous record being that recorded in 1947 when 185 759 heads were sold. The figure for 1959 was 139 644. [2] This shows that the 1960 drought was one of the severest droughts that hit the British colony of Southern Rhodesia. Mr Quinton, the Parliamentary Secretary for Native Affairs said that slaughter cattle were being sold so as to reduce pressure on the land and so preserve the breeding stock. [3] This was the widely adopted relief measure amongst the African farmers and was the most advised as well by the relief committee because it did not involve any costs.

Although the Cold Storage Commission had developed facilities for the slaughter of huge quantities of beef, there was a challenge in the disposal of this meat. There was insufficient freezing capacity for largely increased quantities and at that time it was difficult to export chilled beef at a greater rate. Freezing also lowered the value of the beef. Hence there was a great loss to the beef industry due to these challenges. CSC chairman stated that the assumption that the company would slaughter about 30 000 a month was theoretical based on the assumption that the beef would be moved immediately without freezing, to the local market, Liebigs, the Congo and chilled overseas export. [4] Without this immediate movement, the rate of slaughtering filled up the existing storage within a matter of days. The Secretary for Rhodesia Farmers Union assessed that from July-November 1960,29 994 hindquarters suitable for chilled export were handled by the Commission in Bulawayo and Salisbury. Of these, only 11 680 could be exported as chilled beef, the balance of 18 314 hindquarters had to be frozen

---

① NAZ 1320/F22, Report by the Director of Conservation and Extension dated 18 November 1960.
② NAZ/1080/2/f6/ Report of the National Drought Committee, 1960.
③ *Ibid*.
④ NAZ 1320/F22, Report of the Under Secretary for Economics and Markets dated 19 November 1960.

at a considerable loss. [1]

The Africans were cooperating by reducing their cattle holdings through sales. In the Wenlock Special Reserve, it was agreed between the District Commissioner and the people that they would reduce the 16 000 heads of cattle to the 10 400 figure which was relevant to the carrying capacity of the area as determined by the assessment committee. [2] Chief Matema and his people asked the District Commissioner to allow him a free hand in reducing livestock to the number required by the law and that he would do it allowing each permit holder up to 16 heads of cattle. The rest was sold to the Cod Storage Commission as slaughter cattle. [3] There were some cases however were African farmers were reluctant to sell their cattle. In the South Nata Reserve for example, Africans were reluctant to sell their cattle yet drought condition was causing grave concern. They were under the impression that the drought position will get better each coming month. In the early month of the year, they had the perception that since their cattle were in good condition at that time, they would remain so even later in the year. [4] However, during this time there was a reduction of prices of cattle due oversupply on the market. The Drought Relief Committee indicated that it was necessary for farmers to appreciate that owing to the serious drought conditions and the large numbers of stock being offered for sale, it was not possible to offer prices as high as those obtained in the open market during the past year. [5] Hence the farmers had to cope with the reduced prices that they were offered.

There were also revisions in the cattle pricing structure as a relief measure to the Matabeleland farmers. In order to assist producers in areas

---

[1] NAZ 1080/2/F6, Report from the Rhodesia National Farmers Union.
[2] Mr. E. D. F. Dawson, "South Nata Reserve Africans Reluctant to Sell Their Cattle", *The Bantu Mirror*, 16 April 1960, p. 1.
[3] Ibid.
[4] Ibid, p. 5.
[5] NAZ S2521, Drought Relief Committee Report.

affected by drought the March standard price was used in the calculation of milk prices in respect of those farmers situated in drought stricken areas. This resulted in these producers receiving 5 shillings per gallon more for milk supplied than they received using the January and February standard prices and this additional amount was met by a special subsidy. [1] The additional amount was in relation to feed purchases and to water supplies.

Cattle were brought from drought areas to other areas like Mashonaland were they were allocated to local farmers by the several local Drought Relief Committees of a non-official character composed of conservation officers and farmers. There were some farmers in Mashonaland who had vast tracts of land which was underutilised who were prepared to take in cattle from Matabeleland. Many were tobacco and maize farmers whose farms were under stocked. Three distribution points were set up at Darwendale, Marandellas and Lochinvar were the Mashonaland farmers were given cattle depending with the facilities that they had at their farms. [2] Supplementary feeding was recommended for all classes of stock and this meant that farmers had to make provision for extra feed in the form of hay and silage as well as purchasing protein concentrate to give about ½ lb digestible protein a day. [3] The response to this scheme had been good and there was a demand for more cattle than was distributed. Those farmers who could provide the feeds were given first preference. Some of the cattle were sold to the Mashonaland farmers. Buying was undertaken by a buying team consisting of a cold storage buyer, a representative of Drought Relief Committee, a veterinary officer. [4] If cattle were passed clean by the vet officer the buyer then estimated the weight and type, price was calculated and offered to the seller. If seller accepts then railing instructions were given and cattle were railed a week later

---

[1] NAZ F226/ 1080/F6, Report of the Secretary of the Federal Ministry of Agriculture for the year ended 30th September 1960.

[2] NAZ/1080/2/f6/ Report of the National Drought Committee, 1960.

[3] Ibid.

[4] Ibid.

on seller's responsibility.

Conclusion

The paper has shown that the colonial state had a significant role to play in terms of ensuring food security. Southern Rhodesian government was able to cushion most of the cattle ranchers, especially white farmers, from the impact of the 1960 drought. This was done through a number of measures such as relief slaughtering, movement of cattle to other areas, provision of hay, relief borehole drilling and dam construction and provision of loan facilities. One can say that the colonial land policy had a negative impact on foot security of the African. They were left with small pieces of land which were not adequate to graze their livestock, making them more vulnerable in times of disaster. African farmers had limited access to some of the relief measures, such as the movement of cattle and borehole drilling, by lack of funds since the majority of them were not credit "worthy". Thus the common relief measure among the African farmers was relief slaughter as they were advised by the Drought relief committee to sell their cattle to the Cold Storage Commission. Drought preparedness and mitigation plans were hardly available for the benefit of Africans.

Food security can be ensured if policies and measures are more of preparedness rather than response to situation of crisis. Measure such as storing feeds and water conservation to ensure the availability of these in the drought times can be recommended. Food and water should be kept in reserves during the times of good harvest for future use. The farmers can also be advised to have some funds set aside for emergencies such as drought. By so doing the farmers would be prepared for the droughts and this would help minimise their impact.

Profit Versus Pragmatism: Foot and Mouth Disease and Southern Rhodesia's Cattle Industry, 1930s – 1940s

Aisha Mashingauta and Godfrey Hove

Abstract

Of all the bovine diseases that afflicted Southern Rhodesia between the 1930s to the 1940s, Foot and Mouth Disease (hereafter FMD) had probably the most far-reaching socio-economic and political implications. It shaped the texture and progress of the cattle industry and the colonial political-economy quite profoundly and, in the process, brought to the fore considerable under-currents not only in the livestock industry but colonial society generally. Using archival sources from the National Archives of Zimbabwe (hereafter NAZ) which include, among others, veterinary reports, inter and intra-governmental correspondences and media reports, this article unpacks and disentangles the intricate dynamics surrounding the outbreak and spread of the disease and the socio-economic and political imperatives that lay at the base of the responses of different stakeholders in the industry. Moreover, we delineate the impact such developments had on Southern Rhodesia's fledgling cattle industry, demonstrating that while the state was mostly influenced by a desire to eradicate the disease and safe-guard the long term interests of the industry, (predominantly settler) ranchers appeared more interested in avoiding cattle losses maintaining profits in the short-term. In the main, we argue that avoidance of immediate short-term losses by farmers—which led to

*concealment of the disease, blame shifting and the development of suspicions
between farmers and the state—contributed to the spread of the disease which,
in turn, deleteriously affected the well-being of the industry and the broader
economy. Moreover, the article discusses Southern Rhodesia's changing
economic relations with neighbouring countries in the region in the wake of
unfolding developments regarding the FMD. By offering a detailed and nuanced
historical exploration of the outbreak, spread and impact of FMD, this article
not only makes a modest contribution to the historiography of Southern
Rhodesia's cattle industry, but hopes to contribute to ongoing conversations
and debates around effective responses to livestock diseases in contemporary
Zimbabwe.*

Keywords: Southern Rhodesia, *Foot and Mouth Disease*, cattle,
economy, veterinary

Introduction

Together with the maize and tobacco industries, the cattle industry was
one of the lynchpins around which the Southern Rhodesian agricultural
economy rotated for much of the colonial period. Indeed, given the country's
tropical climate and topography, particularly in the south-western areas,
early colonial authorities concluded that Southern Rhodesia was primarily
suited to a pastoral economy. Eric Nobbs, the state-appointed Director of
Agriculture explained in 1911 that it the cattle industry would play a pre-
eminent role in agricultural development in the fledgling colonial economy. ①
Thus, from 1908, when the British South Africa Company officially espoused
an agricultural policy that would be underpinned by settler capitalist

---

① See Report of the Director of Agriculture, 1911. Successive government authorities repeatedly declared
the centrality of the cattle industry to Southern Rhodesia's agrarian economy throughout the colonial
period, a notion that was also adopted by the post-colonial administration.

production，the cattle industry was primed to play a key role. While various factors that affected the development of such a crucial industry during this time-such as undercapitalisation，lack of expertise and some cattle diseases-have been discussed extensively by historians，the Foot and Mouth Disease (hereafter FMD) and the extent of its impact on the colony's society has not been subjected to detailed discussion.

Focusing on the Matabeleland province where the outbreak was quite severe，this article explores the outbreak of FMD in Southern Rhodesia and the circumstances behind its spread between the 1930 and early 1940s. First，we trace the origins of the disease during the 1930s and the extent of its occurrence in different parts of the colony. In this way，we discuss the different interpretations that existed among farmers and state functionaries regarding the exact origin of the disease and how this，with time，became a precursor to the differences that emerged among stakeholders regarding effective control measures. Second，we discuss the variegated nature of responses by different sectors of colonial society，particularly farmers and the state itself，and socio-economic，veterinary and political imperatives that shaped the said responses. Using a battery of archival sources (including but not limited to inter and intra-governmental correspondence，memoranda and reports from farmers' organisations) and newspaper articles，the article offers a nuanced exposition and discussion of the attitudes and interests that lay at the root of the state and farmers' responses and initiatives and various arms of the state as the disease began to threaten the fledgling cattle industry and the colony's fragile economy. We demonstrate that owing to their different and often competing social and economic interests across the racial and sectorial divides，farmers' responses were sometimes at odds with state policy (itself not homogenous，anyway). These attitudes and sectorial interests，we argue，were responsible for cases of disease concealment，misrepresentation of facts，speculation and blame shifting that emerged within Southern Rhodesian society during the period under review. Moreover，the article evinces that these responses were largely responsible for the rapid spread of the disease.

Third, and with a particular focus on ranching operations, this article discusses the impact of the disease on the Southern Rhodesian cattle industry as well as on regional cattle trade dynamics. It discusses the extent to which the FMD impacted on ranching activities in the colony and how this impact in turn spewed clashes between cattle owners and the state who blamed each other for the tailspin in which the industry found itself during this period. On the whole, the main argument borne here is that farmers' desire to preserve their immediate economic interests and the more long-term approach taken by the state led to an uncoordinated national response which only served to aid the spread of the disease, thus leading to the decimation of the colony's herd and farmers' incomes. In this way, this article shows that although pushed to the fringes of socio-economic historical studies, FMD was one of the foremost determinants of the development trajectory of the colony's (agrarian) economy between the 1930s and the 1940s. Further, we demonstrate that the disease was more than just a veterinary phenomenon: it offers an interesting analytical lens through which the broader Southern Rhodesian political-economy could be analysed.

Historiographical Reflections on Cattle and Diseases in Southern Rhodesia

The cattle industry of Southern Rhodesia has received significant academic attention from numerous scholars, and this is no doubt attributable to the aforementioned historical importance of the industry to the local economy. Admittedly, bovine diseases, including FMD, have come under discussion as historians sought to explore the origins and development of the cattle industry in colonial Zimbabwe. While FMD has been identified as one of the major impediments to the development of the cattle industry in Southern Rhodesia, discussions around the disease have tended to be tangential rather than comprehensive. Ian Phimister has written on the cattle industry of Southern Rhodesia with specific attention on the beef industry. He analysed the development of the beef industry in Southern Rhodesia from the early days of colonial occupation to the establishment of the Cold Storage Commission in 1938, delineating the factors that helped shape the nature, texture and performance of the industry during this period. [1] These factors include undercapitalization, lack of technical expertise and marketing challenges that pervaded the pastoral economy during the early years of colonialism. Taking up from Phimister, Alois Mlambo discusses the performance of the cattle industry under the Cold Storage Commission, noting that one of the chief reasons for the establishment of the CSC was to promote settler ranchers who had faced a myriad of challenges at both production and marketing levels. [2] Taken together, the two scholars' work offer a *longue duree* account of the history of the cattle industry in Southern Rhodesia. They offer a broader context from which a study of the FMD and its impact on the cattle industry may be situated.

In his doctoral thesis, Victor Machingaidze explores the development of settler agriculture in pre-Second World War Southern Rhodesia, outlining the socio-economic, political and geo-political factors that were at play in shaping the fortunes of the beef industry. [3] Given the focus of his work, Machingaidze's work inevitably discusses livestock diseases such as East Coast Fever and FMD and threat they posed to Southern Rhodesia's cattle industry at both production to marketing stages. [4] As a broader study, however, his discussion on FMD is truncated and thus eschews some interesting nuances that influenced responses to the diseases and also its impact on Southern Rhodesian society. This notwithstanding, his work is an important building

[1] I. R. Phimister, "Meat and Monopolies: Beef Cattle in Southern Rhodesia, 1890 – 1938", *Journal of African History*, Vol. 19, No. 3(1978), p. 394.

[2] A. S. Mlambo, "The Cold Storage Commission: A Colonial Parastatal 1938 – 1963", *Zambezia* (1996), pp. 53 – 72.

[3] V. E. M. Machingaidze, "The Development of Settler Capitalist Agriculture with Particular Reference to the Role of the State" (PhD Thesis, University of London, London, 1980).

[4] *Ibid.*

block upon which a more in-depth study of the political economy of FMD may be made, itself the brief of our study. Closely linked to Phimster and Mlambo's work is Samasuwo's doctoral thesis work on the cattle industry. Samasuwo offers longitudinal study of the evolution of the beef industry in colonial Zimbabwe since the Second World War. [1] On the FMD, he rightly observes that one of the problems which further compounded the marketing problems faced by Southern Rhodesia was the outbreak of FMD, particularly to the extent that it led to the imposition of a marketing ban on Southern Rhodesia agricultural products. [2] Focusing on a host of other variables that affected the beef industry, Samasuwo's study does not give an extensive discussion of the FMD. Using these works, this study thus extends the frontiers of analysis of the FMD to offer a more detailed account of the FMD and the socio-economic factors arising out of it.

Mwatwara has worked on the relationship between African traditional livestock regimes and state veterinary services in colonial Zimbabwe. Written from a socio-environmental perspective, Mwatwara's work looks at the interface between "scientific" veterinary and conservation approaches and African traditional livestock regimes. [3] Similarly, William Wolmer has focused on livestock diseases and livestock management systems on ranches and in African reserves in the Lowveld, revealing the role played by colonial science in defining settler and African regimes. [4] Wolmer outlines how veterinary science was employed to organise the landscape into diseased and disease-free zones, adding that veterinary restrictions constituted a disadvantage to both commercial and communal cattle owners. [5] Drawing

---

[1] N. Samasuwo, "'There is Something About Cattle': Towards an Economic History of the Beef Industry in Colonial Zimbabwe, with Special Reference to the Role of the State, 1939 – 1980" (PhD Thesis, University of Cape Town, 2000).

[2] *Ibid.*

[3] See W. *Mwatwara*, *A History of State Veterinary Services and African livestock Regimes in Colonial Zimbabwe, 1896 – 1980*, PhD Thesis, Stellenbosch University, 2014.

[4] W. Wolmer, *From Wilderness Vision to Farm Invasions: Conservation and Development in Zimbabwe's Lowveld* (Harare: Weaver Press, 2007), p. 99.

[5] *Ibid*, p. 102.

from Wolmer's contextual insights, this article seeks to offer give a much more nuanced and modulated discussion of FMD and its place in the Southern Rhodesian political economy. In the process, it attempts to cover a gaping lacuna in the historiography of Southern Rhodesia's agrarian economy while also demonstrating that FMD was not merely a veterinary problem, but a socio-economic and political phenomenon whose study brings to the fore fascinating features of the colony's anatomy.

Origins of FMD in Southern Rhodesia and Early Responses

The circumstances surrounding the arrival of the FMD in Southern Rhodesia in the 1930s are unclear. Nothing definite was said about its exact origins by officials, including the specialist called into the country in 1932 to investigate the disease. In the absence of scientific evidence, most arguments and assertions tended to be speculative. [1] For instance, a Veterinary Inspector from South Africa identified only as Toit admitted that the exact path of the FMD into Southern Rhodesia is unknown, but went on to speculate that infections may have been brought over land from East Africa where the disease existed enzootically in the form of infected meat, hides or hoofs. [2]

Basing its argument on the fact that some Portuguese East African cattle watered on the Sabi River (where some Southern Rhodesian livestock also watered), the Veterinary Department speculated that the disease may have been introduced from Portuguese East Africa. [3] However, no disease was found at Melsetter, the closest area adjoining with PEA, during the first

---

[1] NAZ 1194/182, Foot and Mouth Disease Outbreak Reports, 1931 – 1937, Report on the Position of the Disease for the year ending December 1932.

[2] NAZ S1217/7, Evidence taken by Committee to Enquire into Certain Aspect of the Recent Extension of Foot and Mouth and African Coast Fever in the Colony, Evidence given to the Central Intelligence Department on the Outbreak of the Foot and Mouth Disease, 1932.

[3] NAZ S1217/7, Evidence taken by Committee to Enquire into Certain Aspect of the Recent Extension of Foot and Mouth and African Coast Fever in the Colony.

outbreak of 1931, rendering the suggestion rather unsustainable. The disease was only recorded in Melsetter during the 1934 outbreak. Claims by some farmers that the disease may have come from game were dismissed by the Veterinary Department: the latter argued that had it not been for the comparative freedom of game from the disease, the Union of South Africa could not have escaped the infection at the time of earlier infection, given the fact that game from Southern Rhodesia constantly moved back and forth across the Limpopo River. [1] Thus, to date the exact manner in which the FMD entered Southern Rhodesia remain unknown, although it may safely be argued that the disease was spread by livestock movement.

The first case in Southern Rhodesia was reported at Nuanetsi Ranch in 1931. Cattle at the Ranch began exhibiting symptoms associated with FMD, the most common of which were signs of lameness among cattle, losses in reproduction, lactation, growth, and draught power. [2] Cattle exposed to the infection also became dull, dribbled saliva and seldom grazed normally. In 1931, Archibald Culver, a Cattle Inspector employed at Nuanetsi Ranch reported that several of the examined livestock showed these symptoms and also had bad feet. [3] He estimated that about 150 cattle in the kraal head had these signs and symptoms. [4] It was suspected to have been carried from Nuanetsi to Fort Victoria by transport cattle, from Fort Victoria to the Enkeldoorn District by movement for sale and from Enkeldoorn to Gwelo Township by cattle for sale purpose. [5] Further, the disease was said to have

---

[1] NAZ S1217/7, Evidence taken by Committee to Enquire into Certain Aspect of the Recent Extension of Foot and Mouth and African Coast Fever in the Colony.

[2] D. Perry, T. F. Randolph, S. Ashley, R. Chimedza, T. Forman, J. Morrison, C. Poulton, L. Sibanda, C. Stevens, N. Tebele, I. Yngström.

[3] NAZ S1217/7, Evidence taken by Committee to Enquire into Certain Aspect of the Recent Extension of Foot and Mouth and African Coast Fever in the Colony, Evidence given to the Central Intelligence Department on the Outbreak of the Foot and Mouth Disease, 1932.

[4] NAZ S1185/11, Foot and Mouth Disease, Investigation made in 1935 in regard to Outbreaks at Nuanetsi Ranch, Chief Veterinary Report to the Department of Agriculture.

[5] NAZ S1185/11, Foot and Mouth Disease, Investigation made in 1935 in regard to Outbreaks at Nuanetsi Ranch.

extended from Nuanetsi to Belingwe Native Reserve. [1] Available records indicate that it is from Belingwe that the disease is thought to have moved and extended to the Gwanda Native District and lower portion of Insiza. [2]

The sporadic and intermittent nature of the outbreaks significantly impacted on initial efforts to bring the disease under control. The disease first occurred in 1931, was followed by another outbreak in 1934. The 1934 outbreak was said to have been more obscure and mysterious than that of 1931. Its origins could not be traced to the first outbreak and the virus appeared new altogether. [3] Worse still, fresh waves of FMD were further recorded in 1936, 1946 and 1948. Without substantive evidence on the exact origins of the disease, farmers and the Veterinary Department were left astounded, with some believing new outbreaks were probably fresh infections unconnected to earlier outbreaks. This confirms Wolmer's observation that what further complicated the situation in Southern Rhodesia was the fact that the virus strand that caused the first outbreak was not the one that caused succeeding ones. [4] These circumstances undoubtedly put Southern Rhodesia in a tenuous position and, as discussed later in this article, insufficient information on the real cause and origins of the disease were part of the reasons why other countries considered imposing trade restrictions on Southern Rhodesia.

It is also true that different parts of the country were affected by the disease at different times. While some areas like Meseltter and Fort Victoria escaped the first outbreak, they were hit either by the second of 1934 or the third of 1936. The Secretary of the Department of Agriculture and Lands

---

[1] NAZ S1185/11, Foot and Mouth Disease, Investigation made in 1935 in regard to Outbreaks at Nuanetsi Ranch.

[2] NAZ S1185/11, Foot and Mouth Disease, Investigation made in 1935 in regard to Outbreaks at Nuanetsi Ranch.

[3] NAZ S1194/D4/7, FMD, Chief Veterinary Officer Reports on FMD Research, Letter from the Veterinary Research Department to the Secretary, Department of Agriculture, 20 May 1935.

[4] Wolmer, "Land, Landscapes and Disease", p. 49. Machingaidze also echoes similar observation that the problems of combating the disease were worsened by insufficient knowledge of the disease as it appeared before Southern Africa. See Mashingaidze, "The Development of Settler Capitalist Agriculture", p. 355.

stated that following the 1931 outbreak at Nuanetsi, fresh outbreaks were recorded in Gwelo, Tokwe Ranch, Ardern Ranch in Mazowe and Umvuma Good Hope Farm. [1] Large blocks were infected in the country as fresh outbreaks continued to erupt in the Central and South district of Gwanda, Chibi, Belingwe, Victoria, Selukwe and Chilimanzi. [2] More isolated outbreaks occurred in the Charter District, around Enkoldorn, Salisbury, Mazowe, Gwelo, Bubi, Insiza District among others. Thus, to the extent that the exact source of the disease was never discovered and that the disease broke out irregularly in both spatial and temporal terms, it was always going to present challenges for colonial authorities, farmers and other stakeholders to effectively control its spread.

Early Responses: Denial and Concealment of the Disease

The circumstances surrounding the FMD outbreaks undoubtedly complicated Southern Rhodesia's capacity to effectively deal with the disease with finality. However, beyond these circumstances, which appeared beyond the colony's control, early responses by farmers further muddied the waters. This section discusses farmers' responses to the FMD, the socio-economic fundamentals behind them and the impact of such responses on the cattle industry. From the early 1930s, some white commercial ranchers appeared eager to deny the existence of the disease among their herds with the result that cases of disease concealment were quite common. Although the fact that Southern Rhodesia experienced a relatively mild strain of the disease throughout the period under review was advantageous, it also enabled the disease to escape observation and for farmers to successfully conceal it.

White ranch owners often directed their managers not to report the

---

[1] NAZ 1194/182, Foot and Mouth Disease Outbreak, Report on the Position of the Disease for the year ending December 1931.
[2] Ibid.

presence of the disease. This was so because they feared that their cattle would be banned from the market. The Criminal Investigation Department of the British South Africa Police reported that "deliberate efforts" were made by a ranch manager at Nuanetsi Ranch not to report the first outbreak of the disease, in spite of regulations which stipulated that every FMD case should be reported to the Veterinary Department, adding that approximately 9000 cattle from Nuanetsi were sent to all parts of the country and were subsequently slaughtered for export as a result of the concealment. [1] It was the suppression of the disease and continual migration of infected cattle from the Nuanetsi Ranch that resulted in the spread of the disease to many parts of the country. By 1932, a number of areas were affected by the disease in areas around Chibi. Further hints of concealment of the disease can be deduced from the testimony of one Petrus Stephanus Nel, a cattle owner at Nuanetsi who, in a court of enquiry held by the Criminal Investigation Department in 1934 at Nuanetsi, initially denied that his cattle had FMD and instead attributed the fact that some of his cattle had sore feet to muddy kraals. [2] Later, he admitted that "only" thirty-five cattle in his herd showed all the symptoms of FMD, a situation he strangely argued to have been mitigated by the fact that no deaths had been recorded. [3]

Other methods of concealing the disease included the use of "coded message" between ranch managers and ranch owners to ensure that "outsiders" would not know about the exact state of affairs at Nuanetsi. They did this to avoid alarming cattle owners from neighbouring ranches and, more importantly, veterinary officials. If FMD was detected, one would say, "cows and calves have arrived", and if not, one would say, "Cows and calves have not arrived". [4] For example, one Joseph Cornelius de Blanche, the

---

[1] NAZ S1217/7, Summary of events leading up to the sending of message to the Police on the Outbreak of FMD (Not dated hereafter N/D).

[2] NAZ 1185/11, Foot and Mouth Disease Outbreak Enquiry at Nuanetsi Ranch, Evidence given by Petrus Stephanus Nel on the Outbreak of FMD to the Police, 24 February 1934.

[3] Ibid.

[4] Ibid.

manager in charge of the Dumba Section at Nuanetsi Ranch from 1930 to
1934, testified that the disease indeed appeared in 1931, yet no member of
the Veterinary Department was informed, including Van Heerded, the cattle
inspector. [1] This, he added, was done to spare the cattle from forced
slaughter and burning. John Vernon Hartley who was employed at Nuanetsi
Ranch at Chesi and Mkumi section also confessed that he did not report cases
of FMD to veterinary authorities because the manager had secretly visited his
section at midnight and told him to keep quiet. [2] He also noted that sick
cattle were trekked during the night.

But what was the motive behind such denials and concealment? The
answer may be found in the testimony of Fynn, a rancher who admitted to
concealing the disease because he wanted to preserve the most important form
of capital in his ranching enterprise-cattle. [3] He explained that:

> This disease is not as bad as officials make it out to be. I have lost
> more cattle to slaughter by the Veterinary Department than to (the)
> Foot and Mouth (disease) It has taken me nearly eight years to build my
> herd and to establish a viable cattle business, only for the veterinary to
> use FMD as an excuse to blow everything. I cannot just switch to eggs or
> something like that... [4]

What is incontrovertibly clear, however, is that the denial and
concealment allowed farmers to continue with their marketing activities for a
while, regardless of the disease's existence. The concealment thus led to a

---

[1] NAZ 1185/11, Foot and Mouth Disease Outbreak Enquiry at Nuanetsi Ranch, Evidence given by
Petrus Stephanus Nel on the Outbreak of FMD to the Police, 24 February 1934.
[2] Ibid.
[3] NAZ 1185/12, Foot and Mouth Disease Outbreak Enquiry at Nuanetsi Ranch, Evidence given by John
Fynn on the Outbreak of FMD to the Police, 06 March 1934.
[4] Ibid.

huge conflict between cattle inspectors and cattle owners. [1]

Despite regulations stating that all suspected cases of FMD had to be reported to the Veterinary Department, some Cattle Inspectors connived with ranchers to conceal the disease. For instance, one Cattle Inspector identified only as Peter revealed that he received written instructions from the Fort Victoria veterinary office not to inspect cattle leaving the ranch for export. As a result, over 200 cattle earmarked for export which left the ranch for West Nicholson were not inspected. [2] He further revealed that farm authorities claimed that there were no cases of FMD at the ranch, despite some of the cattle having sore feet, which is one of the symptoms of FMD. However, when the herd was tested at West Nicholson just before slaughter, 75 of the 200 cattle were reported to be "definitely dying from the FMD." [3] Johns Campbell, the Veterinary Officer stationed at West Nicholson, was forced to destroy the entire herd that had left Nuanetsi for West Nicholson. This case not only brings to the fore the desperation of ranchers to continue cattle sales and profits but also reveals the extent to which state officials played differential roles in the process. As indicated above, officials at Nuanetsi were complicit in the concealment of FMD while their counterparts at West Nicholson insisted on testing prior to the sale of cattle.

African ranch workers were also forced to conceal cases of the disease. Janje, who was employed as a "boss boy" at Chesi section at Nuanetsi Ranch, attested that he had told the ranch manager, that he suspected that his cattle were suffering from FMD but from the response he got, Janje was convinced that he had made a mistake by openly speaking about the disease. [4] He added:

---

[1] NAZ S1185/11, Investigations in regard to the FMD outbreak at Nuanetsi Ranch, Report from Detective JE Chubbock to the Criminal Investigation Chief Superintend, 24 February 1935.

[2] NAZ S1217/7, Evidence given by Peter Van Herdern, Cattle inspector at Nuanetsi on the outbreak of FMD on the Ranch, 29 March 1936.

[3] NAZ S1185/11, Investigations in regard to the FMD outbreak at Nuanetsi Ranch, Report from Detective JE Chubbock to the Criminal Investigation Chief Superintendent, 24 February 1935.

[4] Ibid.

I cannot give the names of the people on the Ranch that spoke to
me, but it was made quite obvious to me I should have said nothing.
Gooch the Accountant spoke to me and told me to keep to myself
anything I found on Nuanetsi Ranch. He hinted that my employment
status at Nuanetsi was now insecure. There is no doubt in my mind that it
was the intention of the Acting Manager not to report outbreak of FMD
on the Nuanetsi Ranch. I consider it was their intention to first allow
cattle trekking to West Nicholson and Beitbridge to arrive at their
destinations first before any report could be made. [1]

While African ranch workers were filliped to conceal the disease by their
superiors, Africans who owned cattle appeared to be deliberately hiding the
disease too. In a case heard in a FMD Court of Enquiry in 1934, Chirabi
Alias Magayisa, an African cattle owner admitted that in 1933 he had noticed
FMD amongst his cattle and admitted that he did not make a report to
veterinary authorities. [2] He noted that he neither planned to conceal the
disease nor was he under any instruction to hide it. Magaisa reasoned that he
was afraid his cattle would be slaughtered and burnt, something that would
deplete his herd. [3]

The cases outlined above prove that the main reason why farmers and
farm managers tried to hide the existence of the disease was to avoid their
cattle being killed. However, this was done at the expense of the spread of
the disease to other areas other than Nuanetsi such as Gwanda. It is quite
evident that there was a conflict between the government's veterinary
interests and the farmers' profit motive. Moreover, as indicated above, some

---

[1] NAZ S1185/11, Investigations in regard to the FMD outbreak at Nuanetsi Ranch, Report from
Detective JE Chubbock to the Criminal Investigation Chief Superintendent, 24 February 1935.
[2] NAZ S1185/11, Evidence given by Alias Magayisa on the outbreak of FMD at Nuanetsi Ranch, 22
February 1935.
[3] Ibid.

government officials connived with farmers to ensure that the disease was concealed. Such denial and concealment may have been beneficial to farmers in the short term, but it had a detrimental long-term impact on their ranching operations and the cattle industry in general.

An Unending Blame Game

The FMD outbreak was accompanied by blame shifting within Southern Rhodesia with different sectors accusing each other for the spread of the bovine disease. Revealing the deep-seated racial prejudice and tensions that pervaded Southern Rhodesian society during the period under review, a section of white farmers and authorities blamed Africans and their livestock for spreading the disease, in the process denying that their own behaviour and their livestock may have been contributing to the spread. These accusations, which were apparently driven by racial prejudice and malice, were detrimental to efforts to bring the disease under control.

The outbreaks of FMD occurred at a time when racial segregation, which had been the hallmark of colonial society, had received a considerable stimulus from the passage of the Land Apportionment Act in 1930. [①] In that spirit, the African human body was viewed by sections of the settler community and some state officials as pathological and thus a likely career of most infectious diseases. The same applied to their livestock. Indeed, some veterinary officials suspected that the FMD was spread by African cattle which had either been exchanged for grain with settlers or sold to the state. In a telegram between the Chief Veterinary Offices and the Department of Agriculture in 1934, the former attributed (without providing evidence) the rapid spread of the FMD in Matabeleland to 'reckless' Africans, alleging that infected African cattle which had strayed from the Gwanda Reserve had

---

① For a more detailed discussion on racial segregation and the factors that underlay it see R. Palmer, Land and racial domination in Rhodesia, Berkeley, University of California Press, 1977.

been responsible for the rapid spread of the disease in surrounding areas. [1] Similar allegations arose during the 1934 outbreak, with one veterinary surgeon making assertions that the FMD had been detected in the Matibi Reserve No. 1 in Chibi district in August. Thus, the surgeon added, cattle in the area were not to be allowed to mix with settler herds. On inspection, however, no trace of the disease was found among cattle from Matibi. [2] Embarrassed, the surgeon further claimed that if the Matibi Reserve was not responsible for the outbreak, then the disease must have originated from African cattle in the Belingwe Native Reserve. [3] Such claims did not explain why settler herds that had never been in contact with livestock from African reserves tested positive to the FMD. For instance, an entire dairy herd belonging to one Pasco was infected in 1936 yet it had been kept indoors except during early mornings and late evenings when it allowed onto a very small paddock. [4] It was argued, again without evidence, that Africans in the Victoria District had contracted FMD hence there was every reason to believe that the disease was transmitted to a clean herd during operation of milking by infected African. [5]

In some cases, white cattle owners believed that the disease was only found among African-owned cattle, and that African cattle owners were deliberately hiding the disease, thus leading to the spread of the disease. Checks were therefore put on the slaughter, sale or removal of cattle for *lobola* purposes in African areas from 1932 onwards. [6] It was also suspected that due to the cost of dipping the cattle, Africans would not bring all their

---

[1] NAZ 1223C/12, Veterinary Matters and the Foot and Mouth Disease, 1932 – 1950, letter from the Chief Veterinary Surgeon to the Department of Agriculture and Lands dated 01 June 1934.

[2] Ibid.

[3] Ibid.

[4] *The Rhodesian Herald*, 27 November 1931.

[5] NAZ 1223C/12, Letter from the Chief Veterinary Surgeon to the Department of Agriculture and Lands, 01 June 1934.

[6] NAZ 1692, Assistant Native Commissioner Beitbridge Correspondence 1926 – 1938, Letter from the Department of Agriculture to the Chief Native Commissioner, July 1933.

cattle to the dip tank. [1] The following diagram shows figures provided by the Chief Native Commissioner showing number of African cattle that was suspected not to have been brought to the dip tank for inspection in 1936.

AREA	NUMBER OF CATTLE NOT BROUGHT FOR EXAMINATION	TOTAL NUMBER OF AFRICAN CATTLE
Victoria	193	61,738
Bikita	1 470	36,703
Ndanga	574	60,855
Chikwanda	469	18,955
Chibi	2 587	70,512
Gutu	1 289	60,772

Graph extracted from the National Archives of Zimbabwe file, NAZ S482/ 103/ 39, East Coast Fever and Foot and Mouth Disease.

However, the figures given by the Chief Native Commissioner are questionable for two reasons. First, the number of cattle that they claimed existed in African reserves does not tally with realities on the ground. Given the conditions that existed in the reserves, that of infertile soil and poor rainfall it is doubtful that they had such a carrying capacity. Moreover, given policies and legislation deprived Africans of land and livestock, it is doubtful that Africans owned such huge herds during this time. [2] Moreover, judging from the given figures it is also highly unimaginable that Africans would bring such a large number and leave out a small number. From the foregoing, it is clear that there is no evidence to suggest that Africans were hiding the disease, nor was the FMD predominantly spread by their livestock. If anything available evidence suggests (as discussed earlier) that some white cattle owners were deliberately concealing FMD in order to safeguard their

---

[1] NAZ 1692, Assistant Native Commissioner Beitbridge Correspondence 1926 – 1938, Letter from the Department of Agriculture to the Chief Native Commissioner, July 1933.

[2] Such Legislation include the Land Apportionment Act, Native Land and Husbandry Act, among others.

ranching businesses in the short term. Thus, unfounded blame shifting only served to divert attention away from proper research into the source and the manner of the spread of the disease and work towards dealing with the real vectors in the transmission of the disease. Thus, concealment of the disease by farmers and the playing out of a racially motivated blame game may have contributed more to the spread of the disease, with devastating socio-economic consequences.

Socio-economic impact of the FMD

While the outbreaks of the FMD obviously had a profound economic impact on Southern Rhodesia's cattle industry, the overall consequences were broader: it affected Southern Rhodesia's relations with its regional neighbours leading to bans in cattle trade leading to viability challenges. Moreover, viability challenges within the cattle industry complicated the relations between the settler farming community and the colonial administration. The most immediate impact of the disease, however, was cattle losses. Ranchers across the country lost livestock during the 1930s and 1940s, with a corresponding loss in potential income. For example, the Veterinary Department reported that the first outbreak in 1931 had claimed no less than 70 000 cattle, with most of the casualties occurring in Matabeleland. [1] Similarly, the 1934 outbreak was reported to have killed nearly 60 000 cattle within a period of 10 months. [2] This left ranchers, some of whom had been concealing the disease, complaining that their "only source of livelihood" was under threat as they kept losing cattle to FMD. [3] The

---

[1] NAZ 1223C/12, Veterinary Matters and the Foot and Mouth Disease, 1932 – 1950, letter from the Chief Veterinary Surgeon to the Department of Agriculture and Lands dated 14 February 1933.

[2] NAZ 1223C/12, Veterinary Matters and the Foot and Mouth Disease, 1932 – 1950, letter from the Chief Veterinary Surgeon to the Department of Agriculture and Lands dated 08 August 1935.

[3] NAZ S1193/D4/6, FMD, General, Letter from Thornyby Polled Hereford to the Department of Agriculture, 10 March 1932.

situation was aggravated by the forced slaughter of infected livestock that occurred at the behest of the Veterinary Department. By 1934, the Veterinary Department had mounted enough evidence pointing to the existence of the disease. Large numbers of cattle were killed, quarantined and inoculated. At Nuanetsi ranch by June 1934, about five hundred cattle had been quarantined. [1] In 1934, 264 heads of cattle were destroyed at Retreat farm in Salisbury. [2] Although the state had pledged to compensate farmers whose cattle had been killed on account of FMD, the promise was seldom honoured in most cases, leading to agitation among farmers.

Local restrictions and farmers' responses

The FMD disease outbreaks also disrupted cattle movement and, in the process, disturbed marketing processes in the country. As part of measures to control the disease, cattle sales were prohibited in all districts except Melsetter and Umtali in 1931. The inevitable corollary of this was the country ran out of commercial beef as butchers struggled to obtain cattle. In 1934, one butcher in Victoria lamented that he had "not received any beast for 4 months" and, as a result, he was practically "out of business". [3] Typically blaming the government for instituting control measures, one white cattle owner complained that:

> ... most of the difficulties we are currently facing emanate from sales restrictions. They are not due to lack of market, but there is very little cattle trade at the present because of the difficulty in the way of

---

[1] NAZ S1185/11, Foot and Mouth Disease, Investigation made in 1935 in regard to outbreaks at Nuanetsi Ranch.

[2] NAZ S1217/7 Evidence taken by Committee to Enquire into Certain Aspect of the Recent Extension of FMD and African Coast fever in the Colony, Memo to the Department of Agriculture from the Veterinary Department, June 1934.

[3] NAZ S1193/D4/6, FMD, General, Letter from Saunders, (butcher) to the Department of Agriculture, 16 November 1931.

moving the cattle. Current restrictions have achieved nothing besides impoverishing ranchers. Let us not forget that farmers' poverty ultimately lead to the country's poverty. [1]

As state/farmer interests seemed at odds, the introduction of control measures provided fertile grounds for battles between farmers and the colonial state. For example, in a newspaper article of 1937, cattle owners in Bulawayo evinced a great deal of dissatisfaction over the methods used by the Veterinary Department in dealing with FMD. One farmer noted, "The whole business is now a farce yet the cost and expenses of cattle inspectors running around the country is a huge cost on the colony. "[2] In short, cattle owners were furious about how cattle movement restrictions were affecting their usual business. With cattle sales in the whole Matabeleland region suspended, many ranchers' incomes were adversely affected, and they blamed the state for that. [3] One white rancher expressed his anger thus:

> Does any another country in the world lock up thousands of square miles of the country for two years because of isolated cases of FMD... surely we have some Gilbertian regulations imposed on us by veterinary officers who are not trained to business and do not see the absurdity of their actions. The sooner we adopt safer methods in handling this FMD trouble the sooner will this country once again prosper as far as the cattle industry is concerned. It is time we cattle people say plainly what we feel and think about the rule of non-business people of the Veterinary Department. [4]

---

[1] NAZ S1193/D4/6, FMD, General, Letter from Thornyby Polled Hereford to the Department of Agriculture, 01 January 1932.

[2] *The Rhodesian Herald*, 28 September 1937.

[3] Ibid. A farmer called Hay wrote to the Rhodesian Herald complaining that the suspension of cattle marketing in Bulawayo had left ranchers in a precarious economic position.

[4] NAZ S1193/D4/23, Foot and Mouth Disease Cattle. Proceedings of a meeting of the Cattle Owners of Gwanda, 18 June 1936.

While settler farmers had a business as usual mentality, the government was more concerned about minimising the spread of the disease with the hope that the industry would recover in the long term. That Southern Rhodesia experienced one of the mildest form of FMD in the world during the period under review caused ranchers expressing dissatisfaction with what they considered to be "the most drastic veterinary regulations ever conceived in any country".[1] The Veterinary Department always maintained that the restrictions on cattle movement and sales were "a necessary evil which will cause hardship during these times" but will ensure that that the industry will recover in the foreseeable future.[2]

The whole situation was aggravated by the introduction of the Cattle Levy and Beef Export Act in 1931. Under the Act, every owner of cattle would pay a levy and the Minister of Agriculture imposed a levy on exported cattle.[3] According to Samasuwo, under the Cattle Levy Act No. 11 of 1931, any person who slaughtered more than five head of cattle per year for sale, barter or consumption would, regardless of the weight, quality or price of the beasts involved, pay two shillings and six pence per head to government.[4] While farmers were asked to pay the levy, a number of them were complaining that they could not raise the money because they were in areas locked up owing to foot-mouth restrictions and they were not able to raise the funds by selling their stock. Reacting to the levy, one Rademeyer complained of the low prices they were receiving for their cattle, arguing that the price he secured would not allow him to pay the levy.[5] By introducing a levy during a period of distress, ranchers felt that the colonial administration was not concerned about their welfare.

---

[1] NAZ S1194/SC42/181/6, FMD General, Letter from Cattle Owners Association of Gwanda to the Department of Agriculture dated 13 April 1932.

[2] NAZ 1223C/12, Veterinary Matters and the Foot and Mouth Disease, 1932 – 1950, letter from the Chief Veterinary Surgeon to the Department of Agriculture and Lands dated 10 June 1933.

[3] NAZ SC74/132, FMD and the Cattle Levy and Beef Export Act, 1931.

[4] See Samasuwo, 'There is Something About Cattle', p. 36.

[5] Ibid.

Another issue which exacerbated the conflict between cattle owners and the Veterinary Department was that restrictions were not uniformly imposed: ranchers in FMD free areas were granted permits to transport their livestock while those based in infected areas, for good cause, were not granted. ① It was the refusal by the Veterinary Authorities to grant other cattle owners' permits that became a subject of criticism accusing the authorities of differential treatment emanated. ② For example, in 1933, the Gwanda District Cattle Owners Association wrote to the Veterinary Surgeon complaining that they felt like their district was being victimised with regard to the movement of cattle. ③ Due to the severity of the disease, the district was under restrictions for about two years while other districts had been opened up for movement. ④ Moreover, what dismayed most farmers was the fact that although Southern Rhodesia goods were restricted, the restrictions could not be reciprocated. Owing to the Customs Agreement, imports from the Union were still entering the country free. Some farmers consequently pressed the government to move out of the Agreement until the disease condition had improved in the country. ⑤ The government did not heed this call, hence it fell out of favour with cattle owners.

Agitation between the state and cattle owners was not only on disease control measures but also on how government approached investigations and research on the disease. While the state believed that it was in the best interest to hire investigators from the Union, this was largely contested by cattle owners. For example, Gwanda Farmers Association complained that the visit of Du Toit pertaining to the FMD was contrary to the interests of the

---

① NAZ S1193/D4/6, FMD, General, Letter from Gwanda District Cattle Owner Association to the Chief Veterinary Surgeon Southern Rhodesia, 08 June 1933.

② Farmers in areas where permits were refused came to believe that preferential treatment was given to their farmers hence they began to condemn how the veterinary officials were handling the disease.

③ NAZ S1193/D4/6, FMD, General, Letter from Gwanda District Cattle Owners Association to the Chief Veterinary Surgeon Southern Rhodesia, 08 June 1933.

④ Ibid.

⑤ Ibid.

meat industry in the country. ① The Rhodesian Agricultural Union in 1931 also objected to the state's decision to base their future FMD policy on the recommendations of Du Toit. ② Farmers thus urged the government not to publish the Du Toit Report as they believed that it was damaging the negotiations with the Union in connection with the marketing of cattle. The government, however, insisted it was in the interest of the colony to allow skilled observers such as Du Toit to observe the disease. To the farmers, having an investigator from the same country that had imposed trade restrictions on them was unacceptable. However, to the government it was a gesture as well as an assurance to the Union that Southern Rhodesia had nothing to hide and was making every effort to control the disease. This became a major bone of contention between the two parties. As shown in the next section, Du toit's report significantly contributed to South Africa's introduction of trade restrictions, hence farmers felt that the embargo was self-invited.

The Department of Agriculture and Lands, on the other hand, would insist that honesty was key in handling the disease, and that restrictions on export were not imposed by the government but by neighbouring countries. ③ This notwithstanding, the majority of ranchers believed that the government had exposed them and itself through its decisions. While the state had a long-term goal of eradicating the disease as well as preventing its spread in order to have the trade embargo lifted, the farmers had a short term goal of taking advantage of the then favourable market and getting their products onto the market.

---

① NAZ S1193/D4/6, FMD, General, Letter from Gwanda Farmers Association to the Department of Agriculture Southern Rhodesia, 13 January 1932.
② NAZ S1193/D4/5, FMD, General, Letter from the Rhodesian Agricultural Union to the Agricultural Department dated 10 December 1931.
③ NAZ S1194/SC42/181/6, FMD, General, Letter from the Department of Agriculture to the Rhodesian Agricultural Union, dated 18 April 1932.

Foot and Mouth Disease, Southern
Rhodesia and the regional dimension

Perhaps the most far reaching implication of the FMD was that Southern
Rhodesia lost its traditional cattle trade partners in the region and beyond.
The first country to place an embargo on Southern Rhodesia was the Union of
South Africa in 1931. Armed with every information pertaining to the
position and control of the disease in Southern Rhodesia, The Union imposed
an embargo on Southern Rhodesian cattle in 1931. The South African
Department of Agriculture argued that the spread of FMD into the Union
would ruin the farming community, particularly in the Transvaal where cattle
formed the large proportion of the farming activities. [1]

Restriction on Southern Rhodesia trade products emanated from the
report of Du Toit, who in 1934 argued that "the danger is a common one in
Southern Africa... it may break into Northern Rhodesia, Natal or
Transvaal. "[2] It might be such statements that alarmed the neighboring
countries. He added that he could "not recommend that there is no risk in the
importation of animals and animal products from Southern Rhodesia into
Northern Rhodesia and South Africa". [3] As Southern Rhodesia had been
divided into prohibited areas and semi-prohibited areas by the Veterinary
Department in 1932 for local cattle movement, South Africa simply refused
to accept Southern Rhodesian cattle from prohibited areas, mostly in the
southern areas. The introduction of cattle on the hoof to the Johannesburg
Quarantine Market from Southern Rhodesia other than prohibited areas was,
however, allowed on the basis that they were subjected to strict quarantine

---

[1] NAZ S1180/2/33(13), Foot and Mouth Disease: Letter from the Department of Agriculture, South
Africa to the Department of Agriculture, Southern Rhodesia, 12 April 1931.

[2] NAZS1193/D4/13, Letters of Du Toit, Foot and Mouth Disease in General, Recommendations on the
Outbreak of FMD in Southern Rhodesia 1932.

[3] NAZS1193/D4/13, Letters of Du Toit, Foot and Mouth Disease, in General, 1934.

for three weeks. ① Southern Rhodesia cattle would be accepted if they were accompanied by a veterinary certification certifying that the cattle had not been derived from a prohibited area. Thus, by providing a map of prohibited and semi-prohibited areas to the Union, Southern Rhodesia further undermined her bargaining position as the Union had every detail of affected areas in Southern Rhodesia.

Although restrictions were relaxed in 1933 due to the subsiding of the outbreak, this was short-lived. This because of the reoccurrence of the disease in some parts of the country in 1934. For example, in January, 1938, some restrictions were relaxed but in March of the same year there were reports that the disease had been confirmed in the Victoria and Bulawayo District. ② Two animals with FMD were found at the Cold Storage Abattoirs. This resulted in the removal of the relaxations and meat exports to the Union were again suspended. ③ In some cases, Southern Rhodesia meat was confiscated. ④ In 1946, the Union Castle refused to accept the meat for the Armdale Castle from Southern Rhodesia and the meat was taken to the storage at the port. ⑤

Trade restrictions were also imposed by other countries in the region. As South Africa banned the importation of goods from Bechuanaland due to its proximity to Southern Rhodesia, the latter was left with no option but to impose restrictions on Southern Rhodesia to secure its market in South Africa. ⑥ Nyasaland soon followed suit. In a letter to the Governor of Southern Rhodesia in 1931, the Governor of Nyasaland said that on the account of FMD, he was prohibiting importation into Nyasaland of all

---

① NAZ S1215/1812/2, FMD Correspondence with Agriculture Department Pretoria 1936 – 1937.
② NAZ S1801, Foot and Mouth Disease, Disease, High Commissioner for Southern Rhodesia Crown House.
③ NAZ S1801, Foot and Mouth Disease, Letter from the High Commissioner of Southern Rhodesia Crown House to the Department of Agriculture, January 1938.
④ Ibid.
⑤ NAZ S1801, Foot and Mouth Disease, High Commissioner for Southern Rhodesia Crown House.
⑥ Ibid.

animals' carcasses, hides and skins, horns, hoof, wool among others. ① Northern Rhodesia feared that there was a possibility of FMD infection being carried to Northern Rhodesia by merchandise in cattle trucks, hence in 1931, they called for disinfection of trucks used for the conveyance of cattle. ② In terms of transportation of cattle from affected areas, the governments of Belgian Congo and Northern Rhodesia agreed in 1931 that trucks transporting cattle be disinfected and should carry certificates of disinfection. ③ The trucks were also to carry stated quantity of agreed contents and had to be disinfected under European supervision. ④

In 1931, a conference was held to discuss the nature of the disease in Southern Rhodesia. At the conference on FMD held at Livingston in July, 1931, it was agreed that frozen meat and butter from Southern Rhodesia be transported only if the trucks convoying these products were disinfected after loading the products. ⑤ Another conference was in December, 1933 in Salisbury with representatives from Bechuanaland, Belgian Congo and Northern Rhodesia with a view to review the terms of the embargo. However, countries present refused to relax their restrictions even in times when the disease appeared to have receded. There was fear that the virus might still be present in the bone marrow and meat tissues of some of these products. For example, the Government of Northern Rhodesia informed Southern Rhodesia in 1934 that, in so far as importation into Northern Rhodesia was concerned, the embargoes were not going to be modified

---

① NAZ S1193/D4/22, Foot and Mouth Disease, Cleansing of Cattle Trucks, Letter from the Governor of Nyasaland to the Governor of Southern Rhodesia, dated 26 June 931.

② Ibid.

③ NAZ S1193/D4/22, Foot and Mouth Disease, Memo on Cleansing of Cattle Trucks from Northern Rhodesia Veterinary Department to the Veterinary Department of Southern Rhodesia, December 1931.

④ Ibid.

⑤ This was a conference held in Southern Rhodesia to discuss the possible measure to deal with the disease in Southern Rhodesia. The conference was attended by representatives from Botswana, Malawi, and Portuguese East Africa who also feared that the disease would be spread to their respective countries.

despite signs that the outbreak was subsiding. [①] The position taken by Northern Rhodesia was based on the research conducted in South Africa that concluded that the virus of FMD remained active in the urine of the animal for eight months after they had recovered. [②] The justification they gave was that the Africans employed in the mines had a strong objection to frozen meat, they stated that live cattle was essential for both breeding purpose and slaughter hence their government was not prepared to lift its embargo. [③] Bechuanaland thus guaranteed the supply of live cattle into Congo and this meant that Southern Rhodesia had lost its market in the Congo.

Feeling the adverse financial effects of the embargoes, farmers' organisations met at district and ranch levels to discuss their situation. In these meeting cattle owners were pleading with the government to approach and request the government of Northern Rhodesia and Portuguese East Africa to lift the embargo on agricultural and farm produce, as the area had now been declared free from FMD. [④] Such petitions, which were largely unsuccessful, bear testimony to the deleterious impact of the disease on their businesses. Yet, as demonstrated earlier, their lackadaisical and often deceitful approach to the outbreaks contributed to the escalation of the crisis, leading to international trade partners' withdrawal. Following the trade embargo on Southern Rhodesia, there is no doubt that farmers were affected in terms of market availability, their price bargaining power as well as in their breeding schemes. [⑤] This affected farmers' income and they, in turn, blamed the government for their misfortune. For an already ailing industry

---

① NAZ S1193/D4/15, Paper on the Conference on Foot and Mouth Disease, and the Visit of Montgomery, Northern Rhodesia Position on Trade with Southern Rhodesia, 1934.

② This was research done in South Africa in 1932, to test the possibility of FMD being spread by cattle blood, urine, bones among other things.

③ NAZ S1193/D4/15, Paper on the Conference on Foot and Mouth Disease, and the Visit of Montgomery.

④ Ibid.

⑤ The fact that the virus that was causing the disease in Southern Rhodesia was identified with the virus in Britain led to the placement of restrictions and embargoes on Southern Rhodesia products. The first country to place an embargo on Southern Rhodesia was South Africa in 1931. Countries like Bechuanaland, Northern Rhodesia and Nyasaland followed suit.

from undercapitalization, poor beef quality and marketing problems of the 1930s, FMD was, indeed, an undesirable burden that would only aggravate the state of affairs in the industry.

Conclusion

This article has traced the outbreak of FMD in Southern Rhodesia during the 1930s, tracing the origins and occurrence of the disease in Southern Rhodesia. It has shown that veterinary officials were never able to fully account for the exact source of the disease as it entered the country, nor were they able to explain the manner of its spread in Matabeleland. Moreover, we have discussed initial responses of the farming community and the state, demonstrating that the two entities were driven by different and diametrically opposing interests. While the colonial government, by imposing strict restrictions on cattle movements and sales, sought to eliminate the disease farmers were eager to maintain their business operations. The corollary of this was that farmers often denied the existence of the disease among their stock, and some went as far as concealing clear cases of FMD at their premises. We have argued that that this state of affairs only served drive the spread of the disease, with devastating impact on the farmers themselves and the cattle industry generally. This study has also demonstrated that, as the spread of the disease became more evident, cattle owners began to blame each other along racial lines, with especially settler farmers blaming African stock owners and their livestock for the spread of the FMD. This, we postulate, was done in spite of the fact there was no evidence to prove that one race was responsible for the spread of the disease. Thus, we argue that racially inspired blame shifting within the farming community and also on the part of some state officials worked to prevent the development of effective disease control measures. A historical appreciation of the disease's occurrence and the efficacy of attempts to combat it is essential if such diseases are to be controlled effectively. Agriculture is not only the country's most important economic activity but also contributes to both personal and national income. Hence if not correctly handled an outbreak of a cattle disease can be a source of conflict between farmers and the Government, different Government Departments and inevitably between countries that share border boundaries as disease know no boundaries.

This article has also delineated the impact of the FMD on the cattle industry of Southern Rhodesia. It has shown that, largely because of flawed responses to the outbreaks, the disease spread quite rapidly and adversely the cattle industry. Cattle losses (due both to slaughter and death as a result of the disease) and internal restrictions on the movement and sales of cattle adversely affected the profitability of farming and retail operations. We have also argued that the introduction of trade restrictions by traditional cattle trading partners in the region aggravated the situation of the cattle industry and also potentially complicated relations between Southern Rhodesia and its neighbours. Ultimately, both local and regional restrictions contributed to the souring of relations that emerged between settler farmers and the colonial government during the period under review. Thus, this article has argued that FMD was more than just a veterinary issue, but is a useful window through which larger Southern Rhodesian society and the contradictions that pervaded it may be explored.

Norton Industrial town and the Development of Road Infrastructure in Southern Rhodesia, 1923 to 1965

Shalot Nyaradzo Nhete and Bernard Kusena

Abstract

This study examines the intersection of ambitious road infrastructures and the broader scheme of decentralisation of manufacturing in Southern Rhodesia using the case of Norton, an industrial area in the fringes of Salisbury. Historically, the construction of new road-link projects induced opportunities not only through attracting transport-intensive establishments, but also reorganising production within existing businesses. The construction of urban roads in the Norton suburban area during the early 1920s to the mid-1960s permitted various types of manufacturing to decentralise. Beginning as an administrative and commercial hub in a rich agricultural area, Norton rapidly developed into a strategic industrial centre, thanks to its proximity to water and power supplies. Yet, for researchers who grapple to account for change over time, these spatial dynamics often mask important differences across sectors of the economy. For instance, the fact that land in periphery areas was cheaper also meant a huge reduction in employment costs and an increase in labour productivity, factors which were key to the wider colonial project of cost minimisation and profit maximisation. In addition, this suburbanisation of population provided the motive force for geographical dispersion of retailing, prompting small municipalities on the outskirts of cities to encourage the establishment of shopping centres within *their jurisdictions to attract shoppers from larger towns, thereby, increasing tax revenues. Thus, the study deploys archival evidence and empirical models consistent with these historical developments to generate nuanced understandings of the political economy of capital projects during this period.*

Keywords: Urban Infrastructure, Decentralisation, Manufacturing, Norton, Suburbanisation,

Introduction

While the link between efficient road networks and economic development is quite general and apparent, this study shifts the discourse on the Southern Rhodesian road expansion programme from being predominantly a question of controlling the fledgling agricultural market economy following the failure of the "Second Rand". [1] Palmer reports that, by the 1920s, it was increasingly evident that the gold deposits in the colony did not match the speculated quantities to sustain a mining economy. [2] The article re-situates and reframes this discussion in terms of the compelling need to obviate shrinking state revenues through broadening the tax base via spatial dispersion of retail and other lucrative investments. The newfound capabilities for moving people and goods proved pivotal for the development of the retail economy. As a starting point, the discussion focuses on the development of urban roads in Southern Rhodesia, using the case study of Norton, a town which sprang to importance due to the influence of farming.

Situated off Bulawayo road on the western side of Salisbury (now

---

[1] A major reason for settler occupation was to extract vast mineral resources, especially gold since it was rumoured that the lands beyond the Limpopo were endowed with rich deposits. However, this turned out to be untrue and the Pioneer Column had no alternative but to venture into agriculture.

[2] R. Palmer, "The Agricultural History of Rhodesia," In: R. Palmer and N. Parsons (eds.), *The Roots of Rural Poverty in Central and Southern Africa*, California: University of California Press, 1977.

Harare), Norton grew into a town with as phenomenally rapid and unique network of roads as sufficient to spur on our interest to interrogate. We present an analysis of the whole question of urban road construction and how it impacted the colonial economy. The study acknowledges the overarching role of urban road transportation in enhanced service delivery through improved mobility of goods and people. By facilitating the efficient movement of raw materials and labour, Norton's road transport system supported the colony's overall economic trajectory, an observation confirmed in separate studies by Fishlow and Taylor who argue that similar door-to-door linkages between producers and markets facilitated America's rapid economic growth. [1] These scholars set forth the argument that the economic changes of the first half of the nineteenth century were tied to the development of internal transport, further illustrating he transformational consequences of those changes.

The advent of colonialism in Southern Rhodesia led to the economic development of the country as a British colony. When the British South Africa Company (BSAC) occupied the country in 1890, it concentrated on establishing a railway network that would link Southern Rhodesia with the major ports in South Africa and Mozambique because of the landlocked nature of the colony. A good railway network was established thereafter, but there remained the challenge of accessing road networks from the different centres of production, especially mines and farms. Therefore, a road network had to be established to cover this gap. Mlambo notes that when the Pioneer Column arrived in the country, there were no clear roads and the ones they established were just nothing more than 'dirty tracks' as they were made by the trails of their wagons[2]. For its part, the BSAC did very little to establish good roads throughout its reign up to 1923 when the Responsible

---

[1] A. Fishlow, *American Railroads and the Transformation of the Ante-Bellum Economy*, Cambridge: Harvard University Press, 1965; G. R. Taylor, "The Transportation Revolution," *The Economic History of the United States*, *1815 - 1860*, Vol. 48, No. 4,1962.

[2] A. S. Mlambo, "From Dirty Tracks to Modern Highways: Towards a History of Roads Transportation in Colonial Zimbabwe, 1890 to World War Two" *Zambezia*, *1994*, XX1, II, p. 148.

Government took over. The company, however, managed to put in place such laws as the 1916 Outspan and Road Ordinances, the Width of Steel Wheel Ordinance, Vehicle Tax Ordinance and Road Councils Ordinance in 1921. [1]

The increased operation of white settlers at different economic centres gradually led to the development of urban centres. These developments were not peculiar to Southern Rhodesia. Trends in American history have shown a development of agrarian communities around urban centres because of a rise in population and concentration of people in an area. [2] In Europe, as in the USA, the development of urban transport network contributed greatly to the advancement of economies an example being the complementary role played by the transport revolution in the total process of Britain's industrialisation drive. [3] This paper draws similarities and demonstrates the importance of transport networks in penetrating the African interior and the subsequent creation of urban centres. As Rodney puts it, roads provided a unique service that was very instrumental in the exploitation of African resources during the colonial period. [4]

Literature on Southern Rhodesia's road construction and maintenance programme is growing, most of which establishes the connection between road infrastructure and improved mobility. [5] This body of literature feeds into international discourses on the contribution of roads to economic

---

[1] A. S. Mlambo, "From Dirty Tracks to Modern Highways: Towards a History of Roads Transportation in Colonial Zimbabwe, 1890 to World War Two" *Zambezia*, *1994*, XX1, II, p. 148.

[2] J. S. Gordon, *An Empire of Wealth: The Epic History of American Economic Power*, New York, Happer Perennial, 2005, p. 4.

[3] W. S. Churchill, *A History of the English Speaking Peoples; The Age of Revolution*, London, Cassell, 1957, p. 155.

[4] W. Rodney, *How Europe Underdeveloped Africa*, London: Bogle-L'Ouverture Publications, 1972.

[5] Mlambo, "From Dirty Tracks to Morden Highways; S. Mushunje, "The Development of Road Transport in Southern Rhodesia, 1890 – 1940", (BA Hons. Dissertation, Department of History, University of Zimbabwe), 1986; B. Kusena, "The Development of Road and Road Transport Network in Southern Rhodesia, 1945 – 1965", (BA Hons. Dissertation, Department of Economic History, University of Zimbabwe), 2015.

prosperity. For instance, it speaks to what Verbugh has observed, which is to say that "transport is the lifeblood of any form of activity and, therefore, of economic activities, whether they take place on a remote farm or in a big mining or industrial concern. "[1] This further echoes Berg's conclusion that studying transport networks is indispensable in understanding the general economic development of any country. [2] Some studies on Southern Rhodesia have centred on the colonial period, while others have focused on the post-colonial dynamics. [3] For instance, while Mlambo has published a ground-breaking analysis of the evolution of roads from "dirty tracks" to all-weather highways[4], Mushunje, Kusena and Muchenu have invariably traced the developments in road design and construction all the way up to the end of colonial rule. For instance, Muchenu has examined the impetus of the expanded Rhodesian road scheme in order to illustrate its impact on the performance of the country's tourism sector. Kusena has conceptualised the post-Second World War road programme around issues of post-war reconstruction, given how road and bridge maintenance and construction had stagnated when funds and materials had been directed to support the war effort. [5] His study has brought out the debates that the Roads and Rail Transport Commission was seized with and how the resolutions were implemented by the Road Councils. [6] Kusena has also highlighted some of the incidental benefits of road construction accruing to Africans such as the ease of mobility, improved access to competitive markets and creation of menial jobs. [7]

[1] C. Verbugh, *Road Transport of Goods in South Africa*, Stellenbosch, University of Stellenbosch, 1958, p. 13.

[2] C. N. Berg, U. Deichmann, Y. Liu and H. Selod, "Transport policies and development," *Journal of Development studies*, Vol 53, issue 4, 2017.

[3] R. Muchenu, "The Development and Maintenance of Roads in Rhodesia 1965 to 1979", B A (Hons) Dissertation, University of Zimbabwe, 2017.

[4] Mlambo. , "From Dirty Tracks to Morden Highways . . . "

[5] B. Kusena, "The Development or Road and Road Transport Network in Southern Rhodesia 1923 – 1965", p. 9.

[6] NAZ S3615/5/2/25/2/2, Norton Road Council, Minutes.

[7] *Ibid*.

The Establishment of an Industrial Centre

Since 1890, farm settlement in Norton saw the establishment of progressive agricultural endeavours. Farms in Norton specialised in tobacco and maize whilst a few white settlers established small mines like Beatrice mine. The Norton farming community was in an area that was inaccessible. There were no proper roads or other channels of communication to link farmers to general developments in the country. There was need for a transport network to link them with the market for their agricultural produce. The establishment of important infrastructure as roads was not a new phenomenon to the British. Prior to the colonisation of Africa, they had participated in the exploitation of the American colonies where they managed to establish a viable transport system to support the mercantile system from the 16th Century. [1]

Developments in road transport networks between 1890 and 1923 were largely determined by the need to link different producers to the market. In this case, the available route was the railway network which could be reached through the Norton siding. The provision of a shade at the railway station in 1915 was important as it boosted farmer and miner confidence in relying on the railway as a mode of transport. As a result, all other road routes created thereafter led to Norton railway siding. What now remained was for each landowner to make efforts to continue opening up their farms to the market by providing necessary conditions for construction of branch roads. Evidence of settler adherence to the payment of Road Taxes and Vehicle Tax during this period helps explain the settler role in complementing efforts put by the BSAC government through such legislation to establish a rudimentary transport network in the country capable of satisfying the cost minimisation and profit maximisation principle. The Company government established the

[1] NAZ S3615/5/2/25/2/2, Norton Road Council, Minutes.

Department of Mines and Public Works as the specialised division to manage roads issues within the colony in 1895. [1] Norton siding acted as the port of call for all developmental activities in the area as it was considered central to farmers. It was from this railway station that all commercial, industrial and urban development that later followed in Norton were born. Before this, farmers in Norton sold their produce through Salisbury and Hartley (now Chegutu) depots, an expensive move considering high transport costs.

Through the efforts of the Road Board, farms like Kent, Rocklands, Knock Maroon, Ganga and Austria were given access to the siding. The BSAC cooperated with the farmers in road development by placing the burden of branch roads upon the farmers. As a result it became mandatory that every land owning settler took part in road construction activities. Progress in road construction was guided by proceedings between the Secretary of Mines and the Norton District Farmers and Stock Owners Association (NDFSOA). Farmers in need of a branch road for easy access to and from their farm applied to the Road Board of the district to discuss their plea. This clause was a reinforcement of the 1896 Road Transport Ordinance clause that every settler was obliged to "open up" his farm or mine for easy access and communication throughout the colony. [2] The Norton-Dorton strip road was the first achievement of the combined efforts of the community. This success was crucial as it formed the basis of all other developments resulting from the joint efforts of the NDFSOA and Roads Department.

Change and Continuity? Road Development, 1923 – 1965

The Responsible Government took over administration of the Road Department in 1923. Therefore, the several Ordinances put in place by the BSAC continued to be implemented in Southern Rhodesia. No major changes

---

[1] NAZ S3615/5/2/25/2/2, Norton Road Council, Minutes.
[2] Ibid.

were noticed in the laws to do with road construction and the transport networks of Norton until 1929 when Rhodesia was directly affected by the Great Depression. This policy stagnation could have been a result of the nature of support that the Responsible Government partly relied on international capitalists in terms of funding. This is supported by Arrighi who noted that "economic dependence on foreign capital forced the settler government to adopt middle of the road policies, compromising between the interests of the national bourgeoisie and white workers on the one hand, and of international capitalism on the other."[1]

This sort of financial dependence created a void in the funding of roads in Peri-urban areas as Government concentrated more on the development of trunk roads in order to fully manoeuvre and explore the interior of the colony.[2] For example, the Norton Road Council could not collect enough taxes in 1929 to fund the maintenance and construction of the intended roads. Norton residents were therefore encouraged to do temporary repair work on the roads as they awaited the Road Council to come up with strategies to do permanent road work.[3] The Great Depression then became a major determinant of the infrastructural development not only in Norton but in Rhodesia as a whole. Therefore, this explains the idea brought forward by Newbury that economic policies adopted in Britain had a direct impact on the daily proceedings of the British overseas empire.[4] The development of roads in Southern Rhodesia was determined by the British response to the post First World War depression of the 1920s and the Great Depression of 1929.

The Great Depression had a direct negative impact on the Rhodesian farmers. The falling prices had a bearing on the way farmers paid their taxes. Some members of the Norton-Lydiate Road Council signed a petition

---

① G. Arrighi, *The Political Economy of Rhodesia*, The Hague: Mouton, 1969,6.

② *Ibid*.

③ *The Rhodesian Herald*, August 9 1929.

④ D. M. Newbery, "Road Taxes, Road User Charges and Earmarking", *Fiscal Studies*, 1999. Vol. 20, No 2, p. 15.

requesting a breakaway from the council. [1] Most of the farmers were in the area close to Lydiate so they had common cause for their break away from the Norton-Lydiate Road Council. It was raised in the petition that the 1929 depression affected farming so much that they could not pay the Road tax amid other levies like the Motor Tax which increased in 1929 in response to the Great Depression. In 1919, some farmers at Johannesburg and Clifford farms had suggested that the Council cut its costs by reducing the salaries of the road workers as a way of containing the post war effects that were being felt in the colony but nothing was done. They had suggested a reduction from £25 to £20 pounds but this was not accepted. [2] Their withdrawal was a result of their full support of the road construction and maintenance programmes that they did not want to handicap the Norton-Lydiate Road Council by non-payment of rates and taxes. During the Second World War, the manufacturing industry boosted.

In Norton, this drive towards industrialisation saw the growth of industries related to agriculture. Rhodesian Seeds thrived because it supplied farmers around Norton with seeds. Harold Poole specialised in production of agricultural mechanised tools. [3] However, these industries had a ready local market so there was stagnation in road construction during the Second World War. Local farmers used the already-established road networks for their services in and around Norton. A major change implemented by the state was the creation of an urban centre in a predominantly farming community. Norton was the first experiment in the whole of the British Colonial Empire to be "planned from the first brick and road. "[4] There were deliberate plans to create and develop a town centre in Norton. The establishment of an

---

① Norton District Council: Petition of breakaway signed by fourteen members of the road council, 324/14/, NAZ.
② NAZ GEN/96 Peri-urban roads.
③ Ibid.
④ NAZ S481/627, Norton General. Planned because Austria farm was bought with the intention to develop a township.

expanded industrial centre in Norton was an activity that was planned because it was given preference by the Government. The situation in Norton was different from the rise of other urban centres the world over. Other centres emanated from the concentration of people in an area because of a wide range of political, economic, social or religious factors. [1] For example, Kimberly in South Africa rose to an urban centre around the 1860s because of gold and diamond mining activities in the area. [2] In America, Texas was a result of cattle ranching. [3] A shift in planning policies was evident in 1947 when Government endorsed the creation of an industrial township in Norton to address the various demographic challenges the colony was facing.

A number of factors can explain the government decision to create an industrial centre in Norton. Following the negative impact of the Second World War on Southern Rhodesia, the Rhodesian government initiated a move to decentralise industrialisation in the colony as a means of checking on the free movement of Africans. [4] The war had disrupted such as Bulawayo, Salisbury and Umtali (now Mutare) so industrial workers needed attention as they had resulted in an uncontrolled influx of Africans in a serious rural-urban drift that emanated from the demand for labour in these towns. In 1948, through a parliamentary discussion, it was agreed that Norton be the focus for development because of its proximity to the capital Salisbury. [5] This special arrangement made for Norton was used to examine the provision of roads in the town. Being in the midst of a farming community, developments in Norton were complimented by the construction of the dam on the Hunyani River between 1941 and 1952.

Proximity to Hunyani dam increased human concentration in the area. In a way the creation of Norton epitomised the colony's new town planning

---

[1] B. Freund, *African cities*, Cambridge University Press, Cape Town, 2007, p. 60.

[2] Ibid.

[3] Gordon, *An Epic of Wealth: The Epic of American Economic Power*, p. 8.

[4] NAZ S3615/25/5/2/2/1, Norton Development Panel Correspondences.

[5] Ibid.

policy. ① The new policy was meant to regulate the inflow of Africans into urban areas by putting control measures on the African residential areas in established towns like Salisbury and Bulawayo. ② On paper, planning provided room to come up with measures to limit African influx to Salisbury because Norton was just 40km away. This was supported by a majority of the settlers as evidenced by one press headline "Village May Be Great Industrial Centre; Plan for Norton. "③ The headline shows that there was high anticipation for the new industrial town. A common rural community around Norton was bound to change into a great production centre. In order to boost investor confidence in the town, abnormal methods were to be used to achieve the aim. The Norton Development Panel was established in August 1948 to focus on the creation and development of Norton as a new industrial centre. It comprised of members from various government departments and other experts whose contributions were aimed at ultimately improve the revenue base of through retail activities in the town.

The key consideration towards opening an industrial hub to the north was the construction of an all-weather road with a high level bridge over the railway facility at Hunyani River. The bridge was to lead to an easy servicing of the area. In 1941, the construction of the Hunyani dam was meant to develop into a power generation project for Salisbury. Also, a reliable source of water through the dam was to ensure sustainable industrial activities in the proposed town. However, the coming of the Federation in 1952 diverted attention to Kariba which became a better choice because of shared expenses between Southern Rhodesia and Northern Rhodesia. ④ The construction of Kariba had a direct impact on road network development in Norton. By shifting power generation to Kariba, other industries such as Rhodesian Motors no longer

---

① NAZ S3615/5/25/2/2, Norton Development Panel 1952 – 1958.
② NAZ S3615/5/25/4/, Norton Development Panel 1948 – 1952. Extract from the New Town Planning Policy.
③ *The Rhodesia Herald*, 20 June 1953.
④ NAZ S3615/5/25/4/1, Norton Development Panel 1948 – 1952.

opted for Norton because they relied more on electricity so Salisbury remained a convenient place for them. Therefore, the reduced number of prospective investors in Norton also lessened the chances of road funding in Norton. Even faced with this dilemma, the NDP continued with its mandate.

Norton plan included all necessary facilities such as schools, a hospital, a cinema, a reliable transport network, a sewer system, residential area and an industrial area among others. This was a major step to correct the ever centralisation of population and industry in major towns. According to the plan, the target population was set at 8 500 Europeans and 25 000 Africans. [1] The population limit was meant to avoid the same problems faced in Salisbury and other towns where the settlers were facing problems in regulating African movement. In order to allow the smooth development of the new proposed town, attempts were made to provide public transport as an economic proposition. Norton achieved its intended since manufacturing and retailing developments were complimented by a viable transport network. Also, most amenities in the town were supposed to be accessible by ordinary cycling so as to ease traffic congestion that was posing problems in Salisbury [2]

After 1945, there were serious efforts to upgrade Rhodesian infrastructure as a possible investment destination for international investors. Two main reasons were accountable for this change as stated by Chandler the minister of mines in his parliamentary address in 1950. [3] According to Chandler, there was a feeling in the United Kingdom that the recession there would be greater than elsewhere in the commonwealth outside Europe. Looking for investment elsewhere was the common way of investing in the late 1940s. Another reason was the political situation in the political union of South Africa. [4] Investors were not ready to invest in South Africa because of

---

[1] NAZ S3615/5/25/4/1, Norton Development Panel 1948 – 1952.

[2] Ibid.

[3] NAZ S3615/5/25/4/2/2, Norton Development Panel.

[4] Ibid.

Apartheid system which was under scrutiny the world over. [1] Therefore, the most favourable and nearest destination was Southern Rhodesia. Investors therefore adopted a look to the north policy in Southern Rhodesia since Southern Rhodesia had the most improved infrastructure if compared to Zambia and Malawi. To address this situation, there was need for the Rhodesian government to create an enabling environment to harness investor confidence. This was another reason for the creation of Norton as a new industrial centre.

The Rhodesian government bought Austria farm in 1948 to create room for the development of an industrial centre. [2] Although there were prior efforts towards infrastructural developments in farms surrounding Norton, the acquisition of Austria farm in 1948 by the state was a turning point towards industrialisation and commerce in the area. The Second World War presented opportunities for an industrial boost in Southern Rhodesia. The war cut import supply thereby presenting an opportunity for the growth of the manufacturing sector in Rhodesia. Industrialisation attracted labour from the African areas leading to population concentration in Salisbury and Bulawayo. The idea of creating an industrial centre at Norton was based on government effort to control African population in urban areas. [3] A panel was set up in 1948 with the aim of upgrading, managing and developing Norton as a "self-contained industrial township. "[4] One of the well spelt duties of the Norton Development Panel (NDP) was to develop a road system which was going to make the town easily accessible for the benefit of Southern Rhodesia at large. [5]

Another reason for the creation of Norton was to enable government to free the major roads in Salisbury that were facing frequent traffic congestion. As stated in 1949 by Mr Kerr, Director of Public Affairs, a good road

---

[1] NAZ S3615/5/25/4/2/2, Norton Development Panel.

[2] NAZ S3615/5/25/4/2, Norton Development Panel 1954 – 1958. Note to the NDP Stating Government Position on the Establishment of Norton.

[3] NAZ S3613/5/25/4/1, Norton Development Panel 1948 – 1953 General; Correspondence Rework.

[4] *Ibid.*

[5] NAZ S3613/5/25/4/2, Norton Development Panel 1948 – 1953; Minutes.

network in Norton was going to ease the new demand for every European family to own a car. ① Mr Kerr argued that the new town was going to provide standard tarmac roads that were to help continue the use of bicycles and ease congestion on the roads thereby leading to a longer life for the new roads. The frequent use of roads in urban areas resulted in their rapid deterioration. To ensure a longer life the settlers decided to use a compact town to limit traffic flow in the colony. A compact town would provide all necessary services at a distance comfortably travelled by bicycles or by foot. By adopting a compact town at Norton the responsible government was trying to control traffic flow and conserve roads in the colony.

The effect of developing this town was to divert some of the strains being felt by larger local authorities in coping with extraordinarily rapid growth of the colony. ② Suburbanisation would give them space to consolidate their position. The progressive decrease of overall peasant productivity caused by war effects increasingly worsened this obstacle to economic growth. Goods previously imported became practically unavailable, thus creating a demand for local industries. ③ This economic situation, together with the need for profit making and the enforcement of the Land Husbandry Act of 1951 forced the lawmakers to consider other methods of decentralising towns for easier management. Thus, the Responsible Government continued with the administration of the Roads Department while a new board was set up to try and focus on the development of a new industrial center. For the first time, southern Rhodesia created a town on paper.

Funding and Labour Dynamics in the Development of Norton

The development of roads is guided by a number of variables among

---

① NAZ S3615/5/25/2/3, Norton Development Panel. Mr Kerr was director of Public Affairs from 1946-1960.
② NAZ GEN/96, Roads in Norton.
③ Arrighi, *The Political Economy of Rhodesia*, p. 10.

them are funding and labour supply. These two greatly determine the purposes of the road and who will benefit from the road itself. Under Company rule, the Department of Roads was financed by the government but the farmers themselves had to make contributions towards the construction of roads in their areas as guided by the 1896 Road and Transportation Act. [1] The Act provided that all settlers were to take part in the creation and maintenance of roads in the areas they occupied. With the planned development of Norton, the government pledged to fund the infrastructural developments in the township. However, local and international events directly affected government expenditure resulting in a change of funding strategies for the development of Norton. These funding dynamics also had a bearing on the provision of labour in road construction for both rural and urban areas.

The introduction of Road Tax played a pivotal role in the establishment of a road network in Norton. However, there were challenges to do with the collection of Road Tax. As early as 1895, most farmers were not well established that they could not pay the expected amounts. For example, in the 1914 to 1915 budget a total of £2 000 was set aside in then national budget for the construction of roads instead of the proposed £4 000, an amount grossly inadequate to sustain road construction and maintenance schemes throughout Rhodesia. [2] This explains the introduction of a Road Tax as a subsidy to road development. Road tax was meant to aid government efforts in the provision of roads. It was a direct tax to the road user. Proceeds from the road tax were used to develop roads in the area the tax would have been collected.

This tax was a fee paid by every landowner in accordance with one's possessions with the aim of contributing to the construction and maintenance of roads. The success of road tax can also be seen in Britain when it was used

---

[1] NAZ GEN/96, Roads in Norton.
[2] *Ibid.*

as an aid to measures taken to improve roads during the 1870s when several trunk and link roads were funded by proceeds from the Road Tax. [1] By the 1920s, the impact of post First World War depression made it apparent that the yearly budget of £2000 allocated by the Government could not realistically sustain the construction. [2] Therefore, the various road authorities were faced with a funding dilemma. Other Road Councils such as Marandellas (now Marondera), Que Que (now Kwekwe) and Bindura could not even make any attempts to repair or construct new roads until 1926. [3] Prior to this, the Road Councils Ordinance clearly stipulated that all land owners were to be taxed as a means of collecting revenue for the development of public utilities. Besides funding the actual road construction process the money was also meant for fencing the roads for the protection of animals. [4]

The Great Depression presented a new challenge to the funding patterns for road developments in Rhodesia. In June 1930, one farm owner, Mr. W. I. Parsons resigned from the Norton-Lydiate Road council citing his personal financial position and that he did not agree with the policy of the council. He stated that "during the present depression drastic economics should be affected. No economy has not been affected and as far as I can see no economy is intended to take place in the future. The finance is in a bad state now and is likely to be much worse later on. "[5] Parsons suggested dealing with the depression first before continuing with placing more financial burden upon institutions and individuals. In support of this idea, Arrighi points out the weakness of the government, arguing that it did not make enough efforts to pull itself out of the economic depression that was being felt across the world. The government lacked the initiative sufficient to kick-start development. The result was a stagnation of the economy. After nearly two

---

[1] Newbury, "Road Taxes, Road User Charges and Earmarking", p. 9.

[2] NAZ GEN/96, Roads in Norton.

[3] NAZ GEN/96, Norton-Dorton Road.

[4] NAZ S3615/5/5/2/1, Norton Road Councils.

[5] NAZ Road Councils.

decades of self-government, the country still did not have an industrial sector, save for a railway workshop and small firms engaged in wholly subsidiary activities which were incapable of meeting the challenges of the global depression. [1]

In an effort to approach the funding puzzle, decentralisation of funding for roads construction was granted in 1945. Through section 50 of the new Town and Country Planning Act, "streets were to be constructed at the expense of the owner."[2] This clause placed the burden of extra road construction upon the land owner making it more expensive considering that they were already eligible for all other taxes, road like Vehicle Tax Motor Tax and the Road Tax. Cartwright, Secretary of the Department of Roads in 1931 justified the hike of the taxes saying "the road is the channel of all trade and commerce, and fundamental to social existence, and all this must stagnate unless road communications are extended in order that the country herself may be fully developed for the benefit of all citizens."[3] However, the hike in prices and the shift of the responsibility of street roads from the government to the land owner can be explained as one of the financial effects of the Second World War. The Responsible Government was facing financial difficulties because it was complimenting British war efforts at the same time trying to satisfy domestic need for finished goods whose import had been disrupted by the war.

Loan votes became another source of funding for the creation of roads in Norton. In instances where the Road Council allocation from the Government and the collected taxes could not cater for the road development activities at hand, the councils had borrowing powers. Earlier on in 1932, amid the great economic depression the Norton-Lydiate Road, Council had borrowed £163 under the Government Grant for the purchase of materials

---

[1] Arrighi, *The Political Economy of Rhodesia*, p. 10.

[2] NAZ GEN/96, Roads in Peri Urban Areas, Volume 1.

[3] NAZ S/AS7635, Association of Road Councils: First Congress.

and plant equipment. ① Financial difficulties arising from the Great Depression continued to hit farmers such that not much progress could be traced in the works of the Norton Road Council. Rhodesia's participation in the Second World War between 1939 and 1945 disturbed progress in infrastructural development, councils maintained already established roads other than constructing new ones. A letter by the management of Harold Poole company in Norton, cited quite a number of challenges to do with gravel roads so the recommended the use of concrete roads. ② Gravel roads posed problems when carrying heavy loads during rain seasons so there was need to introduce asphalt roads which allowed a stronger bond between the soil and road surface.

To further ease funding challenges, Mr Aldred a member of the housing board recommended that the construction of houses as a sources of revenue to help in funding road construction. He argued that the construction of houses provided a ready supply of rates from African labourers and those European investors who wanted to spare themselves the burden of building houses in Norton. ③ These financial constrains acted as a stimulus to the full urbanisation of the Norton. It was the availability of African living areas that made it cheap for industrialists to recruit labour leading to an increase in the number of companies that operated in Norton. This rapid urbanisation was not just a result of labour but the presence of key amenities like a school, hospital, reliable transportation system, an independent sewer system and the Hunyani dam nearby for water supply.

The major challenge with financing road construction in urban centres was largely determined by stakeholders who were naturally reluctant to spend

---

① *The Rhodesia Herald*, 10 May 1929.

② NAZ S3615/2/2/3/24, Norton Township Industrial Development 1951 – 1953.

③ NAZ S3615/5/5/25/5/2/. 1 – 5, Road Contracts. NAZ. The funding constraints faced by the NDP were so serious that they compromised road quality. The road between Norton siding and Lucas Battery company was compromised to a 1m gravel depth instead of the agreed 1. 3m. By 1965, funding challenges continued to haunt the NDP.

money on roads which were going to be handed over to another council without realising any reasonable profits from them. [1] However the council could not commit itself financially because it was not aware of its fate after the completion of the industrial township. [2] This uncertainty of road ownership was a major dilemma for the NDP from its inception. The government did not clarify on the ownership of the infrastructural developments put in place by the panel. Thus, both the Norton Road Council and the NDP cautiously invested on the roads because they were not sure of how long they were going to benefit from the roads.

For issues of labour supply in the construction of trunk, branch and urban roads, reliance was placed upon the Africans. Oxen and wagons were used to transport materials. In 1927 letter responding to the Norton District Road Council (NRC), the then Minister on Mines Mr Chandler, Minister of Mines acknowledged the need for the continued use of African 'gangs' as the major source of labour because the government owned just two graders for servicing all roads in the Rhodesia. [3] The aim of this arrangement was to reduce extensive use of tractors to reduce fuel costs. Road construction in Rhodesia was also supplemented by forced labour imposed upon African prisoners. The government aligned the establishment of Norton to its existing forced labour policy of *chibharo*. The development of urban roads in Zimbabwe came at a cost for Africans. They were coerced into wage labour as a way of ensuring tax payment. [4] This shortage of machinery clearly explains the kind of labour Africans were exposed to. They worked for very little or no wages at all.

Although Africans were accommodated in the plan, the town plan itself was racially discriminatory in the bias of transport control mechanisms.

---

[1] NAZ S3615/2/2/3/24, Norton Township Industrial Development.

[2] NAZ S3615/5/5/2/1, Norton District Road Council.

[3] Ibid. Gangs are groups of African convicts who served their jail terms by supplying labour to public works for the government.

[4] Ibid.

Africans could have their own township and amenities adjacent to but separated from the European township by the industrial zone. [①] A justification to this scenario was the need to avoid transport woes at peak hours. This entitled the Africans to separate road networks that they would use to manoeuvre into their own township. As was the situation in Salisbury where suburbs like Highfield and Mufakose were created to serve the same purpose, in Norton, the Ngoni residential area was created in 1955 strictly for African labourers whilst the Europeans lived in the Porsche area of Galloway and Twinlakes. [②] By 1965, the NDP acknowledged that the town had developed well but not to what they anticipated in twenty eight years. One company BMC operated for a few weeks and left because they had reservations for the infrastructure. Their report stated that:

> [W]e will all be grateful if you will place before the Parliament our strong representation regarding the dust nuisance arising from the road leading past the European settlement during dry and wet weather; the houses are surrounded for most of the day in a heavy pool of red dust which settles not only on the garden, washing, and outside of houses but also on food and furniture inside the dwellings. [③]

Apart from the nuisance it must have been most unhealthy for the adults and children living in these houses to leave in such dusty conditions, there was need to pay attention to roads in order to attract more industrialists into the new centre. The Director of Joseph Lucas Limited, a battery company established in Norton since 1925, revealed that "the roads are in extremely dangerous condition and as a result we find that our business associates are very loath to visit us. In consequence, we are placed at a disadvantage with

---

① NAZ S3615/5/25/2/1, Norton Development Panel.
② C. Van Onselen, *Chibharo: African Mine Labour in Southern Rhodesia 1900 – 1933*, London: Pluto Press, 1976, p. 91.
③ NAZ S3615/5/25/4/2/2, Norton Development Panel.

industry in other parts of Rhodesia. It is therefore essential that immediate action be taken. "[1] There was need for NDP to reconsider their effort in road construction and maintenance.

This failure was a result of the lack of funding, diversion of government focus to federal politics, and the absence of a clear ownership plan of the roads after the establishment of the industrial centre. However the NDP managed to establish access roads to the industrial site. The failure of intended industrial take off was not a result of the unavailability of roads but of the quality of roads available. Even the roads in the white settler residential area were not up to standard that by 1962 five white families had relocated to Salisbury citing poor roads. [2] Poor urban roads meant delayed movement of raw materials and produce thereby affecting maximisation of profits which was the focus of the colonial capitalists.

Conclusion

The BSAC rule should be credited for setting the pace. All roads developments in Norton were based on the Norton Road Council's implementation of the provisions of the Road Councils Ordinance of 1921. The Responsible Government managed to finance some road construction activities although the Road Council's subsidised by the collection of Road Tax. By 1930 the council managed to create road network that linked the Norton farming community to the Norton Railway Siding as its market outlet. The choice of Norton as an Industrial centre was largely determined by the existing road network that was established by the NRC. The Council managed to strategically place Norton Siding as a major outlet of produce from both the farming community and the industrial township. The government created a new town in Norton as a way of decentralising

---

[1] NAZ S3615/2/2/3/24, Norton Township Industrial Development.
[2] NAZ S481/1037, Norton Development Panel.

demographic pressure from Salisbury and Bulawayo. The creation of an industrial centre changed the whole town planning policy. Focus was shifted from developing farmer's branch and link roads to establishing urban roads. These were more expensive to construct as their standard had to compete with other roads in the newly created Federation of Rhodesia and Nyasaland.

However, the development of urban roads in Norton was not smooth as expected. There were no clear terms of benefit to those who funded the projects. These funding challenges delayed progress. By the end of the Federation in 1963, the industrial town was not fully developed. Instead of attracting investors, its incomplete infrastructure drove away some potential investors. The failure of industrial take off further marginalised African labourers in the town. Their social amenities remained stagnant until the Unilateral Deceleration of Independence (UDI). The failure to establish many industries remained a worry for Africans who still needed employment to meet the different taxes demanded by the colonial government. Industries grew in Norton during this period. These include Harold Poole Limited (manufacturer of steel farm implements), Lucas Battery Company (battery manufacturer), Rhodesia Seeds Company (processed and supplied agricultural seeds) and Rhodesia Pulp and Paper Millers (produced different types of paper).

Good urban roads guaranteed investor confidence in order to sufficiently secure the interests of the white settler community. As Arrighi has argued, the post-war political economy of Rhodesia is explained in terms of increased demand for industrial goods. [1] Goods previously imported became practically unavailable, thus creating a demand for local industries. It is common cause that the economic impact of the war on Rhodesia was the disruption of the smooth import and export of goods that were needed to develop manufacturing industries in Africa. Increased investment led to advanced exploitation of African resources and realisation of huge profits by the white

[1] Arrighi, *The Political Economy of Rhodesia*, p. 14.

capitalists. The good urban roads in Salisbury, Bulawayo and Umtali help explain the population pressure these towns faced after 1945. The development of urban roads in Norton also failed because of the shift from a Federal government to an independent government in 1963. Evidence has it that from 1963 there were no other significant road developments besides the annual maintenance work initiated by the companies. The government focused more on establishing its political control of the country. African political opposition was also on the increase during this period hence the neglect of the special Norton project.

Funding constraints contributed much to the failure to establish a viable urban road network in Norton. The government as the major financing agent had its expenditure drained by participation in the Second World War. Therefore the loaning conditions were tightened such that the NDP could not easily access funds to use for the construction of roads. Again the standard macadamised roads expected after 1948 were expensive to construct. Funding had a direct bearing on labour supply. The lack of funds resulted in scarcity of African labourers who needed the money to pay their due taxes. The unavailability of proper urban roads in Norton by 1965 was a major contributory factor to the collapse of a carefully planned industrial town. The success of road construction is highly depended on reliable funding and labour supply. The paper provides insights into the empirical models used by the colonial government in trying to harness suburbanisation for industrial and commercial growth of the colony and large.

Revisiting Post-World War II Industrialization in Southern Rhodesia: the Industrial Development Commission 1945 – 1949

Iviny Murombo

Abstract

This paper examines the contributions made by the Industrial Development Commission (IDC) in stimulating the growth of secondary industries in post-World War II period. This work notes that, in as much as industrialisation had gained momentum during World War II, up to the end of the War, industrial development was still at its emerging stages. Industrial development at this stage faced difficulties in marketing and therefore required protection from outside competition. Furthermore, it witnessed shortage of resources, mainly manifest in capital challenges. The paper explores how the IDC endeavoured to stimulate industrialisation in Southern Rhodesia by overcoming these impediments to industrial growth. The paper, engages both primary and secondary documentary sources to demonstrate how the IDC carried out its functions such as establishing, financing, modernising industries, and balancing industrial development in the colony through decentralisation to overrun challenges bedevilling industrial progress. It also assesses the successes and failures of the IDC as well as the problems it faced during the time of operation including political challenges, government's attitude and resistance from industrialists. This is done by comparing what the

IDC intended to achieve and what it actually achieved. The final examination
shows that the IDC presented a sturdy government engagement in the industrial
sector and it was instrumental in the industrialisation process as seen through
the increased pace of industrial growth even in the wake of multiple challenges.

Introduction

It is understood that the Second World War (WWII) was a watershed in
the industrialisation process in Southern Rhodesia. [1] In that regard, it can be
seen that the development of secondary industries gained momentum during
the War and as a result, industrialisation began to take shape throughout the
war years. [2] Conversely, industrial development was still at its incipient stage
and it faced difficulties in marketing and the need for protection from outside
competition, shortages of resources, and, funding. These difficulties pushed
the government to concentrate more on the development of secondary
industries. [3] Against this backdrop, the government became committed to
policies that pushed for an invigorated intervention in industrial
development. With such efforts, the IDC was, therefore, created by the
government to run industrial undertakings and, to increase the pace of
industrial development. Therefore, this paper shows how the establishment
of the IDC stimulated industrial development in Southern Rhodesia. To speed
up the pace of industrialisation, the government of Southern Rhodesia made
use of statutory bodies such as the Industrial Development Advisory
Committee (IDAC) and IDC. Initially, the government created IDAC from

---

[1] E. S. Pangeti, 'The State and Manufacturing Industry: A Study of the State as Regulator and
Entrepreneur in Zimbabwe', PhD, University of Zimbabwe, 1996, p. 63.

[2] A. S. Mlambo et al, *Zimbabwe: A History of Manufacturing, 1890 - 1995*, Harare: University of
Zimbabwe Publications, 2000, p. 31.

[3] National Archives of Zimbabwe S10/39/45 Industrial Development Advisory Committee 1944 - 1945
reports.

1940 to 1944 to enhance war time manufacturing. However, IDAC could not deliver what the government intended leading to its disbandment.

The government dissolved IDAC in 1944 and replaced it with the IDC which had executive powers (compared to IDAC). Through the Industrial Development Act of 1944, the Commission was established. The IDC was tasked with speeding up the growth of industries as well as creating more industries. It was empowered to promote the establishment of new industries and to develop and modernise existing industries, promotion and expansion and better organisation of industries, coordinate industries, balance industrial development as well as determining economic policy relating to matters including subsidies, tariffs, quotas, marketing, transport, and the financing of new industries. [①] By setting such a statutory, the government aimed at diversifying the economy from solely depending on mining and agriculture through improving the industrial sector of Southern Rhodesia laying the base for post-war industrial development.

This paper, thus, seeks to make a modest contribution to economic reconstruction in the de-industrialising world by analysing the roles played by the IDC in post-World War II industrial developments in Southern Rhodesia. The paper begins by tracing the nature of secondary industries at the end of World War II and accounts for the emergence of the IDC and its role in stimulating industrial development. The paper made use of primary data from the National Archives of Zimbabwe (NAZ). It specifically made use of correspondences, minutes, reports, memoranda and manuscripts from the Ministry of Commerce and Industry and its related statutory bodies such as Industrial Development Advisory Committee (IDAC) and Industrial Development Commission (IDC). Equally important secondary sources, journal articles, published and unpublished works also helped in giving a clear picture of the nature of industrialisation in Southern Rhodesia.

---

① *The Rhodesian Herald*, 18 November 1944.

Background to the development of the IDC

Arrighi posits that the Second World War opened up spaces for the development of secondary industries in Southern Rhodesia. [1] Phimister agrees with Arrighi's view arguing that the Second World War provided an opportunity of Import Substitution Industrialisation (ISI) forcing Southern Rhodesia to manufacture goods previously imported. [2] Under ISI, there was a substitution of goods that Southern Rhodesia used to import and as a result, the country experienced a rapid growth of secondary industries when these goods were locally manufactured. It can be noted that the War changed the economy of the colony from being heavily dependent on agricultural and mining products, to a diversified one with the expansion in the manufacturing sector. [3] Given the opportunity for development, Southern Rhodesia's government made strides to maintain the development of industries by improving and developing existing industries. Thus during and after the War, government played a central role in maintaining the growth of industries in Southern Rhodesia. [4]

Worth noting is that government concern with the growth of secondary industries followed the closure of certain market opportunities enjoyed during the War and the possibility that industrialisation could lose momentum. [5] Thus, despite the benefits that World War II brought to the development of

---

[1] G. Arrighi, 'The Political Economy of Rhodesia', New Left Review, No. 39, 1966, p. 35.

[2] I. Phimister, From preference towards protection: Manufacturing in Southern Rhodesia 1940 - 1965 in Zimbabwe: A History of Manufacturing, 1890 - 1995, Harare: University of Zimbabwe Publications, 2000, p. 31.

[3] Paul Mosley, The Settler Economies: Studies in the Economic History of Kenya and Southern Rhodesia 1900 - 1965. Cambridge: Cambridge University Press, 1983, p. 85.

[4] NAZ RG-P/TR44, Secondary Industry in Southern Rhodesia: Department of Trade and Industrial Development Salisbury, May 1953.

[5] V. Gwande, "Foreign Capital, State and the Development of Secondary Industry in Southern Rhodesia", MA Dissertation, Faculty of the Humanities for the Centre for Africa Studies, University of Free State, 2015, p. 35.

secondary industries in Southern Rhodesia, industrialisation remained in its nascent stage. [1] Gwande notes that, "the recurrent debate between the state and industrialists suggests that, despite the fortunes that the war may have brought to secondary industries; the sector was still in its teething stage and continued to be plagued by many challenges. "[2] W. Arnold substantiates this arguing that the industrial development in Southern Rhodesia was hindered by several factors regardless of the fortunes brought about by the War. [3] Arnold highlights that low gross output, protectionism, and funding remained serious problems in the development of industries[4]. He also points out that industrial development for Southern Rhodesia was still lagging considering that it existed as almost entirely a primary producer producing agricultural products at most up to the outbreak of the war. [5] He reckons that:

> Her main export was gold which was the mainstay of the country being supplemented by various agricultural exports, it was so in its early stages to industrialise, thus when the war ended, the shield which it offered for growth was removed calling for a serious concern from the state to deal with industrialisation of the country. [6]

From this, the Minister of Commerce was determined to maintain the development of secondary industries which called for the establishment of the IDC through the Industrial Development Act of 1944. A key feature to the development of the IDC was the nature of industrial development with the

---

① V. Gwande, "Foreign Capital, State and the Development of Secondary Industry in Southern Rhodesia", MA Dissertation, Faculty of the Humanities for the Centre for Africa Studies, University of Free State, 2015, p. 24.

② *Ibid*, p. 24.

③ W. E. Arnold, Southern Rhodesia Industrial Future, in Empire Digest September 1945 Southern Rhodesia Issue, p. 45.

④ Ibid, p. 45

⑤ Arnold, p. 46.

⑥ *Ibid*.

end of the war. Chairman of IDAC, Macintyre noted in May 1953, that the disabilities of the IDAC coupled with other challenges plaguing industrial development pushed the establishment of the IDC. [1]As the Chairman of IDAC, Macintyre noted in May 1953, the Committee's activities had been devoted to the industrial development of the country, and in pursuit of that aim they had travelled widely and conducted many investigations. ... however; the Committee had acted in [an] advisory capacity and had no executive powers hindering the Committee in carrying out its functions. [2]

It is imperative to note that the failures of IDAC in promoting industrial development as the government of Southern Rhodesia intended together with the idea that industrial development was still at its embryonic stage, led to the setting of the IDC. Macintyre asserted that, the IDC was to be established to overcome challenges faced by industrial development and [that] IDAC faced when he lamented that "by establishing IDC, the disabilities of IDAC could, therefore, be removed."[3]

IDC responsibilities

In December 1944 IDC was established under the Department of Commerce and Industries with the sole purpose of stimulating the pace of industrial development for the colony. The Commission was given executive powers (compared to IDAC its predecessor) intending to increase the pace of industrial development in the colony. Under the Bill of 1944, the IDC was authorised to, "promote the establishment of new industries and industrial undertakings and the development of existing industries and industrial undertakings". [4] Other objectives of the Commission were to ensure the expansion, better organisation, and modernisation of industries making a

---

[1] NAZ F292/16/3, Secondary Industry in Southern Rhodesia, May 1953.
[2] NAZ F292/16/3, Secondary Industry in Southern Rhodesia, May 1953.
[3] Industrial Development Commission, *The Rhodesian Herald*, *November*, 1944.
[4] Gwande, 'Capital, State and The Development of Secondary Industry in Southern Rhodesia', p. 35.

balanced industrial development, coordination of industries and advising the government on the economic policy including tariffs, quotas, marketing, and transportation.

The Commission was objected to assisting in financing or promotion of new industries and industrial undertakings as well as existing industries. Under section 7 of the bill, for the purpose of carrying out its objects, the Commission was granted the power (a) to assist the promotion of companies for conducting any industry or industrial undertaking in the colony, (b) to conduct experiments in or undertake research in industrial process, (c) to lend or advance money or to acquire an interest in or provide or otherwise to assist in the subscription of capital for any person engaged in or proposing to establish or to expand or modernise and industry or industrial undertaking (d) to act as a manager or consultant to any person conducting an industrial undertaking (e) to appoint committees to investigate and advise the commission upon any matter (f) to draw, make, accept, indorse, discount, execute and issue promising notes, bills of exchange and other negotiable and transferable instrument (h) to insure with any company or person against any losses, damages, risks and liabilities which the commission may incur (i) to do all such other things as are incidental or conducive to the attainment of any object or incidental to any power or function mentioned in this section. ①

Stimulating industrial development through the IDC

It was the primary duty of the IDC to speed up the development of secondary industries in the colony in the post-World War II period. This became the base of industrialisation in Southern Rhodesia. As Stoneman noted, "the period 1945 – 53 was the phase in which the Rhodesian economy

---

① NAZ S10/39/45, Industrial Development Advisory Committee 1944 – 1945 reports, Bill to constitute the commission.

'took off' under the stimulus of high export demands and substantial capital inflow",[1] in this case primarily from the government. [2] Thus, through roles played by the IDC, the colony was set on a sound foot in industrialisation. Notably, several industries were to be established by the IDC and for the government; this was expected to be speedy. Hence, the IDC would not hold-up actions by cooperating and coordinating industrial development as well as recommending to the government the immediate necessary industries that were supposed to be set for other industries to develop. [3]

With its establishment, the IDC abruptly investigated the demands for the growth of secondary industries in the colony. In the first reports it handed out, the IDC key industries that were critical to be established. It also outlined the need for communication improvement in order for industrialisation to suffice. [4] The chairmen of IDAC upon handing over to the IDC stated that key industries lagged behind and thus, IDC's efforts were to be devoted to the establishment of those industries to pace up the growth of other industries. For instance, IDC noted that starch, cement, textile, transportations were a major factor retarding industrial growth. [5] Also, vital operating industries had no capacity to meet the growing demand as well as the growing industrial base. [6] Hence, for these reasons, the IDC had to establish the mentioned industries. As Macintyre noted, "there was a concern with the establishment of industries that would provide reasonable exports of manufactured goods and resources for both local and outside markets". [7] In line with this, the IDC was obligated to keep up with its mandate which it ultimately carried with immediate effect.

---

[1] Stoneman, 'Foreign Capital and the Prospects for Zimbabwe', p. 38.
[2] Ibid, p. 39.
[3] NAZ F292/16/3, Secondary Industry in Southern Rhodesia, May 1953.
[4] NAZ S/IN 18, Industrial Efficiency, 1945, p. 6.
[5] Ibid.
[6] Pangeti, 'The State and Manufacturing', p. 67.
[7] NAZ S10/39/45, Industrial Development Advisory Committee 1944 - 1945 reports on Industrial Efficiency.

Upon the realization that setting up of critical industries was the core priority of the IDC, it commenced work in 1945. This saw its work devoted to the establishment of the cement industry, textile industry, and the related Rhodesian cables. The IDC believed that these were industries were a key drive for industrialisation to suffice in the colony relating it to infrastructure development. The IDC in 1945 noted that the cement industry was producing at a low output and could not meet the demands of the growing industries in the colony.[1] This had the effect of dragging building and construction of industrial plants at the same time increasing the cost of building when the importation of cement was too high for Southern Rhodesia industrialists.

In the words of Musgrave, Chairman of the IDC:

> The existing company had made appreciated efforts together with its associates in the union of South Africa in keeping the colony going with cement. This, however, does not alter the fact that even with the present time; it is insufficient to meet the demand, even without reckoning on any large programme of public works, irrigation dams, etc. , such as highly probable in the near future. The needs of the private enterprise are not being met, the building is delayed and its already high cost still further increased by the cement shortage.[2]

Musgrave also outlined that in April 1945, the commission began an investigation of the development of the cement manufacturing industry and found that only one factory was operating and it became clear that the full output of this factory would not suffice for the growing needs of the colony. The company operating the factory considered that the risks involved in any real expansion, such as doubling the plant capacity were incompatible with the prospects of the increased business, in view of high costs of machinery

---

[1] NAZ S/IN 18, Industrial Efficiency, 1945, p. 6.

[2] NAZ S/IN 18, Reports of Statutory Bodies-Industrial Development Commission 1945 – 1949: 31 December 1945, p. 4.

and labour, both of which were trending to increase. [1]

Thus, the existence of one cement company was a problem for the growing Rhodesian secondary industries that entailed the establishment of other industries of cement manufacturing within the colony. Through the considerations made by the IDC, the Rhodesia Cement Limited was formed with an authorised capital of £260 000.000, with the first issue of £40 000.000 for cash was heavily over scribed as soon as the shares were offered to the public. [2] The company was energetically engaged in the preparations required to go into production as soon as possible. Thus the aspiration of quick development of secondary industries was realized and set on a sound footing considering the recommendations made by IDAC. Macintyre, in 1944, recommended the IDC that, "the shortage of cement in the colony is considered to be seriously handicapping the development of the colony and the Committee has been at some pains to consider ways and means whereby the production might be increased. Therefore the Committee recommended that the Industrial Development Commission give this matter their early consideration. "[3] Thus, by 1946, the commission had established a cement plant in Matabeleland through its investigations and the determination to increase the development of infrastructure within the colony. In all, this evidenced the role of the IDC in setting industries.

Equally important, the IDC also encouraged the institution of other industries including the textile industry and others including factories to make starch (Cassava Corporation), cutlery, bricks and tiles, plywood and plastic. The IDC also managed to set the Industrial Alcohol distillery at Umtali. [4] As early as 1943, the idea to establish the Industrial Alcohol plant was seen

---

[1] NAZ S/IN 18, Reports of Statutory Bodies-Industrial Development Commission 1945 - 1949: 31 December 1945, p. 6.

[2] Ibid.

[3] NAZ S10/39/45 Industrial Development Advisory Committee 1944 - 1945 reports.

[4] NAZ S225/1, Reports on the establishment of the Industrial Alcohol Distillery, 14 July 1949.

through the recommendations made by IDAC. [1] IDAC advised the Prime Minister, Huggins, to establish the plant in Umtali. [2] However, Huggins argued that this would be established when the colony had set-up an Industrial Commission. [3] Through the IDC, the Alcohol plant was eventually set up in the colony. Thus, important to realize was the roles played by IDC in setting industries that one can consider little or non-existent.

Levelling the financial field

The IDC also increased funds disbanded to industries and to industrialists between 1945 and 1949. This as the chairman stated, was meant to enhance industrial development by ensuring sufficient capital to industrialists. The IDC disbursed funds for establishing and developing industries. By the 1944 Bill, under Section 7, sub-section (c), the IDC was empowered to lend or advance money to any person engaged in or proposing to establish or to expand or modernise an industry or industrial undertaking. [4] This empowerment sought to solve the issue of funding to industrialists as finance was a major problem retarding the development of secondary industries in the colony. It can be noted that IDC obtained capital in two forms, the first being capital advances by the government from loan funds bearing interest at 4 percent per annum and this capital was specifically for investment as required by the needs of industrial development which was secured to the commission by approved securities. [5] The second form involved capital advances from Revenue Funds, free of interest and granted by the

---

[1] NAZ S225/1, Reports on the establishment of the Industrial Alcohol Distillery, 14 July 1949.
[2] NAZ S10/39/45 Industrial Development Advisory Committee 1944–1945 reports.
[3] NAZ S104, Minutes dated 21 April 1943.
[4] NAZ S10/39/45, Industrial Development Advisory Committee 1944–1945 reports, Bill to constitute the commission.
[5] NAZ S/IN 18, Reports of Statutory Bodies-Industrial Development Commission 1945–1949: 31 December 1945, p. 3.

government to meet the shortfall in the revenue of the Commission which was anticipated during the first few years of operation and also the costs of the general inquiries, investigations and research work authorised from time to time. [1]

Thus, between 1945 and 1946, the IDC made financial assistance available to various industries from time to time in varying forms. Musgrave reported to the Minister of Commerce and Industries that "in industrial banking, financial assistance had been extended to various industries and there was industrial progress". [2] In addition, Musgrave concluded that the financial assistance in the year 1946 was made in respect to Cutlery, Coachbuilding, Electroplating, Glass, Printing, Alcohol, Ceramic and other several industries that were of minor importance. It is worth noting that finance extended to industries, increased the pace of industrial growth when the finance allowed the industrialists to develop industrial plants within the colony. A notable example is evident in the Rhodesian Cement Company. It can be noted that from 1945, Rhodesian Cement Limited was straddling to make the industry suffice, however, IDC provided financial assistance amounting to £200 00.00 at an annual interest of 5 percent which enhanced growth to the cement industry. [3] The IDC also loaned the Glass industry in 1947 and the funds were approved on the basis of productivity to further the project. For instance, IDC could not approve the applied loan of £15 000 by May and Partner as the amount was greatly in excess of the capital to be raised by the company and there were no assets except the machinery it had proposed to purchase. [4] Hence, it can be argued that the IDC had a bigger role in the development of secondary industries as it extended loans to industries that appealed for funding. IDC made funds available for the development of secondary industries through loans, in turn increasing the pace of

---

[1] NAZ S/IN 18, Reports of Statutory Bodies-Industrial Development Commission 1945 – 1949: 31 December 1945, p. 4.

[2] NAZ S/IN/18, Industrial Development Commission Reports, 31 December 1946.

[3] NAZ S10/20/1, Cement: Industrial development and plant designs, production and plant control, 1946.

[4] NAZ S/IN/18, Capital and Financing of the Industrial Development Commission.

industrialisation when industrialists were guaranteed financial assistance.

Modernising and Strategically Positioning Industries

In addition to financing, the IDC enhanced modernization and betterment of industries stimulating the development of secondary industries in the colony. The IDC adopted various means in modernizing industries varying from importation of capital goods, experimenting and investigating possible ways to increase the pace of industrialisation. The Industrial Alcohol and the Cement industry were notable examples that indicated the role played by the IDC in modernising industries in post-World War II. [1] IDC was mandated by the government to modernize industries and ensure the betterment of industries or any industrial undertaking within the colony. Throughout, the IDC modernisation and betterment of industries works were seen in several industries including the cement industry, industrial alcohol distillery, glass industry, and plastics. [2] In a way, it can be said that the IDC contributed to the increasing pace of industrialisation in post-World War II period. Mosley resonates well with this, arguing that after the war, there was an increased pace in the growth of the manufacturing industry. [3]

As the chairman of IDC noted, "the Commission purchased equipment, advancing machinery in industries to increase industrial efficiency, therefore, increasing the pace of industrialisation in Southern Rhodesia". [4] Notably, in May 1945, the IDC replaced the wash pump of the alcohol plant in Umtali which threatened the output of alcohol as it was damaged extensively. [5] In April 1946, Industrial Alcohol appealed for the

[1] NAZ S10/16/1, Industrial Alcohol Factory at Umtali monthly reports, 1945 – 47.
[2] NAZ S/IN 18, Reports of Statutory Bodies-Industrial Development Commission 1945 – 1949: 31 December 1945.
[3] P. Mosley, The Settler Economies, p. 85.
[4] NAZ S/IN/18, Growth of Secondary Industries: Industrial Progress, 1946.
[5] NAZ S10/16/1, Industrial Alcohol Factory at Umtali monthly reports, 1945 – 47.

improvement of the steriliser which they lamented that, "the steriliser no longer met the growing industrial business. "[1] The IDC therefore made available a new steriliser replacing the old on the distillation plant keeping production high. Important to note is that the IDC imported a new steriliser worth £15 000 in May 1946 to improve the efficiency of the plant. [2] Thus, IDC became crucial in modernising the alcohol industries as it imported advanced machinery for use in the manufacturing of alcohol. [3]

In addition to these developments, the Industrial alcohol works as the Chairman reported that "a quotation had been received from England detailing laboratory equipment required by the manager totalling something over £1000". [4] It was resolved that the equipment detailed amounting to approximately £445 be ordered immediately by the IDC illustrating the striking determination of the Commission in increasing the efficiency of the Industrial Alcohol works at Umtali. [5] As a result of the importation of new machinery and laboratory equipment, production increased between 1945 and 1947. This is supported by the Chairman of the IDC who reported that, "production of alcohol increased appreciably in the month on November when 2188 gallons were produced from the usual 1456 gallons produced. [6] IDC attributed investments increasing the pace of development. Not only in the Alcohol Plant, did IDC make efforts, but in the glass industry and plastics importing machinery that resulted in increased production, therefore expanding the development of secondary industries. [7]

Interestingly, the IDC made efforts to decrease the costs of production for industries to maximise profits therefore, enhancing industrial development. It is imperative to note that the IDC endeavoured in the

---

[1] NAZ S10/16/1, Industrial Alcohol Factory at Umtali monthly reports, 1945 - 47.
[2] NAZ S10/16/2, Industrial Development Commission and Alcohol Works.
[3] Mlambo et al, *Zimbabwe: A History of Manufacturing*, p. 42.
[4] NAZ S10/16/1, Industrial Alcohol Factory at Umtali monthly reports, 1945 - 47.
[5] Ibid.
[6] Ibid.
[7] NAZ S/IN/18, Capital and Financing of the Industrial Development Commission.

reduction of tariffs for industries across the colony ranging from water, power, and transport costs. The IDC realised that reducing tariffs for industries would decrease production costs and this would increase profits for industries enhancing the continuous establishment of industries. [1] In 1947, the IDC made striking efforts to ensure cheap power supply to industries. From the reports given on tariffs in 1947, it is the considered opinion of the IDC that cheap power together with better communications will increase the flow of investment capital into Southern Rhodesia. [2] Bertram asserts that the Commission at this time was interested in attracting investment capital in the colony to increase the pace of industrial growth through creating conditions conducive for investment. [3] More so, the IDC worked with the Tariff Advisory Committee in rebates (deduction from the amount which was paid) of duty for imported raw materials used in industries. [4] Together with the Tariff Committee, the Commission negotiated the rebates of duties so that industrialists would maximise profits. The rebates on imported goods were crucial in industries as evidenced by the increase in the gross value of the output of all factories and workshops from under £5 million in 1939 to over £20 million in 1947. [5] In so doing, it can be argued that the IDC played a role in increasing the pace of development of secondary industries by its involvement in lowering of tariff rates for industries.

At the same time, the IDC made efforts in finding markets for the growing industries in the colony from 1945 to 1948. From 1945, the IDC interceded between the governments of South Africa and Southern Rhodesia on issues relating to the Customs Union. [6] Through the institution of the

---

[1] NAZ S10/16, Water Tariff Reduction minutes, 27 December 1945.

[2] NAZ S10/43/4, Tariff Advisory Committee Report, 1947.

[3] NAZ S/RH679, N. R. Bertram, An industrialists view of the determinants required for growth of secondary industry in Southern Rhodesia, *in Rhodesia Journal of Economics*, Vol. 3, No. 2, June, 1969.

[4] Phimister, "Secondary Industrialisation in Southern Rhodesia", p . 436.

[5] NAZ S932/14, Industrial Development of Southern Rhodesia.

[6] NAZ S10/43/1 - 2, Industrial Development Commission: Trade Agreements of Southern Rhodesia and South Africa, 1945 - 1947.

Committee of Enquiry into the Protection of Secondary Industries, the IDC carried its role into the protection of industries, quotas, tariffs, and economic policies to be pursued by the government. ① IDC was empowered to appoint committees to investigate and advise the commission upon any matter in the colony, ② and it was responsible for the committee of Enquiry that was established to investigate on the matter. Using information from the investigations made by the Committee of Enquiry, the IDC recommended that "the Union must assist Southern Rhodesia to archive a state of industrial activity within the colony maintaining that, the union is desirous of removing customs barriers". ③ The removal of customs barriers was anticipated by the IDC to assist industries to maximise profits at the same time reducing transportation costs. In respect to that, the report made by the IDC recommended that the Union provide markets for the industries in the colony at the same time protecting infant industries by an external custom duty within the Union. By then, the IDC was active in preparing and drafting the constitution which was to guide trade relations with the Union. It worked together with the investigation body in South Africa and it provided information that favoured Rhodesia's industries at large. ④ For instance, in the draft presented by the committee, the Commission recommended that "imports will not be subject to higher taxation than that on national products. "⑤ It should be added that the commission institution of the Committee of Enquiry in the Protection of Secondary industries was a major step towards the protection of industries in Southern Rhodesia. At the same time, this fell in line with the IDC's ambition in establishing markets for

---

① NAZ S10/43/1 – 2, Industrial Development Commission: Trade Agreements of Southern Rhodesia and South Africa, 1945 – 1947.
② NAZ S10/39/45, Industrial Development Advisory Committee 1944 – 1945 reports, Bill to constitute the commission.
③ Ibid.
④ NAZ S10/43/1 – 2, Industrial Development Commission: Trade Agreements of Southern Rhodesia and South Africa, 1945 – 1947.
⑤ Ibid.

industries within the colony.

Assessing IDC's intervention

The invigorated efforts for increased pace of industrial growth, it can be realised that the IDC had successes in combating de-industrialization. To understand the extent of its intervention capacity, we examine the intended targets and what was achieved when the IDC concluded its activities. Fundamentally, the IDC battled the factors which affected industries causing a slow paced development. Thus, through the IDC, there was an increase in industrial efficiency and with that one can note the achievements of the IDC through the establishment, modernisation, and betterment of industries. [1] This particular sub-section examines several problems the IDC encountered that can also help us in explaining some of the failures of the IDC to meet the intended targets. Notably, the IDC was affected by government policy and attitude towards the body, politics, and conflicts with other statutory bodies and ministries. Therefore, while the IDC had successes, it had also its failures.

It is worth noting that the IDC set industrialisation in Southern Rhodesia on a sound footing considering an increase in the pace of growth. Gwande posits that secondary industries grew at a formidable rate in post-World War II period and the IDC role in the expansion can be noted. [2] Earlier, the work highlighted some of the problems that affected industries and how these problems led to the establishment of the IDC. Nevertheless, IDC became crucial in solving problems including continuous shortages of goods in the colony. In this sense, one can appreciate the role played by the IDC through the establishment of industries within the colony from 1945 up to 1949. By 1946, with only one year in operation, the IDC reported that the expansion

---

① NAZ S/IN 18, industrial progress reports, 31 December 1949.

② Gwande, "Foreign Capital, State and The Development of Secondary Industry in Southern Rhodesia".

of secondary industries was mainly a result of the establishing role it played. The Chairman reported that "there was an increase in the number of industries from 524 in 1946 to a further of 681 by 1949". [1] From that, the chairman argued that the IDC had an important role in the industrialisation of Southern Rhodesia as evidenced by the increase in the number of industries within the colony. In addition, this is attributed to the endeavours of the IDC in establishing industries and encouraging the development of industries.

Furthermore, the IDC also stimulated manufactured exports diversifying the economy from relying on the exports of primary products. [2] There was also an increase in manufacturing exports, which was illustrated in the expansion of secondary industries, further illuminating the success of the IDC. The Chairman reported that, "in 1945, 382 manufacturing industries had a gross output of £14,062 000 and a net output of £6,205 000, by 1950 these had increased to 648 industries with a gross output of £42,414 000 and a net output of £19,102 00"[3] In this light, it shows how the IDC managed to expand industrial exports. Notably, exports of manufactured also expanded due to the modernisation and betterment of industries increasing the output. For instance, in the Rhodesian Cement Limited industry alone, modernization increased the competence of producing cement that by 1949 it was producing 265 000 tons per annum against 65 000 tons produced in 1945. [4] On the same note, the Chairman of the IDC illustrated that the value of exports of the principal produce of secondary industry in 1946 was £2 432 870. 00 which stood at £481 685. 00 higher than the figure for 1945 indicating that there was progress. [5]

For the government, it was imperative to increase the flow of exports

① NAZ S/IN 18, Reports of Statutory Bodies-Industrial Development Commission 1945 – 1949: 31 December 1945.
② NAZ S/225, First Meeting of IDC, 6 March 1945.
③ NAZ RG/TR44, Secondary Industry in Southern Rhodesia: Department of Trade and Industrial Development, Salisbury May 1953.
④ NAZ S10/20/4, The Rhodesian Cement Industry memoranda and progress reports, 1947 – 1948.
⑤ NAZ S/IN/18, 'Industrial Progress, 1945, p. 5.

through developing the industry of colony to reach the greatest possible volume, and this is seen in the years of the IDC, making it an achievement of the Commission. Tow concurs with the view that "the volume and output of manufacturing have grown rapidly in the post-war years and its development has made an important role towards diversifying the economy. "[1] Thus, the IDC played a crucial role in increasing the pace of industrialisation in Southern Rhodesia.

The IDC also worked towards the marketing of goods with efficiency and quality in local factories. This is believed to have also helped the expansion of secondary industries. As noted, the IDC worked towards establishing markets for secondary industry through a Customs Union with South Africa. Thus, with the interceding role, the Customs Union of Southern Rhodesia and South Africa was formed in 1948 and it provided secondary industries in Rhodesia with ready markets. [2] In addition, from the establishment of the IDC, it endeavoured at enhancing the quality of products produced for instance by establishing several industries of the same product creating competition. Phimister notes that Southern Rhodesia exports to South Africa more than doubled, and in 1950 they increased by a further 70 per cent over the figures for 1949. Overall Southern Rhodesia exports to the south jumped from 1. 2 million in 1948 to almost 7 million in 1953. [3] This indicated to the expansion of secondary industries through the responsibility of the IDC.

On the same concept, the provision of funds to industries and industrial undertakings can draw us to the achievements of the IDC. The body ensured financial assistance to industries. It disbanded funds based on efficiency and this resulted in the expansion of secondary industries within the colony. With the availability of funds, industries grew and it ensured the importation of

---

① Tow, "The Manufacturing economy of Southern Rhodesia: Problems and Prospects".

② NAZ S10/43/1, Industrial development Commission: Trade Agreements: Southern Rhodesia and South Africa, 1945 – 1947.

③ I. Phimister, "Secondary Industrialisation in Southern Rhodesia: The 1948 Custom Agreement between Southern Rhodesia and South Africa", *Journal of Southern African Studies*, 17, No. 3, 1991, p. 435.

capital goods that further enhanced the development of secondary industries within the colony. One industrialist lamented that " indirectly, the government made funds available to numerous small industries through the old IDC and to several large industries", with an effect of speeding up industrial development in the colony. [1] Thus, with the availability of financial assistance to industries, there is no doubt that the IDC was successful in disbursing funds to industries. In all, the pace and extent of expansion of industries in Southern Rhodesia were also realised with the promotion given by the Commission to industries and industrial undertakings in the colony. The IDC was a gateway between the government and industrialists, where it promoted companies through investigations, experiments and a consultant to industries giving advice to any person conducting an industrial undertaking. In that epoch, the IDC was of great assistance in the promotion of industries and by the increase and expansion of industries, it can be argued that the IDC had a role in the growth of secondary industries in post-World War II.

In as much the IDC pressed for an increased pace and expansion of industries in the colony, it encountered various difficulties that curtailed its operations. As a statutory commission obligated to engage in industrial undertakings freely, the government however, became an impediment to the IDC executing its responsibilities. [2] The government interfered with the work of the IDC, to the extent of threatening the powers given to the body. [3] Complemented by the politics in Southern Rhodesia, the government limited the functions of IDC. One notable example is when the Chairman of the IDC pointed out to Hargreaves who was an industrialist interested in setting a textile plant with their own spinning mills that:

---

[1] NAZ S/IN 18, Reports of Statutory Bodies-Industrial Development Commission 1945 - 1949: 31 December 1945, p. 17.

[2] NAZ S10/20/3, Industrial Development Commission and Colleen Bawn Limestone, 1946.

[3] NAZ S/225, Minutes of the fifty second meeting of the IDC, 11 February 1949.

While the Commission held this view and there were no legal means of preventing such a company establishing their own spinning plant, the government however, prevented the commission from participating in such a project by limiting the finances available for such participation. ①

This was, consequently, a factor to be taken into account, when the Commission during its epoch failed, therefore, to establish spinning mills with Hargreaves. Since the government at large was the main source of funds that the IDC disbursed to industries, making funds unavailable for the IDC hindered them from establishing a textile plant with Hargreaves. Therefore, government undermined the authority given to the IDC leading to its failures. Thus, if the Commission had been allowed the powers inherent in the act, it could have carried out a first class job but government had restricted its activities to such an extent that members were dissatisfied and had in fact as an earlier date, all handed in their resignations, as it was too evident that political expediency was interfering with their activities. ② Above all, this explained the dissatisfaction members of the IDC had as a result of how government interference with its work curtailed the commission's progress.

More so, the Calico Printers Association, a company which was prepared to expend some £300000 in the colony indicated some of the challenges faced by the IDC. The party in power had agreed to the scheme but it was vetoed by the opposition. ③ In this sense, it is clear that politics hindered the IDC in carrying its operations as Cowen made it vivid that the opposition hindered the establishment of an industry. In 1946, the politics in Southern Rhodesia between the Labour Party and the United Party had an effect of slowing the activities of the IDC. ④ For instance, in a letter to Mr. Mills, Musgrave

---

① NAZ RG/TR44, Secondary Industry in Southern Rhodesia: Department of Trade and Industrial Development, Salisbury May 1953.
② NAZ S/225, Minutes of the fifty second meeting of the IDC, 11 February 1949.
③ *Ibid*.
④ NAZ S10/20/3, Industrial Development Commission and Colleen Bawn Limestone, 1946.

lamented that "it is not decided just how the cement industry will be dealt with and I do not think it will be settled until after elections". [1] This indicated how politics hindered the IDC from striking industrial undertakings with Mr. Mills who was keen to establish a cement industry.

Moreover, the IDC faced challenges with the continuous conflicts with other government ministries and bodies in the colony particularly the Cost of Building and Building Permits Committee. This hindered the IDC to successfully carry its functions leading to some of their failure. One notable example was in the decentralisation of industries to achieve balanced industrial development. Parker reported that "the IDC faced conflicts with other ministerial bodies in carrying its functions", [2] and this was evidenced by the Cost of Building and Building Permits Committee. The Committee held a petition for the IDC when it wanted to assist in the building of the Allied Industries Limited buildings. [3] As the Chairman reported, this delayed the building of the industry as the Committee held the petition for over nine months while the material was available for commencing construction. [4] Thus the IDC, wanted authorisation from the Building Permit Committee when it had already decided to establish allied Industries Limited in Salisbury. With these problems hindering the IDC, it failed to meet some of the intended targets which can make the body to have failed in establishing crucial industries such as the textile industry.

Conclusion

The institutionalisation of the IDC stirred the pace of industrial development in Southern Rhodesia in the post-World War II period. It is important to note that when the IDC took over from IDAC, industrial

---

[1] NAZ S10/20/4, Industrial Development Commission: Letter to Mr Mills, 12 April 1946.
[2] *Ibid*.
[3] NAZ S/225, Industrial Development Commission Minutes of 14 July 1945.
[4] Ibid.

development was still at its early stages and was plagued by several challenges. Thus, with a close association between the government and industries to increase industrial development in the colony, the IDC was established through the Industrial Development Act of 1944 to enhance industrial growth in the colony reflecting the government's position regarding industrial development. From its inception, it began to investigate and research on possible solutions to the problems affecting industrial development in the colony. The IDC was active in granting financial assistance to industries for establishing and modernising industries in Southern Rhodesia. Through such financial assistance, several industries were set up that, to a greater extent, ameliorated the shortage of goods and inputs in the colony. Moreover, an increased expansion of industries was experienced in the colony arising out of the modernisation, coordination, and promotion efforts championed by the IDC. The body also interceded between the South African and Southern Rhodesia governments resulting in the 1948 Customs Union that led to the expansion of secondary industries in the colony considering provision of a ready market. This, therefore, explains the government's intentions in developing the industrial sector of the colony in post-World War II years. The paper has also shown that, despite the increase in the pace of industrial development, the IDC met several problems which hindered its operations. The IDC was hugely affected by the government which undermined the statutory powers given to the body. Political interference by other ministerial bodies in the colony hindered the operations of the IDC. The government interfered with the operations of the IDC thereby restraining the extent of its functions in industrial development. Beyond the interference, the politics in the colony also hindered the IDC's operation through delaying projects approved by the IDC. Hence, for these reasons, the IDC, to some extent, failed to deliver its intended targets as there were delays, denials, and poor of coordination. As such, these failures led to the dissolution of the IDC and all of its powers were transferred to the new Ministry under the Act No 14 of 1949.

Understanding the 1947 Tripartite Labour Agreement: Central African Labour History From 1946 to 1948 in Relation to Southern Rhodesia Labour Needs

Peter Uledi

Abstract

This paper argues that the labour negotiations by the three Central African territories were skewed in favour of Southern Rhodesia which sought to benefit from the labour agreement to fulfil its labour demands. [1] *Southern Rhodesia, aware of the economic status of Nyasaland, sought to offer Nyasaland an alternative of how it could generate revenue through exporting labour to Northern Rhodesia and Southern Rhodesia. It was not only the labour shortage that led Southern Rhodesia to the negotiating table with the other two northern territories but also the need to compete with the Union of South Africa on the labour market. Using archival sources this chapter explores negotiations, debates and conditions which led to the adoption of the Tripartite Labour Agreement between the three Central African territories. Literature on this period has*

---

[1] This paper benefited from Dr Joseph Mtisi's private archive that has conference proceedings and correspondences on the labour question in Central African Territories. Dr Mtisi is a retired senior labour history lecturer from the Department of Economic History at the University of Zimbabwe.

tended to focus more on the economic development of the territories[1], *state-peasant relationship*[2] *as the settlers tried to develop colonial system and the movement of labour from one territory to the other.* [3] *However，this chapter examines the negotiations，conditions，and economic atmosphere which led to the 1947 Amended Tripartite labour agreement between the Central African Territories. The paper uses the agreement signed in 1936 as a footing to explain the reason for need to redraw the 1947 agreement. This paper contributes to the existing body of knowledge by Patton and Phimister. Using Southern Rhodesia as a case study to understand the labour dynamics within the region and showing how important labour was in the development of the settler economies，and how each territory sought to promote its own interest.*

Introduction

The centrality of labour to the development of any economy is undeniably imperative especially so for colonial economies like that of Southern Rhodesia. Settlers sought to assert themselves by imposing，among other measures of control，taxation on Africans to force them to offer their labour to meet taxation requirements. This，however，did not succeed as Africans found ways to frustrate such strategies. Successful peasants found it economic to compete with settlers on producing for the market rather than selling their labour. [4] Those that offered their labour were faced with bad working conditions，forcing them to migrate to the Union of South Africa or desert work. The

---

[1] H. Simson, *Zimbabwe：A country study*, Uppsala, The Scandinavian Institute of African Studies, 1976, p. 23.

[2] J. Herbst, *State Politics in Zimbabwe*, Harare University of Zimbabwe Publications, 1990, p. 124.

[3] B. Patton, *Labour export policy in the Development of Southern Africa*, Harare, University of Zimbabwe publications, 1995, p. 17.

[4] I. R. Phimister, *Rhodes，Rhodesia and the Rand*, Harare, University of Zimbabwe publications, 1980, p. 7.

result was that labour shortages continued to exist much to the discontent of the white settler government which led to the Central African labour agreement which came to be known as the Tripartite Labour Agreement of 1936. The paper examines the negotiations held there after arriving on the 1947 Amendment Act which was more in favour of Southern Rhodesia, which was ear marked to benefit from labour acquired from her northern territories and thereby also forming a labour buffer between the northern territories and the Union of South Africa. However, in as much as it can be argued that the negotiations were skewed in favour of one territory, Nyasaland and Northern Rhodesia refused s terms proposed by Southern Rhodesia for example that remittances be taken at the end of a contract and Northern Rhodesia demanded labour which was enough for its copper mines. Despite the different positions the three territories arrived at an agreement in 1947 to allow movement of labour.

The literature that exists on the period under study concurs that there was labour shortage, so is this paper but differs on what the state did in coming up with solution which among them was to drag the northern territories into an agreement meant to benefit one territory at the expense of the other. Lewis described the state of labour in northern territories as "unlimited labour supply."[1] Arrighi nuanced the sentiment that the Second World War had far reaching consequences on labour[2] as it put to an end what Arrighi argues that labour became scarce because of the developments in manufacturing, agriculture, and growing dominance of the local economy by foreign oligopolies. However, he fails to take note of what Rutherford argued was mistreatment of labour[3] and what Phimister calls successful peasants. [4]

---

[1] W. A. Lewis, *Economic Development with Unlimited Supplies of Labour*, Manchester, The Manchester School, 1954, p. 14.

[2] G. Arrighi, "Labour Supplies in Historical Perspective: A Study of the Proletarianization of the African Peasantry in Rhodesia", *Journal of Development studies*, Vol 6, No 3, 1970, pp. 1 – 38.

[3] B. Rutherford, "Another side to rural Zimbabwe: social constructs and the administration of farm workers in Urungwe district, 1940s", *Journal of Southern African Studies*, Vol 23, No 1, 1997, p. 107.

[4] I. Phimister, "Corporate Profit and Race in Central African Copper Mining 1946 – 1956", *Business History Review*, *85*, 2011, pp. 749 – 779.

Building upon Arrighi's view, this paper is an addition on the literature of labour by exploring states role in labour supply through a labour agreement. Bill Patton attempted to analyse why there was movement of labour in Southern Rhodesia. [1] His reasons are well captured by other scholars but he did not analyse the negotiations that Southern Rhodesia engaged in with Northern Rhodesia and Nyasaland, the conditions leading to the agreement and the economic status prevailing in each territory. For David Johnson, the state continued to play an important role in recruiting labour even up to the Second World War. [2] However, his most important contribution to the socio-economic impacts of the Second World War was how it facilitated more labour for settler farmers, through the Compulsory Native labour Act. [3] However, Johnson fails to critically analyse how Africans were not passive but even refuted compulsory recruitment and how this led the government to engage the northern territories as a labour safety valve.

Rutherford lays the foundation for examining how farm workers were administered using the Urungwe areas in Southern Rhodesia in the 1940s. [4] His analysis is important as it how white farmers treated African labour resulting interalia in desertion and, migration of labour to the Union of South Africa. Maravanyika and Huijzenveld are of the view that labour shortage was endemic in Southern Rhodesia and the colony did not meet its labour demands because of exclusionist policies, [5] their analysis is important as it notes the shortage of labour in the colony. [6] They however did not make an

---

[1] B. Patton, *Labour export policy in the Development of Southern Africa*, Harare, University of Zimbabwe publications, 1995, p. 17.

[2] D. Johnson, "Settler Farmers and Coerced African Labour in Southern Rhodesia 1936 – 46", *The Journal of African History*, Vol 33, 1992, pp. 111 – 128.

[3] Ibid.

[4] B. Rutherford, "Another side to rural Zimbabwe: social constructs and the administration of farm workers in Urungwe district, 1940s", *Journal of Southern African Studies*, Vol 23, No. 1, 1997, p. 107.

[5] S. Maravanyika and D. Huijzenveld, "A Failed neo-Britain: Demography and the Labour Question in Colonial Zimbabwe c. 1890 – 1948", *African Nebula Vol* 1, No 1, 2010, pp. 1 – 16.

[6] Ibid.

attempt to analyse what the government did to meet labour demands and this paper, using the 1947 Tripartite agreement, argues that the government was aware of the tensions between farmers and miners and how other employer's mistreatment of labour and sought to benefit from a natural labour reservoir in Nyasaland through negotiations skewed in its favour.

Madimu interrogates the relation of state on one hand and miner and farmers on the other. The state having favoured miners in the initial years of colonisation was faced with a challenge when agriculture developed and the two sectors fought for labour. [1] Madimu only examines the relations of state and settlers on mining and farming but never dealt with the labour issues, which this paper seeks to explore as to how the state sought to satisfy labour demands in each sector. This paper builds upon the analysis that labour was scarce in Southern Rhodesia because of labour ill administration and the fight for scarce labour.

The Labour Question

Southern Rhodesia faced a number of economic problems; among them were labour,[2] undercapitalisation,[3] and locust invasions.[4] The labour problem was particularly difficult to deal with, as local labour was not forthcoming due to, among other things, "successful" peasant agriculture.[5] A number of measures were taken to coerce Africans into wage labour. The colony's mining and agricultural sectors were growing fast that the labour

---

[1] T. Madimu, "*Farmers, Miners and the State in Colonial Zimbabwe (Southern Rhodesia), c. 1895 – 1961*", PhD Thesis, Stellenbosch University, 2017, p. 45.

[2] G. Arrighi, *The Political Economy of Rhodesia*, The Hague, Mouton, 1967, p. 34.

[3] I. Phimister, "Corporate Profit and Race in Central African Copper Mining 1946 – 1956", *Business History Review*, 85,2011, pp. 749 – 779.

[4] P. Uledi and G. Hove, "A War of Man against Locust"! Locust Invasions and Anti-locust Campaigns in Salisbury, Southern Rhodesia, 1918 – 1940s, *South African Historical Journal*, Vol. 70, No. 4, 2018, p. 692.

[5] G. Arrighi, *The political Economy of Rhodesia*.

problem continued to hamper any meaningful economic development. African reserves were created mostly in infertile areas mainly to force Africans into wage labour. In addition, Africans were forced to pay hut and poll taxes. One of the ways Africans could meet these demands was to enter wage employment. [1] The working conditions were harsh and local labour fled the country to the Union of South Africa where wages and working conditions were relatively better.

The solution to the labour question was thought to be found in securing labour from Nyasaland and Northern Rhodesia. This option was to work for Southern Rhodesia labour problem since Africans in Nyasaland and Northern Rhodesia had been migrating clandestinely to Southern Rhodesia as the country offered better working conditions and higher wages compared to the northern territories. But this was not the only push factor; Nyasaland was a "natural" labour reservoir as there were no natural resources that could be exploited in the protectorate for the benefit of both the indigenous and white settlers. [2] Thus, because of taxation and other colonial pressures, Africans had to seek employment elsewhere. This created tension between the governments as labour was illegally moving to Southern Rhodesia. The Nyasaland administration attempted to monitor labour movements to its benefit. [3] This resulted in talks between the three territories leading to an agreement, in 1936 Tripartite Labour Agreement, on how to control and allow free migration of labour within the territories. It should be noted that the agreement was not easy to administer as the three territories had different expectations, and this took debates and disagreement which eventually resulted in the amended 1947 Tripartite Agreement according to which labour was allowed to move freely within the territories under certain conditions.

---

① R. Palmer and N. Parsons, (ed.) *The roots of rural poverty in Central and Southern Africa*, Los Angeles, University of California Press, 1977, p. 269.

② B. Patton, *Labour export policy in the Development of Southern Africa*, Harare: University of Zimbabwe publications, 1995, p. 241.

③ Ibid.

However, before examining the agreement in detail, different positions should be analysed which influenced each territory in agreeing to the terms of the labour agreement.

The discovery of commercial quantities of gold in South Africa in 1888 came with the exploitation of diamonds in the Northern Cape. This would change the whole labour migration pattern in Southern Africa. Gold and diamond miners, accommodated in compounds and were contracted for 18 months stints. [1] This is the same system that Nyasaland proposed for its exported labour. The extent to which Nyasaland labour flowed to South Africa has been queried by Harrington et al as they argue that the large population of black workers in the Union came from Botswana, Lesotho and Swaziland and those from Mozambique, Zambia and Nyasaland made just a small proportion. [2] Thus, to ensure labour supply, the Witwatersrand Labour Organisation (WENELA) was established in 1900, and was given the mandate to recruit from Nyasaland, Northern Rhodesia and Southern Rhodesia. [3] Given the labour problems in Southern Rhodesia, it was clear that WENELA was going to face challenges since the colony was also in dire need of labour.

Harrington et al claims that the mine management has always provided healthcare for its employees. [4] This was one of the reasons why labour became a problem in the northern territories as workers fled the Rhodesia's and Nyasaland. The Union posed a threat to whatever labour arrangement that was going to be put in place among the Central African territories. The South African war of 1892 – 1902 forced gold mines to virtually shut down and led to a lowered demand for black labour resulting in the loss of 100 000 jobs. Thus WENELA was requested to set up a realistic structure to achieve a

---

[1] J. Parpart, 'The household and the mine shaft: gender and class struggles on the Zambian Copper belt, 1926 – 64', *Journal of Southern African Studies*, Vol 16, Issue 3, 2007, pp. 36 – 56.

[2] J. S. Harington, et al, 'A century of migrant labour in the gold mines of South Africa", *The Journal of The South African Institute of Mining and Metallurgy*, 2004, pp. 64 – 71.

[3] Ibid.

[4] Ibid.

stable workforce. ① This meant they were to penetrate all neighbouring countries in an attempt to cater for South Africa's labour problems. In 1912, Mozambique provided 48 per cent of the labour and by 1930, Nyasaland provided more labour than Lesotho and Swaziland and Mozambique combined making it the richest labour reservoir in Southern Africa. ②

The Second World War had effects on South Africa as gold price was now low and conditions for labour were poor. Strikes broke out in 1946, bringing mines to a standstill as over 60 000 workers withdrew their labour. The 1946 strikes in South Africa, to some extent, influenced the discussions leading to the amendment of the labour agreement in 1947. Jeeves and others state that there was a recruiting crisis which led to more pressure on South African industry, following the 1946 African mine workers' strike. ③

The development dilemma in Nyasaland

Patton argues that labour from Nyasaland has historically developed neighbouring countries than its own. ④ The colonial and post-colonial problem that Nyasaland has had to face was the struggle to control labour export. The development of capitalist agriculture-tea and coffee plantations and tobacco farms among other agriculture undertakings, meant that labour needed to be retained in the country for internal use. It was, however, difficult to retain labour, given the development of settler plantations as the government invested more in settler farms rather than peasant production. The neglect on peasant production and provision of assistance whatsoever for peasants to

① J. S. Harington, et al, 'A century of migrant labour in the gold mines of South Africa", *The Journal of The South African Institute of Mining and Metallurgy*, 2004, pp. 64 – 71.

② Ibid.

③ A. Jeeves, D. Yudelman and J. Crush, *South African Labour Empire: A history of black Migrancy of the Gold mines*, Boston: Westview Press, 1991, p. 134.

④ B. Paton, *Labour export policy in the Development of Southern Africa*, Harare: University of Zimbabwe publications, 1995, p. 241.

meet their food demands and the selling of surplus to meet taxation pressures made staying in and remain in Nyasaland not an option. Paton notes that the dilemma of the colonial administration was on whether to use labourers for internal development in agriculture, mining, and road and railway construction. [1] Both the local officials and farmers realised that the local developments would be more beneficial than sending Africans outside to work outside the country. But as mentioned earlier, taxes and other pressures pushed Africans to seek work and thus look for better employment outside the territory. Planters in Nyasaland were unable to attract the labour they required as they were paying less than employers outside the country. The result was the ban on all emigrant labour, a stricter pass law and redoubled taxes were imposed as a solution to deal with the labour problem. [2] This was, however, not a solution as it made the labour problem even worse and stimulated massive clandestine labour migration. Labour emigration had proven an effective way to lure remittances for the colony as the government was paid for the labour exported. [3]

The labour problem in Nyasaland became perpetual, most certainly given the ill-treatment of African workers by their white employers. Africans working on estates were not allowed to grow crops even on fallow estate land. This meant that food provision was a challenge given the low wages they were paid. Furthermore, African women were frequently raped and men sometimes assaulted. The most infamous instrument of African oppression was forced labour of "thangata" introduced in 1904. In this "thangata" Africans were forced to live on estates and work for two unpaid months as a form of tax payment. [4] The governor is quoted saying that:

---

[1] B. Paton, *Labour export policy in the Development of Southern Africa*, Harare: University of Zimbabwe publications, 1995, p. 241.

[2] File 137/186B, Migrant labour committee (second file) 1945 – 46, letter from A Stepherson to labour Commissioner in Lusaka, 5/6/46.

[3] Ibid.

[4] F137/186B, Migrant labour Committee, (second file) 1945 – 46, The position of Workers in Nyasaland, 26/6/46.

The principle governing the question of Natives proceeding outside the protectorate in search of work is that emigration is to be discouraged so far as possible, but those Natives who have made up their minds to leave the protectorate shall do so under government control. ①

It was becoming clear to the government that labour was migrating out of the country. Thus, despite the need for labour in Southern Rhodesia, economic condition themselves in Nyasaland were pushing labour away at the expense of internal development. It was also clear that the Nyasaland administration could not control clandestine labour emigration as the population of those that worked in Southern Rhodesia increased. ② The Nyasaland government then lifted the prohibition it had imposed on foreign recruiting of labour and began to strive for a degree of compromise on labour supply to neighbouring countries.

Debates leading to the amendment 1947 of the Tripartite Agreement

Having agreed to the first agreement in 1936, the three territories were not satisfied with the terms of the agreement and how it operated, resulting in the need to amend it. The number of workers migrating to other territories from Nyasaland continued to rise. By 1945, 2 207 Nyasalanders were employed in Northern Rhodesia in mines and this was 4.5% of the total employment. ③ All migrant workers working in Northern Rhodesia from

---

① F137/186B, Migrant labour Committee, (second file) 1945 – 46, The position of Workers in Nyasaland, 26/6/46.

② F137/186B, Migrant labour Committee, 1945 – 46, Draft letter from Secretary: Native affairs in Southern Rhodesia to chairman, Central African Council, Migrant Labour committee, 17/7/46.

③ F137/186B, Migrant Labour Committee (second file) 1945 – 46, Stephenson to Labour commissioner (Lusaka), 5/6/46.

Nyasaland numbered 115 000, by the end of 1945. [1] These numbers continued to trouble the Nyasaland government as it was being disadvantaged by the labour outflow. Hence, there was need for regulations regarding labour movement.

The working conditions in Nyasaland and Southern Rhodesia did not go well with Africans. Consequently many of them migrated to the Union of South African to work in mines in Johannesburg. Witwatersrand Native Labour Association (WENELA) provided transport for African from their homes to places of employment and this meant that the Rhodesias were facing stiff problems in securing labour since they did not offer same services. This prompted the need to come up with a legislation to control the flow of labour, and to establish a Native Labour Agency in Southern Rhodesia. [2] This was envisioned to work well with the agency distributing labour that entered Southern Rhodesia and ensuring payment of "good" wages possibly to ensure good payment so as to compete with the South African employers. There were debates on whether or not Africans should be given a choice to work in Southern Rhodesia or South Africa. Allowing Africans to choose was self-defeating for Southern Rhodesia, given the poor working conditions poor housing and low wages they offered, compared to South African employers. This was dismissed as a bad idea hence the need to engage the other two Central African countries on how to regulate labour flow within the territories and possibly prohibit labour to go to South Africa. Southern Rhodesia was being affected the most by a haphazard labour policy. By 1946, there were 165 000 migrant workers in Southern Rhodesia, 6 000 of whom were in transit to South Africa. [3]

---

[1] File 137/186B, Migrant labour committee (second file) 1945 – 46, letter from A Stephenson to Labour Commissioner in Lusaka, 5/6/46.

[2] Ibid.

[3] File 137/186B, Migrant Labour Committee (second file) 1945 – 46, "Notes on Migrant African labour which employer in Southern Rhodesia should understand" secretary Migrant Labour Committee to W. F. Stabbs: Northern Rhodesia Labour Commissioner. Letter dated, 5/6/46.

It seems from the onset that the Tripartite Agreement would benefit Southern Rhodesia more since it was the brains behind the idea to have a labour agreement that would provide a solution to labour shortages. Employers failed to provide accommodation for wives of workers and this caused social friction as men were forced to live without their wives. [1] However, employers later realised how efficient married men were and thus the need to provide accommodation for married men and the need to improve living and working conditions. For Southern Rhodesia, the government regulation compelled employers to provide labour with proper housing and food. This was not enough because labour still found its way to South Africa due to relatively better wages, hence the need to engage with Nyasaland on allowing labour flow into the colony and provide a basis in which it was treated well and contracted to avoid migration. This was expressed by the Migrant Labour Committee which emphasised the need to study Africans and improve the conditions and make them tap into modern industrialisation. [2]

The debates on the revision of the provisional Tripartite Agreement set in motion a long period of contention. This is explained by Crush et al who argue that migrant labour systems of South African gold mines emerged out of the different contradictory interests of the recruiters, the farmers, miners and states in the region. [3] With regards to Nyasaland, the Central Africa Council proposed a revision of the Agreement by including compulsory deferred pay and family remittances. [4] This formed the basis of the agreement in which the government of Nyasaland sought to make profit from the migration of its labour. This is the idea that the Nyasaland administration

---

[1] File 137/186B, Migrant Labour Committee (second file) 1945 – 46, "Notes on Migrant African labour which employer in Southern Rhodesia should understand" secretary Migrant Labour Committee to W. F. Stabbs; Northern Rhodesia Labour Commissioner. Letter dated, 5/6/46.

[2] Ibid.

[3] A. Jeeves, D. Yudelman and J. Crush, *South African Labour Empire. A history of black Migrancy of the Gold mines*, Boston; Westview Press, 1991, p. 134.

[4] File 137/186B, Migrant Labour Committee (second file) 1945 – 46, "Notes on Migrant African labour which employer in Southern Rhodesia should understand".

sold to the Rhodesia if the latter wanted labour from Nyasaland. These terms were refused by Southern Rhodesia which preferred a system in which workers would remit money on voluntary basis not one backed by legislation. The Nyasaland government also proposed that Africans should remit money to Nyasaland by means of postal orders and bank drafts. [1] The system in which remittances were sent back home raised questions on whether the money would benefit the African back home or the Nyasaland government wanted to use that money for its internal development, as the money was sent through the Native Department stations.

The Nyasaland government also proposed a contract system which laid the terms and conditions of work. This issue resulted from the failure of the Labour Committee to deal with non-contract workers. The contract system would help not only the employee from exploitation by the employer but would also enable the government to have statistics of migrant workers and the remittances accruing in the process. The Nyasaland administration complained of Africans leaving their wives, gardens, and families for work outside the country and returning home with cheap clothes and Knick-knack which was not in tandem with labour rendered. [2] This was to set in motion a provision of a contract which included, among its terms, limitation of the period of absence from Nyasaland to a year or eight months, compulsory deferred pay and compulsory family remittance to dependents. These terms did not go well with the Rhodesians. Labour in Nyasaland itself did not understand the demands made by their government and this fuelled clandestine migration to the Union of South Africa. The need to have an act which would regulate labour migration was clear as the Union refused to cooperate. Thus, there was the need to have legislation with sound humanitarian basis and such obvious advantages to the workers. Nyasaland's

[1] F42/4/6 Vol 1, Africans in the federation labour migrant workers Act. Remittances for deferred pay (migrant labour workbook scheme) from supervisor of the native immigration to chief native commissioner, 10. 6. 46.

[2] F42/4/6/1, Africans in the federation. The migrant workers Act, 17/06/1946 – 48.

main argument and criticism was that the terms were littered with 'pious hopes' sincere but unlikely to be unfulfilled. [1] Thus, there was dilemma as to how the issue of migrant labour could be solved. The colonial office in London could not be involved in such deliberations as the responsibility to solve the labour demands in one of its colony was in the hands of the colonial officials in those respective colonies.

The debate on whether labour should be imported into Southern Rhodesia also had dimensions to do with the quality of labour available. The Governor of Southern Rhodesia argued that the labour problem was as a result of employers not understanding Africans, in terms of behaviour, character and culture. His position on the labour question was that "the only way to improve the output of the African and that was to teach him to be efficient and take pride in his work". [2] Thus, if the African workers were to be effective stakeholders in the industry, the Governor stressed it was necessary to provide good accommodation. This, however, failed to materialise because the employers wanted to minimise costs and maximise profits. Consequently employers in Southern Rhodesia concluded that the only solution to the labour problem was to import labour from Nyasaland. But the problem persisted and this forced introspection on the employers. This shows how capitalistic he colonial policy was and its intentions to milk African labour at a minimum cost.

Southern Rhodesia began to appreciate that their treatment of workers labour was the main reason why the labour problem continued. Two camps on how to solve the problem had arisen in Southern Rhodesia. The first advocated good worker treatment and welfare, and was open to the idea of labour import from the Northern territories. [3] However, the point of

---

[1] F42/4/6/1, Africans in the federation. The migrant labour Act, 17/06/46.

[2] G. Huggins, "Africans must be taught to take pride in his work", *Chronicle Newspaper*, 14 June 1946.

[3] F137/186C, Migrant Labour Report, (First file) 1946 – 47, Extract from the Rhodesia Herald dated 13/12/46, Reasons for shortage of labour from Nyasaland suggested change in European attitude towards the Africans.

convergence was to solve the problem and get the best out of the African worker. This led to the idea of employing Africans on a profit sharing basis. Partly to prevent desertion, and strikes, save money and would provide an incentive for the African workers. This was well captured by one writer who wrote: "I wonder we shall ever get the best out of our work people unless they are made partners in running the workshops and factories and partners in sharing profits."[1] One other advantage of adopting the profit sharing approach was that employers would save money by not employing recruiting agencies.

The debate among employers in Southern Rhodesia and between Nyasaland and Southern Rhodesia brought out two important aspects. The first was that Nyasaland wanted to export labour but it was mistreated and hence they were in a dilemma on whether to keep it for local development or send it to Southern or Northern Rhodesia for money.[2] The other issue was that Southern Rhodesian employers who were also in a dilemma on how to get labour: either to improve worker welfare for improved worker efficiency or import more labour from the Northern territories that could be easily exploited unlike local labour. The resolution made by the Rhodesian Mining Industry Federation Congress in 1942 included treating the African labour problem as a natural disaster and the government to adopt and encourage progressive policy and set up a Permanent Native labour Department to deal with the aspects of labour.[3] Solutions suggested included the establishment of a school for the boss boys, set high wages, better food rations, improved housing and medical conditions and to appoint inspectors to weed out inefficient workers.

---

[1] Farm owner, 'Profit sharing schemes', *Herald Rhodesia*, 19 June 1946.

[2] Box 120147, (Ministry of Labour) F42/4/6/1 Vol Africans in the federation labour migrant workers Act, Remittances and deferred pay (migrant labour workbook scheme) letter from Deputy Commissioner of labour of Supervisor of Native labour immigration to chief Native Commissioner, 5/7/46.

[3] F137/186C, Migrant Labour Report, (First file) 1946 – 47, Extract from the Rhodesia Herald dated 13/12/46, Reasons for shortage of labour from Nyasaland suggested change in European attitude towards the Africans.

Attitudes of the Three Territories towards
the 1947 Agreement

All the three territories wanted African labour but they had conflicting ideas, interests and attitudes on how to solve the labour problem and approach a new tripartite agreement. Southern Rhodesia favoured non-contracted labour from Nyasaland in supplementing labour that was unrestricted and unregulated. Otherwise Southern Rhodesia wanted labour to flow on a voluntary basis. Southern Rhodesia maintained this attitude throughout the negotiating period from 1942 to 1947 because it wanted flow of cheap labour and not to be tied to any formal or contract systems. This was meant to force Nyasaland to give in to their demands, but Southern Rhodesia knew very well that Nyasaland needed to be treated with caution because it was ready to sign a deal with the Union and export its labour to more paying mines. Hence, Southern Rhodesia played the card well in accepting some of the proposals and rejecting others. Furthermore, Southern Rhodesia threatened to close its labour market from the three territories. This was to reduce more demands and new proposals from the northern territories. This, however, had impacts on how Nyasaland would propose its labour export demands.

Nyasaland was the main labour exporter in Central Africa. This meant her position was both compromised and could be used to her advantage as she could make demands since the labour market was growing. After 1942, Nyasaland made proposals to amend the Tripartite Agreement because she thought it was not operating effectively. As already stated, Nyasaland wanted labour to be exported on a clear contract system. The contract would serve as a guarantee in which it would be convinced that its labour was employed. [1] Nyasaland's attitude towards the labour system continued to

---

[1] F137/186B, Migrant labour Committee, Letter from E. H. Machell to P. J. Kenworthy Native labour Immigration, 26/6/46.

change as Southern Rhodesia continued to be affected by how the employers in the Union treated labour and this meant that Southern Rhodesia, because it wanted labour so badly, had no option but to accept the compulsory deferred pay, family remittance and a work book scheme controlled by Nyasaland. It appears that Northern Rhodesia was silent but it also made proposals to place its labour representative in Southern Rhodesia to monitor the conditions of service. [1]

Nyasaland had a very negative attitude towards what it called "Machona", Nyasalanders who left the country and never went back. This had two effects; the government was losing its men-power and also sources of tax and this was causing more rural poverty. A survey in the late 1930s was conducted in Nyasaland to assess the way of life of women whose husbands migrated, and it was seen that their ability to survive the economy was very low, prone to starvation and could not work their lands properly. These women were the poorest of the society. This is what led to the contract system and reduction of the period of absence to 18 months. The Migrant Labour Committee reported in 1946 that the provisions of compulsory family remittance would relieve thousands of women and children from hunger during the absence of their menfolk. [2] As a way to deal with the Machona, the Nyasaland government stressed the need for compulsory expatriation but the government of Southern Rhodesia had reservations on the issue. [3] This caused friction between the two governments.

Are we in agreement?

After it was clear to Southern Rhodesia that there was need for labour, the country decided to adopt the terms Nyasaland was proposing for

---

[1] F137/186B, 1945 – 46, Migrant Labour Committee (second file) Code Telegraph from Rumson (Salisbury) to secretary (Lusaka) and secretary (Zomba) 6/7/46.

[2] F137/186B, Migrant labour Committee 21 – 21/03/46.

[3] NLAB102/A, Migrant Workers Act 1947 – 1949, memo dated 02/05/07.

exporting its labour. Nyasaland also came to the realisation that exporting labour was economically viable since it reduced pressure on resources and capital inflow of remittances. The Central African Council drafted proposals on migrant labour, making provisions for deferred pay and family remittances. Since these provisions existed in the earlier agreement, the proposal set that some part of the migrant labour earnings should, "return to his country of origin for his dependents to mitigate the effects of his absence upon the social and economic structure of that country. "[1] It also proposed that work books and stamps be used to capture records. Southern Rhodesia had no option but to accept the scheme.

Nyasaland argued for short term contracts for its workers. The agreement laid terms for Northern and Southern Rhodesia that facilities were to be made available for those who wished to enter into long term contacts. [2] This was to avoid workers being exploited and the contract captured the wage provisions for the worker in terms of food and the period of stay in the country of employment. However, Southern Rhodesia tried to resist the idea of deferred pay and contracts, let alone the limited period of stay away from home which Nyasaland had limited to 24 months. Members of the Chamber of Mines did not like the idea of family remittances and argued that it was only going to adopt it if the money was sent after four months. [3] The railway companies in Southern Rhodesia were against the idea of the Southern Rhodesia Native Labour Supply Commission Bill. The Bill wanted to end the activities of the labour agencies by excellent administration of labour flow and distribution. [4]

Nyasaland made more proposals besides the deferred pay and family

---

[1] NLAB102/A, Migrant Workers Act 1947 – 1949, memo dated 02/05/07.

[2] F137/186B, Migrant Labour Committee 1945 – 46, Letter from W. A. W. Clark to Minister of Finance, 25/6/46.

[3] F137/186B, Migrant labour Committee, Letter from E. H. Machell to P. J. Kenworthy Native labour Immigration, 26/6/46.

[4] F137/186B, 1945 – 46, Migrant Labour Committee (second file) Code Telegraph from Rumson (Salisbury) to secretary (Lusaka) and secretary (Zomba) 6/7/46.

remittances. All migrants were supposed to have a medical examination before leaving the country, and before departing from the country of employment, the contractors were supposed to provide free transport. These proposals were very hard to avoid since Southern Rhodesia had already decided that the only way to solve labour shortages was to import surplus labour from Nyasaland. The initiative by Nyasaland was to increase the profitability of exporting labour by reducing transport cost for its workers to and from Southern Rhodesia. It should be noted that Southern Rhodesia did not accept the proposal as a point of weakness to negotiate but the need to avoid the deplorable effects of emigration of male population out of the country. Thus, the only way to solve this was to use a special stamp operated by the Nyasaland government. Nyasaland made a proposition to Southern Rhodesia that if Rhodesian employers provided the necessary married quarters, Nyasaland was prepared to "allow an employee's wife and children to come to the colony".[1] The Migrant Labour Committee reported in 1946, that the proposals were too cumbersome and had many loopholes to ensure any degree of success. This was a way to dodge such a system and actually encouraged and facilitated voluntary remittances to Nyasaland, and Southern Rhodesia refused labour going back to Nyasaland after 24 months.

The discussion on amending the Tripartite Agreement was going in circles as shown by continued conferences. Mr. Hudson, a representative of the Southern Rhodesian Government, accepted the principle of deferred pay and family remittances but rejected the compulsory stamp and the book scheme as being uneconomic and difficult to implement. Rather they proposed an alternative scheme whereby the whole of the tax collected from all migrant workers would be remitted to the countries of origin where a proportion of it could be put into family remittance. Southern Rhodesia also wanted voluntarily sending of money back home signed on an employee's identity certificate and work book. Southern Rhodesia representatives were

---

[1] F137/186B, Migrant labour Committee, 14/7/46.

opposed to the contractual system as it would prove unpopular, impracticable with tremendous organisation and that it would disrupt the flow of labour. The agreement seemed close yet so far since the territories we not yet agreed on some proposals to revise the early agreements.

These agreements did not please Africans in Nyasaland who wanted to migrate to the Union of South Africa. Southern Rhodesia persuaded the workers by offering them the access to be exempted from paying tax in the first year. Such an act was initiated by Southern Rhodesia to encourage clandestine labour migration from the two northern territories. This was only to discourage them from going to the Union but this did not stop workers from clandestinely proceeding to the Union. [1] The claims by Nyasaland workers forced Southern Rhodesia to agree to the remittance scheme of "temporary deposit and remittance account". The migrant labour Committee reported in 1946 that, "the Southern Rhodesian government appreciates that something must be done to alleviate the position of Nyasaland and provisions for controlled migration is necessary and financial position must be made for family left without support". [2] The ability or inability of the three governments to agree on such matters must be regarded as an indication of their willingness to foster that measure of cooperation. Disagreements on the inter-territorial migration were delaying production in Southern Rhodesia as labour was restricted to come to the colony. [3]

Since the new migrant labour Act was to be put in effect from the first of January 1947, there was need to sort other technical issues before the new Migrant labour Act started working. These included setting up a labour camp at Tete which was one of the new ports of entry for migrant labours from Nyasaland and Northern Rhodesia. This was because 20 000 migrants passed

---

① F137/186B, Migrant labour Committee, 14/7/46.

② F137/186B, Migrant Labour Committee 1945 – 46.

③ Box 283299, (Min of labour) Migrant Workers Act, 1947,1949,10/03/47.

through this camp annually. [1] This was called "Wanderlust labour". Hence there was need to create a system in which this labour was captured and made sure that they reached Southern Rhodesia.

Northern Territories Worker Representatives and the Working Conditions

Nyasaland and Northern Rhodesia had reservation in exporting labour to Southern Rhodesia because of ill-treatment of imported labour. Nyasaland wanted to include the Union of South Africa in the labour agreement because it argued that labour was paid better wages and treated better in South Africa compared to Southern Rhodesia. This argument meant Southern Rhodesia was going to suffer labour shortages, hence it was forced to accept labour representatives from the Northern territories to be stationed in the colony. The labour representatives were mandated to write reports on how employers, especially farmers treated the workers from the Northern territories. [2]

Nyasaland labour representatives proposed that labour be given freedom to choose employers and employment they wanted. The government of Nyasaland knew that bad employers would always get labour through the Labour Bureau that distributed imported labour and this meant that labour from Nyasaland would be exploited and mistreated. [3] By 1945, over 21 000 Northern migrant workers were employed in the mines in Southern Rhodesia. [4] But the wages were way below those paid by the mines in the Union of South Africa. [5] Workers in the mines worked from 8 to 13 hours

---

[1] S482/588/39, Migrant Native Labour: Rest camps, letter from J. N. Kennedy Governor (SR) to Paulo De Rego (Lourenco Marques).

[2] Box 28329, (Ministry of Labour) Migrant workers Act 1947 – 1949, From Mr Bullock to Commissioner of Native labour.

[3] F137/186, Migrant labour committee, 19 March 1945.

[4] F137/186B, Migrant Labour Committee 1945 – 46, Nyasaland Labour Office on African mine workers in Southern Rhodesia.

[5] Ibid.

and were given cooked food especially workers from Shabani mine. Rations of meals, hot tea, or cocoa for underground workers and bread were given before men went underground for work. [1] It should be noted that, at times the food was inadequate to keep a worker really fit to do the hard manual labour.

Furthermore, the living conditions were not good, especially those of the mine compounds. The report of the Migrant Labour Committee in 1946 made clear to Nyasaland and Northern Rhodesia that the living conditions in the compounds were not good. The compounds were overcrowded as more than five workers used a room meant for two people. In addition, compounds were vulnerable to cholera, typhoid and other sanitary diseases. Pass laws were made strict for those in the compound and the compound system denied the workers access to the outside world. The compound system was indeed a quasi-military system in which the compound main gate which was the point of entry and was guarded by boss boys and compound managers who were brutal and could beat and whip men for failing to cooperate. [2] The long working hours, low wages and mistreatment of workers made the worker representatives from the northern territories advise their governments to move the agenda of a contract system which laid the conditions of work or to export its labour to South Africa. It was such mistreatment which stimulated clandestine migration. When Southern Rhodesia in the 1946 - 7 period changed the working conditions, labour flow to the colony increased. This led to workers who were in South Africa fled to Southern Rhodesia, which meant workers wanted to work in Southern Rhodesia but because of the bad living and working conditions they fled to the Union. One can say it was not the improved working conditions in Southern Rhodesia but the worker strikes in the Union from 1946 - 48 that made labour flee South Africa for Southern

---

[1] Box 28379, (Ministry of Labour) F15 Nyasaland Migration 1941 - 47 Vol 1, From W. H. D Walke, Captain staff Officer to the Commissioner of police, to the Chief Native. Commissioner, 13/08/47.

[2] Ibid.

Rhodesia. [1]

The Nyasaland government also sent Chief Kalonga to Southern Rhodesia to investigate on the living conditions. The Chief was from the Central Province of Lilongwe. He visited Darwendale estates compounds and met workers from Nyasaland. The Chief was interviewed and said, "I was instructed by the Nyasa government to see how Nyasa African employees were treated and paid by their employers in this country" (Southern Rhodesia) and I also came with other two Chiefs from Nyasa who visited the Midlands with the same objective. [2] One of the workers stood up and read a letter to the Chief on the working conditions and said that, "Africans from Southern Rhodesia and Nyasaland were not paid enough wages although they were employed in skilled jobs". [3] This made the Southern Rhodesia employers revise their treatment towards African workers.

Chief Kalonga's visit shocked employers in Southern Rhodesia whether his motive was to stop recruitment in Nyasaland or to improve conditions of workers in Southern Rhodesia. This fear was expressed in a letter by the Ministry of Labour:

It appears that no conclusions were arrived at as a result of the visit of Chief Kalonga, his visit was more in the Native working conditions, and his opinions are not known and were not apparently made known during the course of his address. No suggestion was made that recruiting might be stopped or curtailed. [4]

The government in Southern Rhodesia was left wondering what really the motive of the Chief was. One thing was clear, Nyasaland was making an

---

[1] Central Africa council 27/02/47.
[2] Box 28379, (Ministry of Labour) F15 Nyasaland Migration 1941 – 47 Vol 1, From W. H. D. Walke, Captain Staff Officer to the Commissioner of police, to the Chief Native Commissioner, 13/08/47.
[3] Ibid.
[4] Box 28329, (Ministry of Labour) F151, Nyasaland Migration 1941 – 47, Vol 1,15/09/47.

investigation on its workers' conditions and this gave it the ability to propose new terms as it knew the attitude of Southern Rhodesia towards labour.

1947 Inte-Territorial Labour Agreement

The agreement of 1947 was reached as a result of several factors which forced the three territories wanting to amend the 1942 migrant labour agreement. The Northern Territories especially were not satisfied with the clauses and implementation of the 1942 labour agreement. The Colonial Office appointed a mediator and custodian of the Labour agreements to be made within the three territories, in the form of the Central African Council (CAC). This was a result of the disagreements that existed. The three territories were to air their grievances, concerns and dissatisfactions through the CAC and not directly to each other as was previously the case. The Union of South Africa was also roped into the talks and the four governments met for the first time in 1950, after the instigations and mediations of the CAC. [1] However, the Union of South Africa benefited from clandestine migration and even sponsored it because its labour was cheap.

The grievances of Northern Rhodesia and Nyasaland were understood and accepted by the CAC, as explained by W Clark, the Chief Secretary of CAC as "very unsatisfactory and heavily skewed in favour of Southern Rhodesia". [2] The Colonial Office and CAC agreed that although the two territories had grievances, the agreement should be continued until the end of the war, which it did. Negotiations began in 1946 and changes were made that were "fair" to every government. Changes included that, "the Southern Rhodesian governments improves the Camps and constructs permanent structures on land designated for the construction of these camps". [3]

---

[1] F137/186, Migrant Labour Committee (Special). 1945 – 46 Sheet titled "Migrant Labour" enclosure in letter dated 20/12/45 from Colonial Office (W. Clark Chief Secretary Central African Council).

[2] Ibid.

[3] Ibid.

Transport was to be provided by, rail via what became known as "ulele". Remittances and deferred pay were made compulsory. This was to ensure that migrant labour was treated fairly on the area of employment particularly on the Southern Rhodesian farms. Southern Rhodesia was also to go out of its way to ensure that all incoming labour had the right documentation and was to be repatriated after eighteen months. Most importantly, the onus lay with Southern Rhodesia to retain migrant labour; the first call clause in practice was all but scrapped off. [1]

Conclusion

The 1947 labour agreement captures the political economy of the central African countries as they attempted to build their economies on manipulation. Attempts by Southern Rhodesia to arrest the labour shortage were met but without satisfactory results as the labour exporting countries of Nyasaland and Northern Rhodesia made proposals that forced Southern Rhodesia to enter into an agreement it was not pleased with. Southern Rhodesia, as the main importer of labour, was in a dilemma; whether to improve the quality of workers it had or to increase the number by bending to the demands of the Northern Territories. The Northern territories, especially Nyasaland were also in a dilemma; whether to use the labour for internal development or send it for profit. The better policy to adopt was export of labour under certain conditions which the other Central African countries adopted, but it was Southern Rhodesia which was more vocal in labour demand than the other two. The Union of South Africa was the main competitor for labour and it gained from the disagreements between the central African countries. Clandestine migration was beneficial to the Union as it could be exploited. The aspect of clandestine labour also caused political

---

[1] F137/189, Migrant Labour Committee (Special). 1945 – 46 Sheet titled "Migrant Labour" enclosure in letter dated 9/08/46 from W. Clark, to Colonial Office.

tension in the Union as farmers benefited from it while miners needed official labour because clandestine labour was not meeting their labour demands. Southern Rhodesia made attempts to curb clandestine migration but the Union did not cooperate, which led to the final Migrant labour agreement of 1947 in which Southern Rhodesia agreed to the new labour agreement and improved the working conditions to attract more labour. It was Southern Rhodesia which made profits from the labour imports unlike the labour exporters who always had to rely on that system which Southern Rhodesia always manipulated. To avoid this manipulation and mistreatment of workers, the Northern territories placed worker representatives in Southern Rhodesia to monitor the worker conditions and also to overseer the proper implementation of the agreement.

Book Review: A.S Mlambo, E.S Pangeti, I. Phimister, Zimbabwe: A History of Manufacturing, 1890 – 1995, University of Zimbabwe, 2000

Nyasha Blessed Bushu

It is quite befitting that the development of Southern Rhodesia's manufacturing industries be authored by astute scholars such as Alois Mlambo, Ian Robert Phimister and Evelyn Pangeti. The scholars have written extensively on the colonial administration's attitude towards the agrarian and mining industries respectively. David Johnson also attempted a limited examination of the manufacturing industry which he concludes to have been a watershed for Southern Rhodesia's manufacturing industry in a chapter of his book, *World War 2 and the Scramble for Labour in Colonial Zimbabwe, 1939 – 1948.* [1] This book by Pangeti et al is a more in-depth analysis of issues surrounding the progress of manufacturing in Zimbabwe; it also offers a retrospective perspective on the significance of collaborative state and private intervention on issues regarding colonial economic development. The scholars employ a long historical approach covering a vast expanse of issues over nearly a century. The study is broken down by typologies based on chronology making their narrative less cumbersome to

---

[1] D. Johnson, *World War II and the Scramble for Labour in Colonial Zimbabwe, 1939 – 1948*, University of Zimbawe, 2000.

follow. They distinguished epochs which were punctuated by prominent flag points or milestones which were both a consequence of internal and external forces which defined colonial state and subsequent independent government's policies and attitudes towards manufacturing.

In the first chapter which covers the period from 1894 to 1939, Phimister captures manufacturing in its nascence and the factors which militated against its development initially under the British South Africa Company and subsequently the Responsible Government. Phimister aptly describes a lethargic development through his description of the preoccupation with agrarian and mineral export oriented growth under the "spirit of imperialism" under the 1898 Orders in Council. [1] Here, Phimister's main argument is that colonial administrations were more than reluctant to initiate solid protectionism for the manufacturing sector. He further highlights a protracted struggle between the state and industrialists represented by companies like Wright Confectionaries, Joelson Brothers, Paper Industries Ltd who remained resolute in developing a light industry. Manufacturing remained undercapitalised confronted with a banking system which was "unresponsive" to the demands of the manufacturing industry and secondary industry continued to be regarded as a relatively minor adjunct to mining and farming. [2] This notwithstanding, Phimister concludes with the contention that, it was World War Two which galvanised the initiation of manufacturing policy and it was not out of government's "own volition".

The second chapter covers the period from 1940 to 1965. Phimister demonstrates a shift in state policy and a subsequent partnership between state and private capital. During this period, the colonial administration

---

[1] Phimister Chapter.

[2] Phimister demonstrates that there had always been a tendency to favour the interests of the mining and agriculture sectors as the chief sources of foreign exchange. When their interests collided with those of industrialists who were clamouring for protectionist policies, the government tended to be swayed by the former which explains why the government only initiated the Customs and Excise Tariff Act as late as 1937 and subsequent development of manufacturing was only to be thrust upon government through the demands of the War.

grew to become the largest investor in manufacturing. Through a quantitative, exposé Phimister pertinently demonstrates a significant growth in manufacturing sector where investment grew from 1. 2 million in 1948 pounds to 7 million pounds in 1953 and consequently, the number of firms rose from 294 companies in 1939 to 473 in 1948 recording expansion in chemicals, electrical goods and textiles with South Africa becoming a critical trading partner with a wide range of customs and tariff arrangements. Phimister concludes by indicating how the idea of Federation had been initiated to favour industrial expansion and accordingly manufacturing performed buoyantly during this period with the lion's share of investment and subordination of the other two co-federates.

Overall, the chapter demonstrates the strength of collusion between the government and the private sector in influencing economic growth. Pangeti builds on this in the ensuing chapter which covers the period 1965 to 1979 and argues that the colony proceeded out of the UDI period unscathed by the intended punitive sanctions initiated by Britain because of the successes of the preceding decade. By 1963 with the collapse of the Federation, the two co-federates remained agrarian based while Southern Rhodesia's manufacturing flourished. A mixture of import substitution measures and good commercial diplomacy with South Africa rescued the situation and proved to be a critical life line with exports continuing despite sanctions as Rhodesia Iron and Steel Commission's products were exported under South Africa Iron and Steel Corporation. Pangeti argues that a combination of state and private ingenuity, "an ounce of resourcefulness and courage" propelled this excellent growth which was slightly regressed by external factors such as the oil crisis of 1973 which affected inflow of raw materials. This notwithstanding, manufacturing withstood this economic barrage as transport industry, construction, brick cement glass industries prospered.

In his overall conclusion, Pangeti points out that by the end of the decade, the economy was starting to show signs of weakness due to stresses emanating from overproduction and under consumption, regional turmoil which affected the movement of raw materials and the low investment through as the liberation struggle consumed a significant amount on military expenditure. Furthermore, the war contributed to consumption decline due to low demand in rural areas. Mlambo maintains that these structural weaknesses were carried over into the independence era and although the black indigenous government made deliberate attempts to expand manufacturing through encouraging linkages between manufacturing and peasant agriculture, the task was futile. The post-colonial economy witnessed expansion in food processing, textiles, transport, chemicals with the introduction of Zimbabwe phosphates, Sable chemicals and Triangle sugar estates reducing the import bill on oil from 29% to 22% in 1981. This was however short-lived by a number of changing aspects in the economy including capital flight. There is a tendency by contemporary scholarship is to pin the blame for the decline of productivity squarely on the post-colonial regime's mismanagement but Pangeti et al give a more dynamic view their contribution. Although he unapologetically underlines the faultiness of government's socialist rhetoric, the so-called scientific socialism which appeared, "anti-capital" and stringent protectionism, he also considers some inherited problems such as outmoded machines and the subsequent droughts as contributing to a lethargic development in manufacturing during the independence period. His main argument in this chapter does not completely absolve government's contribution to the disaster that occurred but simply offers alternate view that aids in better understanding the economic dynamics of the immediate post-independence period.

The final chapter reveals how the drive towards manufacturing came to a grinding halt through the influence of the IMF through the adoption of the Structural Adjustment Programmes (SAPs). The deregulation and the devaluation of the currency further influenced runaway inflation and dwindling purchasing power of the black majority leading to low consumption which inevitably led to the plummeting of industry. The main argument in this chapter reveals how international capital deliberately rigged the

Zimbabwean economy to fail. The summation made by Mlambo is that the IMF did not intend to initiate curative measures for Zimbabwe's economy but rather, the international organisation made prescriptions that further negatively impacted the Zimbabwean economy in the 1990s period. It further exposes the cut throat nature of international economics and how there is no room for empathy in global economics.

Overall, this book provides insightful details on the development of manufacturing in colonial and immediate post-colonial Zimbabwe. Perhaps the only salient shortcoming is that it glosses over critical epochs for instance the developments during the Depression and Federation periods which are not discussed at length. Admittedly, this task might have been insurmountable given the wide range of issues that needed to be covered in a study that stretches beyond a century. This notwithstanding, I would recommend this book for economic history and industrial development scholars who intend to gain a foundational understanding of the economic history and policy mechanisms of the manufacturing sector in Zimbabwe since colonialism.

图书在版编目(CIP)数据

非洲经济评论.2020：英文/舒运国,张忠祥,刘伟才主编.—
上海:上海三联书店,2021.7
ISBN 978-7-5426-7482-1

Ⅰ.①非… Ⅱ.①舒…②张…③刘… Ⅲ.①经济发展-研
究-非洲-2020-英文 Ⅳ.①F14

中国版本图书馆 CIP 数据核字(2021)第 130472 号

非洲经济评论(2020)

主　　编 / 舒运国　张忠祥　刘伟才

责任编辑 / 殷亚平
装帧设计 / 徐　徐
监　　制 / 姚　军
责任校对 / 张大伟　王凌霄

出版发行 / 上海三联书店
　　　　　 (200030)中国上海市漕溪北路 331 号 A 座 6 楼
邮购电话 / 021-22895540
印　　刷 / 上海惠敦印务科技有限公司

版　　次 / 2021 年 7 月第 1 版
印　　次 / 2021 年 7 月第 1 次印刷
开　　本 / 710×1000　1/16
字　　数 / 300 千字
印　　张 / 22.5
书　　号 / ISBN 978-7-5426-7482-1/F·844
定　　价 / 98.00 元

敬启读者,如发现本书有印装质量问题,请与印刷厂联系 021-63779028